Antonia Karaisl von Karais
The House is in a State

Maecenata Schriften

Edited by
Dr. phil. Rupert Graf Strachwitz,
Dr. sc. Eckhard Priller and
Christian Schreier

Volume 19

Antonia Karaisl von Karais

The House is in a State

Christian Wolff's Oeconomica in the context of public welfare

DE GRUYTER
OLDENBOURG

ISBN 978-3-11-071392-3
e-ISBN (PDF) 978-3-11-071409-8
e-ISBN (EPUB) 978-3-11-071419-7
ISSN 1866-122X

Library of Congress Control Number: 2020948511

Bibliographic information published by the Deutsche Nationalbibliothek
The Deutsche Nationalbibliothek lists this publication in the Deutsche Nationalbibliografie; detailed bibliographic data are available on the Internet at http://dnb.dnb.de.

Druck und Bindung: CPI books GmbH, Leck

MIX
Papier aus verantwortungsvollen Quellen
FSC www.fsc.org FSC® C083411

www.degruyter.com

To
Sabine Freifrau Karaisl von Karais (1948–2017)
and
Karl Viktor Freiherr Karaisl von Karais (1912–2017)

Acknowledgments

First and foremost, many thanks to my father Franz Karaisl von Karais who introduced me to Christian Wolff and thus gave rise to this project, to my sisters Benedikta and Marie for all their support, as also to Rose Gibbs and Alba Gibbs Joffe for their patience at close quarters.

I am very grateful to Adrian Kelly and Adrian Lyttelton for supporting my application after all these years, and to Zane Selkirk who would have done so had it been necessary.

Many thanks to my supervisors Guido Giglioni and Raphaele Mouren for taking on my thesis, the basis for this book, as also Michelle O'Malley, Jill Kraye and everyone at the Warburg Institute for discussion, inspiration and critique along the way. Above all, my deepest gratitude to Marina Warner for all the encouragement and innumerable pointers throughout the years.

Most but last, biggest thanks to Xaxa Panman for her invaluable help rendering this piece more palatable.

生江さん, ありがとうございます。

https://doi.org/10.1515/9783110714098-202

Table of Contents

1 Introduction

1.1 The reception of Wolffian philosophy

This study focuses on the last work of eighteenth-century philosopher Christian Wolff, the *Oeconomica methodo scientifica pertractata*, a rationalist guide to domestic morality. Born in 1679 in Breslau Wolff embarked on a splendid academic career, enjoying the support of contemporary luminaries like Gottfried Wilhelm Leibniz. He accepted a professorship for mathematics at Halle university in 1706 and soon expanded his range to include natural, theoretical and moral philosophy.[1] Wolff ultimately made a name for himself as one of the first scholars to systematically publish in the vernacular at a time when Latin still ruled the day at German universities; in fact, this made him a major figure to spread philosophy amongst the population at large in the eighteenth century.[2] Popular and controversial alike, he was expelled from Halle by Frederick Wilhelm I in 1721, the culmination of an enduring conflict with the theological faculty who dominated the university at the time. The scandal inevitably contributed to his fame; Wolff spent his exile in Marburg as a coveted professor, resisting the eventual pardon of the king. He only returned to Halle in 1740 with the accession of Frederick II where, amply decorated, he passed away in 1754 – midway through writing the *Oeconomica*.[3]

Although Wolff's life is well-attested, his legacy is disputed: revered, reviled, yet indisputably famous throughout his lifetime, the *maître à penser de l'Allemagne* quickly lost in prominence thereafter.[4] And even though Wolff left behind an immense oeuvre covering over 50,000 printed pages, spawned an eponymous movement with his methodology and furnished the German language with a philosophical terminology – in short, even though the impact of Wolffian philosophy can be considered a fact, his name is not as commonplace in modern academia as his erstwhile prominence would suggest.[5] In fact, this discrepancy between lifelong prominence and posthumous oblivion is an oft-repeated theme in contemporary scholarship.[6]

1 Ahnert, Thomas, 'Introduction', in *The Law of Nations Treated According to the Scientific Method*, by Christian Wolff, ed. by Thomas Ahnert, trans. by Joseph H. Drake (Indianapolis: Liberty Fund, 2017), pp. ix–xxiv (xi–xii).

2 Biller, Gerhard, 'Biographie und Bibliographie', in *Handbuch Christian Wolff*, ed. by Robert Theis and Alexander Aichele (Wiesbaden: Springer, 2018), pp. 5–34, p. 11.

3 Biller, 'Biographie und Bibliographie', p. 5.

4 As Wolff was famously dubbed by Voltaire. Quoted in Thomann, Marcel, 'Christian Wolff', in *Staatsdenker in der frühen Neuzeit*, ed. by Michael Stolleis and Notker Hammerstein (Munich: Beck, 1995), pp. 257–83, p. 257.

5 Biller, 'Biographie und Bibliographie', p. 7.

6 See, for instance, Wundt, Max, *Die Deutsche Schulphilosophie im Zeitalter der Aufklärung* (Hildesheim: Olms, 1964), p. 123; Schwaiger, Clemens, 'Christian Wolff', in *The Bloomsbury Dictionary of Eighteenth-Century German Philosophers*, ed. by Heiner F. Klemme and Manfred Kuehn (London:

https://doi.org/10.1515/9783110714098-001

Scant accessibility to Wolff's numerous works may have contributed to his latter-day obscurity. Although various re-editions of his books were published during his lifetime, his works were hard to come by in the twentieth century until Jean Ecole's complete edition secured them for the modern reader 1963 onwards – and prompted a cautious Wolffian Renaissance.[7] The digitisation of Wolff's works removed this issue for good: his entire oeuvre is now freely obtainable in the original on Google Books. The dearth of re-editions of Wolff in the interim may have been symptomatic of the harsh revision his philosophy received in the immediate aftermath: the deconstruction of his philosophical creed set in early with Kant and the rise of idealism in Germany, few decades after Wolff's death.[8] Less than a century later, historians, intellectuals and pundits such as Heinrich Heine, Georg Friedrich Wilhelm Hegel, Karl Marx and Wilhelm Roscher mention Wolff merely in passing, and typically dismissively.[9] In general, scholarship of that time tends to treat Wolff as a necessary evil rather than a venerable precedent.

It seems that the shift from prominence to obscurity must have occurred within only a few decades. Scholars of the nineteenth and early twentieth century still consider Wolff a household name in the history of philosophy.[10] Some fifty years later he

---

Bloomsbury Publishing, 2016), pp. 862–67; Bissinger, Anton, *Die Struktur der Gotteserkenntnis: Studien zur Philosophie Christian Wolffs* (Bonn: Bouvier, 1970), p. 1; Frängsmyr, Tore, 'Christian Wolff's Mathematical Method and Its Impact on the Eighteenth Century', *Journal of the History of Ideas*, 36.4 (1975), 653–68 (653).

7 See e.g. Bissinger, *Die Struktur der Gotteserkenntnis*; Stipperger, Emanuel, *Freiheit und Institution bei Christian Wolff (1679–1754)* (Frankfurt am Main, Bern and New York: Peter Lang, 1984), pp. 25, 4. On the modern revival of scholarship on Wolff, see Schwaiger, 'Christian Wolff', p. 866.

8 Thomann, 'Christian Wolff', p. 257. Fichte is an instructive example, whose early allegiance to Wolff was corroded by his acquaintance with the works of Kant. See Beck, Gunnar, *Fichte and Kant on Freedom, Rights, and Law* (Lanham, MD: Lexington Books, 2008), p. 23. See also Schöffler, Herbert, *Deutsches Geistesleben zwischen Reformation und Aufklärung: von Martin Opitz zu Christian Wolff* (Frankfurt am Main: Vittorio Klostermann, 1974), p. 221.

9 Gerlach, Hans-Martin, 'Christian Wolff – seine Schule und seine Gegner', *Aufklärung*, 12.2 (2001), 3–8 (5–6). Hegel, for example, accuses Wolff of both 'barbarism of pedantry' and 'pedantry of barbarism', see Vidal, Fernando, *The Sciences of the Soul: The Early Modern Origins of Psychology*, trans. by Saskia Brown (Chicago; London: University of Chicago Press, 2011), p. 90. For Wolff's reception by Marx, Engels and Lenin, see Krause, Gunter, 'Christian Wolff and the Classics of "Scientific Socialism"', *European Journal of Law and Economics*, 4 (1997), 285–297. Roscher acknowledges Wolff's importance yet attributes his success to his comparative lack of sophistication: 'Allerdings hängt der glänzende Erfolg, den Wolff bei seinen Zeitgenossen hatte, wesentlich damit zusammen, daß er so wenig über das geistige Niveau seiner Zeit hervorragte.', Roscher, Wilhelm, *Geschichte der National-Oekonomik in Deutschland*, Vol 14 (München: R. Oldenbourg, 1874), p. 347.

10 See, for instance, the following statement by Ernst Kohlmeyer: 'Christian Wolffs Name ist populär, unzertrennlich von ihm auch das Schlagwort der Demonstriermethode', Kohlmeyer, Ernst, *Kosmos und Kosmonomie bei Christian Wolff: Ein Beitrag zur Geschichte der Philosophie und Theologie des Aufklärungszeitalters* (Göttingen: Vandenhoeck & Ruprecht, 1911), p. 7.

is presented as a forgotten spectre, overshadowed by the likes of Leibniz and Kant.[11] Since then, a number of scholars have worked on recovering the thought of the erstwhile famous philosopher to better understand his role in the German Enlightenment, and, in fact, the period as a whole.[12] And whilst the earlier attempts were focused on Wolff's theoretical philosophy, more recent times have seen a budding interest in his work from scholars of a broader disciplinary range – including the social sciences.

A particular school of thought has rediscovered Wolff as an early representative of economic theory, first and foremost Jürgen Backhaus. In Backhaus' view, it was Wolff who 'established economics as the science of the modern welfare state', a precedent to influence early representatives of cameralism such as Johann Heinrich Gottlob von Justi (1717–1771).[13] In a similar vein, the economists Erik Reinert and Arno Mong Daastøl pronounce Wolff and Leibniz the representatives of 'a legal tradition which consciously tried to construct the basis for a modern welfare state'.[14] Reinert goes as far as declaring Wolff 'pivotal in laying the theoretical foundation for Germany's economic ascent', associating him with the German Historical School of Economics as an alternative to classic economic theory.[15] This brand of economic analysis traces its origins to the traditions of didactic literature on moral conduct and state administration, and is given a rationalist core with the natural law codified by Wolff, according to Reinert.[16] Backhaus further argues that the German Historical School

---

11 Bissinger, Die Struktur der Gotteserkenntnis, p. 1.

12 Gerlach, 'Christian Wolff – seine Schule und seine Gegner', pp. 6–7. Recurring names in the postwar bibliography for Wolff include Jean École, Marcel Thomann, Michael Albrecht, Marcel Thomann, Charles Corr, Hans Werner Arndt, Mario Casula, Anton Bissinger, Hans Poser; see Biller, Gerhard, 'Die Wolff-Diskussion 1800–1982. Eine Bibliographie', in *Christian Wolff 1679–1754. Interpretationen zu seiner Philosophie und deren Wirkung, mit einer Bibliographie der Wolff-Literatur*, ed. by Werner Schneiders (Hamburg: Felix Meiner, 1986), pp. 321–45, pp. 332–345.

13 Senn, Peter, 'What Is the Place of Christian Wolff in the History of the Social Sciences?', *European Journal of Law and Economics*, 4 (1997), 147–232 (183); Backhaus, Jürgen G., *The Beginnings of Political Economy: Johann Heinrich Gottlob von Justi* (New York: Springer, 2009), pp. 11, 14. The discipline of 'cameralism' established itself as the science of statecraft at German universities such as Halle, Heidelberg and Kaiserslautern in the early modern period; the curricula were designed to furnish future civil servants with the expertise of political and economic administration of Germany's princely realms. See Gray, Marion W., *Productive Men, Reproductive Women: The Agrarian Household and the Emergence of Separate Spheres during the German Enlightenment* (New York: Berghahn Books, 2000), p. 91.

14 Reinert, Erik S., and Arno Mong Daastøl, 'Exploring the Genesis of Economic Innovations: The Religious Gestalt-Switch and the Duty to Invent as Preconditions for Economic Growth', *European Journal of Law and Economics*, 4 (1997), 233–83 (236).

15 Reinert, Erik S., and Rainer Kattel, The Visionary Realism of German Economics: From the Thirty Years' War to the Cold War (London: Anthem Press, 2019), p. 110.

16 Reinert, Erik S., and K. S. Jomo, (eds), *Origins of Development Economics: How Schools of Economic Thought Addressed Development* (London and New York: Zed Books, 2005), p. 51.

functions as the spiritual continuation of Wolffian thought and as the theoretical bridge to Joseph Schumpeter, with his stress on technology, innovation and learning as pillars of a national economy. As a result, they conceive of Schumpeter's explicit excision of Wolff from his *History of Economic Analysis* as a

> fundamental and far-reaching mistake on Schumpeter's part, one that prevented him from understanding the historical and philosophical foundations of German economics, and thus possibly also prevented him from appreciating the deep discrepancies that exist between English and German-type economics at the most fundamental level.[17]

Schumpeter's omission of Wolff is understandable if we consider their vastly dissimilar understanding of the conduct of science. In Schumpeter's definition, the basic tenets of a scientific analysis of economics are the 'sum total of the historical, statistical and theoretical technique... with the results they help to produce'.[18] None of these elements feature in Wolff's methodology. Firstly, Wolff explicitly disclaims that a theory derived from a set of statistics can warrant the degree of certainty his demonstrative method would.[19] Experience and experiment are valid forms of scientific proof.[20] Yet collected statistical information does not proffer the requisite certainty to qualify as scientific in the Wolffian sense. Secondly, Wolff's works are written in an entirely a-historical fashion. Whilst the assumed natural state of man serves as a philosophical point of departure, he very rarely considers the historical development between this abstract era and the present. Lastly, Wolff does not probe a positive inquiry into human behaviour to develop a theory to explain the world as an economist would, but a normative exploration of possibilities to describe the world as it should be.[21] It further needs to be mentioned that Wolff – in tune with the general conception of social sciences in the eighteenth century – does not single out the economy as a

17 Reinert, Erik S., 'Steeped in Two Mind-Sets: Schumpeter in the Context of the Two Canons of Economics', in *Joseph Alois Schumpeter: Entrepreneurship, Style and Vision*, ed. by Jürgen Backhaus (Boston: Kluwer, 2003), pp. 261–92, pp. 264–6.

18 Schumpeter, Joseph A., *History of Economic Analysis: With a New Introduction*, ed. by Elizabeth Boody Schumpeter (New York: Oxford University Press, 1996), p. 21.

19 As Wolff notes in a preface to a statistical work on demographics that we would consider a lot closer to our contemporary conduct of social science – see Süssmilch, Johann Peter, *Die göttliche Ordnung in den Veränderungen des menschlichen Geschlechts, aus der Geburt, dem Tode und der Fortpflanzung desselben erwiesen*, ed. by Christian Jacob Baumann (Berlin: Verlag der Buchhandlung der Realschule, 1765), pp. 11–12.

20 See, for instance, Wolff's meticulously recorded experiments with grain in: Wolff, Christian, Entdeckung der wahren Ursache von der wunderbahren Vermehrung des Getreydes, dadurch zugleich der Wachsthum der Bäume und Pflantzen überhaupt erläutert wird (Halle: Renger, 1725).

21 Wolff considered his own definition of philosophy as the science of possible things, *scientia possibilium*, as idiosyncratic and original. See Lüthje, Hans, 'Christian Wolffs Philosophiebegriff', *Kant-Studien*, 30 (1925), 39–66 (39–40).

separate sphere of study.[22] In his discourse, economic activity is chiefly state-directed, not the result of individual decision-making processes. Remarks on price, trade or production only exist within the context of political theory but do not form a theoretical body akin to modern economics.[23]

On account of the above it is clear that the retroactive association of Wolff with the history of economic thought is not necessarily a fruitful one. Yet even if we have to decidedly set his work apart from economic analysis, we can agree with Wolff's modern supporters that his political philosophy touches upon a particular subsection of modern economics: public welfare. Wolff's early work on politics, the *Deutsche Politik*, does not give any detailed policy suggestion, but specifies welfare as the founding purpose of a state. The individual can achieve his or her highest possible degree of well-being only within the framework of a state – conversely, the aim of the state is the welfare of its members.[24] Concrete policy suggestions can be found in his works on natural law, chiefly the eighth and last tome of his *Jus naturae*, ranging from public health concerns to poor relief and public services. Examples include the regulation of medical practitioners and provisions, fixed wages and working hours, re-education and placement of unemployed citizens and support for the needy.[25] As Martina Komm remarks, in this idealized blueprint of the body politic human welfare is effectively decoupled from divine providence and mandated to the private initiative and moral conscience of the ruler.[26] Wolff is no liberalist and casts a mould for an absolutist monarchy, not a democratic body politic.[27] Yet taken out of context, these policies have a surprisingly modern ring and are by no means unfamiliar to contemporary welfare states.

A crucial difference, however, remains between modern and Wolffian welfare theory: the former seeks to alleviate the consequences of social inequality, pre-empting informal networks where they cannot be trusted to perform this function;[28] the latter considers inequality within household and body politic as instrumental, presenting the family as a natural building block for the state and its social welfare function. According to Backhaus, this framework is consistent with the modern concept of subsid-

22 Schabas, Margaret, *The Natural Origins of Economics* (Chicago: University of Chicago Press, 2005), p. 1.

23 Frauendienst, Werner, *Christian Wolff als Staatsdenker* (Berlin: Matthiesen Verlag, 1927), p. 130.

24 Wolff, Christian, Vernünftige Gedanken von dem gesellschaftlichen Leben der Menschen und insonderheit dem gemeinen Wesen, §§ 214, 223 (Frankfurt and Leipzig: Renger, 1747), pp. 162, 165–166.

25 Frauendienst, Christian Wolff als Staatsdenker, p. 143.

26 Komm, Martina, 'Zu einigen Aspekten von Christian Wolffs Ökonomik', in *Christian Wolff als Philosoph der Aufklärung in Deutschland*, ed. by Hans-Martin Gerlach, Günter Schenk, and Burchard Thaler (Halle: Martin-Luther-Universität, 1980), pp. 83–89, p. 83.

27 Lutterbeck, Klaus-Gert, Staat und Gesellschaft bei Christian Thomasius und Christian Wolff: Eine historische Untersuchung in systematischer Absicht (Stuttgart: Frommann-Holzboog, 2002), p. 12.

28 Girvetz, Harry, 'Welfare State', *International Encyclopedia of Social Sciences*, ed. by David L. Sills and Robert K. Merton (New York: MacMillan, 1968), p. 512.

iarity whereby the lowest possible level of administration is entrusted with the care for its subjects – except that this level is not created or mandated by the government, but privately organised: the household.[29] Yet it is necessary to consider Wolff's philosophy in detail to understand whether his theory of socio-economic relations presents a harbinger of modernity or a buttress to tradition.

1.2 Wolff's Oeconomica in the literary context

The household has its own place in Wolff's Latin oeuvre and the work dedicated to its moral exploration is the focal point of this study: his *Oeconomica methodo scientifica pertractata*.

The book presents a scientific analysis of the social infrastructure of the household, divided up into sections dedicated to husband and wife, parents and children, masters and servants and the house as a whole. Wolff planned to cover a broad range of topics from wedding and wooing to spousal duties, pedagogy, education of children and proper conduct of staff in this rationalist primer to domestic bliss. Yet having died midway through writing the section about parenthood, his book was posthumously published in 1754. Subsequently, a scholar from Danzig, Michael Hanov (1695–1773), added and published the missing half in1755. He delivered the rest of the chapter on parenting and the two last sections, that is, on masters and servants and the composition of the household as a whole.

The name *Oeconomica* might suggest a topical link to modern economics. Contrary to these expectations, the work has to be understood within a diffuse tradition of didactic literature both old and ubiquitous. Branded low-brow and practical, this type of wisdom literature offers advice on the household as a sphere of production and the family as its definitive social composite. Wolff further reduces the scope of the genre from practical realities to moral comport only: his *Oeconomica* is exclusively concerned with the social infrastructure of a household – the relationships between husband and wife, parents and children, masters and servants and their embedment within the household as constitutive unit.

With its sole focus on the domestic realm, the *Oeconomica* is rarely mentioned by scholars of economics or other social sciences, historically and more recently. This may be due to the fact that it uses the old Aristotelian model to describe the domestic order, a notion already outdated at the time of the book's publication.[30] Schumpeter's *History of Economic Analysis* groups comparable works together as a literary category

29 Backhaus, Jürgen G., 'Christian Wolff on Subsidiarity, the Division of Labor and Social Welfare', *European Journal of Law and Economics*, 4 (1997), 129–146 (136).
30 Priddat, Birger P., and Christoph Meineke, 'Ökonomie', in *Handbuch Christian Wolff*, pp. 291–313, p. 297.

that specifically does *not* belong in the history of economic thought.[31] Only Wilhelm Roscher in his *Geschichte der National-Oekonomik in Deutschland* (1874) mentions the work in the context of political economy, which might signal his confusion about the purpose of the work rather than its significance within economic discourse.[32] This scholarly disinterest illustrates the topical split in spite of the etymological commonality between the Latin terms *oeconomica* or *oeconomia* and modern economics. Their linguistic origin rests with its Greek beginnings, subject to a significant shift in meaning by the eighteenth century.[33] As Germano Maifreda notes, when 'the seventeenth century neared its end, the ways in which the term "economy" and its derivatives were employed in the principal Western languages seem to expand.'[34] In tune with this development, both *oeconomica* and *oeconomia* seem to have lacked a firm definition at Wolff's time, making their meaning strongly dependent on the context.[35] Yet whilst the term *Oeconomia* assumed a broader meaning alluding to dispensation in general, also beyond the context of the household, the derivate *Oeconomica* as a literary category seems to have been exclusively applied to domestic matters. With the exception of certain local or historical trends, style and format of this latter genre is too fluid to make for a securely defined genre – works associated with this group include poems, philosophical treatises, novels or simply aphorisms.[36] Fluid not merely in form, these works also cover a broad topical spread: subject matters include administrative affairs and family conduct, agricultural tips as well as medicinal, legal,

31 Schumpeter, History of Economic Analysis, p. 156.

32 Wilhelm Roscher, *Geschichte der National-Oekonomik in Deutschland* (Munich: R. Oldenbourg, 1874), pp. 349–350.

33 Duve, Thomas, 'Der blinde Fleck der "Oeconomia"? – Wirtschaft und Soziales in der frühen Neuzeit', in *Wirtschaft und Wirtschaftstheorie in Rechtsgeschichte und Philosophie*, ed. by Heinz Mohnhaupt and Jean-François Kervégan (Frankfurt am Main: Klostermann, 2004), pp. 29–61, p. 32.

34 Maifreda, Germano, *From Oikonomia to Political Economy: Constructing Economic Knowledge from the Renaissance to the Scientific Revolution* (Farnham, Surrey: Ashgate, 2012), p. 189. Chapter 6 of Maifreda's book, 'The Economic System', maps this development in more detail.

35 Schabas, *The Natural Origins of Economics*, p. 3. The range of different associations made with *oeconomia* or *oeconomica* can be glimpsed from universal and philosophical lexica of the seventeenth and eighteenth centuries. According to Rudolph Goclenius, 'Oeconomica' is commonly defined as 'ars bene dispensandi' (Goclenius, *Lexicon philosophicum* [Frankfurt: Widow of Matthias Becker, 1613], p. 546). 'Oeconomia' features simply as 'Haushaltung' in Johann Jablonski and Johann Theodor, *Allgemeines Lexicon der Künste und Wissenschaften* (Leipzig: Hartung, 1721), p. 510; Zedler's *Universal Encyclopedia* defines different types of *oeconomia*, depending on the specific use case: *oeconomia divina, oeconomia privata, oeconomia sylvatia*, even *oeconomia animalis*; *oeconomica ars* or *oeconomie* is associated with household management while *oeconomicae societates* designate the different relationships within family communities, a term central to Wolff's *Oeconomica*. See Zedler, Johann Heinrich, 'Oeconomia', in *Grosses Vollständiges Universal-Lexicon aller Wissenschafften und Künste*, Vol. 25 (Halle and Leipzig: Johann Heinrich Zedler, 1731–1754), p. 277.

36 Cossar, C.D.M., ed., The German Translations of the Pseudo-Bernhardine 'Epistola de Cura Rei Familiaris' (Göppingen: A. Kümmerle, 1975), p. 273.

and technical advice. Hence, it is not content or format but the domestic realm as the sphere of interest that makes for the securest categorisation. The reference to either house or family in the titles of these works suggests that the two were considered interchangeable terms for the same social construct. Eventually, the *paterfamilias* as the recipient of the advice would become the definitive pole of *Oeconomica*-related literature. This is evident in the name *Hausväterliteratur*, the brand of German wisdom literature Wolff's *Oeconomica* is commonly ascribed to. Judging from the vast expanse of information transmitted in the classics of this genre, the household as a unit historically exceeds the private realm that we have come to associate with it.

The *Desiderata oeconomica*, a doctoral thesis submitted in 1731 by Philipp Casselmann, illustrates this spread and the concomitant dilemma. The thesis demands a systematic and concentrated treatment of domestic disciplines based on existing literature: from Aristotle, Xenophon and Hesiod to Roman agricultural treatises to concurrent works and collections on technology, medicine or politics. The material on offer purveys a spread of subject matter and genre: Hesiodic verse, Xenophon's dialogue, Pseudo-Aristotelian discourse, Roman agricultural primers, More's *Utopia* as well as encyclopaedic collections of prosaic household wisdoms.[37] The thesis does not yield a closer definition of term, subject matter, audience or genre, but illustrates burgeoning interest in *oeconomica* as a subject matter in the academic sphere and breadth of topics associated with the term at the time.

Christian Wolff's *Oeconomica* is not the systematic treatment Casselmann called for. Rather, it presents the continuation of a specific genre of household literature, aforementioned *Hausväterliteratur*: primers for the householder.[38] Pragmatic more than philosophical, literature of that sort crystallised into a popular type of advice genre on all matters domestic between 1500 and 1750 in Germany.[39] As the household and the economically productive sphere of its members were not necessarily kept separate at the time, extant examples of *Hausväterliteratur* tend to treat domestic relationships as embedded within the setting of a self-sufficient agricultural unit.[40] In spite of this rural element, the audience was not restricted to farm owners – it was written for the *paterfamilias* as a private individual presiding over a household, be that poor or rich, city or country.[41] Three extant examples of this genre, which in the course of this study will be used as means of comparison with Wolff's work, are as

37 Casselmann, Philipp C., and Johann Hermann Fürstenau, *Desiderata oeconomica* (Rinteln: Enax, 1731).

38 Duve, 'Der blinde Fleck der "Oeconomia"?', p. 33.

39 Lichtblau, Klaus, Das Zeitalter der Entzweiung: Studien zur politischen Ideengeschichte des 19. und 20. Jahrhunderts (Berlin: Philo, 1999), p. 25.

40 Wehler, Hans-Ulrich, Deutsche Gesellschaftsgeschichte, erster Band: Vom Feudalismus des alten Reiches bis zur defensiven Modernisierung der Reformära 1700–1815 (München: Beck, 1989), p. 82.

41 Hahn, Philip, Das Haus im Buch: Konzeption, Publikationsgeschichte und Leserschaft der 'Oeconomia' Johann Colers (Epfendorf/Neckar: Bibliotheca Academica Verlag, 2013), p. 66.

follows: the *Oeconomia christiana* (1529) by Justus Menius (1499–1558), teaching the correct conduct of a Christian family in direct reference to the Bible; the *Oeconomia ruralis* (1593–1601) by Johannes Coler (1566–1639), an expansive household manual combining a range of farming advice with sparser dispensation of moral precepts; and the *Oeconomus prudens et legalis* (1702) by Franz Philipp Florinus (1649–1699), touching upon both moral and practical, complete with juristic annotations.[42] These works cater to an encyclopaedic breadth of topics, both culturally particular and highly comprehensive. Coler's manual, for example, covers all from traditional agriculture to kitchen recipes, from dream interpretation to animal husbandry, listing no less than two methods to catch monkeys – arguably information of secondary importance to a German target audience.[43] And whilst the above differ in content, all of them share a practical attitude and a religious overtone that establish the direct connection between mundane dealings and divine ordinance: the ultimate source of authority remains the Christian religion. This may seem most obvious in Menius' work who derives precepts for the householder straight from the Bible; yet Florinus's book, too, which is devoted to mostly practical matters, makes the religious tangent explicit: every household task is declared a Christian duty, effectively a spiritual revaluation of otherwise self-directed economic activity.[44]

If Wolff's *Oeconomica* is to be considered the last proponent of this genre, its systematic treatment and rationalist bearing suggests a departure from the freely assembled, lone-standing works of Christian *Hausväterliteratur*. Wolff may follow the tradition of combining practical and ethical advice, but the material is worked over in his own scientific style and incorporated into his philosophical system following the Aristotelian model of practical philosophy, placing the *Oeconomica* between ethics and politics.[45] His methodological overhaul in particular presents the genre in a new light and his method with a new challenge. His previous projects clarify and systematise philosophical thought to render it comprehensible to a broader audience – in the *Oeconomica* he is reworking an ultimately mundane body of information in order to elevate it to the academic realm. Divine ordinance as a source of instruction for the good life retreats into the background – all moral advice is ultimately abutted by man's rationality, not revelation.

The integration into his philosophical system, as part of practical philosophy, presents a challenge of historical proportions. Aristotle as the chief source of philo-

---

42 On the categorisation of these works as Hausväterliteratur see Müller, Rainer A., 'Die Oeconomia ist ein Monarchia. Der (deutsche) Fürstenhof der Frühmoderne als Objekt der Hausväter- und Regimentsliteratur', in *Hof und Theorie. Annährungen an ein historisches* Phänomen, ed. by Reinhardt Butz (Cologne: Böhlau, 2004), pp. 145–64, and Duve, 'Der blinde Fleck der "Oeconomia"?', pp. 33, 39.

43 Coler, Johannes, *Oeconomia ruralis et domestica* (Mainz: Nicolaus Heyl, 1665), pp. 602–3.

44 Florinus, Franciscus Philippus, *Oeconomus prudens et legalis* (Nuremberg, Frankfurt, Leipzig: Christoph Riegel, 1750), Ch. 1, § 11, p. 4.

45 Duve, 'Der blinde Fleck der "Oeconomia"?', p. 34; Lichtblau, *Das Zeitalter der Entzweiung*, p. 26.

sophical categories postulated ethics, *oeconomica* and politics as the triad of practical philosophy, but rather than delivering all three parts the ancient philosopher wedged his theory of the household into the first book on political theory. Meanwhile the Pseudo-Aristotelian *Oeconomica*, a work long presumed to be Aristotle's fulfilment of this category, seems to have never attained full status within the academic sphere, even where its authenticity was not disputed.[46] Wolff resolves the resulting debate over whether the household should be discussed as part of the body politic or independently. He justifies his decision to give the *Oeconomica* its own place with the idea of progressive stages of society: the *societates simplices* of the household are recast as natural societies preceding the civil society as a post-natural state. The family thus demands theorisation as a pre-stage and active component of the civil state.[47]

Classic examples of *Hausväterliteratur* might have promoted the good life within the domestic sphere but would not explicitly place the household as a functional unit within a political context. By reviving and reappraising the category of *Oeconomica*, however, Wolff reinvents the household as a necessary composite of the body politic and the instruction of its members as a necessary prerequisite to not just a functioning household but a functioning civil society.[48] This naturally prompts questions about the relationship between the family as the traditional unit of provision and Wolff's social welfare as state-organised programme. The reciprocity and complementarity of family and state within Wolff's socio-political philosophy is the main concern of this book.

1.3 Research question and methodology

The central hypothesis of this study proposes that Wolff takes on the old genre of household wisdom and updates it to serve a political purpose. The *Oeconomica* not only demonstrates domestic morality for the sake of the household but re-evaluates the family as a functional unit to preserve the continuity of human race and, explicitly, the state. Considering Wolff's household within the context of specifically the welfare elements of his political theory shows how household and government have reciprocal functions to serve the common purpose of the body politic, the *bonum commune*. Putting his welfare state model into the historical context furthermore illustrates that Wolff's socio-political construct not only combines ideas traditional and

46 Cranz's and Schmitt's list of commentaries on the Pseudo-Aristotelian *Oeconomica* lists only seven contenders, none of which seem to be scholastic commentators. This is a mere pittance compared to the reception of Aristotle's other works. See F. Edward Cranz and Charles B. Schmitt, *A Bibliography of Aristotle Editions, 1501–1600* (Baden-Baden: V. Koerner, 1984), p. 185.

47 Christian Wolff, *Oeconomica methodo scientifica pertractata* (Halle: Renger, 1754), § 1, p. 1.

48 Wolff, Vernünftige Gedanken von dem gesellschaftlichen Leben der Menschen, § 15, p. 9; § 209, p. 155.

novel, but also documents a very specific point in socio-political history: a time when Germany's territorial princes, and the Prussian monarchy in particular, sought to centralise government functions, subsuming and recasting existing social welfare practices in the process to serve the purpose of the state. In tune with his times, Wolff's political theory charges the state with the regulation and provision of the citizen body; the *Oeconomica* seeks to inculcate domestic and civic virtue to match. This linkage between the domestic and the political sphere presents a modification of traditional *Hausväterliteratur* whilst offering a segue between this more recent genre and Aristotle's tripartite practical philosophy – at a time when *Hausväterliteratur* as a genre was on the wane or about to be subsumed by its subcategories. Countering the trend by systematically integrating domestic philosophy with politics, Wolff is creating a connection between the 'unadulterated etymological economics of the ancient and medieval world' and the nascent state bureaucracy of the present using contemporary forms of advice literature.[49]

The driving impulse behind this research has been the question whether Wolff's political theory really presents the harbinger of the modern welfare state, as Backhaus and Reinert suggest. As it is, the retroactive application of such a label is not necessarily constructive. Instead, this analysis attempts a contextual reading to modify what seem to be overly positive but also exceedingly negative contemporary interpretations of Wolffian philosophy. The latter-day assessment of Wolff as a political theorist oscillates between extremes. Where Ernst Cassirer proclaims Wolff the 'father of human rights', Ernst Bloch considers his theories a mere 'apology of the mercantilist welfare and police state'.[50] In Ere Nokkala's reading, Wolff sketches a paternalist government that casts citizens as passive subjects, 'treated as immature children'.[51] Notably, these readings all depart from a modern point of view, comparing notes between Wolff and the present as the ideological end point. Rather than reading his philosophy from such a teleological point of view, this study aims to proceed from the other direction: by establishing what sources and discourses fed into the phenomenon that was Wolff in his own time.

---

49 Menut, Albert Douglas, 'Maistre Nicole Oresme: Le Livre de *Yconomique* d'Aristote', *Transactions of the American Philosophical Society*, 47 (1957), 783–853 (785).

50 Kadelbach, Stefan, Thomas Kleinlein, and David Roth-Isigkeit, eds., *System, Order, and International Law: The Early History of International Legal Thought from Machiavelli to Hegel* (Oxford: Oxford University Press, 2017), p. 220.

51 Nokkala, Ere, *From Natural Law to Political Economy: J.H.G. von Justi on State, Commerce and International Order* (Münster: LIT Verlag, 2019), pp. 89–90: 'Under a paternal government subjects were only obliged to behave passively and rely on the judgments of the head of the state regarding the way in which they ought to achieve happiness. ...In a paternalistic government (*väterliche Regierung, imperium paternale*) citizens were treated as immature children. Wolff wrote explicitly that ruling persons were to their subjects as fathers to their children. The task of the ruler was the same as that of fathers, providing their children with the means necessary for advancing the perfection of their internal and external condition.'

In terms of methodology, the argumentation is based on a contextual analysis of Wolff's *Oeconomica* and the parts of his natural law that postulate state-led welfare institutions. Rather than a hermeneutical exercise, the analysis will draw on the historical context to illustrate the inspirations, impulses and pressures acting upon the author. This background information also helps to trace Wolff's tacit assumptions, where they differ from a modern view and how this affects an interpretation of his work. There are some obvious intricacies to the task. Wolff's philosophical system first found expression in a vernacular version early on in his career, followed up by a full cycle covering the same disciplines in Latin. Whilst the German works are a good introduction, only the Latin cycle can give a full understanding of his mature thought – albeit Wolff did not live to complete his oeuvre.[52] The author died midway through the *Oeconomica* and the completion of Wolff's philosophical system was entrusted to a scholar from Danzig, Michael Hanov (1695–1773). Hanov not only finished the *Oeconomica* but also *Politica* and *Physica*, the last parts of the cycle. Whilst this leaves the primary sources for the analysis truncated, it offers an attractive opportunity for a comparative examination of Hanov's and Wolff's joint work.

Secondly, Wolff's oeuvre is generally assumed to be consistent throughout his publication history. As will be seen on closer inspection though, there is a progression and the odd change of heart with regards to certain concepts in the early and later works. And although Wolff's philosophy was conceived as a static edifice, beginning to end, identifying malleabilities within helps to map the development of his thought throughout his lifetime. On the downside, this means that reconstructing a truncated Latin system from the German forerunner may not always be reliable. Moreover, secondary literature that considers only Wolff's vernacular works has to be treated with caution as it can only yield a limited view of the full theoretical framework the philosopher had established by the end of his life. The fresh exploration of Wolff's work by contemporary social scientists thus stumbles over a linguistic border that poses the reversal of an old problem. Where Wolff wrote in Latin to reach an international audience back then, the international audience of our own days seems to struggle less with his German than with his Latin works – and potentially miss out on some of the finer points exclusive to the latter.[53] For the purpose of this research, therefore, the German works cannot be considered fully representative of Wolff's mature thought which is codified in his unfinished Latin cycle.

To return to the principal aim, the driving concern of this study is to explore the relationship between government, family and individual in Christian Wolff's philosophy of the welfare state theory. In structure and methodology, it presents itself as a case study of the philosopher's last work, the *Oeconomica*, considered within the con-

52 Bissinger, Die Struktur der Gotteserkenntnis, p. 32.

53 The works of Reinert, Nokkala, Komm, Priddat and Meineke cited above all exclusively use Wolff's German works.

text of his philosophical system with a view to its declared role as the *prodromus Politicae*: as the forerunner and building block to the political philosophy Wolff never lived to write. The reciprocal, complementary relationship between family and state within the philosopher's socio-political theory is the main concern in question. Even so, the genesis, context and afterlife of his philosophical system and methodology, *prima facie* of secondary importance, are given a prominent role in the argumentation; understanding these factors is indispensable for analysing any part of his philosophy and the same is true the *Oeconomica*.

Accordingly, the second chapter, after the introduction, discusses the pillars of Wolff's philosophy: his scientific method, which presented a universalist way of obtaining knowledge through logical, deductive reasoning; his philosophical system, designed to integrate all sciences into one consistent body of truths; and his theory of natural law, which sought to provide a supra-confessional, theology-free theory to inform moral practice. The summary draws on these findings to derive the ramifications of these predicaments for Wolff's particular interpretation of the genre of *Oeconomica*.

The third chapter presents an analysis of the *Oeconomica* with the help of these three guiding ideas, comparing Wolff's arguments to other works of comparable content. The first section illustrates how the Wolffian method is meeting a challenge in terms of genre: it has to prove by practice that ultimately non-systematic material, the typical substance of wisdom literature, can be sensibly described through deductive demonstration and presented in a rationalised, abstract form. This section covers how Wolff refashions pre-existing practices informed by norm and tradition as logically self-evident morality. The second part illustrates how Wolff's understanding of systematic philosophy dictates a rebuilding of integral topics through other disciplines in the Wolffian universe – sometimes successfully, sometimes less so. The argument specifically examines the *Oeconomica*'s integration with the works on which it is ostensibly based: Wolff's *Psychologia*, *Ethica* and *Jus naturae* as the theoretical foundation to the *Oeconomica*.[54] The third part discusses how Wolff shifts common precepts from religious ideology to the rationalist footing of natural law, operating at a distance from theology. This reconciliation of traditional norms with an assumed order of the world at large is the ultimate step to put culturally relative norms onto a universalist footing.

Chapter 4 considers the *Oeconomica* and its role as *prodromus Politicae* in conjunction with Wolff's welfare state, insofar as it is retrievable from his natural law. The first part will establish the ideological foundation to Wolff's welfare state from his natural law, with specific reference to the absolutist framework given. The second, third and fourth part will consider three specific areas of social welfare and how they are treated in both *Oeconomica* and natural law: school education and universities,

54 Wolff, *Oeconomica*, § 2, pp. 2–3; § 3, pp. 3–4; § 4, pp. 4–6.

prosperity and poor relief, and public health programmes. Wolff's thought will be placed in the historical context, with respect to both policy and ideology, to understand what he merely documents and where he also innovates.

Chapter 5, by way of a coda, offers a comparison between Hanov's completion of Wolff's system with the original author's own work, to further illustrate the idiosyncrasy of the philosopher's universalist discourse. Wolff himself advertised his method as a universal approach to any science, open to anyone with the good sense of applying his rules – and comparing Hanov's half of Wolff's system to the part written by the philosopher himself provides a litmus test to this very proposition. The first part covers Hanov's own literary background to establish an idea of his purpose and focus as an intellectual. The second part probes an analysis of Hanov's half of the *Oeconomica* through the same prism as used before: Wolff's very own understanding of method, system and natural law. The last section establishes whether and how Hanov uses Wolff's postulate for social welfare in his *philosophia civilis*, written to complement the philosophical system. As is easily apparent, Hanov and Wolff differ significantly in their understanding of social welfare. These discrepancies further highlight where either author, instead of building an endogenous scientific discourse as intended, was responding to exogenous influences, such as literary sources or their socio-political environment.

The concluding remarks argue that Wolff's proclamation of social welfare as a core responsibility of the state is not a novel trend; at his time the Prussian rulers who also governed the duchy of Magdeburg and therefore the philosopher's mainstay Halle had established a number of centralised welfare institutions that Wolff is witness more than vanguard to. The association with modern welfare states, however, has to be qualified further – granted institutional similarities, the ideological backdrop is significantly different. The moral justification for Wolff's welfare regime is not based on the idea of universal rights and equality as a liberal democracy would argue. Rather, it serves to fortify existing hierarchies by building citizens' welfare into the moral code of the ruling power. In that sense, the deliberate inclusion of the nuclear family in the socio-political process is not an act of subsidiarity and empowerment but of subordination of private purpose under public interest.

2 The hallmarks of Wolffian philosophy

2.1 Introduction

The purpose of this chapter is to show the idiosyncrasy of Wolff's philosophical project on the basis of three core components: his scientific methodology, the philosophical system and his concept of natural law. All three principles are derived from his philosophy and shape it in turn – in terms of content, integration and ideological thrust, and the same is true for the Oeconomica. Household wisdom as a genre has a markedly different provenance from Wolff's scholastically informed philosophy; understanding the difference and distance between this literary category and his customary discourse helps to elucidate where they prove a challenge to combine.

Wolff's systematic philosophy has the goal to create an all-encompassing network of philosophical truths, covering all of the cosmos that is rationally intelligible to man. This discourse seeks universality in abstraction – and utility in universality. For his theoretical philosophy, the escape into pure abstraction may work well. Its application to household wisdom, however, is a challenge as the subject matter is intrinsically rooted in the fabric that makes up the world of relative truth and material mess: culture, norms and daily practicalities. In order to understand the full extent of the *Oeconomica* as a project and how it fits with the literary tradition, it is necessary to establish what the hallmarks of Wolff's philosophy demand – and the ramifications these demands have for the *Oeconomica* as part of his moral philosophy.

Wolff is not the first one to attempt an academic treatise on the household, and the flagging reception of his work reflects a lasting conundrum in that tradition: that a discourse vastly successful at a popular level rarely carried the day in the university realm. The consistent reproduction of the classics of domestic wisdom literature signal an appeal more than nominal, at least to lay readers.[55] This presents a stark contrast to the lack of scholarly interest for the mundane subject matter and almost generic precepts of wisdom literature, even if found in revered sources such as Hesiod or the Old Testament. Christa von Bauer-Kayatz ascribes the long-lasting scholarly disappointment with the wisdom books of the Old Testament to the 'monotonous theological subject matter', a 'conspicuously rational faith' and a 'eudaemonistic way of thinking defined by practical considerations' which does not seem to sit well with the

55 Whilst Renaissance works such as Leon Battista Alberti's *Della famiglia* (1435–1444) or post-Reformation *Hausväterliteratur* show numerous reprinted editions, the reproduction of the medieval *Epistola cura rei familiaris*, transmitted in manuscript form, proves that content of this type was popular enough to warrant even costly reproduction. See Cossar, *The German Translations of the Pseudo-Bernhardine 'Epistola de cura rei familiaris'*, p. ii. Philip Hahn offers a comprehensive reception history of Coler's *Oeconomia ruralis* and its several editions in Hahn, *Das Haus im Buch*.

https://doi.org/10.1515/9783110714098-002

idea of the sublime sought in cult and revelation.[56] Regardless whether this really is the dominant opinion, her statement signals that these straightforwardly practical passages do not garner as much attention in academic research. A similarly telling sign is the scholarly bewilderment about the second, practical part of Hesiod's *Works & Days*: contrary to the interpretative scope of Hesiodic mythology, his farming advice seems hopelessly dated, fragmentary and rife with superstitions to modern commentators.[57] It is true that, from a transmission point of view, household-focused wisdom literature seems to neither age nor travel well, presumably because it is both too generic and too specific in terms of content, and the subject matter not a good foil for universalist truths about the human condition.

Regardless, the rediscovery of ancient texts sparked a movement to treat these mundane matters from a more learned perspective. Works of various genres, such as the Pseudo-Aristotelian treatise *Oeconomica*, Hesiod's epic *Works & Days*, Xenophon's dialogue *Oikonomikos* and the Roman Rustic writers, served as canonical blueprints and were translated, cited and reworked numerous times between the Renaissance and the French Revolution.[58] Broadly speaking, two trends emerge that correspond with the stylistic opposites presented by Xenophon and Aristotle: discursive prose and theoretical works. On the one hand, there is moral-didactic literature, often with stylistic pretensions, which addresses the layman and can have a varying display of learned content. *Hausväterliteratur* would fall under this heading. On the other hand, *Oeconomica* developed as an academic discipline, which tried to package private life into theoretical, philosophical terms. This academic discipline of *Oeconomica* rose and fell with the canonical power of Aristotle. Within Aristotle's system, practical philosophy was comprised of ethics, economics and politics, each of them analysing man's condition in his role as an individual, as a member of a family and a citizen of a body politic. As mentioned before, other than the pseudo-Aristotelian *Oeconomica*, no text seems to have been discovered to date that could be credibly seen as Aristotle's own take on this philosophical category. The text's varying reception is reflected in scholastic and Renaissance translations, commentaries and scholarly references. There was a demonstrable scholarly interest in the philosophical is-

56 von Bauer-Kayatz, Christa, *Einführung in Die Alttestamentliche Weisheit* (Neukirchen-Vluyn: Neukirchener Verlag des Erziehungsvereins, 1969), p. 9: 'Lange Zeit hat man in der alttestamentlichen Forschung ... bedauernd festgestellt, daß in den Weisheitstexten nur eine sehr eintönige theologische Thematik erklingt, daß sich in ihnen eine auffallend rationale Gläubigkeit äußert, ein eudämonistisches, von Nützlichkeitserwägungen bestimmtes Denken...'.

57 See Hesiod, *Works & Days*, ed. by M. L. West (Oxford: Clarendon Press, 1978), p. 252. Commenting on lines 381–617, the editor says: 'the instruction offered, however, is remarkably sketchy and lacunose, and descriptive passages such as 504–68 and 582–96 make it clear that the poet's aim is not severely didactic'. At p. 333, commenting on lines 724–59, he cites 'silly superstition' as the reason for Wilamowitz condemning 724–59, and doing so with wide-spread scholarly approval.

58 Gray, Productive Men, Reproductive Women, p. 50.

sue of matrimony, even if not necessarily within the context of a household, and Aristotelian texts were consulted on the matter.[59] Yet the Pseudo-Aristotelian *Oeconomica* seems to be mentioned only marginally and not been regarded a standard reference work in that area.[60]

The humanists' break from the scholastic discourse seems to have created a new space for the *Oeconomica* to be reconsidered as a less sublime but meaningful work and category of moral philosophy, now also pursued by non-celibate intellectuals with an interest in the practical side of life, in stark contrast to the medieval scholarly sphere largely dominated by celibate clerics exempt from family life.[61]

The Reformation created a pressing need for teaching materials to be used and circulated in the newly established universities in Germany; in the process, *Oeconomica* gained a new lease of life in the academic realm. Philip Melanchthon (1497–1560) was the first driving force of this effort and, in spite of a conscious break with the scholastic past, he sought to reinterpret Luther's religious experience with the help of the Aristotelian categories in order to create a new university curriculum for philosophy.[62] In that spirit Joachim Camerarius (1500–1574), a contemporary of Luther and Melanchthon, delivered a translation and a commentary of the pseudo-Aristotelian *Oeconomica*.[63] The renewed interest in the philosophical canon further established *Oeconomica* as its own category in the second half of the sixteenth century, where Protestant academics started to publish philosophical textbooks specifically suited to their local university curricula.[64] In the course of this development, the Aristotelian triad of practical philosophy was adapted, reinvented and executed several times over, well into the seventeenth century, by scholars like Camerarius, Bartholomäus Keckermann (c.1572–1609), Johann Alsted (1588–1638) and Clemens Timpler (1563–1624). With this rise of textbooks, the academic trend of *oeconomica* started to become self-referential and to develop its own discourse beyond the original source

59 Albertus Magnus (c.1200–1280), for example, wrote an exposition on economics and included some Pseudo-Aristotelian arguments on matrimony in his commentary on the sentences of Peter Lombard. See Menut, 'Maistre Nicole Oresme', p. 797, and Blažek, Pavel, *Die mittelalterliche Rezeption der aristotelischen Philosophie der Ehe: Von Robert Grosseteste bis Bartholomäus von Brügge (1246/1247–1309)* (Leiden and Boston: Brill, 2007), p. 124.

60 For instance, the *Relectiones theologicae* by the Spanish scholastic Francisco de Vitoria (1483–1546), written in the sixteenth century include a whole treatise on marriage replete with references to Aristotle drawn from the *Politics*, *De anima* and *De animalibus*, but not the *Oeconomica*. See de Vitoria, Francisco *Relectiones theologicae XII* (Lyon: Jacques Boyer, 1557).

61 Blažek, Die mittelalterliche Rezeption der aristotelischen Philosophie der Ehe, p. 391.

62 Ibid., p. 55.

63 Printed posthumously, see Camerarius, Joachim, *Politicorum et oeconomicorum Aristotelis interpretationes et explicationes accuratae* (Frankfurt: Andreas Wechel, 1581).

64 Kusukawa, Sachiko, 'Nature's Regularity in Some Protestant Natural Philosophy Textbooks, 1530–1630', in *Natural Law and Laws of Nature in Early Modern Europe*, ed. by Lorraine Daston and Michael Stolleis (Farnham: Ashgate, 2008), pp. 105–21 (116).

texts. Keckermann's *Systema disciplinae politicae* (1606), a textbook for the disciplines of ethics, economics and politics, departs from the translation-commentary model to provide a broader exposition for household morality as a discipline. His references show that he is using Camerarius' division of chapters of the pseudo-Aristotelian *Oeconomica* and summarizes scholarly views on the authenticity of the work.[65] Alsted's *Encyclopedia* includes a section entitled *Oeconomica*, structured according to new, Ramist principles.[66] Thus, *Oeconomica* in the Aristotelian sense had re-gained the standard of a scholarly discipline in the Schools in Protestant Germany – albeit, the small publication runs show that its influence as a discourse was marginal and confined to localised curricula only.

The small print runs of academic *Oeconomicae* stand in curious contrast to the vast if ephemeral popularity of the classic works of *Hausväterliteratur*, which stand out for their frequent reproductions within specific time frames. Coler's work was reprinted numerous times in the seventeenth century, and even adapted – that is, purged from anti-Catholic remarks or references to Reformation figures – to the Catholic readership.[67] Florinus's *Oeconomus prudens* was first printed in 1702 and last republished in 1750, only four years before the publication of the first part of Wolff's *Oeconomica*. The books must have found enough readers to make one or more republications a profitable venture, which implies that the market responded to the utility value of these works – hardly pleasure reads given their prosaic execution. On one hand, the works of Coler, Florinus and Menius reflect the re-evaluation of the spiritual importance of family life during the Reformation.[68] On the other, they clearly responded to a practical need at the time.

The academic renditions of Keckermann, Alsted and Camerarius proved nowhere near as successful as their popular, vernacular equivalents. This implies that the success of wisdom literature hinged on its perceived utility, its connection to cultural context and a specific audience. The academic tendency to universalise the discourse rendered it void of genuine utility without making the subject matter substantially interesting to an academic audience. It is the prominence of practice over theory, cultural specificity over universality that lends the lay tradition its poignancy. Ephemeral as it may have been, this tradition lasted longer than their universalist renditions in academia. All this bodes badly for a universalist approach to this type of work. Yet Wolff's *Oeconomica* tries to wed two factors that seem to live separate lives in the literary tradition: practical utility and universality – in fact, practical utility *through* universal appeal. To Wolff, wedding theory and practice is of utmost necessity: every

65 Keckermann, Bartholomäus, *Systema disciplinae politicae* (Hanover: Peter Anton, 1616), p. 12.
66 See the chart dividing the field up into dichotomies, in Alsted, Johann Heinrich, *Encyclopedia: Septem tomis distincta* (Herborn: Christoph Corvin, 1630), p. 16.
67 Hahn, *Das Haus im Buch*, pp. 233–6.
68 Gause, Ute and Stephanie Scholz (eds.), *Ehe und Familie im Geist des Luthertums: Die Oeconomia Christiana (1529) des Justus Menius* (Leipzig: Evangelische Verlagsanstalt, 2012), p. 11.

human, with very, very few exceptions, is somehow born into and part of a basic family structure; and given the universality of this predicament, instruction is expedient.

The following will discuss the three basic elements of Wolff's philosophy – scientific method, philosophical system and natural law – and their relation to said purpose. The first part will discuss his very own scientific method which Wolff considered a universal approach to any field of science – even morality. In the second instance, Wolff's philosophical system will be discussed as a structural obligation and a metaphysical concept. Lastly, a discussion of his natural law shows where Wolff takes a literary tradition and utilizes it as a new foundation for a moral philosophy independent from Scripture. Since Wolff's work is synthetic in approach and execution alike, the discussion will take sources into account that the philosopher was known to consult. This will help to see where Wolff chooses, amends and fuses concepts from other authors – and whether the result follows or breaks with tradition.

2.2 Wolff's scientific method

2.2.1 Wolff's method in context

The scientific method is a trope born early in Wolff's work, and persists throughout. Inspired by mathematics, Wolff sought to extract methodological constants from the fields of algebra and geometry to apply them to less certain, no less important fields of human knowledge – moral philosophy in particular.[69] Initially designed as an alternative to existing modes of scholarship, the method quickly crystallised into an intrinsic aspect of Wolffian philosophy. Parallel to practice, the theory also expanded: Wolff's method does not merely serve to format content – the content of his philosophy increasingly serves to justify his method. According to Wolff's own, professedly original definition, philosophy in general is the science of all possible things.[70] In that sense, 'philosophy' does not refer to a specific branch of inquiry but serves as an umbrella term for categorised human knowledge. Under this heading, different 'philosophies', or disciplines, exist, as transpires from the names of his Latin works: *philosophia prima*, *philosophia moralis*, *philosophia physica*, amongst others.

---

69 Wolff, in fact, credits his interest in mathematics to his methodological quest: 'Also machte ich mich anfangs über die Mathematick aus keiner anderen Absicht, als damit ich ihr Art im Erfinden und Beweisen zu Schlüssen genauer erkennen möchte, in Hoffnung dadurch geschickt zu werden, auch die Erkäntniß GOttes, der Seele und der Tugend zu Überzeugung aller Menschen, die dem Lichte der Vernunfft Raum geben, zu einer ungezweiffelten Gewißheit zu bringen.' in: Wolff, Christian, *Mathematisches Lexicon* (Leipzig: Son of Johann Friedrich Gleditsch, 1716), sig. a2v.

70 Wolff, Christian, 'Discursus praeliminaris', § 29, in *Philosophia rationalis sive logica, methodo scientifica pertractata* (Frankfurt and Leipzig: Renger, 1740), p. 13.

The titles further declare that these disciplines were written out *methodo scientifica*, i.e. in the scientific method. In contrast, Wolff's German writings do not carry *Philosophie* or the German term *Weltweisheit* in the title but simply point to the subject matter under the heading of *Vernünfftige Gedancken* – that is, 'rational' or 'reasonable thoughts'.[71] The term *vernünfftig* provides the programmatic analogue to *methodus scientifica* in his Latin books: 'science', by definition, is a mode of secure demonstration, based on *Vernunft*, that is, reason.[72] Conversely, method becomes the definitive element to each *scientia*, or discipline, and of *philosophia* in general as the summary of all sciences objectively explained through deductive reasoning.[73] The same relationship between subject matter and methodology is defined for the *Oeconomica*: *oeconomica* is the science of small societies, in Wolff's definition, and since it is a science it has to be treated with the scientific method.[74]

Wolff's idea of true *mathesis*, real learning, aspired to the clarity mathematical sciences could achieve with heuristic means. Yet rather than replicate the mathematical format his scientific method sought to identify and utilise shared universal principles. Throughout his work, there is a palpable progression from formalistic imitation to conceptual kinship: Wolff's doctoral thesis, written *methodo mathematica*, is structured into axioms, definitions and corollaries that inform each other, mirroring the appearance of a mathematical treatise. His later philosophical works, *methodo scientifica*, follow a different pattern: they present a progressive series of arguments packed into uniform syllogisms.[75] Thus, the mathematical format of Wolff's earlier work eventually gives way to the scientific method. The actual method is described in the 'Discursus praeliminaris', the programmatic work to Wolff's philosophical system, in the form of a user-friendly list of rules. Briefly said: no principles can be used that have not been sufficiently proven, no terminology that is not sufficiently defined; all propositions have to be based on the principles validated in the discourse; newly introduced terminology needs to build on the terms introduced beforehand; all propositions need to be

71 See, for example, the full title of what is otherwise known as Wolff's *Deutsche Politik*: Wolff, Christian, *Vernünfftige Gedancken von dem gesellschaftlichen Leben der Menschen und insonderheit dem gemeinen Wesen* (Frankfurt and Leipzig: Renger, 1747); the Latin counterpart would be *Philosophia civilis*.

72 Wolff, *Philosophia rationalis*, § 30, p. 14: 'Per *Scientiam* hic intelligo habitum asserta demonstrandi.' On *Vernunft* and *methodus scientifica* as semantically equivalent expressions, see Günter Gawlick, *Wolff-Index: Stellenindex und Konkordanz zu Christian Wolffs 'Discursus praeliminaris de philosophia in genere'* (Stuttgart-Bad Cannstatt: Frommann-Holzboog, 1999), p. xi.

73 Lüthje, 'Christian Wolffs Philosophiebegriff', p. 63.

74 Wolff, *Oeconomica*, §1, sig. A: 'Per *Oeconomicam* intelligimus scientiam dirigendi actiones suas liberas in societatibus minoribus.' Ibid., § 4 *nota*, sig. A2v: 'Supponimus nimirum Oeconomicam methodo scientifica esse tradendam...'.

75 See, Wolff, Christian, and Laurent David Bollhagen, Philosophia practica universalis, mathematica methodo conscripta (Leipzig: Christian Goez, 1703), in contrast to Christian Wolff, Philosophia practica universalis, methodo scientifica pertractata. Pars prior (Halle: Renger, 1744).

formally demonstrated before they can act as the basis for further propositions; a correct proposition needs to accurately determine the condition under which the predicate conforms with the subject.[76] In principle, the method consists of nothing other than a definition of scientific rigour where, similarly to a Euclidean treatise, all definitions and predicaments are built from scratch and concatenated into one successive, stable chain of arguments – a self-sustaining train of thought without the need to resort to authoritative sources. Laborious though it seems, this strict rigour is imposed to keep incertitude at bay by not letting any vague propositions or unclear definitions slip into the discourse. Hypotheses, for that matter, are only allowed where they can still further the thought process, even though they can never attain the same status as valid propositions.[77] Mid-explanation, Wolff returns to stressing the utility of sound propositions, labouring a point that seems self-explanatory.[78] Yet this illustrates that with the absence of a methodological standard for science or philosophy, a new mode of scientific inquiry had to stand its ground vis-à-vis established modes of scholarship.[79] Indeed, critics may have proven recalcitrant; yet to Wolff and his followers, the method promised an actionable, sure-footed approach to science, progress from traditional teaching methods and the neutralisation of confessional battle grounds through the examination of the world rather than articles of faith.[80]

Wolff's method is synthetic in nature, although its simplified guise is stripped of all reference to his borrowings. Its composite parts transpire throughout the Wolffian corpus where its loans from logic, mathematics and rival epistemological approaches are explained in more detail. Whilst an explanation of the method needs to precede the corpus to explain its method, it is only throughout Wolff's entire philosophy that the reader comes to understand the premises and tacit assumptions the method itself rests on. Here as elsewhere, Wolff adopts and fuses elements from other thinkers where he recognizes conceptual parallels in accord with each other and his own ideas. His debt to Leibniz, who is regularly mentioned in prefaces, essays and footnotes, is unmistakeable. Wolff also names several inspirations for his method in his *Ratio praelectionum*, amongst them Peter Ramus, Melanchthon, Descartes, Locke, Malebranche and Tschirnhaus.[81] Tracing concepts intertextually is not always easy

---

76 Wolff, 'Discursus praeliminaris', §§ 117–121, pp. 54–57.

77 Ibid., § 127, p. 61.

78 Ibid., §§ 122, pp. 57–58.

79 Wolff, at unrelated points, uses examples to promote the utility of his method, for example in his illustration of a *syllogismus biformis*, see Wolff, *Logica*, § 489 *nota*, p. 374: '*Omnis liber methodo demonstrativa conscriptus certiorem cognitionem largitur lectori, quam liber secundum scholae methodum conscriptus*'.

80 Wolff specifies this particular objective in his autobiography. See Christian Wolff and Heinrich Wuttke, *Christian Wolffs eigene Lebensbeschreibung* (Leipzig: Weidmann, 1841), pp. 4–5. See also, Lutterbeck, *Staat und Gesellschaft bei Christian Thomasius und Christian Wolff*, p. 146.

81 Bissinger, Die Struktur der Gotteserkenntnis, p. 14.

since Wolff rarely references his borrowings *in situ*. Still, affinities with other thinkers help to place the method within its historical context. Wolff's keenness on a rule-based method – in fact, the postulate of a universal, deductive method to weed out everything hypothetical or falsifiable – is strongly reminiscent of Descartes.[82] In fact, Wolff and Descartes share the optimism regarding the wide-ranging capacity of the human intellect, the conviction that all sciences can be treated with the same method and that all disciplines are interconnected. Wolff's modification of Descartes' premises, however, demonstrates how his scientific method picks and mixes from different, sometimes opposing traditions to reconcile them in one single approach. For Descartes, the criterion of truth in a proposition is that something can be understood clearly and distinctly – a beguilingly simple repartee to the obtuseness of scholastic logic.[83] Wolff's early days saw him accepting this rationale in his own practice. His approach changed under the auspices of Leibniz, whose criticism of Descartes' truth criterion led Wolff to adopt the scholastic 'Principle of Non-Contradiction' as a more formal approach to testing veracity.[84] The Principle of Non-Contradiction, simply put, says that for a statement to hold true, it must not contain a contradiction. In practice, this condition is guaranteed in a statement where the subject is contained in the predicate – so Wolff *qua* Leibniz.[85] Furthermore, Wolff claims that the principle is compatible with Tschirnhaus's *conceptabilitas*, the intellectual grasp of human beings that can conceive the conceivable only. Ehrenfried Walther von Tschirnhaus (1651–1708), a Cartesian and acquainted with Spinoza, was no friend of scholastic philosophy.[86] His writings treat certainty not as some exogenous quality assured by logic but as an operation of the mind and intrinsic to the intellect: if we can think an entity, the potentiality of its existence is implied – the impossibility to conceive of something means it cannot be possible either. By implication, therefore, the cosmos, or all things that can rationally be, are coextensive with the reach of the human mind; and *con-*

---

82 Schneiders, Werner, '"Deus est philosophus absolute summus." Über Christian Wolff's Philosophie und Philosophiebegriff', in *Christian Wolff: 1679–1754: Interpretationen zu seiner Philosophie und deren Wirkung*, ed. by Werner Schneiders (Hamburg: Felix Meiner Verlag, 1983), pp. 9–30, p. 13. In fact, Descartes had laid out a similar methodological checklist before Wolff, see Descartes, René, *Regulae ad directionem ingenii = Rules for the direction of the natural intelligence: a bilingual edition of the Cartesian treatise on method.*, ed. by George Heffernan (Amsterdam: Rodopi, 1998).

83 'Verum est quod clare et distincte intelligitur', quoted in Linke, Paul Ferdinand, *D. Humes Lehre vom Wissen: Ein Beitrag zur Relationstheorie im Anschluss an Locke und Hume* (Leipzig: Wilhelm Engelmann, 1901), p. 9.

84 Wolff, Christian, *Ausführliche Nachricht von seinen eigenen Schrifften* (Frankfurt a.M.: J.B. Andreä and H. Hort, 1733), p. 227; Corr, Charles A., 'Christian Wolff and Leibniz', *Journal of the History of Ideas*, 36 (1975), 247.

85 Wolff, *Philosophia rationalis*, § 513, p. 392: 'Veritas est determinabilitas praedicati per notionem subjecti'. See also Bissinger, *Die Struktur der Gotteserkenntnis*, p. 75.

86 Winter, Eduard, Der Freund B. Spinozas E. W. v. Tschirnhaus: die Einheit von Theorie und Praxis (Berlin: Akademie Verlag, 1977), p. 6.

ceptubilitas becomes the yoke to join ontology and epistemology together.[87] Wolff furthermore uses this concept as a bridge to link the Principle of Non-contradiction to his vision of philosophy as the science of all things, not insofar as they are material but simply possible: possible in the sense of non-contradictory, that is, possible in the sense of conform to his truth criterion.[88] Wolff's truth criterion hence lives a double life as a practical tool inherited from the scholastics, and as an epistemological principle adopted from anti-scholastic sources.

The same goes for the Principle of Sufficient Reason, another scholastic inheritance via Leibniz. The Principle of Sufficient Reason formalizes the notion that everything existent in this world happens on account of an identifiable cause. This inevitable relationship – successive or simultaneous – prescribes the order in which philosophical arguments and disciplines have to be concatenated.[89] Just as the Non-Contradictory and the Possible are conflated in Wolff's world, the quest for the 'why' rather than the 'that' marked the distinction in the Wolffian philosophy between mere historical and philosophical cognition: the fact that cognition did not stop at recording facts and their cause and consequence, but sought to discover the causal links between intrinsic, universal principles.[90] By its very definition, method is synonymous with order, for Wolff believes that the philosophical method coincides with the order through which the philosopher ought to present his teachings, proceeding along the lines of cause and effect.[91] His idea of proceeding, *pulchro nexu*, along the natural linkage of arguments rather than from general to specific, recalls the understanding of the Renaissance Aristotelian Jacopo Zabarella (1533– 1589) – and further-

87 van Peursen, C. A., 'E.W. Von Tschirnhaus and the Ars Inveniendi', *Journal of the History of Ideas*, 54.3 (1993), 395–410 (406).

88 Wolff, Christian, *Philosophia prima sive ontologia, methodo scientifica pertractata* (Frankfurt and Leipzig: Renger, 1736), p. 65, § 85: '*Possibile* est, quod nullam contradictionem involvit, seu, quod non est impossibile.'

89 van Peursen, C. A., 'Ars inveniendi im Rahmen der Metaphysik Christian Wolffs: Die Rolle der ars inveniendi', in Christian Wolff 1679–1754. Interpretationen zu seiner Philosophie und deren Wirkung, mit einer Bibliographie der Wolff-Literatur, ed. by Werner Schneiders (Hamburg: Felix Meiner, 1986), pp. 67–88, p. 81.

90 Waibel, Violetta L., 'Natur als "Aggregat" und "System". Kants implizite Auseinandersetzung mit Wolff und Lambert in der "Ersten Einleitung in die Kritik der Urteilskraft"', in *Kant und die Berliner Aufklärung: Akten des IX. internationalen Kant-Kongresses*, ed. by Ralph Schumacher, Rolf-Peter Horstmann, and Volker Gerhardt (Berlin: De Gruyter, 2001), pp. 667–675, p. 669: 'Intrinsisch sind alle zureichenden Gründe, Wolffs Kriterium, mit denen er das philosophisch-wissenschaftliche Denken von bloß historischem Wissen unterscheidet.... Der zureichende Grund eines jeden Sachverhalts beruht nach Wolff auf den ontologisch notwendig anzunehmenden, verborgenen Zusammenhängen, den geheimen Vollkommenheiten der Natur, die es durch die allein dazu fähige philosophische Erkenntnis aufzudecken gilt.'

91 Wolff, 'Discursus praeliminaris', § 115, p. 53: 'Per *Methodum philosophicam* intelligo ordinem, quo in tradendis dogmatis uti debet philosophus.'

more evokes early Christian imagery of *pulchritudo mundi*, the beauty *qua* regularity of cosmos and creation.[92]

On paper, Wolff's method is a simple set of rules to ensure veracity *qua* rigour. In practice, his ideal of heuristics superseded pure method, embodied in the *ars inveniendi*, the skill to find hidden truths. Before Wolff, the term had been formulated by Peter Ramus (Pierre de la Ramée, 1515–1572) and Tschirnhaus, who exported it from the context of oratory and reinvented it as a type of logical thinking, an acting principle middling between human reason and applied method.[93] Wolff himself further formalised it as a skill capable of identifying hidden truths, be that in existing knowledge or unexplored fields.[94] The *ars inveniendi* is less a logical than a psycho-logical concept: it is the capacity to identify the truth in disparate places through analogies and similarities, glimpsing regularity and order in a complex world. Epistemologically, the net is cast wide in terms of admissible evidence, as long as all happens under the guidance of rationality. Wolff tacitly endorses a bigamy of reason: truth can be uncovered where reason is wedded to experience, *connubium rationis et experientiae*, or to imagination, *connubium imaginationis cum ratione*.[95] Under the guidance of rationality both empirical and theoretical evidence are allowed although the latter – using definitions, propositions and axiomatic statements – is a purer form of science than the exploration of the truth on an empirical basis.[96] But rather than taking sides, Wolff places himself somewhere between pure rationalism and raw empiricism whereby both forms of inquiry complement each other. This is evident in the way in which he explores certain disciplines both through thought and observation. Cosmology, for example, is divided up into *cosmologia generalis*, pure theory, and coupled with the *cosmologia experimentalis*, which seeks to stabilise the theory in experiment.[97] Psychology is divided up into

---

92 See, for instance, Zabarella, Jacopo, *Opera logica*, ed. by Wilhelm Risse (Hildesheim: Olms, 1966), Ch. 12, p. 155; Poppi, Antonino, 'Zabarella, or Aristotelianism as a Rigorous Science', in *The Impact of Aristotelianism on Modern Philosophy*, ed. by Ricardo Pozzo (Washington, DC: Catholic University of America Press, 2003), pp. 35–63, p. 39. The concept of *pulchritudo mundi* as the natural regularity of the world appears in the Middle Ages already, e.g. in the writings of the Dominican monk Ulrich Engelbert von Straßburg (c.1220–1277). See Schneider, Norbert, *Geschichte der Ästhetik von der Aufklärung bis zur Postmoderne: Eine paradigmatische Einführung* (Stuttgart: Reclam, 1996), p. 7.

93 Schneiders and van Peursen, 'Ars inveniendi im Rahmen der Metaphysik Christian Wolffs', p. 75.

94 Wolff, 'Discursus praeliminaris', § 74, p. 35: 'Definitur adeo Ars inveniendi per scientiam veritatem latentem investigandi.'

95 Wolff, Christian, *Psychologia empirica, methodo scientifica pertractata* (Frankfurt and Leipzig: Renger, 1732), § 496, p. 379: 'Concursus rationis & experientiae in cognoscendo Connubium rationis & experientiae dici solet'; ibid., § 150 *nota*, p. 104.' [p]atet adeo usum imaginationis rectificari per connubium imaginationis cum ratione, ut adeo ars communis inveniendi ... fiat proba opusque producat perfectum...'.

96 van Peursen, 'Ars inveniendi im Rahmen der Metaphysik Christian Wolffs', p. 80.

97 Wolff, Christian, *Cosmologia generalis, methodo scientifica pertractata* (Frankfurt; Leipzig: Renger, 1731), p. 3 § 4: 'Datur Cosmologia duplex: altera scientifica, altera experimentalis. *Cosmologia generalis scientificae* est, quae theoriam generalem de mundo ex Ontologiae principiis demonstrat:

psychologia rationalis and *psychologia empirica* to the same end. Wolff's assumes that either form of inquiry should lead to the same results, to the real truth, if done correctly.

Where authors like Descartes, Malebranche, or Locke and Newton, sought to formulate scientific approaches that combine rules for inquiry with a restriction on admissible forms of evidence, Wolff doubles the stringency of the rules but also the range for material allowed. A demonstration can only build on 'definitions, indubitable experience, axioms and propositions already proven'.[98] What sounds like a restriction in theory turns out a permission in practice: the permission to combine experience, accepted wisdoms, elements from other authors with his own ideas – if they can but be made to conform with his methodological criteria. Often, this methodological overhaul simply spelled verbal clarification. In the preface to his *Deutsche Metaphysik*, for example, Wolff prides himself on having improved material from St Augustine and Leibniz in his demonstrative manner, so as to eliminate any trace of doubt from their arguments.[99] Once clarified, Wolff announces, he adapted some of those 'Leibnizian truths' into the Wolffian chain of reasons. His revival of scholastic *termini* is guided by the same approach: Wolff proclaims to have adapted their material to a post-Cartesian world by refining their badly defined terminology, improving obscure expressions and updating the proofs of their principles.[100] Just as with the borrowings for his method, it becomes permanently unclear where Wolff's content is feeding on other authors or on his own ideas, for on the surface Wolff's works tend to chiefly cite Wolff himself, true to his methodological predicament. As he says quite openly, Wolff is only intent on truth, regardless whether someone else has said it before.[101] Authorship and authority lose relevance where method can ascertain universal veracity. This approach was a poignant departure from the scholastic idea of scholarship and did not lose legitimacy after Wolff but continued with Kant.[102] This

---

Contra experimentalis est, quae theoriam in scientifica stabilitam vel stabiliendam ex observationibus elicit.'

98 Wolff, Christian, *Philosophia rationalis sive Logica, methodo scientifica pertractata*, (Halle: Renger, 1740), § 498, p. 379: 'In specie autem probatio *Demonstratio* dicitur, si in syllogismis, quos inter se concatenamus, non utamur praemissis, nisi definitionibus, experientiis indubitatis, axiomatis & propositionibus jam ante demonstratis…'.

99 Wolff, Christian, Vernünfftige Gedancken von Gott, der Welt und der Seele des Menschen, auch allen Dingen überhaupt, den Liebhabern der Wahrheit mitgetheilet, (Halle: Renger, 1743), § 10, p. 6.

100 Wolff, Philosophia prima sive Ontologia, § 7, pp. 3–5.

101 'Ich suche nichts als Wahrheit, und bekümmere mich im übrigen nicht, ob sie einer vor mir auch gesagt oder nicht.', Wolff expresses in all frankness in a preface to a selection of Leibniz's works, see Leibniz, Gottfried Wilhelm, *Kleinere philosophische Schriften*, ed. by Caspar Jacob Huth and Christian Wolff (Jena: Mayer, 1740), p. xv.

102 Schneider, Ulrich J., 'Leibniz und der Eklektizismus', in *Neuzeitliches Denken: Festschrift für Hans Poser zum 65. Geburtstag*, ed. by Günter Abel, Hans-Jürgen Engfer and Christoph Hubig (Berlin: Walter de Gruyter, 2002), p. 234.

emancipation of truth from authorial context through methodological verification also meant that Wolff could build an entire, self-contained corpus of knowledge from scratch, like Euclid did and Descartes aspired to.

2.2.2 Demonstrative morality

Arguably, it is exactly this epistemological permissiveness that allowed Wolff to build a methodologically consistent corpus across a whole range of disciplines. Trusting his method to be ideologically agnostic, he felt justified to touch upon natural and moral philosophy under one and the same heading. Historically, this attitude was not without controversy at the time: the idea of applying a scientific – or geometric method – to the field of moral philosophy had long been viewed with suspicion. According to the natural law philosopher Samuel Pufendorf (1632–1694), one of Wolff's major sources, this opinion sprang from the Aristotelian dogma that the subject matter of morality – unlike mathematics – was not suitable for this kind of treatment: natural science and human behaviour were made of different fabrics that required different treatment; natural philosophy explored necessary cause and consequence; moral, or human sciences, could only be explored under the predicament of contingency.[103]

A paradigm shift occurred in the seventeenth century when new scientific approaches brought fresh epistemological wind into the debate. Pufendorf took it upon himself to make an argument for systematic, logical exploration of practical philosophy, in the context of his natural law. Certainty, so Pufendorf, was not hindered by the spectre of contingency in theory; and the apprehension about determinism in moral discourse was unnecessary insofar as one could logically explore probabilities and weigh them against one another with a degree of certainty, as suggested by the English natural law philosopher Richard Cumberland (1631/1632–1718).[104] Moreover, possibilities could be just as much subject to positive inquiry as realities: it did not matter whether a triangle existed in reality for a mathematician to make sound conclusions about it, and the same, argued Pufendorf, was true for the possibilities in human action, in reference to Erhard Weigel (1625–1699).[105] Weigel had indeed deliv-

---

103 Pufendorf, Samuel Freiherr von, *De iure naturae et gentium libri octo*, Vol. 1, Bk I, Ch. 2, § 1 (Frankfurt and Leipzig: Knoch-Eslinger, 1759), p. 23.

104 Pufendorf, *De iure naturae et gentium*, Vol 1, Bk I, Ch. 2, §IV, p. 26: 'Licet enim sciri possit, quid possibile sit, possibiliaque inter se comparari queant, ac certo sciri, quidnam ex duobus possibilibus non modo pluris aut minoris valiturum fit, si quando exsistant, sed etiam quodnam e pluribus causis, quod a paucioribus nunc existentibus aut mox extituris fieri possit; quod autem pluribus modis fieri potest, magis probabile sit futurum esse, plerisque valeat eius expectatio: (vid. Richardus CUMBERLAND de legibus naturae c. 3. §. 4. n. 4).'

105 Pufendorf, *De iure naturae et gentium*, Vol 1, Bk I, Ch. 2, § II, p. 24.

ered ground-breaking work on the application of the *mos geometricus* in the field of morality. Wolff's own education was tinged with Weigel's thought through the reception of the mathematician Johann Christoph Sturm (1635–1703) and the mediation of his successor Georg Albrecht Hamberger (1662–1716), who taught at his alma mater in Jena at the time.[106] It was also upon Weigel's instigation that Pufendorf had tried his hand at writing a practical philosophy in a mathematical method at an early point of his career, quite similar to Wolff's early attempt *methodo mathematica*.[107] Yet he, too, abandoned the strictly mathematical mode for common-sense, rational analysis of canonical sources – not in strict application of logic nor in pure servitude to the written law. Perhaps this lack of stringency was the reason why Leibniz considered him a *parvus philosophus*. Leibniz agrees that exploring the relationship between cause and effect is not an argument for but a cure against determinism.[108] Yet he claims that Pufendorf did not understand that the rules of logic were congruent with the 'nature of things' and thus representative nothing other than the divine order.[109] Still, Pufendorf's pledge for seeking certitude in possibilities lives on in Wolff's definition of philosophy as *scientia possibilium*. The important paradigm shift that Pufendorf bears witness to is the conviction that Right and Wrong can be laid down like a law, in absolute terms: as true and false. Given this predicament, consummation was merely a matter of method.

The scientific foray into moral philosophy did not progress uncontested. The idea of establishing a moral code through scientific means, *more geometrico*, gained notoriety with Spinoza's *Ethica*. The work may also have caused the outcry it did not merely for the method it used but for the unorthodox opinions it defended. Combining pantheist leanings, a disavowal of miracles, prophecy and revelation with an individualistic concept of happiness, Spinoza's discourse caused unease amongst philosophers and theologians alike for a host of reasons. It was not just that the rational

106 Bissinger, *Die Struktur der Gotteserkenntnis*, p. 12; Neveu, Sébastien, 'Secondary Authors' Influence on the Formation of the Wolffian "System of Truths"', in *Handbuch Christian Wolff*, pp. 55–71, pp. 65–66; Menzel, Wolfgang Walter, *Vernakuläre Wissenschaft: Christian Wolffs Bedeutung für die Herausbildung und Durchsetzung des Deutschen als Wissenschaftssprache* (Tübingen: Niemeyer, 1996), p. 76.

107 Thomasius, Christian, *Historia juris naturalis* (Stuttgart, Bad Cannstatt: Frommann-Holzboog, 1972), § 28, p. 6.

108 Leibniz, Gottfried Wilhelm, *Die Theodicee*, trans. by Robert Habs (Leibniz: Philipp Reclam jun., 1883), p. 57: 'Es ist nämlich falsch, daß das Ereignis eintrete, was man auch immer thun möge: es wird eintreten, weil man das thut, was es herbeiführt, und wenn das Ereignis geschrieben steht, so steht die Ursache, welche es herbeiführt, ebenfalls geschrieben. Anstatt also die Lehre von einer das Handeln beeinträchtigenden Nothwendigkeit zu bestätigen, dient die Verknüpfung zwischen Wirkung und Ursache vielmehr dazu, sie zu widerlegen.'

109 Thomann, Marcel, 'Ideologische Aspekte der praktischen Philosophie Wolffs', in *Christian Wolff, 1679–1754: Interpretationen zu seiner Philosophie und deren Wirkung*, ed. by Werner Schneiders (Hamburg: Felix Meiner, 1983), pp. 193–202, p. 196.

ordering, the implication of necessary cause and consequence within human action reeked of determinism.[110] Spinoza also shook up some fundamental conceptions of Christian philosophy, downgrading hope and charity from virtues whilst trying to rationally explore human affects considered otherwise vicious and sinful – and boldly proposing that nature and God alike are subject to some form of necessity.[111]

Postulating logical necessity in the realm of divine and human action was considered an affront to dominant Christian philosophy where the concession of a space for free will was a moral imperative. Traditionally, the topic had already caused a headache. Bible passages documenting God's omnipotence and influence upon man's intent suggested a fatalism of their own, a problem Erasmus amply discusses.[112] Spinoza's ethics threaten the concept from below, by insinuating that human affects and actions are subject to nature, not merely intellect and will, and it was this brand of determinism that Wolff's bitter opponent Johann Joachim Lange (1670–1744) claimed to identify in his vision of the 'world as a machine'.[113] Yet regardless of associations made by political detractors, the logical patterns Wolff seeks in morality are a far cry from Spinoza's nexus of necessity. The focus of Wolff's philosophy on possible rather than existent things was the definitive distinction setting his creed apart from atheism or determinism.[114]

On the surface, the restriction of moral theory to contingent matters recalls Pufendorf's argument for certainty in moral philosophy. But Wolff's quest for certitude in the field of morality is not actually interested in probabilities in the real, material world but certainties in the possible world. Following the metaphysics of the late scholastic Francisco Suárez (1548–1617), Wolff's universal propositions are not built on material necessity but are non-contradictory entities in the abstract.[115] Real or not, they are descriptive of the perfect world order not as it is but as it *could* be – or *meant* to be, rather; and whether these moral propositions actualise in the real world is contingent upon the free will of the individual. To further illustrate this point, Wolff draws another distinction between the necessary and the contingent: in his reading, the opposite of something necessary would be impossible or a contradiction in itself;

110 Israel, Jonathan I., *Radical Enlightenment: Philosophy and the Making of Modernity, 1650–1750* (Oxford: Oxford University Press, 2001), p. 296.

111 Spinoza, Benedict de, *Die Ethik, nach geometrischer Methode dargestellt*, trans. by Otto Baensch (Hamburg: Felix Meiner, 1967), p. 100, pp. 187–8; for Spinoza's quite liberal attitude towards sex, see Israel, *Radical Enlightenment*, p. 86.

112 Erasmus published a disputation dedicated to the topic, see Erasmus, Desiderius, *De libero arbitrio diatribe, sive collatio* (Basel: Johann Froben, 1524).

113 Bianco, Bruno, 'Freiheit gegen Fatalismus. Zu Joachim Langes Kritik an Wolff', in *Halle. Aufklärung und Pietismus*, ed. by Norbert Hinske (Heidelberg: Lambert Schneider, 1989), pp. 111–56, pp. 117–8.

114 See, for instance, Wolff's proof of God's existence: 'Probe notandum est, Deum existere non concludi ex eo, quod mundus existit, sed quod contingenter existit.', Wolff, Christian, *Philosophia moralis sive ethica methodo scientifica pertractata. Pars tertia* (Halle, Magdeburg: Renger, 1751), § 12 *nota*, p. 13.

115 Darge, Rolf, Suárez' transzendentale Seinsauslegung und die Metaphysiktradition (Leiden: Brill, 2004), pp. 37–38.

for the contingent, however, there *is* a possible opposite.[116] To use an example, a pebble that drops will not spontaneously fly – a man at the crossroads can go left or right, i.e. his action is contingent upon his decision. In that sense, he not only defends a morality based on the contingency of its actualisation in the real world – he also links up the necessarily moral in the possible world to the non-contradictory; that link justifies its exploration with the Principle of Non-Contradiction, Wolff's chosen truth criterion. Moreover, Wolff's idea of sufficient reason not only refers to relationships of cause and consequence – a nexus also exists between an intelligent being's purpose and the impulse to an action; the motive of an intended outcome impels will to cause action.[117] Wolff here builds on Thomas Aquinas's postulate linking motive and moral action through the fulcrum of the will. The will as a moveable, malleable force behind moral action is in itself prompted by a motive as perceived by *ratio*, reason. In that context, something reason has identified as good can function both as motive and end to the will prompting action.[118] Suárez had developed this concept further. He identified the motive not just as any but as the qualifying factor behind moral action whereby an individual only acts according to a bidding with the bidding in mind.[119] Wolff, finally, combines this argument directly with the concept of sufficient reason: the motive is the sufficient cause for the will to effectuate moral action.[120] Yet again, this conceptualisation renders both psychological and moral discourse susceptible to logical argument; and as will be seen, Wolff reverse-engineers the motives from universal purpose in order to direct moral action.[121]

---

116 Wolff, Christian, De differentia nexus rerum sapientis et fatalis necessitatis, nec non systematis harmoniae praestabilitatae et hypothesium Spinosae luculenta commentatio, (Halle: Renger, 1737), p. 18: 'Evidens adeo erat necessarium hic dici, cujus oppositum impossibile, seu contradictionem involvit; Contingens vero vocari, cujus oppositum possibile deprehenditur.'

117 Wolff, Cosmologia generalis, § 31, p. 28.

118 Thomas Aquinas, *Contra Gentiles*, Bk 3, Ch. 10, n. 15: 'Dictum est autem quod in ordine actionum moralium duo principia voluntatem praecedunt: scilicet vis apprehensiva; et obiectum apprehensum, quod est finis. Cum autem unicuique mobili respondeat proprium motivum, non quaelibet vis apprehensiva est debitum motivum cuiuslibet appetitus, sed huius haec, et illius alia. Sicut igitur appetitus sensitivi proprium motivum est vis apprehensiva sensualis, ita voluntatis proprium motivum est ratio ipsa.' See also ibid., Bk 3, Ch. 10, n. 16: 'Rursus, cum ratio multa bona et multos fines apprehendere possit; cuiuslibet autem sit proprius finis: et voluntatis erit finis et primum motivum, non bonum quodlibet, sed bonum quoddam determinatum.'

119 Suárez, Francisco, *De pace, de bello: Über den Frieden, über den Krieg*, Vol. 2, ed. by Markus Kremer and Josef de Vries (Stuttgart-Bad Cannstatt: Frommann-Holzboog, 2013), p. XXXI: 'Zu einem sittlich vollständigen Akt sei es nämlich erforderlich, dass ausdrücklich auch aus dem Motiv des Gebotes heraus gehandelt werden will. Die hierin angesprochene motivationale Kraft der Tugend wird durch die Bedingung bestätigt, die verlangt, dass unter jeglichen Umständen gut gehandelt werden soll.'

120 Wolff, *Psychologia empirica*, § 887, p. 669: 'Ratio sufficiens actuum volitionis ac nolitionis dicitur Motivum.'

121 The idea of the motive as a sufficient reason to volition also appears in Leibniz. See Antognazza, Maria Rosa, *Leibniz: An Intellectual Biography* (Cambridge: Cambridge University Press, 2009), p. 103; Dyck, Corey, 'Power, Harmony, and Freedom: Debating Causation in 18th-Century Germany', in

Three important elements are therefore synthesised in Wolff's scientific approach to morality: the existence of norms good and bad in the absolute; their necessary linkage in a possible, ideal world, whilst their realisation in the real world remains contingent upon the human will; and the motive as a sufficient reason for the will prompting action, be that moral or not. In that sense, Wolff's method applied to morality is as synthetic as it is conciliatory. It offers a systematic approach to morality whilst incorporating Christian imperatives like freewill within his theory. Still, even though Wolff's mode of thought reads like a rationalised offspring of Christian philosophy, his purposeful separation of theology and morality called the Pietists, a prominent force in Halle University, to action. Things came to a head with Wolff's public endorsement of a purely rationality-based morality in a speech about Confucius in 1721 that eventually catalysed his expulsion in 1723. Wolff was openly vocal about his conviction that natural law could be sufficiently derived from human reason, better said, that a concept of morality could be attained through the pure use of rationality, without taking recourse to Scripture.[122] The theologians saw the role of the Bible eclipsed where prominent Pietists had been intent on retaining a space for revealed truth, as a source of truth beyond the grasp of reason.[123] Given the fertile grounds for conflict, Wolff's speech served as the catalyst to the conflict in Halle that eventually led to his expulsion. Yet the accusations on paper went beyond the initial disagreement, branding Wolff a materialist, a fatalist, a determinist and, crucially, a Spinozist.[124]

In response to these accusations Wolff claimed that even where the roles of philosopher and theologian needed to be separate, the two modes of investigation, that is, faith, *fides*, and reason, *ratio*, would never disagree when pursued correctly.[125] In his defence he sought to actively distance himself from Spinoza, and also from some of Leibniz's teachings that had incurred the suspicion of a determinist worldview. In the preface to the fifth part of the *Ethica*, for example, Wolff stresses that Leibniz's

Oxford Handbook of Eighteenth Century German Philosophy, ed. by Frederick Beiser and Brandon Look (forthcoming), p. 4; Rodriguez-Pereyra, Gonzalo 'The Principles of Contradiction, Sufficient Reason, and Identity of Indiscernibles', in *The Oxford Handbook of Leibniz*, ed. by Maria Rosa Antognazza (Oxford: Oxford University Press, 2018), pp. 204–215.

122 Hochstrasser, Tim J., *Natural Law Theories in the Early Enlightenment* (Cambridge: Cambridge University Press, 2000), pp. 158, 164, 161.

123 The Pietists presented their case in a publication to that purpose. See Budde, Johann Franz *Bedencken über die Wolffianische Philosophie, nebst einer historischen Einleitung zur gegenwärtigen Controversie* (Frankfurt am Main: Johann Benjamin Andreä 1724). An in-depth analysis of the background to the conflict is presented in Szyrwińska, Anna, 'Die Pietisten', in *Handbuch Christian Wolff*, pp. 383–403.

124 Israel, *Radical Enlightenment*, pp. 542–544.

125 Wolff, Christian, *Philosophia moralis sive Ethica, methodo scientifica pertractata. Pars secunda* (Halle: Renger, 1751), sig. *2v: 'Nos agimus quod Philosophi est, agat Theologus quod suum est. Si penes utrumque stet veritas, non metuenda est ullae contradictio: de conformitate enim rationis ac fidei nulla superest dubitatio, modo rationis decempeda metiri non audeamus quae captum rationis transcendunt.'

monads were of no use to him, nor could they be. The same applied to Leibniz's pre-established harmony, which he explains as a hypothetical concept in the *Psychologia rationalis* but dismisses as a foundation for his practical philosophy; rather, morality is based on the 'notion of perfection'.[126] Lange, Wolff's opponent, considered the pre-established harmony symptomatic of a fatalist perception of the world, and Wolff's eventual distancing from this Leibnizian model may have been a response to the resulting accusations.[127] Yet Wolff's main defence remains the safe distance between material reality and philosophy as the science of possible things. The philosopher demonstrates duties in the world as it should be, not the world that materially is. Back in the actual existence, human morality rests upon the freedom to act upon rights and obligations – and to Wolff, natural rights and obligations arise from this freedom.[128] These rights and obligations are subject to a true and immutable order, so that they can be discovered by means of scientific demonstration, i.e. Wolff's method.[129] Yet this immutable order is not determining man's action per se; it only provides a guideline to his decisions. Based on this argument, Wolff starkly protests against the accusation of moral determinism.[130] Technically speaking, he cleared himself of the accusations, even though one cannot deny that revelation is bracketed out entirely from the discussion of morality, and logically enough angered the theologians.

It could have been Wolff's ominous degree of epistemological self-confidence, too, that left his Pietist colleagues at unease. His idea of God as the ultimate philosopher, endowed with a perfect intellect that only differed by degree from the human equivalent, presented a vision practically opposite to the voluntarist notion of the divine harboured by the Pietists.[131] Furthermore, Wolff had no doubt that humans could discover the working principles of the God-ordained world by means of mere intellect. Since God could only do the non-contradictory, according to Wolff, man could, by implication, discover what world God had chosen of all possible options, better said, what God really wanted – just not why, or, in Wolff's wording, God's motive behind

---

126 Wolff, Christian, *Ethica sive philosophia moralis. Pars quinta* (Verona: Marco Moroni, 1769), sig. *4: 'Monades vero nulli mihi usui fuerunt, nec esse potuerunt. Idem esto judicium de Harmonia praestabilita.' For the difference between Wolff's idea of perfection and Leibniz's *harmonia praestabilita*, see Kohlmeyer, *Kosmos und Kosmonomie bei Christian Wolff*, pp. 49–53.

127 Wolff, in fact, first defended the legitimacy of the pre-established harmony against Lange. For an in-depth account of their exchange see Bianco, 'Freiheit gegen Fatalismus. Zu Joachim Langes Kritik an Wolff', pp. 120–126.

128 Wolff, Christian, *Philosophia practica universalis. Pars prior*, sig. b3: 'Ob agendi libertatem homini multiplicia competunt jura, nec minus multiplices in eum cadunt obligationes, quibus satisfacere tenetur, nisi censuram meritam incurrere velit.'

129 Ibid., sig. b2.

130 Ibid., sig. b5.

131 Hinrichs, Carl, Preussentum und Pietismus. Der Pietismus in Brandenburg-Preußen als religiös-soziale Reformbewegung (Göttingen: Vandenhoeck & Ruprecht, 1971), p. 391.

this choice.[132] In that sense, Wolff pushes the boundaries for what can and should be discovered through human reason and grants himself the license to lay down with human hand what he pronounces divine design. In contrast, Protestant Aristotelian Henning Arnisaeus (1570–1636) made sure to steer clear of this quandary by declaring the will of God unknowable, and theology impossible without revelation – but using this boundary as an impetus to focus on worldly sciences.[133]

Still, it is out of question that rationalist though he is, Wolff stands squarely in the tradition of Christian philosophy. Rationalising philosophy also meant the rational fortification of Christian dogma, whereby the method uses accepted truths and repackages them into logically self-evident syllogisms, proving the existence of God, his omnipotence and other non-negotiable elements of Christian teachings.[134] In terms of content, therefore, he is more a reactionary than a revolutionary and this is implicit in his defence of the freedom to philosophize, *libertas philosophandi*, that concludes the 'Discursus praeliminaris': philosophers who correctly philosophise do not pose a danger to the existing order but help to fortify religion, individual virtue and state alike – which would explain the ancillary role Wolff assigns to philosophy vis-à-vis theology.[135] Rather, there is a new form of orthodoxy baked into his epistemological view of the world: the idea that there is one uniform truth that every right-thinking person can attain – and in terms of thinking rightly, Wolff's way provides not the royal but a long and winding road.[136] His scientific method is a heuristic tool by name, analysis in practice and didactic by effect: the stringency of logic must infallibly convince the reader, convince him into following the right path of reason to virtue without having to take a leap of faith or waiting upon spiritual experience. In a sense, Wolff harnesses the power of reason not to broaden the mind but to achieve conformity – not material but intellectual determinism.

---

132 Wolff, Christian, *Theologia naturalis, methodo scientifica pertractata. Pars prior* (Verona: Dionigi Ramanzini, 1738), §§ 345–349, p. 176.

133 Dreitzel, Horst, Protestantischer Aristotelismus und absoluter Staat: Die 'Politica' des Henning Arnisaeus (ca. 1575–1636) (Wiesbaden: Steiner, 1970), p. 71.

134 Considerable effort goes into proving the existence, the omnipotence and omniscience of God; see e.g. Bissinger, *Die Struktur der Gotteserkenntnis*, p. 199; see also Kohlmeyer, *Kosmos und Kosmonomie bei Christian Wolff, passim.*

135 Wolff, 'Discursus praeliminaris', § 167, p. 65: 'Si libertas philosophandi integra conceditur iis, qui methodo philosophica philosophantur, nullum hinc metuendum est religioni, virtuti ac Reip. periculum.'

136 See also Kadelbach et al., *System, Order, and International Law*, p. 225.

2.3 Wolff's philosophical system

2.3.1 The concept of system in context

Judging from Hanov's introduction to the second part of the *Oeconomica*, Wolff's philosophical system, unfinished though it was, was hailed as an unprecedented achievement of international proportions, a national treasure, a scientific foundation to the German nation for the generations to come.[137] In reality, Wolffianism found a quicker demise than these high-flying expectations predicted. Still, this laudation illustrates the yearning for a comprehensive, methodologically consistent philosophical curriculum as an international desideratum – and that even an unfinished version such as Wolff's was considered a breakthrough of proportions.

At the time, the idea of a full, systematically ordered body of knowledge was not a novelty but received fresh impulses from new and old approaches to processing information. As Sebastien Neveau remarks, 'the requirement to order, to clarify and to distinguish philosophical thought was not only Cartesian, it was also, contrary to what one might think, scholastic, or in the lineage of the scholasticism of Suárez, represented in particular in Germany by Clemens Timpler and his successors.'[138] Wolff's essay on the systematic intellect, *De differentia intellectus systematici*, lists a similar breadth of intellectual heritage; in it, Wolff positions himself amongst the likes of Euclid, Aristotle and Descartes.[139] Still, he himself was convinced that he was the first person to write out a full system true to his definition, *systema veri nominis*: a system built on the concept of *nexus*, the interlinkage of arguments and disciplines within one comprehensive framework.[140]

The concept of a knowledge system defined by an organising principle stems from a historical need in the universities. The idea of using systematically ordered philosophical systems as teaching curricula gained ground in the seventeenth century with the rise of textbooks vis-à-vis the study of original sources. At the time, the canonical grip of the Aristotelian corpus and the humanist zeal for original texts was losing strength in the face of the unwieldy learning experience – a development particularly strong in Northern European universities, according to Leo Catana: thus, '[b]efore 1620, editions of Aristotelian commentaries outnumbered editions of textbooks expounding Aristotle's philosophy; after 1620, however, the textbooks out-

137 Hanov, Michael, *Oeconomica methodo scientifica pertractata. Pars reliqua* (Halle, Magdeburg: Renger, 1755), sig.)(2v.

138 Neveu, 'Secondary Authors' Influence on the Formation of the Wolffian "System of Truths"', p. 58.

139 Wolff, Christian, 'De differentia intellectus systematici & non systematici: Über den Unterschied zwischen dem systematischen und dem nicht-systematischen Verstand', trans. and ed. by Michael Albrecht, *Aufklärung*, 23 (2011), 229–230 (240).

140 Neveu, 'Secondary Authors' Influence', p. 57.

numbered the commentaries'.[141] Textbooks, in fact, were the first impulses for reordering of existing knowledge systems – and the idea expanded to not only systematise school learning but all information accessible to mankind.[142]

One of the most influential textbook movements for post-Reformation Germany was Peter Ramus's reform of the academic teaching curriculum. Ostensibly a break with form and method of the Aristotelian disciplines, Ramus, according to Howard Hotson, was 'pursuing efficiency and utility with a unique single-mindedness born of his personal experience', transforming 'humanist dialectic from a heuristic tool for identifying and imitating the dialectical strategies implicit in ancient texts into a canon of rules required for the proper "methodical" organisation of any treatise'.[143] Ramus was intent on a pedagogical revolution that allowed students (and teachers) to skip the circuitous journey through the sprawl of the ancient canon and its many commentaries. Instead, students would obtain the requisite knowledge through a systematic curriculum presenting information in a manner easy to ingest and remember. Ramus, like Wolff, does insist on a uniform method; and Wolff is self-professedly inspired by Ramus as he admits himself.[144] Yet, differently from Wolff's *nexus* as driving principle behind order, Ramus's curriculum structured knowledge in dichotomies: each concept, category or science is divided into two subcategories, progressing from general to highly specific. These divisions, in Ramus's opinion, would arise organically from the subject matter, making memorisation an easy feat.[145] A visual legacy of this movement were the so-called Ramist charts used in books of all kinds, a simple graphic way to list categories and sub-categories. Carl Günther Ludovici's list of Wolff's Latin works in Johann Heinrich Zedler's universal lexicon, for example, includes just such a chart.[146]

Ramism crucially inspired some influential figures in Germany's academic landscape. Notable followers in the seventeenth century include the aforementioned Keckermann, Althusius, Timpler and the Encyclopedists from Herborn, Johann Heinrich Alsted (1588–1638) and Amos Comenius (1592–1670). Keckermann in particular became one of the main personages to popularise the idea (and execution) of 'system-

141 Catana, Leo, The Historiographical Concept 'System of Philosophy': Its Origin, Nature, Influence, and Legitimacy (Leiden: Brill, 2008), p. 179.

142 Naturally, there had been much earlier encyclopaedic efforts, even in the Middle Ages; yet it is the conjunction of systematic thought and comprehensive coverage in the post-Reformation textbook movement that is conceptually important for Wolff.

143 Hotson, Howard, Commonplace Learning: Ramism and Its German Ramifications, 1543–1630 (Oxford: Oxford University Press, 2007), p. 97.

144 Bissinger, Die Struktur der Gotteserkenntnis, p. 14.

145 See Walter Ong's Introduction in Petrus Ramus and Walter J. Ong, *Scholae in liberales artes* (Hildesheim; New York: G. Olms, 1970), pp. ix–x.

146 Ludovici, Carl Günther, 'Wolfische Philosophie', in *Grosses vollständiges Universal-Lexicon aller Wissenschafften und Künste*, ed. by Jacob August Franckenstein, Paul Daniel Longolius and Carl Günther Ludovici, 68 vols (Leipzig and Halle: Johann Heinrich Zedler, 1731–1754), LVIII, cc. 883–1232 (909).

atic philosophy' in the seventeenth century. Like Ramus, Keckermann believed that instead of passing on learning through original sources and commentaries, the same content could be organised through principles extrinsic to the text.[147] Methodologically, he moved away from the Ramist dichotomies and returned to Aristotelian ways advocated by the Paduan academic Jacopo Zabarella, whose writings on order, method and logic would impart a great influence on the Protestant part of Germany. Keckermann adopted Zabarella's classification of disciplines, for example, alongside a poignant Paduan peculiarity: following Zabarella, Keckermann reinvented logic as an instrumental discipline, not a self-contained philosophical one as Aristotle would have it.[148] With these predicaments in mind, Keckermann started on a philosophical curriculum for the gymnasium in Danzig covering all sciences: a *cyclopedia*, incidentally built on theology as the foundational science. Keckermann died before its completion, a fate Wolff was to replicate a century later; but the posthumous publication of Keckermann's cycle proved popular, spawning translations and imitations alike.[149]

This effort to create comprehensive, methodologically clear and consistent textbooks lived on with Alsted and Comenius. Alsted sought to create a systematic compendium of Keckermann's writings, 'an integrated whole, unified by the *praecognita* of logic and philosophy which open the two volumes and by consistent application of the method outlined in the system of logic'.[150] The result, the *Encyclopaedia septem tomis distincta*, was first published in 1630 and secured Alsted a lasting reputation – as lasting as the impression it left on Leibniz.[151] These efforts to collect and organise information in unified compendia certainly spoke to ideological and economic stimuli of their own time. Ramus sought to solve problems he had personally experienced whereby people of his own humble background were put under financial pressure by the lengthy Aristotelian curriculum.[152] As it turned out, the efficiency of the textbooks also suited 'the needs of financially pressured smaller states' in particular that could not afford to follow the ostensibly more elevated humanist scholarship at more prestigious universities but desperately needed educated men to staff church and state.[153] Keckermann and the Herborn encyclopaedists were professors whose teaching materials came into direct use not just in universities but also in the gymnasia where they

147 Catana, The Historiographical Concept 'System of Philosophy', pp. 178–179.

148 Hotson, *Commonplace Learning*, pp. 137–139.

149 Ibid., pp. 154–157.

150 Ibid., p. 164.

151 Loemker, Leroy E., 'Leibniz and the Herborn Encyclopedists', *Journal of the History of Ideas*, 22 (1961), 323–338 (324).

152 Hotson, Howard, 'The Ramist Roots of Comenian Pansophia', in *Ramus, Pedagogy and the Liberal Arts: Ramism in Britain and the Wider World*, ed. by Emma Annette Wilson and Steven J Reid (Farnham: Ashgate, 2011), pp. 227–52, p. 230.

153 Hotson, *Commonplace Learning*, pp. 94, 98.

were working. Theirs was an ideology based on a moderate form of Calvinism, eclectic more than sectarian and open to new scientific discoveries. Their pedagogical zeal readily crossed confessional boundaries – as Leroy Loemker says, '[t]he mission of teaching provided the goal or final cause for philosophy both in the Protestant circles inspired by Melanchthon and in the circles of the Counterreformation'.[154] In the same grain, the material impetus behind Wolff's system might have been the provision of textbooks for his courses in Halle and Marburg, as was common practice for professors at German universities at his time.[155] And after all, a work that guaranteed a minimum readership in the form of students also posed an economic stimulus to publishers – all the better if it were a whole system.

These teaching programmes are not solely structural in spirit – they are loaded with the authors' metaphysical and epistemological assumptions. Ramus surmised that a natural order transpired through an analytical process, by dividing up categories into narrower and narrower confines – breaking down temples into bricks, essentially. The Herborn thinkers adopted Ramist classification structures but followed the Aristotelian spirit with respect to the metaphysical interpretation of the world; their philosophy did not descend into dichotomies but started from a fundamental philosophy, proceeding from general principles to the particularities of single disciplines. Within this fusion of new, empirical sciences with theoretical traditions, *a priori* and *a posteriori* knowledge overlap within a unity of truth sought through new methodical approaches to science.[156]

Amos Comenius, Alsted's student, saw the key to all knowledge in 'Panharmonia': secure foundations, the recognition of their order and succession, their reciprocity and inner workings would be the basis of ultimate wisdom. The key to achieving this in form of an encyclopaedic project was the *scientia universalis*.[157] Comenius even suggested in his *Panpaedia* to rework subject matters in a mathematical rather than discursive style, so as to avoid prolixity.[158] This mathematically organised system remained a mere spectre, but the idea of a comprehensive, methodologically unified knowledge system anchored on secure first principles lived on with Leibniz – and furthermore informed Wolff's ideas for educational reform.[159]

---

154 Loemker, 'Leibniz and the Herborn Encyclopedists', p. 325.

155 On German professors' teaching methods and materials, see Tribe, Keith, *Strategies of Economic Order* (Cambridge: Cambridge University Press, 1995), p. 9.

156 Loemker, 'Leibniz and the Herborn Encyclopedists', p. 326.

157 Keller, Vera, *Knowledge and the Public Interest, 1575–1725* (New York, NY: Cambridge University Press, 2015), p. 276.

158 Moll, Konrad, 'Der Enzyklopädiegedanke bei Comenius und Alsted, seine Übernahme und Umgestaltung bei Leibniz – neue Perspektiven in der Leibnizforschung', *Studia Leibnitiana*, 34 (2002), 1–30 (16).

159 Cerman, Ivo, 'Die Rolle der Akademie im naturrechtlichen Staatsrecht Christian Wolffs', in *Aufgeklärte Sozietäten, Literatur Und Wissenschaft in Mitteleuropa* (Berlin; Boston: De Gruyter, 2019), pp. xxiv–xxx, p. xxix.

Each exponent had an idiosyncratic idea about what the definitive quality of a system was and hence the terminology itself is in flux, specifically for terms like *encyclopedia* and *systema*. Clemens Timpler and Keckermann both used the word *systema* in the titles of their textbooks. Alsted's knowledge collection was called an *Encyclopedia*, the term he and Comenius proposed as a synonym for *systema systematum* – a system of all systematic disciplines.[160] Both in reference to single disciplines and comprehensive teaching curricula, the idea of *systema* carried the notion of method within.[161] Crucially, Leibniz's specific idea of an encyclopedia was a '*systema* of all propositions true, insofar as possible, useful and hitherto acknowledged'.[162] An encyclopedia might refer to an expanse of knowledge – the system might mean the same if not a methodological requirement or metaphysical predicament. Wolff's understanding of the word 'system'– *systema* – likewise requires contextualisation. When he discusses the role of hypothetical models of the relationship between body and mind and their implications for the notion of free will, the word *systema* is used in the sense of doctrine, to describe the three dominant theories of his day: occasionalism, physical influx and pre-established harmony – *systema causarum occasionalium*, *systema influxus physici* and *systema harmoniae praestabilitae*.[163] The topic of the three *systemata* recurs throughout Wolff's work, presumably due to its controversial nature – controversy less for the argument than by association with controversial intellectual leanings. Thus, so Wolff assumes, the idea of free will is entirely independent from the choice of *systema*; however, he claims that people intent on negating free will are drawn towards the *systema influxus physici*, to then explain our actions through material impulse only.[164] Furthermore, while the pre-established harmony is a more probable construct than the other two systems, it still offers no more than a hypothesis, in Wolff's opinion.[165] The debate over these three *systemata* may have been heated for the implications it bore beyond the purely human context. As Markus Friedrich says, any supposition regarding the soul not only

160 Hotson, Commonplace Learning, p. 165.

161 Catana, The Historiographical Concept 'System of Philosophy', p. 181.

162 Leibniz to Magnus Hesenthaler: 'Est enim utique Encyclopedia Systema omnium, quousque licet, propositionum verarum, utilium, hactenus cognitarum', as quoted in: Moll, 'Der Enzyklopädiegedanke bei Comenius und Alsted', p. 14. See also *ibid.*, p. 7.

163 For the usage of these terms, see Wolff, Ausführliche Nachricht von seinen eigenen Schrifften, pp. 288–289; Wolff, Philosophia moralis sive Ethica. Pars quinta, sig. b2.

164 Wolff, *Ausführliche Nachricht von seinen eigenen Schrifften*, p. 289: 'Derowegen kan einer, der die Freyheit leugnet, so wohl als ein anderer, der sie vertheidiget, ein jedes von diesen Systematibus erwehlen: wie wir denn auch finden, daß Leute, welche keine Freyheit erkannt, dem gemeinen Systemati influxus zugethan gewesen.'

165 Albrecht, Michael, 'Die philosophischen Grundüberzeugungen des Wolffianismus', in Christian Wolff und die europäische Aufklärung: Akten des I. Internationalen Christian-Wolff-Kongresses, Halle (Saale), 4.-8. April 2004. Teil 5, ed. by Jürgen Stolzenberg and Oliver-Pierre Rudolph (Hildesheim, Zürich and New York: Georg Olms Verlag, 2010), pp. 13–30, p. 15.

touched upon what man could know about himself but also about the existence of God.[166] In that sense, the debate ceased to be purely intellectual but attained political dimensions. Wolff excises the matter from political precariousness by stripping down the idea of body-soul interaction to a simple mechanism: in his opinion, the body is merely responsible for perceptions and for performing the soul's decisions but does not have any influence on the soul which makes the decisions and imparts them on the body; therefore, he contends, the controversy over the relationship between body and soul is irrelevant to the debate over freewill.[167] This simplified view is a *systema* in its own right – it is just that he does not consider this theory hypothetical but scientific. And although he does not seem to single it out as a rival *systema*, his conglomerate conception of the cosmos, the soul and morality *is* the *systema* his philosophical corpus is built on as the full expression of Wolff's didactic ideal – built to explain and teach the soul the proper conduct, in practice and theory. Wolff's *systema* of the soul is the *raison d'etre* and programme for Wolff's system alike.

The term *systema* also leads a life outside the context of the soul. Wolff defines a true system, a *systema veri nominis*, as a system of truths interlinked.[168] The *pulcher nexus* as a transcendent, verbalizable connection between universal truths is what defines a *systema* in the Wolffian sense. The *ars inveniendi* is the heuristic capacity to find truths; its younger brother, the *intellectus systematicus*, is defined as the capacity to interlink these universal truths to a network of doctrines, *systema doctrinarum*.[169] With respect to his predecessors, therefore, it is not only the organising principle and methodological consistency fundamental to the endeavour; it is the seamless integration of all branches of knowledge with one another that renders the system truly so.

2.3.2 Wolff's system in practice

With respect to Wolff's whole body of work, most of his publications conform to the same methodology but not all are part of Wolff's philosophical system. The treatise

166 Friedrich, Markus, 'Das Verhältnis von Leib und Seele als theologisch-philosophisches Grenzproblem vor Descartes: lutherische Einwände gegen eine dualistische Anthropologie', in *Spätrenaissance-Philosophie in Deutschland 1570–1650: Entwürfe zwischen Humanismus und Konfessionalisierung, okkulten Traditionen und Schulmetaphysik* (Tübingen: Niemeyer, 2009), pp. 211–249, p. 227.

167 Wolff, *Ausführliche Nachricht von seinen eigenen Schrifften*, pp. 288–9: 'Der Leib ist weiter nicht interessiret als bey dem Ursprunge der Empfindungen und bey der Ausführung der Rathschlüsse der Seele, keinesweges aber bey der art und Weise, wie die Seele zu ihren Rathschlüssen gelanget.'

168 Wolff, Christian, *Philosophia practica universalis, methodo scientifica pertractata. Pars posterior*, §§ 81–82 (Verona: Dionigi Ramanzini, 1742), p. 36: 'In genere nimirum *systema doctrinarum* est compactio veritatum seu propositionum universalium inter se connexarum.'

169 Christian Wolff, Horae subsecivae Marburgenses anni MDCCXXIX, MDCCXXX et MDCCXXXI: quibus philosophia ad publicam privatamque utilitatem aptatur, 3 vols (Frankfurt and Leipzig: Renger, 1735), I, § 3, pp. 4–7.

on the difference between the systematic and non-systematic intellect, for example, is executed *methodo scientifica* but stands apart from the corpus. The essay *De differentia nexus rerum sapientis et fatalis necessitatis* is neither part of the cycle nor formulated in syllogisms. In contrast, the works of Wolff's system are specifically compiled to form one conclusive body of knowledge, covering all necessary sciences; and as an integrated knowledge system, they only refer back to other works of the cycle, not to any extrinsic writings and be they of his own making.

Wolff's earlier German works cover the same disciplines as does his Latin system, but in significantly less detail. For a real appraisal of Wolff's system we have to turn to his Latin works.[170] Yet to really understand the single elements of the Latin series, they have to be understood as part of a system.[171] The disciplines are listed in the 'Discursus praeliminaris', the programmatic work to Wolff's Latin cycle. The correct ordering of these disciplines is the fundamental step of the whole philosophical programme: the disciplines are consciously arranged so that each builds up and draws from the preceding one.[172] Conversely, where each discipline builds up on the previous ones, it is uniquely informed by its precedents.

The schema in Zedler's universal lexicon divides up the whole Wolffian corpus into theoretical and practical sciences, in that order. In the theoretical part, the system was to first explain the premises of human cognition with the *Logica*. After that, the actual disciplines fall into two camps: first *Metaphysica* (consisting of *Ontologia, Cosmologia generalis, Psychologia empirica, Psychologia rationalis, Theologia naturalis*) and *Physica*, comprised of the *Physica experimentalis* and the *Physica dogmatica*, itself divided into one part treating efficient and one part treating final causes. After the theoretical philosophy follows the practical part, consisting of the *Philosophia practica universalis, Ethica, Oeconomica* and *Politica*.[173] Altogether, the system presents a self-contained primer to the world in its totality. On the downside, one cannot arbitrarily consult single books of the system; since all terminology is purpose-built throughout, the reader would have to start from the beginning of the system to understand any of its parts.[174]

Although the order should naturally follow from the nature of the disciplines, Wolff's fulfilment of his programmatic promise shows that practice stumbles over theory at times. The 'Discursus praeliminaris', for example, declares that the treatise on logic should precede the system so that all other disciplines can be understood in their logical execution. Yet, if one were to strictly follow the order expounded by the

---

170 Bissinger, Die Struktur der Gotteserkenntnis, p. 32.

171 Stipperger, Freiheit und Institution bei Christian Wolff (1679–1754), p. 7.

172 See Chapter 3 of the 'Discursus praeliminaris', entitled 'De partibus philosophiae', with a specific note on the order in § 115, p. 169, in: Wolff, *Philosophia rationalis*, pp. 28–52.

173 Ludovici, 'Wolfische Philosophie', p. 909.

174 This is a complaint the natural law theorist Emer de Vattel (1714 –1767) also lodged. See Kadelbach et al., *System, Order, and International Law*, p. 220.

method, the *Logica* should come only after *Ontologia* and *Psychologia* as these two disciplines yield the basic predicaments for Wolff's logic. The method alone – so straightforward in theory – has contradictory demands in practice. Wolff solves this problem by putting the *Logica* first but reserving some space within for basic principles of *Ontologia* and *Psychologia* necessary to understand the work.[175] This order, however, is not merely of practical importance – it also definitively casts logic as less a philosophical discipline than a tool, following Zabarella.[176]

After having faithfully finished the metaphysical part, Wolff seems to have skipped the *Physica* and moved straight on to practical philosophy. He completed the *Philosophia practica* (1738–9), added eight tomes of natural law previously unaccounted for, finished the *Ethica* in five volumes (1750–3) and commenced the *Oeconomica*. After his death, *Oeconomica*, *Politica* and the *Physica* were completed and posthumously published by Michael Hanov who vowed to follow in Wolff's methodological footsteps.[177] Of the disciplines listed, the majority were canonical categories in the scholarship of Wolff's day even if his system yoked them together in novel ways. Some disciplines, however, are completely new or new to the philosophical curriculum. According to Wolff, the *Philosophia practica universalis*, for example, had led a shadow existence until he took it upon himself to coin and popularise it as a discipline.[178] Wolff also tests new waters by treating psychology in two parts, *Psychologia empirica* and *Psychologia rationalis*.[179] Most poignantly, of all the disciplines present, natural law had never been explicitly incorporated into a curriculum chiefly dedicated to natural, theoretical and practical philosophy. Wolff can thus be credited not just with the intent of re-systematising existing structures but with an idiosyncratic arrangement of disciplines old and new.

Comenius considered the *pansophia* a metaphysical image of his knowledge system; Leibniz thinks the same of his *harmonia praestabilita*; and Wolff, too, has a vision of the cosmos his system represents: the *mundus rationalis*. His system can be understood as a verbal representation of the world as Wolff understands it in the ab-

175 Wolff, 'Discursus praeliminaris', §§ 88–9, pp. 39–41.

176 Aristotle himself begged to differ here; Zabarella preceded Wolff in recasting logic as 'instrumental' rather than a purely 'philosophical discipline', influencing Keckermann. See Hotson, *Commonplace Learning*, pp. 139–140.

177 Prantl, Carl von, 'Hanow, Michael Christoph', in *Allgemeine Deutsche Biographie*, Vol. 10 (Munich: Bayerischen Akademie der Wissenschaften, 1879), pp. 524–525.

178 Wolff, *Philosophia practica universalis. Pars posterior*, § 592 *nota*, p. 298: 'Philosophia practica universalis hactenus deserta & neglecta jacuit, ita ut nec ejus quidem nomen auditum fuerit in Scholis Philosophorum. Et quamvis ejus aliquod specimen jam An. 1703 dederimus, & ejus usum inculcaverimus, nemo tamen hactenus fuit, qui animum huc adverteret.'

179 Wolff, Christian, *Psychologia Rationalis*, ed. by Jean Ecole (Hildesheim and New York: Olms, 1972), sig. b: 'Novum est, fateor, hoc ausum: nemo enim hactenus philosophorum ex essentia animae rationem a priori reddere conatus est, cur istiusmodi potius insint facultates, quam aliae, & cur anima has potius in modificationibus suis sequatur leges, quam alias.'

stract. And since Wolff understands the world as a 'series of finite, interconnected entities', the system, too, had only to be of finite dimensions to count as comprehensive coverage.[180]

The *mundus rationalis*, a framework of abstract universals comprising the cosmos, is a concept wedded to a specific mode of cognition. At the lowest level exists the *mundus sensibilis* or *adspectabilis*, which we can discover through our senses. One level up exists the *mundus intelligibilis*, where we can establish cause and consequence relating to the circumstances on the ground. Yet only the *mundus rationalis* yields the universal principles and their connections that the true philosopher is after. These worlds are not apart from each other; rather, the *mundus rationalis* is embedded in the real world. The philosopher can obtain truths about it by observation in the real world, experimental verification, even.[181] Yet since the *mundus rationalis* ultimately consists of universals, observable particulars of the *mundus sensibilis* yield no more than a guidance for extrapolation, not absolute truths.

What combines all branches of science, in Wolff's view, is in fact the possibility to abstract from them and extrapolate *principia generalia*, which – linked up – describe the *mundus rationalis* – no matter whether we are talking about positive sciences or normative discourses. The world as it should be and the world as it is are congealed in the *mundus rationalis*, and accordingly, Wolff's idea of morality banks on the human discovery of abstract, interconnected principles of the *mundus rationalis*, in a world where we mostly act according to primary wants and needs. Ultimately, morality must go conform with rationality – and in order to conform with rationality, the nexus between the general principles has to be recognised and acted upon, rather than resorting to the nexus between particular instances visible to us in the world.

In his philosophy Wolff sidesteps a problem that had been ultimately keeping philosophers from using mathematical methods for the realms of moral philosophy: the reluctance to proclaim any definite rules or moral axioms in a world ruled by complexity and circumstance. Wolff solves this problem theoretically by focusing on universal precepts rather than actions, which – he admits – given the many different circumstances would be too many to report. Instead, Wolff means to inculcate virtue as the habit of acting according to natural law.[182] Within Wolff's system, therefore, there is no question that general principles can and must be derived for moral philosophy, but he reconciles it with the idea of virtue not as mediating the circumstances but as both paving the path to these general principles and also enacting them. Con-

180 Wolff, *Theologia naturalis methodo scientifica pertractata, pars prior*, § 393 *nota*, p. 192: 'Cum enim mundus sit series entium finitorum inter se connexorum (§. 48 Cosmol.); ens unumquodque, quod in hoc mundo existit, est pars quaedam hujus universi seu mundi totius (§. 341 Ontol.)'.

181 van Peursen, 'Ars inveniendi im Rahmen der Metaphysik Christian Wolffs', p. 67.

182 Wolff, Philosophia practica universalis. Pars prior, sigs. b3–b3v.

versely, the recognition of these universal principles already relies on an abstraction away from the thicket of circumstantial information. The *principia generalia* of Wolff's *mundus rationalis* are practically embedded in the real world, albeit hidden and have to be uncovered through human reasoning. Concretely this means detaching an argument from mere particularities on the ground and instead basing it on particularity-free universal principles that are invisibly represented in the situation on the ground. The difficulty about the *mundus rationalis* is exactly that these principles are only principles in terms of existence, with no essence attached to them. This sounds abstract in theory; but Wolff makes the point clearer in laying out what the different *nexus* in either world related to the same sequence of events would look like.

With a view to practical philosophy, therefore, the aim is ultimately to move away from information inferred from the *mundus sensibilis* and start acting in recognition of the universal interconnectedness of the general principles in the *mundus rationalis*. The *mundus sensibilis* is not a bad or sinful world – the onus is on the observer to correctly understand it, both *mundus sensibilis* and *mundus rationalis*. Wolff compares this with someone using a telescope or a microscope to get to the bottom of certain natural phenomena, seeing beyond what is usually visible to the eye – and understanding the true causes and connections between things.[183] The conceptual premises for a system à la Wolff have an impact on the definition and execution of the single disciplines involved, and the same goes for practical philosophy. As noted above, putting the single disciplines in the right order was not a straightforward feat and subject to change and much justification. In the end, they remain interlinked and reciprocal as elements rather than straightforward arguments in a demonstrative chain. The changes in his system throughout conception and execution illustrate the weight these premises bore on the content.

As per the 'Discursus praeliminaris' Wolff saw natural law as the theory put to practice in moral philosophy. Yet although a discourse in its own right, Wolff here contends that natural law could just be folded into the traditional parts of practical philosophy, i.e., ethics, economics and politics. Judging from the list of German writings, Wolff indeed had not given natural law a dedicated space in the early days. Ludwig Philipp Thümmig's (1697–1728) *Institutiones philosophiae Wolfianae* (originally published in 1725), an abridged account in Latin of Wolff's teachings, written and verbal, assigns the natural law corpus its own space.[184] A pupil and one of the earliest followers of Wolff, Thümmig taught philosophy at Halle until 1723, when he was expelled together with his former teacher. Thümmig's *Institutiones* therefore serves as a good indicator for tectonic shifts in Wolff's system of knowledge. Although the 'Dis-

183 Wolff, Christian, Philosophia moralis sive Ethica, methodo scientifica pertractata. Pars prima (Halle: Renger, 1750) § 328 nota, p. 510.

184 Thümmig, Ludwig Philipp, Institutiones philosophiae Wolfianae, in usus academicos adornatae (Frankfurt and Leipzig: Renger, 1760)

cursus praeliminaris' suggests that natural law should not be given its own specific niche, the final execution of Wolff's Latin corpus agrees with Thümmig's abridged version: in the end the Latin cycle contained eight tomes of natural law. There is, however, a significant progression from Thümmig's blueprint to Wolff's final version. Perhaps a nod to its long-time exclusion from the philosophical canon as an official discipline, household matters do not have their own discipline in the German cycle nor is an *Oeconomica* to be found in the *Institutiones*. Rather, and this is similar to Aristotle's *Politics I* and Keckermann's *Systema disciplinae politicae*, matters concerning the family are folded into political theory in both Wolff's *Deutsche Politik* and Thümmig's *Politica*.[185] The 'Discursus praeliminaris' does mention the *Oeconomica* as part of the practical philosophy, but more as an afterthought – prime status of this field is conceded to *Ethica* and *Politica*. Even so, in the final corpus, the *Oeconomica* duly stands as an independent discipline – and its topical range significantly expanded from the ancillary status it led as first part of Wolff's political theory.

These editorial vicissitudes are symptomatic of the murky status of household morality as a discipline and not without mention. As discussed above, in the introduction to the *Oeconomica* Wolff makes a reference to the debate whether the field should be included in politics or stand on its own. In the end, the question is dismissed as futile: it may be true, Wolff says, that these societies exist within the state and may be subject to political discourse since a ruler has to look after them. Yet these small, primeval societies precede the state as a social structure and therefore have a theoretical standing external to it, even if a state or body politic is the right medium to cater to their welfare.[186] It helps to read this change of heart within the context of other innovations made in the system rather than as purely a progression in thought about the discipline itself. To be precise, it seems that the integration of the *Oeconomica* is helped along greatly by the development and inclusion of natural law into the system – and a Pufendorfian invention it adopts along the way: the *status adventitius*. The commonplaces of natural law had always been *status naturalis* and *status civilis*, the juxtaposition of man's natural and political state. Thümmig's *Institutiones* retains this division and explicitly nominates the two states as theoretical frameworks for the two parts of moral philosophy: ethics and politics.[187] The natural law works in Wolff's Latin cycle expand on this original division by adding a third *status* between the natural and the political state of man. This condition is called *status adventitius*, describing man in the context of social relations which are added to the original nucleus of natural commitments and prerogatives. Man's natural state circumscribes his innate

185 In the *Deutsche Politik*, this is simply the first part; in Thümmig's *Institutiones*, the index calls out the 'philosophia civilis partis oeconomicae' as first part of the *philosophia civilis*. See Thümmig, *Institutiones philosophiae Wolfianae*, index on p. 460.

186 Wolff, *Oeconomica*, § 1 *nota*, p. 2.

187 Thümmig, Institutiones philosophiae Wolfianae, §§ 3–4, pp. 47–48.

rights and obligations; the *status adventitius*, by contrast, describes rights acquired and obligations contracted in basic social frameworks, not naturally.[188] The focus is now not the individual but shared purpose and communal utility. In this way, Wolff retains perfect equality in the *status originarius*; the *status adventitius*, however, introduces property, *dominium*, power, *imperium* – and inequality.[189]

The *status adventitius* was not invented by Wolff. As already mentioned, Pufendorf had already introduced the concept in his natural law.[190] In Pufendorf's rendering, the *status adventitius* had not existed from the beginning of humanity but emerged once families and societies started to form, or, as Pufendorf said, once the communal or familial instinct superseded instincts of communality on a mere human, universal basis.[191] Pufendorf evidently sees a historical dimension in the genesis of these states, and the original state of man extinct. In contrast, Wolff seems to interpret either as coexistent pseudo-legal principles. Although the social and the political state supersede the natural state, natural rights or obligations lodged with the *status originarius*, though changed, still exist. An interpretation of any social legislation has to start with the natural state as its origin.[192] Wolff not only adjusts but further utilizes this extra category: he now has three states of natural law – *naturalis, adventitius* and *civilis* – to match with the traditional parts of practical philosophy: *Ethica, Oeconomica* and *Politica*. In that sense, one change in Wolff's system helped along another – the actual execution of natural law provided a framework to anchor the *Oeconomica* structurally amongst the other, traditionally more prominent disciplines.

By including the *Oeconomica* in the Latin cycle Wolff casts the discipline as an exclusively moral and theoretical science, a measure to both broaden and limit its scope in nature. Where the classic works of *Oeconomica* had expanded across a range of morality and practicality, dispensing advice on family matters as much as agriculture, Wolff's classification strips the discipline of all matters practical to leave ethical concerns only. *Oeconomica* is now the science of small societies that informs free ac-

188 Wolff, Christian, *Jus naturae methodo scientifica pertractata. Pars prima*, § 128 (Frankfurt and Leipzig: Renger, 1740), p. 79: '*Status naturalis originarius* est, qui determinatur per jura connata connatasque oblgationes (sic): *Adventitius* vero, qui determinatur per jura acquisita & obligationes contractas.' Wolff differentiates between *status naturalis* and *status adventitius* with ease whereas *status adventitius* and *status civilis* are not as cleanly divided; in fact, the *status civilis* is one specific incarnation of the *status adventitius*. See ibid., *nota*.

189 Ibid., § 130 *nota*, pp. 81–82: '*Quodsi adeo in statu originario perstitissent homines, omnimoda omnium fuisset aequalitas*.... Enimvero postquam a statu originario recessere, inaequales facti sunt tum quoad jura, tum quoad obligationes, introducto scilicet dominio & imperio.'

190 Pufendorf, *De iure naturae et gentium*, Bk 1, Ch. 1, § 7, pp. 7, 9.

191 Ibid., Bk 1, Ch. 1, § 7, p. 9: 'Adeo licet ab initio generis humani ille status actu non exstiterit; idem tamen deinceps lapsu temporum emersit, postquam communis stirpis memoria, aut ex eadem ortae necessitudinis sensus foret extinctus.'

192 Wolff, Jus naturae methodo scientifica pertractata. Pars prima, § 129, nota, p. 80.

tion within this social realm.[193] This does not mean the excision of practical matters from the Wolffian sphere of interest as a whole; instead, these would be separately treated in other parts of the corpus dedicated to natural science and technology. The definition of the *Oeconomica* marks its scope and its positioning in the cycle further informs its content. As system is tantamount to order in Wolff's view, each discipline builds on the preceding ones in a demonstrative manner. The categories of moral philosophy are the practice matching the theory given in natural law; yet they also feed explicitly from Wolff's theoretical philosophy. Wolff justifies this with the definition of *Oeconomica* concerned with morality; since morality teaches the correct use of the faculties of the soul, the *Oeconomica* needs to draw related principles from the *Psychologia* and the *Ethica* where they have been defined. In theory this means that progressive demonstration would naturally lead to the subject matters the *Oeconomica* expounds; in practice this begs the reinterpretation of traditional content within the confines of Wolff's idiosyncratic corpus.

What are the implications for the *Oeconomica* reborn within Wolff's philosophical system? They are the same as the implication for *any* discipline reborn within Wolff's philosophical system, one might say. As the above aims to illustrate, Wolff's philosophical system is not a list of categories and their fulfilment; it is a meshwork with an idiosyncratic metaphysical programme where the different sciences are integrated with each other to make up one comprehensive knowledge system. This structure rests on the assumption that all forms of scientific knowledge – that is knowledge codified through scientific method – are compatible with each other. In theory, each discipline grows out of the previous one; this means that the historical body of knowledge associated with each discipline is now supposedly a natural part of this network – or has to be reinvented as such, to make practice fit the theory. The order of the system and the categories within were not completely set from the beginning, as we have seen above; there is a degree of flexibility in Wolff's planning, and some creative flexibility when it came to making disciplines fit to the system as it grew.

In practice this means the following: the *Oeconomica* is not an isolated accumulation of knowledge – it is now interlinked with the rest of Wolff's philosophy and informed by other parts of it; secondly – similarly, but on a metaphysical level – the discipline has to be adjusted with what Wolff's *systema*, the fundamental interpretation of the nexus man-cosmos, really is: a translocation into the *mundus rationalis*. Concretely, this means the integration of one discipline with others it had previously been touching upon; and, novel enough, the attempt to abstract a practical discourse from the realities on the ground.

193 Wolff, *Oeconomica*, § 1, p. 1.

2.4 Wolff's natural law

2.4.1 Wolffian natural law in the historical context

The concept of natural law plays a role early on in Wolff's philosophy, even though it lacked a corpus of its own until his Latin system came to be. Yet even as a disembodied discipline, it delivered a conceptual framework to reinvent moral philosophy by. Conceptually more than by execution, therefore, natural law strongly pervades Wolff's early writing: as a moral compass per se, or, the rational capacity to distinguish right from wrong.[194]

As already pointed out, Thümmig's *Institutiones* give testament to Wolff's ample teaching on natural law as an actual code, not concept, prior to the Latin cycle, with a summary account of what Wolff must have been teaching at the time. Still, it is not clear whether Wolff ever meant to put this practice into writing at the time he started his Latin system. Moreover, inconcinnities exist between Thümmig's summary, the programme set out in the 'Discursus praeliminaris' and the system's eventual incarnation, hinting at the flux the system was in throughout its long and difficult birth. Particularly the case of natural law sheds light on the conceptual evolution of this field which was not as monolithic as its end result makes it seem. Natural law exists as a term of reference, not a body of work in the German cycle. Still, Thümmig's *Institutiones* imply that Wolff's teaching must have filled in that blank at least to some extent. Here, natural law features in two instalments: *jus naturae ethicum* and *jus naturae civile*, corresponding to the natural state of man and the political state.[195] The *status adventitius* is not present yet but each body of natural law commands its own space. The status of natural law in the *Institutiones* seems to have been subject to flux down to the eventual execution of Wolff's natural law corpus. Thus, the 'Discursus praeliminaris' describes natural law as the theory within practical philosophy but not as an independent corpus: since Wolff thinks that practice and theory do not need to live separate lives in his discourse, natural law would not have to be treated as an individual discipline – it could simply transpire in the volumes about politics and ethics.[196] Yet in the end Wolff included no less than eight tomes on natural law in his

---

194 The abstract notion of a faculty rather than an actual set of precepts is actually much closer to the conception of natural law that the School of Salamanca advanced – a 'facultas quaedam moralis', as Suárez called it, or the Thomist idea of a divine light God had implanted in us, see Pagden, Anthony, 'The Preservation of Order: The School of Salamanca and the "Ius Naturae"', in *Mediaeval and Renaissance Studies on Spain and Portugal in Honour of P. E. Russell*, ed. by F. W. Hodcroft, D. G. Pattison, R. D. F. Pring-Mill, and R.W. Truman (Oxford: The Society for the Study of Mediaeval Languages and Literature, 1981), pp. 155–166, pp. 158–9, 163.

195 Thümmig, Institutiones philosophiae Wolfianae, §§ 3–4, pp. 47–48.

196 Wolff, *Philosophia rationalis*, § 68 nota, p. 31: 'Facile patet, jus naturae esse theoriam philosophiae practicae (§. 62), Ethica scilicet, Politicae atque Oeconomicae (§. 64. & seqq.). Quamobrem cum non opus sit, theoriam a praxi distingui; jus naturae in ipsa Ethica, Oeconomica atque Politica tradi potest.'

Latin corpus, rather than treating the material within his moral philosophy. By the time Wolff commenced the *Oeconomica*, therefore, natural law had been born a discipline with a definition, a mandate and a corpus of its own. In its eventual incarnation, natural law is defined as the science that is required to differentiate bad from good action. Its function is to supply moral philosophy with the precepts to inform practice. It covers, in eight tomes, a melee of topics traditionally found in practical philosophy and traditional jurisprudence, discussing the position of humans within various frameworks: *Jus naturae I-VI* cover the innate rights and duties of man as an individual; *Jus naturae VII* the responsibilities arising for members of small societies, such as a family or a household; and *Jus naturae VIII* is concerned with the entitlements and obligations of citizens and rulers in a state.

The distinction of natural law within moral philosophy is in tune with a general development in the eighteenth century, whereby the hierarchy between natural jurisprudence and formerly ancillary categories of knowledge was reversed: as Schumpeter observes in particular reference to Scotland and Germany, natural law became a special division of moral philosophy, philosophy in the old sense of collective sciences – the social sciences in a new sense of the word; natural philosophy, in contrast, came to refer to the mathematical and physical sciences.[197] The reconfiguration of natural law as its own special division rather than one of the other 'social sciences' is therefore not unique to Wolff. But his idiosyncratic interlinkage between natural law as the theoretical basis and practical philosophy as its implementation is arguably a novel attempt.

The combination of the two disciplines is starkly representative of Wolff's idea of systematically integrated science, and their respective development speaks of his eclectic approach. Eclecticism itself had become a topic of debate across Europe's universities in the last part of the seventeenth and beginning of the eighteenth centuries, seeking to reconcile new scientific approaches with ancient legacies, combining Descartes with Aristotle.[198] Wolff less discusses than practices eclecticism, crossing borders of time, space and discipline. As a result, the reach of natural law is expanded into purely ethical realms; and Wolff's moral philosophy sidles up to its new bedfellow in format and language, reinterpreting social relationships as natural forms of contracts. According to Hasso Hofmann, this blurring of boundaries between morality and legality may even be the definitive point of Wolff's philosophy with respect to other natural law theorists.[199] But as with method and system, natural law in Wolff's system is still widely indebted to his predecessors.

---

197 Schumpeter, History of Economic Analysis, p. 141.

198 Schneider, Ulrich Johannes, 'Leibniz und der Eklektizismus', in *Neuzeitliches Denken: Festschrift für Hans Poser zum 65. Geburtstag*, ed. by Günter Abel, Hans-Jürgen Engfer, and Christoph Hubig (Berlin: Walter de Gruyter, 2002), pp. 233–50, p. 233.

199 Hofmann, Hasso, 'Recht und Staat bei Christian Wolff', *JuristenZeitung*, 59 (2004), 637–643 (640).

From a historical perspective, the two disciplines of natural law and moral philosophy had been developed by separate faculties. Christian Thomasius claims in his *Historia juris naturae* that natural law as a discipline had long been lodged between philosophy and jurisprudence, overlapping with both but belonging to neither. The philosophers did not care for a discipline Aristotle did not know; and the jurisprudents took natural law for a faith-based matter, theoretical rather than practice-based and a potential jeopardy to the authority of the Justinian law code. As a consequence, it was left to the theologians to develop natural law as a discipline.[200]

This observation does not hold up all the way to Wolff's times – in the seventeenth century, for example, natural law had been developed further by non-theologians such as Samuel Pufendorf. Further down the line, Wolff saw in natural law a chance to emancipate morality from revelation and create a scientific, perfectly rational code of conduct. Under the heading of Wolffian eclecticism, the content of his natural law does not shun theology by principle but subsumes scholastic influences as much as traditional law codes, Protestant theorists and, in fact, natural science. Basing natural law on the notion of perfection, Wolff integrates normative constructs with the positive inquiry of the cosmos as a teleological, rationally ordered system.[201]

Natural law as a normative framework under rational participation is already alive with Thomas Aquinas, who elevated 'this anthropological natural law to a dogma by giving it a specific place in God's creative ratio.'[202] Yet Aquinas, and after him the School of Salamanca thought of natural law not as a code or a set of rules but a quality God had implanted in man, allowing him to evaluate good and evil. The School of Salamanca in particular sought to capitalise on this capacity to sort through some bewildering legal conundrums of their own times, using pagan philosophers, revelation and common-sense alike to sort through morally relevant situations that were served badly by existing law codes.

A collection of lectures by its founder, Francisco de Vitoria's *Relectiones*, provide jurisprudential interpretations for new legal issues without a precedent: in *De matrimonio*, de Vitoria seeks to clarify the legal boundaries of a marriage contract so as to make sense of Henry VIII's divorce; *De Indis insulanis* discusses universal property rights of the natives in newly discovered and conquered lands. Here, de Vitoria is trying to find a theologically and philosophically acceptable code of conduct, combining

200 Thomasius, Historia Juris Naturae, §§ 5–12, pp. 2–3. On Thomasius's contribution to Enlightenment discussions on natural law, see Ahnert, Thomas, Religion and the Origins of the German Enlightenment: Faith and the Reform of Learning in the Thought of Christian Thomasius (Rochester, NY: University of Rochester Press, 2006).

201 Kadelbach et al., *System, Order, and International Law*, p. 225. On Wolff's usage of Thomas Aquinas, see Bissinger, *Die Struktur der Gotteserkenntnis*, pp. 10–11; Casula, Mario, 'Die Beziehungen Wolff-Thomas-Carbo in der Metaphysica Latina: Zur Quellengeschichte der Thomas-Rezeption Bei Christian Wolff', *Studia Leibnitiana*, 11 (1979), 98–123 (103–104).

202 Pagden, 'The Preservation of Order', pp. 155–166 (158).

Aristotle and the Bible to clarify legal loopholes.[203] Natural law, in that sense, made a claim on universality by using extra-legal means with a claim to universality, rationality and revelation. The universality in natural law not only sought certainty to counter homegrown ambiguities, but a common form of legality for people beyond the cultural realm, in the sense of *jus gentium*: a law for all people.

Again, the doctors of Salamanca did not seek to write out legislation by the letter; rather, they expounded the existence of a universal, self-evident code of conduct to inform positive legislation.[204] The tension between universal principle and actual circumstance still called for mediation – mediation in form of *recta ratio*, human discretion to apply these principles to situations on the ground. The discourse, even though appealing to reason alongside faith, would always be subject to a degree of probabilism.[205] The engagement with other cultures, such as the native American tribes in the newly conquered lands, however, brought another pitfall to the fore: in the minds of the Spanish scholastics, rationality as the founding principle of natural law was manifest in a particularly Eurocentric form – and the encounter with other cultures did not widen that concept, but only fenced it off further.[206]

After the Reformation, a new need arose with the dismissal of Catholic curricula and practices in new Protestant institutions. Such scholars as Philip Melanchthon sought to fill this gap with a Protestant reformulation of constitutive sciences for schools and universities, complete with nascent ideas on natural law. The image of God is impressed onto humans, Melanchthon argued; the purpose of humans, therefore, should be to recognise God within themselves and reveal his glory in their actions.[207] In that spirit, Melanchthon's work reflects on the existence of an eternal, immutable order for human relations instilled by God – with the proviso that there was a gap between ontological realities and epistemological possibilities: in spite of the existence of a stable normative order, Man after the Fall was not reliably able to identify it.[208]

203 See the section 'De matrimonio' in Vitoria, *Relectiones theologicae*.

204 Pagden, Anthony, 'The Preservation of Order', pp. 159–160.

205 Gómez Camacho, Francisco, 'Later Scholastics: Spanish Economic Thought in the XVth and XVIIth Centuries', in *Ancient and Medieval Economic Ideas and Concepts of Social Justice*, ed. by S. Todd Lowry and Barry Gordon (Leiden: Brill, 1998), pp. 502–562 (506–508).

206 The native Indians and their customs, for example, were considered perverted and 'unnatural' insofar as they were 'irrational'. Natural law for the School of Salamanca was not based on cultural relativism as much as the basic assumption of the Christian world as a universal norm. See Pagden, 'The Preservation of Order', p. 163.

207 Philipp Melanchthon, *Philosophiae moralis epitomes libri duo*: 'Homini enim impressa est imago Dei ut in ea luceat et agnoscatur Deus. Imago enim debet ostendere archetypum. Ergo finis hominis est agnoscere Deum et patefacere eius gloriam', quoted in Dreitzel, *Protestantischer Aristotelismus*, p. 90.

208 Kusukawa, 'Nature's Regularity in Some Protestant Natural Philosophy Textbooks', pp. 105–121 (112, 113).

Instead, natural law could be approached through the Bible.[209] The decalogue in particular presented the summary expression of God's will.[210] In terms of interdisciplinarity, therefore, Melanchthon narrowed the path in comparison to the medieval times: where the scholastics sought to reconcile Aristotle, Roman law and Christian doctrine, the *praeceptor Germaniae* reduces the scope to Scripture as the sole source of authority.

Responding to the changing world order of the seventeenth century with a fresh legitimacy crisis, Hugo Grotius developed a new concept and corpus of natural law.[211] Drawing new lines between ethics, divine and natural law, Grotius built up natural law as a median discipline that up to this point had only been developed by theologians.[212] The impending blend of morality and jurisprudence is implicit in Grotius's definition of law as a moral faculty or moral capacity.[213] But alongside creating a new configuration for the discipline, Grotius widened the scope of source material again. Rather than subscribing to a particular school or dogma, he sought to work with the liberty of ancient Christian thinkers: seeking and unifying the truth from wherever it could be found scattered, thus devising an eclectic approach self-consciously in the spirit of original Christianity.[214]

To Grotius, the novelty of his work did not only lie in codifying natural law implicit in divine law and human custom; his main aim was to counter the trend where expediency meted out law and the interests of the strong presided over the weak.[215] Grotius, perhaps due to the practical appeal of his project, seems to have cast off Melanchthon's frustration with the human intellect and his adherence to the Bible. Although he considered natural law a fundamentally Christian project, he looked at the emancipation from theology as a conceptual preparation to the path for bolder epistemological exploits to come.

Samuel Pufendorf inherited the idea of a comprehensive law code from Grotius but sought to apply a fresh methodological approach to emancipate natural law from the authority of tradition – the *ipse dixit*. Upon Erhard Weigel's instigation, Pufendorf first attempted to write a work on natural law *more geometrico*, by dividing it up into

---

209 Witte, John Jr., *Law and Protestantism: The Legal Teachings of the Lutheran Reformation* (Cambridge: Cambridge University Press, 2002), p. 127.

210 Dreitzel, Protestantischer Aristotelismus, pp. 90–91.

211 See Thomann, 'Ideologische Aspekte der praktischen Philosophie Wolffs', p. 194; Dreitzel, *Protestantischer Aristotelismus*, pp. 191–2.

212 Thomasius, Christian, *Historia juris naturalis*, §16, p. 4, on Grotius's division between natural, divine and positive law. See Albee, Ernest, 'The Ethical System of Richard Cumberland I. ', *The Philosophical Review*, 4 (1895), 264–290 (265).

213 Thomann, 'Ideologische Aspekte der praktischen Philosophie Wolffs', p. 195.

214 Grotius, Hugo, *De iure belli ac pacis libri tres: in quibus ius naturae et gentium, item iuris publici praecipua explicantur*, ed. by P. C. Molhuysen and Cornelis van Vollenhoven (Leiden: A. W. Sijthoff, 1919), p. 17.

215 Ibid., pp. 3, 8–9.

axioms, corollaries, propositions and recasting the material in the shape of a mathematical treatise.[216] He then abandoned this style in his later works but retained the belief that certitude and deductive demonstration in the moral sciences – natural law being amongst them – would be possible.

Although firmly within the Christian tradition, Pufendorf updated some of the underlying concepts: stepping away from the Thomist view and Melanchthonian doctrine, he renounced a teleological view of nature and the universe. He redefined 'morality and politics as the extrinsic imposition of moral concepts and laws by a superior on to an unordered realm of human movements that lack any intrinsic moral properties and of human agents who lack any innate dispositions to moral and political life.'[217]

The fairly pessimistic view of humans was dangerously close to the Hobbesian camp. In contrast to Hobbes, however, Pufendorf affirmed a universal code prior to man-made legislation, and the notions of justice or injustice as universal concepts rather than social constructs.[218] In his writings, the discovery of these universal norms was not achieved through deduction and syllogisms but resorted to a pragmatic, common-sensical comparison of sources ancient, Christian and jurisprudential.[219] In all this, however, he sought to separate natural law as a discipline from both theology and jurisprudence so as to avoid criticism of either faculty.[220] In this sense he emancipated the discipline from much of its early beginnings.

Wolff was a prolific commentator of Pufendorf and Grotius, and had studied the scholastics and Melanchthon (who in his view was deservedly called the *praeceptor Germaniae*) in detail.[221] His natural law project, unsurprisingly, synthesizes elements from these different points in the development of natural law with his usual eclectic attitude, and fuses them with the scientific scope of his work. Wolff's *scientia possibilium* as a realm equally suitable to positive and normative science rests on Pufendorf's argument which allows for a systematic quest for certainty in moral matters. Melanchthon's influence is particularly visible when it comes to the integration of Church with State, *de facto* the fusion of two authorities. Wolff's natural law is rational but not secular; the authority of God as its author is inherently inbuilt.[222] All the

216 Thomasius, *Historia juris naturalis*, § 28, p. 6.

217 Tully, James, 'Introduction', in Pufendorf, Samuel, *On the Duty of Man and Citizen according to Natural Law*, ed. by J. Tully, tr. by Michael Silverthorne (Cambridge: Cambridge University Press, 1991), pp. xvii–xviii

218 Pufendorf, *De iure naturae et gentium*, Vol. 1, Bk 1, Ch. 2, § 5, pp. 27–26.

219 Ibid., §§ 1–2, pp. 22–24.

220 Tully, 'Introduction', p. xxii.

221 Wolff, Christian, *Ratio praelectionum Wolfianarum in mathesin et philosophiam universam*, § 7 (Halle: Renger, 1718), p. 4:'...qui communis Germaniae Praeceptoris nomen dudum meruit, *Philippus Melanchthon*.'

222 Wolff, *Oeconomica*, § 61 *nota*, p. 95: 'Quamobrem cum autor Juris naturae Deus sit (§. 275. part. 1. Phil. pract. univ.), & nos ad legem naturae servandam obliget... '.

while, Wolff introduces scholastic elements in his methodology, but also conceptually: his idea of natural law and natural order rely on a teleological world view, abandoned by Pufendorf and resuscitated by Leibniz, that safely recoups the discipline as a reflection upon the divine working order within a concert of scientific disciplines. Moreover, the relationship between God, man and natural law is epistemologically redefined. It does appear that Wolff considers natural law imprinted into man, like most scholastics and Melanchthon proclaimed, but that does not make it relative to man. Natural law is a scientific discourse and, like factual truth, extrinsic to humans, authored by God, and waiting to be found – by means of reason, or better, deductive demonstration.[223]

2.4.2 Natural law as a theoretical foundation for moral philosophy

The truly Wolffian novelty in comparison to his predecessors in the natural law tradition is the methodological stringency and the integration of the subject area into his philosophical system. The idea of a codified jurisprudence as part of a systematic corpus unified by a single scientific method was already advanced by Leibniz. Wolff's innovative re-ordering of disciplines is foreshadowed in said mentor's publication in 1664, where he proclaims that both ethics and jurisprudence rest on the 'ultimate truths of nature' and that aspiring lawyers would need to acquire a knowledge of metaphysics before all else.[224] In other words: Leibniz thought it of ultimate importance for students to have a metaphysical grounding that would allow them to differentiate – ontologically – between the just and unjust: a thoroughly Platonic interpretation of ethics that considered the good and the bad subject to epistemological effort.[225] All the while, Leibniz thought that natural law could be derived from the observation of mankind.[226] Wolff takes this bidding to heart but reconciles it with an Aristotelian understanding of virtue as a habit: virtue is, by definition, not the habit of acting appropriately given certain circumstances, but the habit of acting out natural law. The task

223 Wolff, *Philosophia moralis sive Ethica. Pars prima*, § 328 *nota*, p. 510: 'Quemadmodum vero veritatis omnis autor deus est (§. 290. *part. 1. Theol. nat.*); ita quoque autor est mundi rationalis, nec inventores veritatem efficiunt, sed tantummodo in cognitionem ejus penetrant, & aliis tectam revelant...'.

224 Mercer, Christia, 'Leibniz, Aristotle and Ethical Knowledge', in *The Impact of Aristotelianism on Modern Philosophy*, ed. by Ricardo Pozzo (Washington, DC: Catholic University of America Press, 2004), pp. 113–47, pp. 145–146. See also Luig, Klaus, 'Leibniz's Concept of Jus Naturale and Lex Naturalis, Defined with Geometric Certainty', in *Natural Law and Laws of Nature in Early Modern Europe: Jurisprudence, Theology, Moral, and Natural Philosophy*, ed. by Lorraine Daston and Michael Stolleis (Farnham: Ashgate, 2008), pp. 183–98, pp. 183–4.

225 Mercer, 'Leibniz, Aristotle and Ethical Knowledge', pp. 146–147.

226 As Luig puts it, 'The natural law of justice derived, for Leibniz, from observation of mankind.', Luig, 'Leibniz's Concept of Jus Naturale and Lex Naturalis', p. 184.

of natural law is to differentiate between good and bad; the task of moral philosophy is to inculcate virtue to ensure its habitual enactment.[227] By introducing natural law as a definite, scientifically demonstrated yardstick, Wolff avoids the Aristotelian pitfall of virtue and morality being relative to a situation, simply by relating moral principles to universal constants rather than judging them according to circumstances in real life.

By joining positive logic and normative theories in one synthetic construct Wolff also reconciles different understandings of natural law which was forever teetering between descriptive and prescriptive discourse. The related terminology, such as *lex naturalis* and *ius naturae* were clearly in flux at Wolff's time. Where the term *ius* and therefore *ius naturae* always relate to a jurisprudential idea, *lex naturae* or *naturalis* oscillated between normative universalisms expounded in jurisprudence and moral philosophy, and positive concepts or formulae in natural sciences.[228] On the surface, the difference between the juridical idea of 'natural law' and the natural law of scientific inquiry seems easy to define: inquiry into the former produces a normative, value-based framework of rules and obligations whilst the latter yields a set of positive observations, or formulae. Yet on closer observation it becomes clear that within the scholastic jurisprudential concept, even the idea of a value-based natural law presumes an analytical dimension because it rests on the assumption of a regular world order reason could explore. The processes of positive inquiry and normative postulate become conflated: with the application of *recta ratio*, of logical reasoning, to a social or political context, the normative values derived draw their justification from the internal logic of demonstration, not an external authority.

The term 'natural' itself is already philosophically loaded. In Aristotle we witness the association of the 'natural' with the intrinsically 'good'. The good and the natural are not bedfellows by necessity as things can be good without being natural. But nothing with that label is ever pronounced bad by the ancient philosopher.[229] The association of 'natural' with 'good' in itself is not so problematic but it seems there is a progressive confusion about what can justifiably be termed 'natural' just *because* 'natural' is supposed to be 'good'. Spinoza had ruffled feathers by proclaiming some impulses value-free and natural that were considered *a priori* damnable by Christian

227 Wolff, *Philosophia moralis sive Ethica. Pars prima*, § 6, p. 4: 'Quamobrem cum habitus actiones suas legi naturali conformiter dirigendi virtus sit (§. 321. *Part. 1. Phil. Pract. univ*); in philosophia morali demonstrandum est, quomodo unaquaeque virtus acquiratur.'

228 Stolleis, Michael, 'The Legitimation of Law through God, Tradition, Will, Nature and Constitution', in *Natural Law and Laws of Nature in Early Modern Europe: Jurisprudence, Theology, Moral, and Natural Philosophy*, ed. by Lorraine Daston and Michael Stolleis (Farnham: Ashgate, 2008), pp. 45–55, pp. 52–3.

229 Schumpeter, *History of Economic Analysis*, p. 108; Schumpeter also refers to the mixing up of 'natural' and 'just' in Aristotle's discourse without clearly defining either, a trend that continues down to the beginnings of classical economics in England.

philosophers, such as for example sexual libido.[230] There are a whole lot of natural bodily functions that could be considered value-free at best but would rarely be upgraded to 'good' in common parlance – defecation, for that matter, does not inspire admiration anywhere in history, but can hardly be considered unnatural. Wolff, judging from his usage of the word, characteristically chooses a middle path. The 'natural' is good and right where it is co-equivalent with the 'rational'. With regards to what is actually natural or not, 'rational' need not apply to all behavioural patterns considered 'natural'. In fact, the functions of body and soul are divided into *actiones naturales* or *necessariae* and *actiones liberae*: actions that occur automatically (the example here is urination) and those that are subject to our free will, that is, conscious decision-making by our soul.[231] And since the use of natural faculties and bodily capacities as instituted by God and their use is an end in itself, these natural functions are by definition sanctioned by God.[232] Yet there exist also 'natural obligations' that we should obey, 'whether we know it or not', that are intrinsically good; and *jus naturae*, insofar as it is intrinsically rational, is not a value-neutral category, but designed to differentiate the good from the bad and therefore intrinsically normative. Although the *leges* themselves are normative propositions, Wolff assumes a positive, logical link – a sufficient reason – between them that can be explored analytically. The seamless incorporation of his Natural Law corpus into his philosophical system marks this development of normative discourse as positive science complete.

The axiomatic beginning of Wolff's science of natural law marks obligation as innate to human beings. *Ius*, in Wolff's understanding, arises from these obligations: '[t]he capacity, or the moral ability to do or not do something, is called Right.' In the context of natural law, it is the right *qua* ability to fulfil one's natural obligation: 'hence, where the law of nature obliges us to an end, it also gives us the right to the means.'[233]

By yoking natural right to moral obligation Wolff further deepens the integration between ethics and natural law. There had been previous attempts to put natural law and practical philosophy into a working relationship, or rather: to put the theory into practice. In the 16th century, for example, Nicolaus Hemming, a Danish professor and follower of Melanchthon, applies an axiomatic method in his *De lege naturae apodictice methodus concinnata* (1562) in the understanding that natural law and morality

230 Israel, Radical Enlightenment, p. 86.

231 Wolff, *Philosophia practica universalis. Pars prior*, § 12, sig. B: '*Actiones* tam *animae*, quam *corporis* dicuntur *naturales* vel *necessariae*, quae per essentiam & naturam animae & corporis determinantur: *Liberae* autem appellantur, quae per essentiam & naturam animae ac corporis non determinantur, sed a libertate animae pendent.'

232 Ibid., § 46, p. 39: 'Usus facultatum animae & organorum corporis sunt fines a Deo intenti.'

233 'Wenn uns also das Gesetze der Natur zu einem Zweck verbindet, so giebt es uns auch ein Recht zu den Mitteln', quoted in Aichele, Alexander, 'Naturrecht', in *Handbuch Christian Wolff*, pp. 269–90, p. 282.

build up on one another. Hemming, according to Mads Jensen, is part of a 'genealogy of Protestant natural lawyers' that started with Melanchthon and continued through to Grotius, Pufendorf and Wolff who was clearly aware of him.[234] *Lex naturae*, for him, is defined as the certain recognition of principles of knowing and acting, inculcated by divine inspiration; from these principles, a secure moral direction can be deduced which are conform with the aim of human living.[235] Hemming wrote in response to Machiavelli's postulate that a state could never be governed without injustices. Justice and right were not just human figments, so Hemming – they were universal constants that existed naturally and internationally.[236] The existence of natural law is clear but to Hemming's knowledge nobody has ever attempted or proposed to apply a scientific, certain method to the project. The Euclidean method, in his opinion, is no less applicable to moral than mathematical subject matters. The axioms necessary for a demonstrative discourse of natural law are drawn from moral philosophy.[237] In that way it is possible to achieve the actual aim: to rebuild the corpus of Danish law into one consistent, deductive system in conformity with divine order, each law retraceable to its ethical origin.[238]

Hemming's work anticipates Wolff's and Pufendorf's early attempts to mathematise moral philosophy, less in content than in format: his treatise is structured into formal proofs that comply with the Euclidean model. Additionally, Hemming's emphasis on the *nexus*, the logical and stringent connections between proofs, are reminiscent of Wolff's definition of a system where the idea of logical order and divine ordinance are conceptually conflated. In that sense, Hemming is a precedent case applying Melanchthon's ideas to existing law codes by means of a scientific method, a project not dissimilar to Wolff's. There is, however, a crucial difference between the structure of Wolff's practical philosophy and Hemming's natural law: Wolff deducts natural law from the notion of perfection in order to provide stable propositions for his moral philosophy; Hemming proceeds in just the opposite order, drawing axioms

---

234 Jensen, Mads L., *A Humanist in Reformation Politics: Philipp Melanchthon on Political Philosophy and Natural Law* (Leiden: Brill, 2019), p. vii. Wolff mentions Hemming as a Lutheran proponent of *computatio canonica*, an ecclesiastic method used to determine degrees of consanguinity, a topic amply discussed in Wolff's *Jus naturae VII*. See Wolff, Christian, *Horae subsecivae marburgenses quibus philosophia ad publicam privatamque utilitatem aptatur* (Verona: Marcus Moroni, 1770), p. 149.

235 Schüling, Hermann, *Die Geschichte der axiomatischen Methode im 16. und beginnenden 17. Jahrhundert* (Hildesheim: Olms, 1969), p. 95: 'Lex naturae ist die durch göttliche Eingebung dem Geist des Menschen eingeprägte sichere Erkenntnis der Prinzipien des Erkennens und Handelns und der aus diesen Prinzipien abgeleiteten mit dem menschlichen Ziel übereinstimmenden Schlüsse, die der Verstand aus den Prinzipien als notwendige Konsequenzen zur Lenkung des menschlichen Lebens aufbaut.'

236 Ibid., p. 94.

237 Hemming, Nicolaus, *De lege naturae apodictica methodus* (Wittenberg: Crato, 1564), sig. A7v: 'Habent & leges ciuiles suam methodum, quibus axiomata suppeditat Philosophia moralis.'

238 Ibid., sigs. B2, B2v.

from moral philosophy *for* natural law. In that sense, Hemming considers moral philosophy the theoretical foundation and natural law its practical consummation, whereby Wolff understands moral philosophy to be the practice built on a theoretical footing of rights and duties. Yet both philosophers seek to provide a framework to formalise the relationship between natural law and moral philosophy.

A century later, Richard Cumberland published *De legibus naturae disquisitio* to counter a new threat, seeking to fight Thomas Hobbes with weapons similar to those Hemming forged against Machiavelli. Like Hemming, Cumberland tries to establish scientifically certain principles in the realm of morality to fight the notion that law and justice are mere social constructs – albeit in response to Hobbes, not Machiavelli.[239] Challenge and solution are quasi-parallel: the task at hand is to prove that norms are universal – the means is the application of scientific or axiomatic methods as transferable models from mathematics to moral philosophy.[240] Cumberland's work is often regarded as an early foundation to English utilitarianism. Whether this is true or not, its central concept that leads to this association is strongly reminiscent of a core element of Wolffian ethic. Cumberland believed that happiness was rooted in perfection and intrinsic to the observance of natural law, an idea also strongly pervasive in Wolff.[241] The result is a form of ethics both deontological and eudaemonic, fusing the idea of duty with the lure of felicity. The poignant difference between the three theories is the axiomatic point of departure for their arguments: Hemming starts from the preservation of human nature and believes that the capacity to identify the right patterns of cognition and action has been divinely impressed upon the human mind.[242] Cumberland sees his framework rooted in the essence of Divine Benevolence.[243] For Wolff, the starting axiom is the statement that duty is essential and natural to man – an anthropocentric more than a heavenly foundation.[244] This relocation of the focus from God to man supports Wolff's move to break with the traditional authority over natural law. Granted that obligation is intrinsic to man, human rationality is perfectly sufficient for deriving universal laws on its own account. The obvious problem of deriving natural law from the observation of the natural – and the natural in human behaviour includ-

239 The refutation of Hobbes' theory is, in fact, the chief purpose of the work, as Cumberland already declares in title and dedicatory preface. See Cumberland, Richard, *De legibus naturae disquisitio philosophica* (Dublin: Jacob Carson, 1720). See also Ewald, William, 'The Biological Naturalism of Richard Cumberland', *Jahrbuch für Recht und Ethik*, 8 (2000), 125–41 (126).

240 Mohnhaupt, Heinz, '"Lex Certa" and "Ius Certum". The Search for Legal Certainty and Security', in *Natural Law and Laws of Nature in Early Modern Europe: Jurisprudence, Theology, Moral, and Natural Philosophy*, ed. by Lorraine Daston and Michael Stolleis (Aldershot: Ashgate, 2008), p. 84.

241 Albee, 'The Ethical System of Richard Cumberland I.', p. 264.

242 Schüling, Die Geschichte der axiomatischen Methode, p. 95.

243 Ewald, 'The Biological Naturalism of Richard Cumberland', p. 128.

244 Wolff, *Jus naturae methodo scientifica pertractata. Pars prima*, sig. b: 'Essentia atque natura humana fons est omnis obligationis, qua tenentur mortales, omnisque Juris, sine quo illi satisfieri nequit.'

ing social patterns – is the problem of differentiating the culturally or individually specific from the universal. Here the scientific method would provide an unerring path past cultural premonitions towards universal morality.

Beyond methodological certainty, Wolff frequently takes recourse to one specific nation as the blueprint for a rationality-based society: the Chinese. Wolff is subject to a fair portion of Orientalist enthusiasm and often cites the Chinese people as a nation in full accordance with his own natural law, presumably inspired by the Jesuit reading of Confucius: conveniently, the Latin versions of Confucius' teachings by Philippe Couplet (1623–1693) and François Noël (1651–1729), which he was familiar with, translate the 'heavenly principle', the fundamental source of human morality, as a universal and natural law, not a principle of revelation.[245] Confucius thus lends himself as a source to Wolff's arguments, perhaps for the fact that the translation by the Jesuits Noël and Couplet was already adjusted to the normative expectations of a Western, Christian reader.[246] In that way Jesuit mediation already pre-adjusted the interpretation of Confucian morale to the scholastic lens of natural law that Wolff was familiar with. Yet also with a view to the reality on the ground, Wolff was convinced that the Chinese to his day sustained the longest unbroken tradition of moral philosophy based entirely on natural reason, not religion.[247] This was clearly informed by the Jesuits who proclaimed Confucian ideas to be alive and at work in the Chinese reality of their own time, in contrast to the difference between ideas and realities of Aristotle or Plato and the contemporary society.[248] Wolff thus works on the assumption that the Chinese lifestyle on the ground reflected the Confucian order by the letter. His controversial speech on China in 1723 presents the actual crux of his understanding of natural law: as Chinese practice demonstrated, morality and virtue could be attainable without the mediation of religion or Scripture – according to Wolff, they derived their ideas of virtue exclusively from the observation of nature.[249] In that sense, Wolff not only presented natural law as a supra-confessional force as his predecessors did; he goes a step further and severs ties between moral philosophy and traditional theology proper. The challenge, and his predecessors felt the scourge of it, too, was to explain God's relationship to a natural law that was considered immutable and universal – without putting divine omnipotence into jeopardy. Grotius is already somewhat ambiguous on the subject: God is implicitly the author of natural

---

245 Meynard, Thierry, The Jesuit Reading of Confucius: The First Complete Translation of the Lunyu (1687) Published in the West (Leiden and Boston: Brill, 2015), p. 61.

246 Kanamori, Shigenari, 'Christian Wolff's Speech on Confucianism: Confucius Compared with Wolff', *European Journal of Law and Economics*, 4 (1997), 299–304 (301).

247 Schaper, Annegret, Ein langer Abschied vom Christentum: Johann Christian Edelmann (1698–1767) und die deutsche Frühaufklärung (Marburg: Tectum Verlag, 1996), p. 61.

248 Meynard, The Jesuit Reading of Confucius, p. 64.

249 Wolff, Christian, *Oratio de Sinarum philosophia practica. Lateinisch-deutsch*, ed. by Michael Albrecht (Hamburg: Felix Meiner, 1985), p. 27.

law 'because it was by his will that such principles came to exist in us'; however, God has to play by the rules himself and cannot alter them – he can neither make two times two anything other than four nor alter an intrinsically bad to a good action.[250]

The issue is diplomatically delicate if not infinitely regressive. These authors proclaim to derive the real, divinely ordained law through means other than revelation. They essentially put down a law with a human pen that God has created but is subject to himself – and the human pen, again, is guided by the laws of nature which God is responsible for, too. This ambiguity lives on in Wolff, who probes an escape with the help of his definition of philosophy: God cannot do the impossible – but by definition, everything God wants to do and is able to, is possible.[251] In a way he hints at the fact that God is subject to limitations, but the limitations depend on his will and might. Similarly, Wolff redraws the epistemological boundaries so as to avoid absolute blasphemy: we can, by means of science, discover *what* God wants; but it can happen that we do not know *why* he wants it, what his motive, i.e. the *ratio sufficiens* of his action is.[252]

Wolff's epistemological self-confidence ruffled the feathers of Halle's theologians for a reason. The quest of certitude within morality had been advanced before, by figures like Weigel and Pufendorf, but Wolff combines the self-confidence of jurisprudence with the dictate of reason in a novel way, redrawing the boundaries of a territory previously subject to theology. The science of felicity now had to focus on the nature of the human spirit and the realm it can explore; and by definition, a moral code would have to be built on the realm reason can explore on its own account lest we demand something impossible. Of course, to the theologians, the impossible could be achieved with God's grace, and revelation yielded a moral code where the world would not make much sense.[253] Yet by foregoing the impossible or even hypothetical and explaining morality through natural law, Wolff not only puts theology out of a job – he brings morality back to the ballcourt of rationality, to the realm of possibility: as a part of *scientia possibilium*.

---

250 Albee, 'The Ethical System of Richard Cumberland. I.', p. 267.

251 Wolff, *Theologia naturalis*, § 345, p. 176: 'Deus nec velle, nec facere potest contradictoria. Etenim nec velle (§. 313), nec facere potest impossibilia (§. 344), sed quicquid vult & facere potest, possibile est (§. 314.343.).'

252 Ibid., § 399, p. 194: '*Deus velle potest, quae cur velit, homo intelligere nequit*. Voluntas enim Dei homini imperscrutabilis est (§. 398).'

253 Wolff responds directly to this opinion in his speech on Confucius, see Wolff, *Oratio de Sinarum philosophia practica*, pp. 22–23.

2.5 Summary

At first sight, the idea of a Wolffian *Oeconomica* seems like a paradox in its own right, from the mere predicaments his conduct of science and the genre of wisdom literature bring to the table. Wolff works in the abstract world of the *mundus rationalis* – household wisdom, economics as it used to be, is steeped in the practice of the real world, not 'an epistemic paradigm', as Giorgio Agamben calls it, but 'a praxis, with a practical activity that must face a problem and a particular situation each time.'[254] As the name already implies, wisdom literature hinges on the experience and authority of the speaker – Wolff decouples science from this notion and seeks epistemic stability through internal coherence.

To Wolff, scientific method, systematic philosophy and natural law were intellectual prerequisites to understanding the world in full, mundane matters included. As seen above, these concepts did not always fit smoothly with the material at hand; as a consequence, method, system and natural law in Wolff's philosophy adjust to and accommodate issues appearing in their practical consummation. This is particularly visible in the changing order of disciplines in the system, the permissive epistemological boundaries in the method and the fluid categorisation of natural law. Additionally, exogenous pressures mould Wolff's philosophy as much as matters of practice: first and foremost, the pressure to defend and define himself within a field ruled by theology under fire from new scientific approaches. In the end, Wolff's conceptual approach remains conciliatory and synthetic more than rebellious and subsumes the influence of many authors from either camp, even if not explicitly referenced. The same can be expected from his *Oeconomica* which warrants reconciliation not just of old and new but also a lay discourse with academic rigour. In some ways the normative concern and the theoretical thrust of the two transmission strands come naturally together in Wolff's conception of science: moral conduct is contingent upon knowledge where an understanding of behaviour and consequences correctly shapes an individual's motives. The scientific discourse in the Wolffian world already bears the idea of the normative within. Conversely, the normative world of traditional morality is the point of departure for scientific analysis about its deeper meaning.

An analysis of the *Oeconomica* would have to bear in mind that practice and theory impact one another in Wolff's work. Differently said, since the system has to fulfil the proleptic plan set out in the 'Discursus praeliminaris', the execution of the *Oeconomica* and its placement within the corpus are in themselves requirements to vindicate the system as a whole. Treatment of domestic philosophy does not arise from the material at hand but departs from the theoretical framework laid out beforehand. The elements crucial to an analysis are the Wolffian dogmata that build his system: the

254 Agamben, Giorgio, 'What Is an Apparatus?', in *What Is an Apparatus? And Other Essays*, trans. by David Kishik and Stefan Pedatella (Stanford, CA: Stanford University Press, 2009), p. 22.

reformulation of all content in a Euclidean guise, directly enacting the Principle of Non-Contradiction and the Principle of Sufficient Reason; the strict adherence to internal terminology only; the integration of different branches of knowledge with one another; and lastly, the re-interpretation of domestic life conform with a universal moral standard of natural law. The fusion with natural law and the application of the scientific method allows for an emancipation from the traditional sources for household wisdom. The deliberate dissociation from the canonical literature and its scholarly treatment sets Wolff's project apart from the academic *Oeconomicae* of the Herborn encyclopedists. Where Keckermann and Alsted still worked in a scholarly fashion, citing from authoritative sources from Aristotle to modern times, Wolff might occasionally refer back to sources or inspirations, but not in a single instance does he call upon the authority of classic works of household literature. Instead, the *Oeconomica*, with its mandate to remain internally self-referential, relies exclusively on self-evident truths – and as is to be seen, this does not exclude intrinsically practice-based content in spite of the pledge to pure theory.

3 A contextual reading of the Oeconomica methodo scientifica pertractata

3.1 Introduction

The aim of this chapter is to document Wolff's translation of commonplace wisdoms typical for household literature into the rationalist format of his philosophy. As the previous chapter discusses, Wolff's approach to science is abstract by definition and the gap to such an intrinsically practical discipline is wide. The combination of both within his system and the reinvention of customs and norms on the basis of natural law changes format and purpose of the common precepts Wolff adopts – even though their essence is largely left alive.

Wolff's *Oeconomica* is not merely an attempt to promote a mundane subject to an academic level. The application of method, system and natural law have a specific impact on the content – with a purpose in mind. Traditional norms are supplied with logical foundations; the classical household topics integrated with Wolff's knowledge system; and the ideological basis shifted from a theological foundation to an underpinning framework of natural law, not secular, but rational. Through this idiosyncratic transformation Wolff takes on a subject of little academic regard and turns it into a theoretical discourse intended for impact: by rationalising the household and aligning the domestic sphere with the interest of the state, he ultimately renders the social sphere political.

Back in 1628, Johannes Avenarius's *Synopsis oeconomica* had lamented the lack of popularity and definition of economics as an academic discipline.[255] The universities' failure to engage with the subject matter was also admonished by prominent philosophers like Christian Becmann (1580–1648) and Daniel Gerhard Morhof (1639–1691).[256] A century later, the tables had turned, albeit not in the way anticipated. Universities in German principalities were developing a growing interest in state-organised resource management and the field of economics started to experience a considerable paradigm shift: the discourse of *Oeconomica* as a morality-based, private household affair was gradually replaced with the academic study of management of natural and human resources within the princely realm.[257] Cameralism, the new science of the day, likewise proceeded from the household, albeit that of the sovereign, as a 'point of crystallization' intent on organising, centralising and systematising the administration of

255 Johann Avenarius, *Synopsis oeconomica* (Wittenberg: Selfisch, 1628), sig. A3.

256 Maier, Hans, Die ältere deutsche Staats- und Verwaltungslehre (Polizeiwissenschaft) (Neuwied am Rhein: Luchterhand, 1966), p. 215.

257 Ibid., pp. 210–1; Keller, *Knowledge and the Public Interest*, pp. 311–312.

https://doi.org/10.1515/9783110714098-003

the state domain.[258] Cameralist sciences did not simply fill the academic gap *Oeconomica* never met but reinvented the discipline from a political perspective.

The transition from one discipline to another was not sudden nor seamless but experienced some growing pains, complete with piecemeal terminological and topical adjustment, as Hans Maier notes.[259] This conceptual flux surfaces with the very advent of cameralist sciences in Wolff's long-time institution, Halle University, which founded a chair for administration, public policy and finance – 'Oeconomia, Polizey und Cammersachen'– in 1727.[260] The overall shift in the discipline from moral to practical affairs was obvious at this point, but it seems to have been unclear whether economic management in general was a matter of organising possessions or populations. The nadir of the Aristotelian interpretation of *Oeconomica* as a moral discourse transpires in the chair's inauguration speech made by the university chancellor, Johann Peter von Ludewig. Ludewig decries these times where a professor of *Oeconomie* would know his Aristotle but not the literal wheat from chaff. His speech suggested Florinus's *Oeconomus prudens* as a textbook for the faculty: a manual covering *moralia*, agriculture and estate management, the first volume addressed to the householder in general, the second, posthumously published volume addressed to the landed aristocrat.[261] In the end, the first professor to hold the chair, Simon Peter Gasser, used Seckendorf's *Teutscher Fürstenstat* as a textbook, before he had written one himself as was customary at the time. Seckendorf's work discussed the political organisation of a principality, not a private household; although estate management and agriculture take up a portion of the manual, the bulk of the content is dedicated to matters of public management and good governance. The textbook Gasser eventually supplied, the 'Introduction to the administrative, political and cameral sciences', swerved in the opposite direction again: chiefly concerned with resource management and revenues, it left matters of political organisation and governance entirely aside.[262] Moreover, where Seckendorf's works were directed at the territorial ruler, Gasser's manual was intended for future public servants.[263] Whilst the discipline of *Oeconomica* graduated onto the academic level in Halle, concern and audience were palpably in flux.

258 Rosen, George, 'Cameralism and the Concept of Medical Police', *Bulletin of the History of Medicine*, 27.1 (1953), 21–42 (24).

259 Maier, Die ältere deutsche Staats- und Verwaltungslehre, pp. 211–212.

260 Goldie, Mark, and Robert Wokler, eds., *The Cambridge History of Eighteenth-Century Political Thought, Vol 1* (Cambridge: Cambridge University Press, 2006), p. 526.

261 Tribe, *Strategies of Economic Order*, pp. 13–14; Müller, 'Die Oeconomia ist ein Monarchia.', p. 152.

262 See for example the table of contents, in Gasser, Simon Peter, *Einleitung zu den Oeconomischen, Politischen und Cameral-Wissenschaften* (Halle: Verlag des Waisenhauses, 1729), p. 24. Tribe, *Strategies of Economic Order*, p. 9.

263 Gasser, Einleitung zu den Oeconomischen, Politischen und Cameral-Wissenschaften, sig.):(3v.

Wolff's *Oeconomica*, published decades after Gasser's appointment in Halle, seems to reverse the trend pushing the field towards a semblance of political economy. Counter to the rise of cameralism, Wolff re-instates the focus on private morality as an academic discipline. True to Wolff's definition of economics as a theory of purely social relations, material topics concerning resource management, self-provision or money-making are entirely excluded. Both structure and content show a strong allegiance to Florinus's *Oeconomus prudens* and its discussion of family morals; yet by excising all of the practical advice Wolff entirely omits the part that would have been of interest to the utility-bent spirit of Halle's new chair for *Oeconomie*. As will be seen, however, Wolff updates Florinus's morality discourse not merely to fit modern standards of science – he reinvents the family from a self-serving to a politically relevant social unit, incorporating cameralist concerns. The first book is dedicated to the *societas conjugalis*, that is, the moral codes for married couples. It is divided into three chapters, mirroring exactly the content of the fourth and fifth chapter of Florinus's first book: the factors governing the choice of a spouse; marriage rites and rituals; and rights and duties of husband and wife. Wolff's second, unfinished section covers the duties of parenthood in general, to then dispense more specific advice on education and the upbringing of children. Here again, content and tone are starkly reminiscent of Florinus. In its essence, the advice is practically the same with one important difference: whilst the concept of duty is central to both authors' ethical framework, Florinus considers Christianity the source of obligation while Wolff derives it from his natural law.

Although the content is very similar, Wolff achieves a significant overhaul of the original precepts through his methodological rendering, systematic integration and fusion of morality with natural law. Where Florinus offers a Christian reading of domestic life and its duties, customs and traditions, complemented with a guide through the bewildering legal landscape, Wolff's *Oeconomica* presents itself as a rationality-based primer absolved from the particularities of legal, traditional or ecclesiastic organisation. In effect, Wolff handles a transition from one source of legitimisation to another but notably, this transition only refers to the arguments – on the surface the code, the resulting practice, remains the same. By and large, in fact, Wolff's discourse remains in step with traditional assumptions about the genre. With regard to some commonplace notions, though, he departs from previously trodden paths in small but seminal ways. The central appellation of the *paterfamilias*, for example, is abandoned in exchange for the gender-neutral term of *conjuges*, addressed to both spouses. Moreover, for the most part he applies the same rules to both husband and wife rather than constructing separate sets of responsibilities.[264] Wolff also

264 In contrast, Menius and Florinus dedicate separate chapters to the duties of husband and wife each. See Menius, Justus, *Oeconomia christiana* (Nuremberg: vom Berg und Newber, 1556); Florinus, *Oeconomus prudens et legalis*.

supplements the original precepts with scientific arguments modern and old, creating an interdisciplinary discourse beyond the traditional confines of morality. Scholastic arguments make an appearance but also contemporary views on medicine and biology, not to forget Wolff's predilection for Chinese wisdoms. This shift marks the graduation of the discipline to an academic field in Wolff's sense. The concerns remain the same – but the discourse is now unwedded from the authority of previous authors and built on what Wolff understands to be science only.

The following chapter aims to illustrate how Wolff achieves this paradigm shift, and where the inherent challenges come to the fore – that is to say, where subject matter buckles under his method; where different traditions of thought defy systematic reconciliation; and where natural law proves an anchor to peculiarities of Wolff's time rather than an abstraction beyond. The first part will discuss the scientific method in the *Oeconomica*. It will examine the application of the principle of Non-contradiction and the Principle of Sufficient Reason as foundations to Wolff's method to then consider the problems of integrating arguments of different epistemological provenance under one methodological heading. The second part considers how Wolff integrates the *Oeconomica* into his knowledge system by rebuilding its topics from material supplied in his Latin cycle; here, too, inconcinnities appear where Wolff fuses different schools of thought under the same systematic principle. The third and last step considers the reinvention of household morality as a science based on the principles of natural law. Wolff replaces traditional modes of Christian duty with a contractual interpretation of social bonds, aiming to pass beyond the trap of confessional relativity. As will be seen, his quest to go beyond traditional norms and sources, particularly through resorting to Chinese philosophy, does not universalise his philosophy but chiefly ends up a reaffirmation of his own cultural entrapment. In the entire discussion, comparisons to the representative works of *Hausväterliteratur* – the books of Coler, Florinus and Menius – help to illustrate where Wolff's *Oeconomica* bows to the tradition of this genre and where he departs from it.

3.2 Oeconomica – methodo scientifica pertractata

3.2.1 Truth, non-contradiction and household wisdom

Christian Wolff's method presents itself as a heuristic tool that served to clarify and sort information old and new. Following a strict protocol, it helps to build up definitions and propositions from scratch with the help of the Principle of Non-contradiction and the Principle of Sufficient Reason. This degree of formalism is classically unfamiliar to *Oeconomica* literature, which tends to busy itself with unstructured and not necessarily logical but experience- and authority-based advice. Wolff's methodological overhaul, however, seeks to form absolute statements from accepted wisdoms and as a consequence changes the basic intent of advice literature – explaining *how* something is done – to a rationality-based affirmation of duty: *that* something should be done.

The introductory paragraphs to the *Oeconomica* show the scientific method at its best. Starting with the definition of economics as the science of small societies, Wolff deduces a number of predicaments, step by step: firstly, that by virtue of being a science, the *Oeconomica* will have to be written in Wolff's scientific method;[265] that natural law, which outlines duties in those societies, is to provide the supporting principles for the demonstration by nature of the content;[266] that, since the faculties of the soul and their correct use in relation to natural law are laid out in the *Psychologia* and the *Ethica*, the *Oeconomica* needs to draw principles from there, too;[267] that the end of the *Oeconomica* is the domestic welfare, and that it should teach the single members of the household how to direct their actions in that light;[268] and lastly, that since everybody will be part of such a simple society at some point, the *Oeconomica's* teachings are of utter necessity.[269] This introductory section does nothing other than present an outline of purpose and structure of the work ahead. Yet it is a telling read that illustrates how Wolff employs demonstration in a context where we might not expect nor require it. Other authors might list the programme of a work, perhaps with some prefatory background information. Wolff not only does that but logically demonstrates what topics, purpose and method should be. The *Oeconomica* therefore, by starting with its very definition, logically establishes its own purpose and format prior to proceeding to the actual content.

Logical demonstration is, in fact, used for every part of the work bar the title as Wolff redefines all concepts in new, scientific terms. The structure of each paragraph shows this Wolffian formalism at work, putting the Principle of Sufficient Reason and the Principle of Non-Contradiction into practice. Officially, all paragraphs take the same format: a statement or a definition followed up by a number of supporting arguments; the final sentence is typically an affirmation of the initial proposition, very much in the spirit of a mathematical *quod erat demonstrandum* as we know it from Euclid. The first and last sentence directly enact the Principle of Non-Contradiction, putting subject and predicate in relation to each other. The supporting statements supply sufficient reasons for why this relationship holds true.[270]

265 Wolff, *Oeconomica*, § 1, p.1.
266 Ibid., § 2, pp. 2–3.
267 Ibid., § 4, p. 4.
268 Ibid., § 5, p. 6.
269 Ibid., § 6, p. 7.
270 See for example the opening paragraph in Wolff, *Oeconomica*, § 7, pp. 9–10: 'Matrimonium contrahi non debet sine animo maxime deliberato...Matrimonium itaque, ...contrahi debet animo maxime deliberato.' Within this repeated statement, Wolff inserts all essential features of marriage to be considered. The exact repetition of an opening statement at the end of a proof is indeed familiar from old

Wolff employs this format to restructure content putatively unsuitable to logical treatment. This can be best seen where he upgrades Florinus's moral biddings to scientific statements. The first chapter of the *Oeconomica*, for example, opens with a syllogistic proof that a marriage should be thought through carefully. This dictum is well-known from the *Oeconomus prudens*: a single man should deliberate the topic of marriage well, preparing his mind to consider it a gift from God, not a necessary evil. Proceeding with that thought in mind, so Florinus, will make a marriage propitious.[271] Wolff echoes this advice but replaces the pious base with a logical footing by proving the non-contradiction of this statement. Drawing from natural law he lists all intrinsic ingredients of marriage one has to be aware of, such as its procreative purpose, associated duties, and its indissolubility. The logical consequence has it that because a person will have to be aware of these intrinsic features of marriage before pursuing it, they will have to be deliberated.[272] Taken out of context, this statement seems almost absurdly self-explanatory; yet if understood as a straightforward conversion of a Christian duty rendered natural, it becomes evident what Wolff's idea of 'reconciling reason with religion' means in practice: the recommendation remains the same, but the reasoning behind it shifts from religious to rational motivation. A similar rerendering of Florinus's idea of parenting shows how Wolff not only rationalizes these arguments but introduces the state into the purpose of the household. The opening statement of Wolff's chapter on parenthood proves the parental obligation to educate their children, in the same manner as with marriage.[273] Florinus proclaims the same duty under the guise of Christendom. Here, the main purpose of marriage is procreation and education of children to serve the continuation of the human race and Christian creed.[274] In comparison, Wolff's rationalist adaptation of the argument plays to more than one master, not just God: here, too, the main purpose of marriage is procreation and education, yet not merely for the sake of God's glorification and the propagation of Christianity but for the continuity of the state.[275] In that sense, procreation ceases to be exclusively a duty towards God and his heavenly kingdom but doubles up as an obligation towards the worldly body politic. Wolff thus takes a middling position between the traditional Christian *Hausväterliteratur* and cameralist interpretations of the second half of the eighteenth century. Heinrich Gottlob von Justi's *Staatswirthschaft*, for example, first published one year after the *Oeconomica*, de-

surviving manuscript editions of Euclid. This exact format was intended to aid memorisation, as Viktor *Blåsjö* has helpfully pointed out to me.

271 Florinus, *Oeconomus prudens et legalis*, Bk. I, Ch. 4, § 4, pp. 12–13.

272 Wolff, *Oeconomica*, § 7, p. 9.

273 Ibid., § 216, p. 360,.

274 Florinus, *Oeconomus prudens et legalis*, Vol. 1, Bk. 1, Ch. 7, § 1, p. 38.

275 Wolff, *Oeconomica*, § 74, pp. 114–115.

clares procreation and education the duty of parents towards ruler and state – without any mention of a religious motivation.[276]

For Wolff, the purpose intrinsic to each *societas* thus provides the ontological starting point to derive duties and best practices in the household, such as in the case of marriage: as per his demonstration, a shared household, spousal concord, even mutual love cease to be ends in themselves; they are now means to fulfil the obligations commanded by natural law.[277] Moreover, based on the intrinsic purpose Wolff can weed out forms of marriage that do not comply with his definition. The union between infertile people, for example, for the sake of a shared life and household is not forbidden, but simply by definition does not classify as marriage but something other.[278] Conversely, practices contravening the end of a *societas* can be logically demonstrated as morally wrong. In the case of marriage, this means a curb on anything that could jeopardise fertility. Wolff uses the occasion to blame masturbation or excessive lovemaking for rendering a man physically ineligible for marriage and culpable moreover. This means that Wolff has logical proof for chastity as an intrinsic good because it curbs the causes for deteriorated fertility and potential hindrances for man to fulfil his purpose within procreative wedlock.[279] The case against masturbation may not be all too scientifically sound. Yet it provides a good case for the ontological clarification Wolff seeks to achieve vis-à-vis legal unclarity. Sodomy was considered a *delictum publicum* by all means; masturbation, or *crimen onaniticum*, was officially classified as a type of sodomy but only punished arbitrarily, and also rarely discovered.[280] Wolff, based on putative science, creates a logically moral case against either. On other occasions, the purpose of each *societas* serves to qualify rather than fortify traditional legal concepts. The *societas paterna*, for example, has the

---

276 Justi, Johann Heinich Gottlob, Staatswirthschaft oder Systematische Abhandlung aller Oekonomischen und Cameral-Wissenschaften, die zur Regierung eines Landes erfodert werden (Leipzig: Breitkopf, 1758), p. 407: 'Die Aeltern haben dannenhero eine doppelte Pflicht auf sich. Sie müssen nicht nur selbst durch thätige Bemühungen zu der Wohlfahrt des Staats das Ihrige beytragen: sondern sie müssen auch ihre Kinder dergestalt erziehen, daß sie dereinst würdige und nützliche Mitglieder des gemeinen Wesens werden.'

277 Wolff, *Oeconomica*, § 26 *nota*, p. 37.

278 Wolff explains this on the example of a marriage with a woman too old to bear children. See Wolff, *Oeconomica*, § 17 *nota*, pp. 24–25: 'Quamvis enim indies videmus, matrimonia cum vetulis contrahi; vi tamen definitionis matrimonia non sunt (§ 270. *part. 7. Jur. nat.*), sed societates aliae, quae quoad effectus civiles matrimonio aequiparantur, & per abusum hoc nomine compellantur.'

279 Wolff, *Oeconomica*, § 12 *nota*, p. 17.

280 Döpler, Jacobus, *Theatri poenarum, suppliciorum et executionum criminalium oder Schau-Platz derer Leibes- und Lebens-Strafen Anderer Theil* (Leipzig: Heirs of Friedrich Lanckisch, 1697), Ch. 5, CCCXXVI, p. 148: 'Erstlich die MASTUPRATIO, si nimirum quis propriis manibus, aliove instrumento se polluat, quam Speciem Sodomiticam Apostolus Paulus MOLLITIEM vocat, mit der Landes-Verweisung/oder andern willkürlichen Strafe: wiewohl dergleichen selten auskömmet/in dem es heimlich getrieben wird.'

upbringing of sound children as its end. Employing parental power beyond the children's interest, e.g. by using excessive severity or brutality, is counted as abuse of this power as it is logically contradictory to its purpose.[281] Wolff therefore puts a moral check on a legal principle that stipulated sweeping rights in his days still.

The Principle of Non-Contradiction meets its biggest challenge when it comes to a quite irrational slice of life: emotions and their stake in ritualised behaviour. Wolff's discussion of the practice of grieving is such an example. Here he picks up on another topic from Florinus to translate a culturally and personally relative practice into absolute norm.

The *Oeconomus prudens* insists on the duty of a *Hausvater* to mourn the death of household members appropriately, and to cater to their burial; in fact, not doing so is the sign of a 'stony, unnatural, un-Christian heart deserving bad repute.'[282] The reasons to mourn a beloved member of the family are emotionally obvious; however, less popular characters should be mourned doubly, as a matter of decency. Here, the question how long this mourning should last and in what format is determined by the emotional state of the mourner, his social environment and his local customs.[283] The basic predicaments of Florinus's advice are clear: mourning the death of any close relative, be they beloved or not, is a Christian duty, but should not exceed due measure.

Wolff takes this exact bidding and translates it into pure abstraction, absolved from cultural or personal parameters. The argument starts with the ontological definition of a calamity in general: as a bad material circumstance that befalls us through bad luck.[284] The next paragraph demonstrates that the death of a spouse can be classified as a calamity – more specifically, the death of a spouse who is fulfilling their role correctly. A virtuous spouse bestows many good things upon the partner, by definition, and their death will deprive the partner of the same; and since the deprivation of good things constitutes a material evil, *physicum malum*, whilst said death is beyond their control, the classification as a *calamitas* – a physical evil beyond our control – is established.[285] Since a calamity logically incites sadness, and the death of a good spouse counts as a calamity, it will naturally inspire sadness.[286] Thus far the argument seems laboured but holds no surprises. The second half, however, takes an unexpected turn: Wolff sets out to prove that natural law does not *prohibit* the mourning of a spouse. The logical reason is that natural law would not bid something im-

281 Wolff, *Oeconomica*, § 205, p. 342.

282 Florinus, *Oeconomus prudens et legalis*, Vol. 1, Bk 1, Ch. 13, § 3, p. 86: 'Es ist dem Christenthum nicht gemäs, sondern eine Anzeigung eines steinernen, unnatürlichen, unchristlichen Herzens, verdienet auch daher schlechten Ruhm, wo man bey dem Tode der seinigen aus einem Stoischen Starr-Sinne, seine Unbeweglichkeit des Gemüths auch in Trauer-Fallen zu zeigen.'

283 Ibid., Vol. 1, Book 1, Ch. 13, §§ 3–4, p. 87.

284 Wolff, *Oeconomica*, § 164, p. 271.

285 Ibid., § 165, p. 273.

286 Ibid., § 166, p. 275.

possible and since sadness is a logical consequence of calamity, it would be impossible not to grieve; hence mourning is not contrary to natural law, even though it should not be excessive and moderated by patience as the virtue responsible for moderation in general.[287]

The case is further discussed for the case of a bad spouse's death – strictly speaking not a calamity, but in fact good fortune.[288] Just as with grief over the good spouse, the happiness, *hilaritas*, inspired by the death of a bad spouse has to be mitigated and pragmatically concealed beneath 'voluntary grief', to maintain good repute and avoid badmouthing the dead.[289] Regardless the convoluted argument, Wolff affirms exactly what Florinus associates with good Christian practice: that public grief over the death of a spouse, beloved or not, is mandatory but should not be excessive. Without mentioning religious motives, Wolff keeps to a purely rationalist format that relies on *a priori* deduction from axiomatic assumptions about human emotions.

Wolff's discussion of mourning leads his method safely *ad absurdum*. The topic does not naturally lend itself to logical treatment and it seems he considered the matter canonical rather than a necessary consequence of his method. In a way this suggests that Wolff considered the programme of the *Oeconomus prudens* mandatory, mourning included, be that because it represented an accepted commonplace or that the text itself carried authority. Regardless Wolff's declared abstinence from canonical sources this implies that Florinus's text, perhaps on account of Ludewig's endorsement, still carried the day as to what was definitive of *Oeconomica* as a moral science – and that Wolff, in spite of his declared rationalist independence, follows a covert canon all the same.

3.2.2 A house built on sufficient reasons

The principle of sufficient reason serves to corroborate and interlink Wolff's arguments.

'Sufficient reasons', in Wolff's logic, can be efficient and final causes alike.[290] What is more, the concept of sufficient reason has a three-fold existence in the *Oeconomica*: in the efficient sense, as a necessary prerequisite to a situation; in a final sense, where an intention or motive functions as a prompt to moral action; and in a pseudo-legal sense, where the motive serves to justify an action, or qualifies it as moral. His arguments do not discuss cause and consequence within the material

287 Ibid., § 167, p. 276; § 168, p. 278.
288 Ibid., § 169, p. 278.
289 Ibid., § 170, p. 281.
290 Waibel, 'Natur als "Aggregat" und "System"', p. 669.

world but within an abstract framework linking universal duties: they do not explain how to respond to certain situations but demonstrate what is universally obligatory.

The triple incarnation of the principle of sufficient reason surfaces in Wolff's casual usage of the term *ratio sufficiens*. In the context of body parts, for example, correctly functioning genitalia pose the sufficient – i.e. efficient – reason for generation.[291] When talking about the division of labour in the household, the *ratio sufficiens* for any duty or simple task is simply the purpose of a *societas* as driving motive or final cause.[292] Lastly, when discussing the circumstances of dissolving an engagement, Wolff declares that financial reasons or aesthetic qualities are not sufficient reasons for either party to retract from their promise.[293] Rather, the motive needs to be honest, that is, in agreement with natural law to count as a sufficient reason.[294] The meaning of sufficient reason here is less as a cause driving a consequence or a motive prompting an action – the *ratio sufficiens* serves as a justifiable cause to an action that qualifies it as morally acceptable, in a pseudo-legal sense of the word.

The largest part of the *Oeconomica* is dedicated to establishing sufficient reasons for the duties pertinent to any household and their relevance to the pursuit of happiness. A prime example of this is Wolff's discourse about conjugal life. The eternal paradox he seeks to solve is why marriage, even though a God-ordained warrant of felicity, leaves people so proverbially unhappy with their lot.[295] The question is not new and, in fact, echoes almost verbatim a statement in Seckendorf's Christian primer for princes, the *Christen-Stat* (1685). Wolff's answer likewise agrees with the cameralist's assessment: a bad marriage is the consequence of hasty, undeliberated choices made on the basis of ill-informed motives.[296] The problem is not just bad judgment with regard to the partner's character but ignorance of the cosmological purpose of wedlock: marriages fail because spouses are not chosen with the morally correct outlook in

291 Wolff, *Oeconomica*, § 10, p. 14: 'Quoniam itaque in hisce functionibus continetur ratio sufficiens generationis (§. 56. *Ontol.*), iis positis ponatur quoque generatio necesse est (§. 118. *Ontol.*).'

292 Ibid., § 29, p. 39: 'Quoniam enim ratio sufficiens operarum obsequialium in fine matrimonii continetur ...'.

293 Ibid., § 65, p. 100: '...ut dissolvantur sponsalia, ratio sufficiens non est, quod personas alia videatur pulchrior, quod ex splendidiore familia nata, quod sit ditior, aut ea, cum quibus sponsalia celebrata, putabatur ditior, quam est.'

294 Ibid., § 64, p. 99: 'Quoniam qui a sponsalibus recedere vult, honestas, hoc est, legi naturae conformes rationes habere debet.'

295 Ibid., § 7 *nota*, p. 10: 'Non infrequentes sunt querelae de infelicitate matrimonii, ita ut apud nos in proverbium abierit, atrimonium esse statum miseriae, Ehestand Wehestand.' Ibid., § 94 *nota*, p. 142:'Apud nos in proverbio est: Ehstand Wehestand, quasi matrimonium sit status miseriarum, molestiarum multarum genitor. Ast talis non est ex intentione Dei, cui convenienter dicentum potius: Ehestand, Wohlstand.'

296 Seckendorf, Veit Ludwig von, *Christen-Stat in drey Bücher abgetheilet.* (Leipzig: J.F. Gleditsch, 1685), II.III. § 1, p. 220: '...also ists dann auch kein Wunder/daß der Ehestand ein Wehestand bey so vielen/wo nicht bey den meisten werden müsse.'

mind. God intended the union of husband and wife with procreation and education of offspring as its goal; marriage is less an end in itself than a fulfilment of human purpose and divine duty.[297] This agrees with Seckendorf's reasoning.[298] Yet Wolff, again, extends this religious interpretation into the worldly realm: marriage is not just a nod to God but the duty of a good citizen, pursued with the continuity of the state in mind.[299]

Where a person may regularly base the choice of a wedding partner on attraction, affection, utility or similar qualities, Wolff's rational abstraction from these circumstantial preferences aligns the motives behind matrimony with the cosmos, the state and God as their creator. Accordingly, he sets out to deconstruct commonplace motives for marriage and counters them with the correct set of sufficient reasons. The core qualities to seek out in a marriage partner are both physical and moral in kind – legality or social acceptability is deliberately bracketed out, different from Florinus's discourse.[300] Wolff demonstrates the essence of physical aptitude with a scientific excursus on human fertility. Moral aptitude, however, forms the bulk of Wolff's discourse, or more specifically, the virtues required to fulfil the duties intrinsic to marriage: a shared household, procreation, and moral education of a child, management of a household in order to provide for necessities and pleasantries alike and the sharing of responsibilities between the partners.[301] With the stress on virtue over other attributes Wolff is perfectly in line with the traditional literature on the topic. Just like his predecessors, Wolff tries to deliver arguments why superficial factors like beauty, wealth and social status should be subordinate to the consideration of inner values. In the line of his rationalist overhaul, however, Wolff updates the arguments from authority-based wisdom to logical argument, re-validating virtue over other attributes that popularly make a match. This is particularly visible for a theme puzzling the experts for millennia: beauty and whether it is a good or a bad thing. Where the matter of beauty is discussed in advice literature from ancient to present times, the prevailing sentiment is predominantly negative: beauty is a pleasing but problematic and ephemeral quality. Florinus, in his *Oeconomus prudens*, for example, dispenses with

297 Wolff, *Oeconomica*, § 73, p. 113.
298 Seckendorf, *Christen-Stat*, II.III. § 1, p. 219: 'Also ist der Ehestand zwar eine heilige Ordnung Gottes/aber für diese zeitliche Leben/dienet jedoch zur Beförderung es Haupt-Zwecks auff gewisse Masse und in vielen Stücken/welche anderswo von denen Gottes-gelehrten ausgeführet sind/sonderlich aber in Fort-Pflantzung des Menschlichen Geschlechts und Vermehrung derer/die das Himmelreich ererben sollen.'
299 Wolff, *Oeconomica*, § 74, p. 114.
300 See, for instance, Wolff *Oeconomica*, § 9, p. 11. The legal eligibility for a couple, *habilitas civilis*, is treated almost like an afterthought since it is not subject to natural circumstances but positive legislation, see ibid., § 44, p. 63: '*inhabilitatis civilis ad matrimonium ratio nulla naturalis, ... inhabilitas civilis a superior in civitate tolli & dispensari potest, quemadmodum ipsi commodum visum fuerit.*'
301 Ibid., § 35, p. 49.

it as a fleeting and perishable good.[302] Avenarius in the *Synopsis oeconomica* decries beauty a 'deceptive pleasure', *fallax gratia*, root cause of haughtiness and jealousy. As a merely physical quality, it can attract but not corroborate love in the absence of good morals.[303] In the synthesised view of poets, theologians, philosophers alike, beauty is not just not essential to a good partnership, but actively harmful and occasionally associated with bad character traits – extolled in millennia worth of love poetry but vilified in moral literature. Somewhat cognizant of this disparity, some authors such as Francesco Barbaro in *De re uxoria* (1415) and Leon Battista Alberti in *Della famiglia* present a conciliatory view. Although virtue should still be the prime quality of consideration, a beautiful wife could bear beautiful children, and a beautiful exterior can often secure a friendly reception by third parties – an almost utilitarian assessment.[304] Wolff solves the riddle by considering beauty within the context of procreation as the definitive purpose of marriage. As for his demonstration, beauty does not contribute to this goal, or at least is not essential as a physical or practical prerequisite.[305] Logically speaking, therefore, it must be considered an irrelevant factor when it comes to choosing a marriage partner. Wolff admits that beauty can cause attraction, but real, rational love is identified with the genuine pleasure virtue inspires; hence love based on physical attraction can be considered negligible in the discussion.[306] Beauty, therefore, is neither an intrinsic good nor an intrinsic evil – it simply is not a sufficient reason for marriage and hence primarily irrelevant to the question, according to Wolff's argument.

A similar discussion surrounds the question of wealth, another divisive issue in moral literature. Avenarius' *Synopsis* warns that although riches are not irrelevant in a partner, the prospect of a sizeable dowry can obscure less salubrious factors, such as a vicious disposition.[307] As with the problem of beauty, wealth is grudgingly acknowledged as a common motive for marriage where from the moral point of view it should not be. This state of affairs is logically scrutinised in Wolff's *Oeconomica*: since it is the philosopher's task to explain why something is rather than not, he has to consider why riches, beauty and fame so commonly detract people from the true factors to match-making.[308] The answer is, quite simply, improvidence and ignorance;

302 Florinus, *Oeconomus prudens*, § 12, p. 15.

303 Avenarius, *Synopsis oeconomica*, p. 20.

304 Alberti, Leon Battista, *Über das Hauswesen: Della famiglia*, ed. by Fritz Schalk, trans. by Walther Kraus (Zürich: Artemis Verlag, 1962), p. 140; Barbaro, Francesco, *Das Buch von der Ehe – De re uxoria*, trans. by Percy Gotheim (Berlin: Die Runde, 1933), p. 33.

305 Wolff, *Oeconomica*, § 35, p. 48.

306 Ibid., § 35 *nota*, p. 50.

307 Avenarius, *Synopsis oeconomica*, p. 20–1.

308 Wolff, *Oeconomica*, § 46, p. 65: 'Quoniam tamen Philosophi inquirere debent in rationem, cur quid potius sit, quam non sit; ideo ostendendum est, quomodo divitiae, forma & natalium claritas omnem cogitationem ab iis avertat, quae in habilitate morali ad matrimonium expendenda sunt.'

and the solution, therefore, is to root out the misconception that riches are the route to true happiness, and to explain the necessity of virtue for true felicity.[309] This is exactly what Wolff sets out to do in his treatise, deconstructing the myth of wealth and demonstrating the nexus between happiness and morality. In that sense, the *Oeconomica* not only presents an analysis of the problem as a cognitive matter but also the solution, in form of an argument to correct the reader's disposition.

In the case of matchmaking, the correct motive, *motivum*, guides moral decision-making. Elsewhere in the *Oeconomica* Wolff explores the relationship between action and motive in reverse: the *motivum* is used to establish whether or when a deed retroactively qualifies as moral. The reciprocity between motive and activity is not only used to reaffirm traditional practices but also to clarify specific scenarios, such as the ever-difficult relationship between sex and morality. It is here that Wolff reconciles what must have been another moral conundrum to most at the time: why sexual intercourse could be considered laudable within the context of matrimony and in fact obligatory, as the *debitum conjugale*, but in itself is no more than a sin. Premarital sex is unsurprisingly considered anathema to Wolff – although not 'naturally illicit', it qualifies as shameful within a political society.[310] But even within the context of marriage, the question of sex presents an issue to the theological debate. Wolff cites Thomas Aquinas and Hieronymus on the occasion, who discuss whether a husband approaching his wife with lust in mind commits a sin of the flesh or a deadly sin.[311] Wolff leaves these theological distinctions aside and simply translates Aquinas' definition into a logical argument: a man approaching his wife for libidinous motives treats her by implication as if she were a prostitute. In that sense he does not act in accord with natural law – a husband who truly honours his wife sleeps with her not with lust but only chastity, procreation and God in mind.[312] Although the activity in question does not actually differ, it is the associated motive that qualifies it as moral or not. Wolff simply renders a theological argument scientifically plausible by replacing the religious justification with a reference to natural law.

As has been mentioned above, in Wolff's philosophy the *motivum* can thirdly function as a sufficient reason for moral action in the efficient sense of the word. The *Psychologia empirica* declares the motive as the sufficient reason for the will or aversion, as it were, which in turn is responsible for an action or its avoidance.[313] In the

---

309 Ibid., § 47, p. 69.

310 Wolff, Oeconomica, § 75, p. 116: 'Concubitus ante nuptial solennes naturaliter licitus; ast cum civiliter illicitus efficitur, turpitudo naturalis in eum derivatur, qua-tenus obligatio civilis naturali sustinetur.'

311 Wolff, Christian, *Jus naturae methodo scientifica pertractatum. Pars septima.* (Halle: Renger, 1747), § 310, pp. 218–219.

312 Wolff, *Oeconomica*, §. 147, pp. 234–235.

313 Wolff, *Psychologia empirica, methodo scientifica pertractata*, § 887, p. 669: 'Ratio sufficiens actuum volitionis ac nolitionis dicitur Motivum.'

Oeconomica this construct is literally put into practice by logically demonstrating the correct motives that will prompt moral action. These motives can feed on deontological or eudaemonic principles: sometimes the end of an action is a duty, as in the example of marital sex, and sometimes Wolff uses motives of self-interested sort, such as the prospect of felicity. This kind of instrumentalization of human self-interest to stimulate ethical behaviour was an idea that Leibniz had already advanced in one of his letters, as a 'mediation between self-interest and morality'.[314] He suggested that self-interest could be employed as a suboptimal but effective means to prompt the soul towards a higher, divine bidding the end of which was beyond the grasp of human reason. Wolff himself explicitly ratifies self-love as a natural cause for humans to seek felicity; and conveniently, self-love, governed by the intellect, is a self-explanatory urge that does not require a motive.[315] The utilisation of this inherent urge for moral betterment, very much in Leibniz' sense, is directly applied in the *Oeconomica*. Wolff argues, for example, that marriage is the cause of conjugal happiness, a happiness everybody wants to attain; but since nobody can be truly happy without virtue, the spouses need to be virtuous to experience true bliss.[316] Since everybody wants to be happy, the outlook of spousal felicity is presented as the self-interested motive for the acquisition virtue.[317]

This argument also functions in the negative. The prospect of discomfort, *incommoda*, that comes with a hasty marriage provides the *motivum* to put some effort in the selection process of a spouse.[318] The motive to cater to parental duties is the tedium that are naughty children, but also the joy that well-educated children bring.[319] The motive to preserve concord in marriage is the fact that felicity requires the absence of unpleasantries; when the spouses are in harmony, they want to make life enjoyable for each other and avert anything bothersome.[320] Naturally, concord and well-educated children are ends that serve a greater cosmological purpose. Harmony is necessary for a functioning household; well-educated children are necessary for the continuity of the state if not humanity. Yet this particular mode of argument illustrates how Wolff's didactic strategy employs self-interested motives to achieve a higher end – in the reader.

---

314 Ahnert, Thomas, 'Zum "Epikureismus" im Naturrecht der deutschen Frühaufklärung', in *Das Naturrecht der Geselligkeit: Anthropologie, Recht und Politik im 18. Jahrhundert*, ed. by Frank Grunert and Vanda Fiorillo (Berlin: Duncker & Humblot, 2009), pp. 39–54, p. 43.

315 Wolff, Christian, Philosophia moralis sive Ethica, methodo scientifica pertractata. Pars quarta, §§ 45–46, 61 (Halle: Renger, 1752), pp. 61–2; 72.

316 Wolff, *Oeconomica*, §§ 91–92, pp. 138–139.

317 Ibid., § 93, pp. 139–140.

318 Ibid., § 43, titled: 'Motivum studii in eligendo conjuge collocandi'. The advice is as follows: 'Ne in persona ad matrionium habiti eligenda simus negligentes, perpendenda sunt incommoda matrimonii non satis circumspecte uniti.'

319 Ibid., § 179, p. 298.

320 Ibid., § 111, p. 160.

The same predicament also explains Wolff's peculiar use of the word *remedium. Remedium* is not a remedy or a fix to a bad situation; it postulates a change of heart by demonstrating the absurdity or unfavourable consequences of immoral action.[321] The *remedium* against choosing a marriage partner for his wealth is to consider the true bliss that virtue brings vis-à-vis the fake bliss of riches.[322] The *remedium* against falling for beauty is to keep in mind that beauty as such does not contribute to the purpose of marriage.[323] A remedy against the proclivity toward adultery, in fact, is to consider Wolff's demonstration about how to avoid vice and prompt virtue – not just by doing but by first willing it.[324] In that sense, Wolff's *Oeconomica* is not only a primer to duty – it presents itself as an autodidactic treatise proving and logically inculcating the motives that are the sufficient reasons to moral action. The necessary link between human purpose and happiness lives on a plane of abstraction, a framework of obligations that can be logically derived. Wolff's discourse unearths this relationship to prove why choosing duty is in the individual's own interest, instrumentalising natural self-love for the sake of moral education.

3.2.3 Sources of knowledge in the Oeconomica – empirical, rational, practical

Wolff's epistemological allowance is wide: from the purely theoretical to empirical to intuitive knowledge. Still, his philosophy does not permit the kind of sources *Hausväterliteratur* customarily draws from: experience and authority. This is already evident from his footnotes which never refer back to canonical sources. Instead, Wolff bolsters his arguments with a mix of rational inference, empirical findings and generalist observations, sometimes his own, sometimes another's. Particularly with a view to biology, Wolff approaches practical questions scientifically, through a mix of empirical evidence, teleological interpretation and rational inference. In the process he folds unfamiliar discourses into a traditional genre whilst seeking common ground between different modes of argument and evidence.

Interdisciplinarity is a traditional feature in *Hausväterliteratur* but not in the Wolffian sense whereby the breadth of knowledge stretches in a different, a scientific direction. This is most apparent when it comes to a topic generally absent from wis-

---

321 Wolff, *Oeconomica*, § 159 *nota*, p. 263: 'In Philosophia morali supponimus hominem rationi aures praebentem eidemque obedire volentem ideoque in ea praescribitur, quae hominibus ratione utentibus prosunt. Atque his efficacissimum remedium adversus actiones pravas ut minus rectas earum absurditas intimius perspecta.'

322 Ibid., § 47, p. 69.

323 Ibid., § 48, p. 70.

324 See the theoretical proof in Wolff, Christian, *Ethica sive philosophia moralis, pars secunda*, § 227 (Verona: Marco Moroni, 1768), pp. 187–188, and its application to adultery in Wolff, *Oeconomica*, § 146, p. 233.

dom literature: the physical facts of procreation. Apart from occasional advice on breastfeeding and musings on female fertility, explicit content is excised from the context of morality on the charge of indecency. Telling in that regard is Lionardo's apology in *Della famiglia* for talking 'too directly', i.e. about carnal matters: pleasure, debt or necessary evil, sex is not an altogether savoury topic within the realm of wisdom literature, it seems.[325] None of the classical works of *Hausväterliteratur* even touch upon this topic. Wolff rescinds this self-imposed censure. In his teleological interpretation of biology, God would have created nothing in vain. Accordingly, even unseemly body parts, genitals included, are part of God's purpose and design, and should be discussed without shame in philosophy and medicine.[326] That does not mean that the genitals themselves are not cause for shame in a non-scientific context.[327] Yet in the *Oeconomica* Wolff can talk about physical facts traditionally considered obscene or unsuitable for the context of domestic discourse because he discusses them in a medical, not a moral capacity. Wolff's candour is unprecedented in the context of moral literature, but not necessarily elsewhere. In fact, the popularity of the happily explicit Pseudo-Albertan *De secretis mulierum*, presumed to be authored in the 13th century and reproduced numerous times since then, signals the popularity of and demand for this sort of information, albeit kept apart from moral confines.[328] In contrast, Wolff practices modern sex education not sequestered from morality but in its very service, using the latest scientific knowledge about reproduction, genitals and sex to inform best practices. More specifically, procreation is the purpose of wedlock and hence the physical ability to procreate becomes the central prerequisite to marriage from the point of view of natural law: God himself has endowed man with the physical and psychological capacity to beget and bring up children, so that in spite of our individually limited lifespan the human race as a whole may persist.[329] Since this the physical ability to procreate is the lynchpin to marital decision-making, Wolff is trying to give practical guidelines to help judge fertility in men and women. Anyone wishing to get married will have to be as certain as possible about his or her state of fertility; conversely, all considerations of marriage should cease when a per-

325 Alberti, *Über das Hauswesen*, pp. 148–149.

326 Wolff, *Oeconomica*, § 11, p. 16.

327 Elsewhere, Wolff supports *pudor*, shame, when it comes to the promotion of chastity: chastity is preserved if children are taught from a young age onwards to be ashamed of uncovering 'obscene' body parts, i.e. the genitals in particular, because they arouse *libido* by touch or sight. See Wolff, *Oeconomica*, § 153, pp. 246–247: 'Quoniam enim partes corporis obscoenae sunt, quae conspectae, vel contactae ad libidinem stimulum addere solent (§. 447., *part. 1. Jur. nat.*), ad eas inprimis pertinent membra genitalia.'

328 Lemay, Helen Rodnite, *Women's Secrets. A Translation of Pseudo-Albertus Magnus's* De Secretis Mulierum *with Commentaries* (Albany, NY: State University of New York Press, 1992), p. 2.

329 Wolff, *Oeconomica*, § 73, p. 113.

son knows that he or she is physically unable to have children.[330] The ability to judge one's own or another person's fertility is therefore crucial to make a morally correct decision and Wolff shares the current state of composite knowledge quite freely.

Biology, as part of the *Physica*, is by Wolff's definition not the science of what bodies do but what is possible through bodies.[331] By explaining conception through sexual intercourse, Wolff logically establishes not how genitals work but what they have to be capable of. For conception, a man's semen has to be ejaculated into the female womb, thus the male capacity to procreate – *habilitas physica* – consists in the ability to produce sperm and the female *habilitas* consists in the physical capacity to receive the sperm. Ergo, a man who has not reached puberty yet is as ineligible for marriage as a castrated man.[332]

On other occasions, Wolff uses ethnographic anecdotes to successfully debunk what must have been a tenacious superstition at the time: that of a pair of testicles one was responsible for producing male, the other female children. Wolff cites the example of an African tribe where testicular amputation is mandatory without causing any reproductive imbalances – and thus solves the question whether unusually few or many testicles disqualify a man from marriage.[333] With regards to the female capacity to conceive, evidence is sparser. Wolff concedes that there is more to conception than simply the introduction of semen into the womb. Given the range of hypotheses proffered by physicists and medics, Wolff dismisses the possibility of absolute certainty; and since nothing secure can be said about the matter, it cannot have any relevance in a scientific debate about morality.[334] Wolff here deliberately dispenses with hypothetical knowledge in the same way he does in the context of the body-mind relationship: if nothing secure can be said about a matter, it self-disqualifies as a valid proposition. Granted that Wolff cannot infer much about female fertility in the absolute, he is using logical inference to give some advice about what could just be a relative incapacity to conceive. This *inhabilitas respectiva* does not necessarily disqualify a person from marriage but perhaps from marrying a specific person. As Wolff declares quite earnestly, a woman's vulva may be too narrow to admit a penis, perhaps because she is too young; therefore, her physical capacity may merely be a matter of growing up. But if one man's penis may be too wide, a differently sized man may do.[335]

As scattered references in the *notae* betray, Wolff's biological knowledge is fed from a number of sources: ethnographic reports, anatomical studies by William Harvey (1578–1657), medicinal works of Daniel Sennertus (1572–1637) and some Chinese

330 Ibid., § 17, p. 23.
331 Wolff, Philosophia rationalis sive logica, § 59, p. 30.
332 Wolff, *Oeconomica*, § 12, p. 17.
333 Ibid., § 15 *nota*, pp. 20–1.
334 Ibid., § 13 *nota*, p. 19.
335 Ibid., § 15 *nota*, p. 21.

doctors but also Wolff's own ideas. This blend of *a posteriori* and *a priori* reasoning at times upends itself – in particular where Wolff is trying to combine arguments derived from different epistemological foundations. An extant example are the several paragraphs on breastfeeding that pick up a debate of varied nature from ancient to early modern times. As the second-century Roman writer Aulus Gellius wrote and Leon Battista Alberti duly picked up on, breastmilk was believed to be responsible for more than just physical nutrition – it was thought to have an influence on the formation of intelligence and character in a child.[336] Based on this idea, Alberti proposed that a healthy mother should suckle her child herself rather than employ a wet-nurse, counter the seemingly prevalent trend.[337] His view rests on the idea that milk is essentially a concoction of the mother's blood and would carry her nobility, character and intelligence within. A mother suckling her own child did not only ensure its nutrition – she ensured that the apple would fall as close to the tree as possible. Rather than a wet-nurse imbuing the infant with her own crude qualities, the *paterfamilias* should be intent on his wife feeding the child with her own milk and character features.[338] As Julia Hairston aptly notes, Lionardo's argument in *Della Famiglia* is curiously followed by a much longer passage on how to choose the right wet-nurse. She suggests this might be an indication of how customary it was for an affluent woman in the Renaissance to employ a wet-nurse rather than breast-feed. That motive of privilege gives way to necessity in Coler's *Oeconomia ruralis:* a mother should by all means suckle her child herself but if she is not healthy enough, the wet-nurse to replace her should eat well and, most importantly, be pious.[339]

Wolff's passage on breastfeeding echoes Coler and structurally mirrors Alberti's argument: breastfeeding is declared the duty of a mother and preferential – but the advice on how to pick and treat a wet-nurse is almost as long as the section actually dedicated to the mother.[340] Yet where Alberti argues for the transmission of nobility, character and talent, Wolff translates the idea of milk as a vehicle of stock into a health-based argument resting on two pillars of eclectic build: firstly, that the blood of a pregnant woman circulates through the embryo in the womb, becoming the child's own after birth. Secondly, he contends that the mother's milk shares specific aspects intrinsic to that mother's blood and hence accommodates the child, which had been fed on maternal blood prior to its birth, better than any nurse's milk.[341] Blood and hence milk are considered to be directly subject to the nursing woman's eating

336 Alberti, *Über das Hauswesen*, pp. 45–46.

337 Hairston, Julia L., 'The Economics of Milk and Blood in Alberti's Libri Della Famiglia: Maternal versus Wet-Nursing', in *Medieval and Renaissance Lactations: Images, Rhetorics, Practices*, ed. by Jutta Gisela Sperling (Farnham, Surrey: Ashgate, 2013), pp. 187–212, pp. 190–193.

338 Alberti, *Über das Hauswesen*, pp. 45–46.

339 Coler, *Oeconomia ruralis*, Ch. 8, p. 349.

340 Wolff, *Oeconomica*, §§ 220–225, pp. 366–378 on mothers; §§ 226–232, pp. 379–386 on wet nurses.

341 Ibid., § 220, pp. 363–367.

habits and her moods. A nursing woman, mother or nurse, needs to maintain level emotions, avoid shocking impressions and keep up sound eating habits – a mandate reinforced by Chinese cultural practice, Malebranche's cautionary tale of maternal imagination and Wolff's supplemented anatomical explanation of the womb as the scientific insight to back up both theory and custom.[342]

With the benefit of hindsight, the *Oeconomica*'s anatomical blueprint of a blood circulation shared between mother and child is obviously wrong. In the eighteenth century, it did find support by figures like John Maubray (1700–1732) and Daniel Turner (1667–1741), a follower of Malebranche, but also drew criticism from physicians like James Augustus Blondel (1665/6–1734).[343] One of the most authoritative voices on the subject was William Harvey, whose ground-breaking anatomical experiments successfully challenged the Galenic interpretation of blood circulation. Harvey explicitly rejects the idea that the maternal blood flows through the umbilical cord into the foetus. He correctly proposed a system by which the foetus has its own circulation and is nourished in the womb like unborn chicks in eggs.[344] Wolff was demonstrably aware of Harvey's work, yet changes his view on the matter throughout his publication history.[345] Wolff's German *Physica*, originally published in 1723, credits the placenta for the unborn child's nutrition but adds the concept of a shared blood circulation as an additional feature in reference to Malebranche's theory.[346] A German treatise on his teleological view of biology first published in 1730, on the other hand, develops the view that the mother's blood is not directly coursing through the child, but feeding into the placenta responsible for its nutrition. The idea of a shared blood circulation is not mentioned; rather, a reference to the analogy between chicks and babies suggests that Wolff refers to Harvey's theory.[347] It is only in the *Oeconomica* that these two incongruous interpretations come to a head when they are joined in logical support for a cultural practice: in the examples cited above, the mention of the shared blood circulation only appears where Malebranche's theory is mentioned, too; the placenta is still mentioned but not in its actual function. In the *Oeconomica*, then, Wolff omits its role entirely and cites the blood circulation shared between mother and child as the sole form of nutrition. The new analogy for the foetus's nourishment

---

342 Ibid., § 222, p. 374; § 221, pp. 371–2.

343 Epstein, Julia, 'The Pregnant Imagination, Fetal Rights, and Women's Bodies: A Historical Inquiry', *Yale Journal of Law & the Humanities*, 7 (1995), 139–62 (147, 149, 152–4).

344 William Harvey, *Exercitatio anatomica de motu cordis et sanguinis in animalibus* (Leiden: Johannes van Kerckhem, 1737), pp. 391–2.

345 Wolff, *Oeconomica*, § 13, p. 19.

346 Christian Wolff, *Vernünfftige Gedancken von den Würckungen der Natur* (Halle: Renger, 1723), § 447, p. 735.

347 Christian Wolff, Vernünfftige Gedancken von dem Gebrauche der Theile in Menschen, Thieren und Pflanzen, § 199 (Frankfurt and Leipzig: Renger, 1730), pp. 556–557.

in the womb is not the chick in the egg, but the fruit on a tree.[348] Officially, the argument is built on *a priori* inference; yet curiously, Wolff claims that this has been proven beyond doubt by anatomical observation, albeit without naming a source. He thus implies against better knowledge that empirical and purely rational argument would agree in the end.[349]

The changing imagery of chicks and eggs or fruit and tree shows how Wolff progressively reconciles different contemporary theories about the nutrition of the foetus to provide both a teleological and an empirical account. What is telling about his method in this regard is its incapacity to critically compare rather than merely combine different theories. In the end, Wolff presents an amalgamized snapshot of different scientific theories contemporary to him – and in spite of his universalist appeal anchors his discourse firmly to the errors of his own era.

3.3 Oeconomica in the philosophical system

3.3.1 Crosspollination in the systema doctrinarum

Typically, classical works of *Hausväterliteratur* such as the books by Coler and Florinus were works of encyclopaedic dimensions – in terms of expanse they posed *corpora* of knowledge in their own right, covering anything considered relevant to the sphere of the householder. Wolff's *Oeconomica* brackets out the topical breadth typical of *Hausväterliteratur*; instead, he translates the theoretical expanse of his whole philosophical system into concrete precepts for the householder. In that sense, Wolff rebuilds classic *topoi* of household literature from the material available in his system. The *Oeconomica* not only self-consciously builds on the preceding part of the corpus – it paves the way for politics as the subsequent discipline.[350]

Wolff's definition of a system emphasised the *nexus*, the connection, between arguments and disciplines. Analogous to body parts, the disciplines have their own ends, but are interdependent with a view to a common goal and parts of the same fixed order.[351] The same principle is visibly active in the *Oeconomica*. In practice this means that, differently from its traditional predecessors, it rebuilds all content from a methodologically defined corpus rather than external sources or experience. As that, it presents not a lone-standing work of encyclopaedic dimensions itself but an integrated part of a knowledge system.

---

348 Wolff, *Oeconomica*, § 220, p. 366.

349 Ibid., § 221, p. 369.

350 The first section of the *Oeconomica* notably carries the title 'Oeconomicae, politicae prodromi', identifying the *Oeconomica* as the precursor of the *Politica*. See Wolff, *Oeconomica*, p. 9.

351 Wolff, *Oeconomica*, § 4, p. 5.

In general, Wolff tends to only cite himself in the main paragraphs, adding external references in the footnotes at best. This practice ensures the stability of his self-sustained corpus. The ample inclusion of biological information in the *Oeconomica* presents a small dilemma in that regard: Wolff had treated all relevant matters in his previous German writings but at the time he commenced the *Oeconomica*, the *Physica*, which would have included biology, had not been written yet. The system's programme in the 'Discursus praeliminaris' generally places the *Physica* after metaphysics, and potentially right after it, that is, before practical philosophy, since it does not depend on the latter's principles. In the footnote, however, Wolff qualifies this thought, claiming that teleology, a part of the *Physica*, seeks its principles from practical philosophy and that therefore the whole of natural philosophy would best be placed at the end of the corpus.[352] The order of natural and practical philosophy seems somewhat undecided, perhaps for the reciprocal more than sequential relationship of the respective areas. When it came to the execution, Wolff decided to tackle practical philosophy first; his *Oeconomica* hence cannot refer its share of biological information back to the *Physica* but can only foreshadow it.[353] Instead of drawing on fully developed arguments, the respective syllogisms lack the usual inner-corpus references and use the footnotes to point cursorily – and atypically – to Wolff's German writings and to a mix of sources in the accompanying footnotes, for example Daniel Sennertus, William Harvey, Chinese doctors and non-medical sources like Malebranche.[354] Wolff himself even comments on this state of affairs as suboptimal.[355]

In that sense, biology provides both a great case for and bad example of the integration of knowledge in Wolff's corpus. Other subject areas fare better in that regard. Wolff's home brand of pedagogy is such a case. Here the auxiliary status of theoretical

352 Wolff, 'Discursus praeliminaris', § 106, p. 48: 'Metaphysicam praecedere debere Physicam supra demonstratum est (§. 95). Quoniam vero Physica ex Philosophia practica principia nulla mutuatur, non opus est ut ea ipsi praemittatur (§. 87). Potest igitur statim post Metaphysicam tradi.' See, in contrast, ibid., § 106 *nota*, pp. 48–49: 'Quoniam tamen Teleologia principia ex philosophia practica supponit, post hanc adeo tractanda (§. 87.), Teleologia autem Physicae pars est (§. 85.); consultius videtur, ut Physica integra demum post Philosophiam practicam tradatur: nisi forsan Philosophiam practicam universalem cum Jure naturali Metaphysicae jungere, Ethicam autem atque Politicam Physicae demum subjungere velis, quatenus quaedam ipsius dogmata in iis usum habere possunt & Technologia, a Physica pendens (§. 71), Politicae principia nonnulla praebere valet.'

353 See, for instance, Wolff, *Oeconomica*, § 11 *nota*, p. 16; § 216 *nota*, p. 360; § 220 *nota*, p. 368.

354 See, for instance, a mention of Daniel Sennertus in Wolff, *Oeconomica*, § 15 *nota*, p. 21; of William Harvey in § 13 *nota*, p. 18; a reference to Chinese doctors in § 222, p. 374; in at least one instance Wolff refers to his German writings about biology: 'Quomodo tantum malum accidere potuerit foetui in utero, dum mater vidit latronem crucifragio plecti, me uberius exposuisse memini in Physica dogmatica idiomate patrio conscripta.', § 221, p. 372.

355 Wolff, *Oeconomica*, § 221 *nota*, p. 372: 'Monui jam longe uberiori disquisitione opus esse, si quae in propositione praesene habentur, pro dignitate explicari & confirmari deberent. Supponunt nimirum multas observationes anatomicas & principia physica... Physicam enim cum Philosophia nostra nondum copulavimus.',

disciplines comes into full view in their practical fruition in the *Oeconomica* – and demonstrates how Wolff shifts the weight of legitimacy from the shoulders of tradition to the pillars of science. Pedagogy and the education of children is a central concern in *Hausväterliteratur*, and understandably so – bringing up children in the spirit of their fathers' ideology spells continuity for household, society and religious community. Menius' *Oeconomia christiana*, to that purpose, declares it the primary goal of a *paterfamilias* to bring up pious, obedient and virtuous children.[356] Coler, in his general pragmatism, features some pedagogical guidelines in the section on medicine, combined with tips on pregnancy and breastfeeding, general advice about infant illnesses, but also hands-on pedagogy. At an infant age, for example, children should not be treated too harshly lest they grow timid or dumb. Reaching the sixth year they should be sent to school, bathed occasionally and fed in moderation, briefly said.[357] As it seems, these works of traditional *Hausväterliteratur* structure their pedagogical advice straightforwardly: by describing the behaviour necessary to achieve a certain outcome, ideology served by experience.

In contrast, pedagogy in Wolff's *Oeconomica* steps away from this practical train of thought. Instead of drawing upon commonplace knowledge and the authority of experience, Wolff constructs an education strategy from scratch: as a scientific, systematic theory of pedagogy buttressed by his theoretical philosophy – more specifically, the doctrine of the soul. Wolff abandons the idea that each period of education should correspond with a specific age. Instead, the different stages should follow the psychological development of a child; and rather than building skill sets, pedagogy should focus on building up the different faculties of the soul as they develop. The soul, the decision-making agent behind our actions, is comprised of lower and upper faculties. The ultimate goal of education is to spur on and guide the development of these faculties, based on the assumption that they develop during different phases of a human's development; education has to take into account that each age corresponds with a different developmental stage.[358] New-born infants classify as imperfect humans: they still 'live the life of animals', as Wolff puts it.[359] We are born with our *facultates inferiores*, i.e. sense perception, imagination and memory, naturally in place, but the upper faculties – intellect and free will – are not innate and need to be trained.[360] Without schooling these capacities, a child cannot grow up to live the life of a human.[361] Education, therefore, is not just a plus – it is an existential necessity.

356 Menius, *Oeconomia christiana*, p. 66: 'Sonder seine haußhaltung sol aller ding dahin gerichtet sein/das der fromme/Gotsförchtige/gehorsame und tugentsame kinder aufziehe.'
357 Coler, *Oeconomia ruralis*, p. 359.
358 Wolff, *Oeconomica*, § 233, p. 388.
359 Ibid., § 215, p. 356: 'Infantes recens nati vitam animalem vivunt, eamque imperfectam...'
360 Ibid., § 215, p 357.
361 Ibid., § 233, p. 387.

Even before that, childcare in Wolff's understanding starts with physical preservation at a young age. An infant may possess the same faculties of the soul as an animal would but unlike animals it lacks the strength to take care of itself. The parents' mandate is therefore to preserve and perfect its life in this rudimentary stage – feed it, clothe it, give it shelter, protect it from strong light, sound or wind.[362] This mandate also extends backwards, to the child's life in the womb. Using Malebranche's idea of uterine memory, Wolff explains that impressions, inclinations and proclivities of the mother can be passed on to the infant's soul in the uterus, including confused notions of good and bad. This stipulates the mother's mandate to shield herself and thus the child from any impressions that will leave a moral dent on his or her life, prior to and after birth.[363] Beyond mere physical needs, the moral education of a child should progressively form the upper faculties of the soul. The goal of education is not to suppress the inferior faculties of the soul but to bring them into accord with the upper ones.[364] In between these two registers there are furthermore intermediate faculties – Wolff singles out *attentio* – that are instrumental to the process.[365] On this occasion, Wolff describes in detail how the intermediary faculty of *attentio* has to be trained from the early childhood onwards.[366]

The concept of *attentio* has been developed in the *Ethica* in the abstract, absolved from any pedagogical context: a conscious, concentrated sense perception, *attentio* procures a clear idea of an object in view and facilitates its representation in the mind.[367] Wolff then utilizes this concept to support his pedagogical discourse. In order to stimulate the most basic form of *attentio*, a child's eyes have to be proactively directed towards and fixed on an object – a sense perception achieved by parental intervention, so to speak.[368] Eventually, infants, children and adolescents should be instilled with a 'desire to see and hear everything' so that natural curiosity can take care of a process that the parents would otherwise have to drive themselves.[369] Since the child is lacking judgment and reason at this point, *attentio* and the innate qualities of memory and imagination only suffice to attain confused and unclear ideas of perceptible things.[370] As children discover and observe more and more things, they will learn

362 Ibid., § 216, p. 359; § 234, p. 390.
363 Ibid., § 221, pp. 368–369.
364 Ibid., § 233, p. 387.
365 Ibid., § 235, p. 392.
366 Ibid., §§ 235–240, p. 391–402.
367 Wolff, Christian, *Philosophia moralis. Pars prima*, § 17, pp. 22–25: 'Quodsi animum ad rem sensu perceptam attendamus, perceptio ejus efficitur clarior perceptione ceterorum, quae simul percipiuntur (§. 237. *Psych. empir.*), consequenter eam agnoscere, vel a perceptibilibus ceteris distinguere valemus (§. 31. *Psych. empir.*) atque ita apta efficitur, ut vi imaginationis reproduci (§. 92. *Psych empir.*) & beneficio memoriae recognosci possit (§. 175.*Psych. empir.*).'
368 Wolff, *Oeconomica*, § 236, pp. 392–393.
369 Ibid., § 238, pp. 398–399.
370 Ibid., § 237, p. 395.

to reflect on them, discern regular occurrences and take note of them.[371] Finally, the child can be taught the names of things – or 'substances', in Wolff's wording – simply by means of *attentio*. A second intermediate faculty, *reflectio*, helps to understand the names of different qualities inherent to a substance.[372] The more often children see things of the same kind and learns to associate them with the correct names, the more their intelligence, *ingenium*, is stimulated, and also their intellect once they learn to discern different qualities in a substance – better said, learn to isolate and abstract certain properties from objects in real life.[373]

The chapter breaks off mid-explanation but even this rudimentary account demonstrates how Wolff's pedagogy tries to put pure theory into literal practice by building on concepts established elsewhere in his system. This stands in stark contrast to a teaching practice that had established itself since the beginning of the eighteenth century in Halle, specifically in Francke's *paedagogium*, which approached education from just the opposite direction: through purposeful interaction with real-life objects. Christoph Semler (1669–1740), a theologian and pedagogue, laid the foundations to this new method with a treatise in 1705 offering suggestions for a 'mathematical school for craftsmen', intended as a supplementary education path for poorer students in need of vocational training.[374] An improved curriculum in 1709 shows Semler's list of suggestions, including activities such as the building of architectural models; to that purpose, he even published a model blueprint of the city of Jerusalem in collaboration with the *Franckesche Stiftungen*.[375] Although Semler's own attempts to run a school in that spirit foundered and eventually ceded with his death, the idea was successfully picked up by the pedagogue Johann Julius Hecker (1707–1768) and developed further into institutions offering practical training instead of abstract knowledge as part of a universal school system – the first beginnings of what lives on in the institution of *Realschule* in Germany.[376] In contrast to his contemporaries' approaches intent on practice and experience, Wolff's teaching aims seem doubly abstract and speak volumes of his quite literal translation of philosophical principles into pedagogical practice: to Wolff, the child is not taught how to speak, how to recognise and name objects – it learns how to identify substance and qualities, by means

371 Ibid., § 240, p. 401.

372 Ibid., § 241, p. 403.

373 Ibid., § 242, p. 406.

374 Semler, Christoph, Nützliche Vorschläge von Auffrichtung einer Mathematischen Handwercks-Schule bey der Stadt Halle (Halle: Henckel, 1705). See Schiller, Hermann, Lehrbuch der Geschichte der Pädagogik (Leipzig: Reisland, 1894), pp. 233–4.

375 Semler, Christoph, Neueröffnete mathematische und mechanische Real-Schule (Halle: Renger, 1709); Semler, Christoph, Die Stadt Jerusalem mit allen ihren Mauren, Thoren, Thürmen, Tempel, Pallästen, Schlössern, auch übrigen publiquen und privat-Gebäuden. (Halle: Verlag des Waisenhauses, 1718).

376 Schiller, Lehrbuch der Geschichte der Pädagogik, pp. 234–6.

of *attentio* and *reflectio*. It is not taught how to behave or how to concretely do something – it is inculcated with the ontological predicaments to act virtuously and think scientifically.

The section on pedagogy ends before Wolff can explain how further mental operations can be stimulated, and how intellect and the sensitive appetite of the child can be brought into accordance with each other to guide the free will. Yet as a procedure, this is already implicit in function and structure of the *Oeconomica* as a didactic treatise itself – in fact, of Wolff's whole system, culminating in practical philosophy. It starts with building up clear notions – in fact, clear notions of what clear notions are – to then demonstrate his way through the mechanism of the world and the human purpose within, logically inculcating the motives that should drive us towards moral action. Wolff's pedagogy is not only a specialised section on childcare but a glimpse of his didactics at large: weaving ontology, logic, psychology and the real world into the minutiae of his practical philosophy.

As the middle part of his practical philosophy, the unfinished *Oeconomica* gives a mere glimpse of what the complete picture of a cosmologically informed morality would look like. As *prodromus Politicae*, however, it methodically teaches domestic morality with a higher purpose: Wolff's systematic integration of the household in the world at large consciously redefines the household as a building block for the state. The idea of the family as a pre-political structure preceding the state is not always consistent. For example, the fact that a marriage can only be verified by a state official means it cannot really exist in a natural guise, outside the *status civilis*. The intertwinement between state and household also means that family duties in a supposedly pre-political stage are proleptically informed by the public interest of a body politic that should technically not exist at this level. This is reflected in the morally approved motives for household activities: simple, private actions now count as a service towards God but also the state as divinely sanctioned form of human organisation. Educating one's children well might be done in one's own interest; but it is the mark of a good citizen in particular to do so.[377] In fact, as the *prudentia civilis* will show, education is of primary importance for the state – not just for the individual.[378]

The *Oeconomica*, in that sense, demonstrates not just domestic morality but civic-mindedness. And although the *Politica* was never written, the *Oeconomica* already illustrates how proactive citizen virtue is complemented with state regulation of private lives. 'Civic aptitude' for marriage, for example, is not a natural factor but a predicament born with political organisation and the subject matter of public

377 Ibid., § 212, pp. 353–354: 'Optime igitur parentes de liberis suis merentur & ipsis optime consulunt, si eos recte educant. Et quoniam liberos hominibus aliis utiles, & dignos Reip. immo mundi cives efficiunt (*not*. §. 176); bene de humano genere & Rep. merentur & quod Deo placet faciunt.'

378 Ibid., § 200 *nota*, p. 335: 'Videbimus etiam suo loco in Philosophia civili, quantum intersit, ne recta educatio ignoretur.'

policy.[379] The topic is therefore bracketed out from the *Oeconomica* but Wolff still makes it clear that the state has an interest and the right to intervene in this realm of decision-making, prohibiting marriage or intermarriage in certain cases.[380] Such legislative intervention sounds like an overreach to the modern ear but it should be remembered that the a regulation of this kind was less novelty than standard at Wolff's time. As Keith Tribe describes the situation, '...the politics and economics of the territorial state turn out to involve a constant work of regulation in which no sharp distinction can be made between "political" and "economic" tasks', and the same holds true for public and private interest.[381] Complementary to this top-down regulation, Wolff's *Oeconomica* formalizes the bottom-up force of civic virtue, turning a one-way street into a two-lane highway. The purpose of house and body politic blend into one universal concern: the continuity of state and human race.

3.3.2 The household as a structural liability

The reconstruction of pedagogy from Wolff's system as a whole works quite seamlessly, possibly because didactics are intrinsic to system and *systema* alike. What Wolff suggests explicitly in the chapter on education is put into practice through the very discourse of the *Oeconomica* itself, albeit on adults: the inculcation of virtue. This is achieved by rationally demonstrating the motive to push the will into a moral direction, putting all the different pieces from the system together for the ultimate fulfilment of Wolff's *systema*, the operational principle of philosophy.

Some other topics are not as smoothly recouped through this mode of argument. In particular, inconsistencies appear where elements from different parts of the system do not blend well with each other, even though they are cogently established at their point of origin. This is most evident on the different – positive and normative – ideas about love that Wolff is trying to reconcile in the *Oeconomica*. His moral philosophy bids love a duty for its positive effects, similarly to virtue; his psychology offers a rational explanation for the sufficient reasons of love as an emotion. Where Wolff tries to bring love as duty and love as phenomenon together in the *Oeconomica*, the two theories resist combination; in the end this goes to show that a scientific discourse derived from how people *do* act does not always logically agree with how they *should* act.

---

379 Ibid., § 44, p. 63: '...inhabilitatis civilis ad matrimonium ratio nulla naturalis, quae scilicet ex ipsa hominis natura derivatur, dari potest.'

380 Ibid., § 23 *nota*, p. 33: 'Non jam quaeritur, quinam a matrimonio sint arcendi, id quod ad Politicam spectat; sed quid ad matrimonii rectitudinem omnimodam requiratur, cum lex naturae, quae urget actionum humanarum rectitudinem ... rectitudinem quoque in contrahendo matrimonio praescribat.'

381 Tribe, Keith, *Governing Economy: The Reformation of German Economic Discourse, 1750–1840* (Cambridge; New York: Cambridge University Press, 1988), p. 34.

Where Wolff's pedagogy focuses on building up basic intellectual capacities of the soul, his adult didactics take a complete soul for granted. The path from heuristic beginnings to moral action, however, is the same: the inculcation of virtue starts with the delineation of clear concepts, of the intrinsic features of duties and virtues involved. The arguments then link up duties and virtues to then demonstrate the motives requisite for moral action.

Wolff's own definition of virtue combines the notion of natural law as the science of right and wrong with the Aristotelian notion of habituation. As a result, virtue is defined as the habit of acting out natural law. Natural law as the theory behind moral philosophy teaches what needs to be done and moral philosophy demonstrates how – but how, in Wolffian terms, is not the explanation of actual tasks at hand but cognitive path to virtue in order to act morally as a matter of habit.[382] Wolff demonstrates not what to do but what to think in order to become a moral person. The *Oeconomica* structures this task into three steps: outlining the duties; identifying the requisite virtues; and by demonstrating – both from a deontological and a eudaemonic point of view – that these virtues and duties serve God, the state and the individual itself. The latter step, quite literally, provides the motive to prompt the reader to acquire virtue.

The duties of a married couple, for example, are as follows: sexual intercourse; a communal household; and a shared way of life.[383] The virtues associated with these duties are *castitas conjugalis*, that is conjugal chastity, frugality and parsimony when it comes to the household, and in general all the virtues required for social living: patience in bad and moderation in good times, and piety above all.[384] The corresponding motives are logically commended through duty or self-interest. To stay chaste, a spouse will have to keep in mind that sex is intended for the purpose of procreation and illicit where only for the sake of libido.[385] Parsimony is desirable for the advantages it brings to the household and the detriment its opposite, prodigality, bestows.[386] Given the centrality of cognitive adjustment to Wolff's didactic approach, it is unsurprising that the *Oeconomica* is suffused with critiques of rivalling epistemologies.[387] In that

382 See for example in reference to the spousal duties, Wolff, *Oeconomica*, § 90, p. 135: 'Qui habitum faciendi officia conjugis acquirere vult, operam dare debet, ut virtutibus omnibus abundet, iis praesertim, quibus praxis officiorum erga alios continetur, vitae consuetudinem, quam matrimonium continet, intimius perspectam probe ponderare & firmo proposito eam colendi matrimonium contrahere.'

383 Ibid., § 90, p. 135: 'debitum conjugale'; 'communis oeconomia'; 'vitae consuetudo'.

384 Ibid., § 90, p. 136.

385 Ibid., § 148, p. 236.

386 Ibid., § 133, p. 208.

387 Wolff here scolds Locke and the followers of Newton, 'lovers of lazy philosophy', for reviving the Aristotelian idea of *tabula rasa* that Wolff so rejects. See Wolff, *Oeconomica*, §. 237, p. 396: '[N]on tamen propterea nostram facimus rasam tabulam *Aristotelis*, quam a recentioribus expulsam ab orco quasi resuscitavit *Lockius* & hujus auctoritas splendore quodam a *Newtono* mutuato collustrata mirifice commendat Philosophiae pigrae amatoribus.'

context he mentions Rorarius, whose book on the rationality of animals had sparked a debate about the soul between Bayle and Leibniz. Wolff does not touch upon his contemporaries' altercation but returns to Rorarius' original suggestion that animals possess reason – and by extension, the divide between animals and humans, between nature and nurture, instinct and intellect. Wolff postulates that nature would not let animals err from the path she defined. Only humans are subject to error in their actions because they possess free will; yet in order to make correct decisions, free will needs to be guided by reason. Animals do not have the scope of free will and if they seem to act conform with reason – or act more reasonably than humans, as Rorarius would have us believe – then this is because they are naturally incapable of erring. Nature compels them to act according to truth. Humans, however, are presented with the spectre of moral choice; they are not fully compelled by nature but have to employ reason to abide by natural law.[388] The presence of reason does not spell the absence of nature in human behaviour and Wolff distinguishes necessary functions of both body and soul from voluntary ones.[389] A similar divide between natural and rational seems to reign over emotions. The prime example in question here is love – and love is the chapter where not only nature and nurture come to a head, but the challenge of integrating different traditions under one *systema* comes to the fore.

Natural love for one's children, Wolff argues, is instilled by nature, an impulse driven by the *appetitus sensitivus*.[390] Natural love in animals and humans is a necessary component that causes them to look after their young as they should. Yet unless informed by rationality it drives humans to spoil their children rather than turn them into morally impeccable human beings. Natural love hence must be brought into accord with rational love, better said, it must be governed by virtue.[391] But love is not only discussed within the context of child education. A considerable space in the *Oeconomica* theorizes on love as the emotional glue to a marriage. The topic is a familiar trope in moral literature throughout the ages, even though by the Renaissance love looked 'more like a mixture of Christian charity and tolerance than passionate attachment' on paper, according to Ian Maclean.[392] In comparison to Aristotle's and Xenophon's prag-

388 Wolff, *Oeconomica*, § 216 *nota*, p. 361.

389 Wolff, Christian, *Philosophia practica universalis. Pars prior*, § 12, sig. B: '*Actiones* tam *animae*, quam *corporis* dicuntur *naturales* vel *necessariae*, quae per essentiam & naturam animae & corporis determinantur: *Liberae* autem appellantur, quae per essentiam & naturam animae ac corporis non determinantur, sed a libertate animae pendent.'

390 Wolff, *Oeconomica*, § 184, p. 306: '...natura inditus est tam brutis, quam hominibus amor prolis suae (§. 257. *part.* 7. *Jur. nat.*).'

391 Wolff, *Oeconomica*, § 189 *nota*, p. 314: 'Amor naturalis, nisi rationalis efficiatur, rectae educationi nocet, ad quam parentes impellere debebat... Vitium non haeret in amore naturali, qui in se bonus est, sed culpa parentum efficitur nocuus.'

392 Maclean, Ian, The Renaissance Notion of Woman: A Study in the Fortunes of Scholasticism and Medical Science in European Intellectual Life (Cambridge; New York: Cambridge University Press, 1980), p. 59.

matic treatment of spousal relations, it seems that Christianity and its focus on *caritas* as central virtue gave love in general a contextual boost. Aquinas stressed that 'the spouses enjoyed the fulfilment of virtue in their experience of the 'deepest friendship', *maxima amicitia*, more so than carnal love.[393] Florinus, more Protestant traditionalist than philosopher, ardently defends the importance of love in marriage: a life without love is hardly a life, and a marriage without love only half the bond. Simultaneously he sets out clear and clearly non-egalitarian principles between husband and wife.[394] Menius, finally, simply stipulates love the duty of a Christian husband.[395] The idea of marital love in moral literature indeed seems to fall short of passion; but as Florinus's *Oeconomus* betrays, the household in theory is not entirely devoid of feeling.

Wolff's *Oeconomica* treats the topic of love from two different angles: as a duty, akin to the Protestant tradition;[396] and as a psychological phenomenon, inspired by virtue and fostering friendship, similar to Aquinas.[397] The psychological reading discusses how love comes about – the deontological interpretation stipulates love as a natural mandate towards the spouse. Both draw from previous literary traditions in philosophy and what is more, both have a theoretical foundation in the rest of Wolff's system. Yet taken together in the *Oeconomica*, the two prove a challenge to combine. The discussion starts with premarital deliberations. Love, from the Wolffian perspective, is not a sufficient reason for marriage, but an essential factor. A means rather than an end, it is a necessary prerequisite for the perfect concord needed for matrimonial life.[398] Whoever wants to get married, should therefore seek to choose a person he can love.[399] Up to this point, Wolff's argument is almost identical with Florinus's discourse, down to the recommendation that people ought to get to know each other well before getting married.[400] The matter becomes complicated where he is trying to

---

393 Outlined in the *Summa contra Gentiles*, see Haar, Christoph P., 'Tomás Sánchez and Late Scholastic Thought on Marriage and Political Virtue', in *The Concept of Law (Lex) in the Moral and Political Thought of the 'School of Salamanca'*, ed. by Kirsten Bunge, Marko J. Fuchs, Danaë Simmermacher, and Anselm Spindler (Leiden; Boston: Brill, 2016), pp. 81–105, p. 91.

394 Florinus, *Oeconomus prudens*, Bk. 1, Ch. 4, § 10., p. 14: 'Denn wie ein Leben ohne Liebe kaum ein solches Leben zu nennen, also ist eine Ehe ohne Liebe kaum eine halbe Ehe.'

395 Menius, Oeconomia christiana, p. 73.

396 Wolff, Jus naturae methodo scientifica pertractatum. Pars septima, § 461, p. 310: 'Conjux unus qua conjux alterum diligere debet tanquam seipsum.'

397 See Wolff, *Oeconomica*, §§ 96–9, pp. 143–6 (on p. 142, the page number erroneously reverts to 137).

398 Ibid., § 107, p. 153: 'Si conjuges amore conjugali se mutuo prosequuntur, concordes sunt, & concordia constans ac perpetua est.' See ibid., § 108, p. 157: 'Concordia conjugum maxime convenit vitae consuetudini…'.

399 Ibid., § 25. p. 34: 'Qui matrimonium contrahere vult, personam eligere debet, quam impense amare potest.'

400 Florinus, *Oeconomus prudens*, Bk. I, Ch. 4, § 13, p. 15. Wolff recommends personal conversation as a means of getting to know a person which might sound more self-explanatory nowadays than it might have been at the time. See Wolff, *Oeconomica*, § 42, p. 60.

match this mandate with the idea of love as a sentiment. As it is, there can be a host of reasons for why we fall in love – some reasons more obvious than others and none of them really under our control.[401] In principle, however, Wolff has a scientific theory of love available: as established in the *Psychologia empirica*, love comes about when we observe something in another person that we like.[402] More specifically, in the ideal scenario, this is not the appreciation of just any quality – true, rational love is fostered through observing and appreciating virtue in another person.[403] Love, just like Wolff's idea of virtue, is a warranty for moral conduct in a marriage, with very practical implications: it renders spouses diligent and prudent in the running of their household.[404] Moreover, love exists in a reciprocal relationship with virtue: since a person's virtue inspires love in the other, a virtuous person in love will actively try to conserve and foster virtue in the beloved.[405] This explains therefore why love fosters love as it breeds virtue reciprocally.[406] By conclusion, love is not a sufficient reason for a match, but a crucial ingredient to wedlock. Wolff deigned the emotion of sadness a necessary consequence of certain circumstances. Love, in contrast, is cast as a rational sentiment subject to the intellect: *amor ordinatus*.[407] A definition of *amor ordinatus* is presented in Thomas Aquinas' *Summa Theologiae*: love in general is not ascribed to vice or virtue, but *amor ordinatus* is implicit in every virtue – every good man loves what is essential to virtue.[408] In the *Oeconomica*, the same concept is applied directly to the relationship between husband and wife: rational love or *amor ordinatus* means loving the virtuous aspects in one's spouse. The scenario of rational, virtue-based love, however, collapses where wife and husband have uneven degrees of virtue, where it is not reciprocated or actively corroded through misbehaviour like adultery – briefly said, where love cannot logically happen.[409] This would not be an issue if it were not

401 Wolff, *Oeconomica*, § 25, p. 34–35.

402 Wolf, *Psychologia empirica*, § 649, p. 487: '*Amor* est affectus, qui oritur ex eo, quod quid in altero observamus, quod nobis placet, seu si quid in altero nobis repraesentamus tanquam bonum, praesertim respectu nostri.'

403 Wolff, Oeconomica, § 96, p. 143: 'Amor rationalis, quo conjugem prosequimur, virtute ejus concitatur.'

404 Ibid., § 135, p. 211: 'Si conjuges amore conjugali se mutuo prosequuntur, in oeconomia diligentiam, prudentiam & providentiam suam desiderari non patiuntur...'.

405 Ibid., § 97, p. 144.

406 Ibid., § 138, p. 217: 'Amor conjugalis mutuus seipsum conservat.'

407 Ibid., § 95, p. 142.

408 Thomas Aquinas, *Summa Theologiae*, II–II, q. 125 a. 2 co.: 'Respondeo dicendum quod, sicut supra habitum est, omnis timor ex amore procedit, nullus enim timet nisi contrarium eius quod amat. Amor autem non determinatur ad aliquod genus virtutis vel vitii, sed amor ordinatus includitur in qualibet virtute, quilibet enim virtuosus amat proprium bonum virtutis; amor autem inordinatus includitur in quolibet peccato, ex amore enim inordinato procedit inordinata cupiditas.'

409 Ibid., § 114 *nota*, p. 165: 'Quamobrem cum amor oriatur,si quod nobis placet in altero observamus (§. 645. *Psych. empir.*), odium vero concitetur, si quod nobis displicet in altero observamus (§. 674. *Psych. empir.*); si uxor maritum amore conjugali minime prosequitur, causa amoris abest, causa odii adest.' Much for the deontological bid of love: the mandate of love does not disappear where its cause expires – and a spouse is still obliged to unilaterally extend this feeling, even if their better half defaults on that obligation.[410] As a solution to this impasse, Wolff takes resort to a medium he sought to abstain from in the first place: Scripture. True, he says, it is hard to love a person who is treating us with disregard. But as the Bible teaches, thou shalt love thy enemy.[411] The virtues commend themselves by logical argument, in the theory and practice of Wolff's moral philosophy. Love is not expressly a virtue in Wolff's philosophy, yet Wolff retains the mandatory character familiar from Protestant household literature. The problem Wolff runs into is that as a sentiment, love is not exclusively ruled by cognitive effort but through an external stimulus. Accordingly, Wolff cannot supply a motive for love, as he does for the virtues, but only describe the circumstances which foster it – and stumble upon the impossibility of a psychological rendering of love combined with a normative mandate. The logical shortcoming does not arise from erroneous deduction rather than combining different exogenous theories in one discourse. This upsets the underlying assumption to the whole system: that two theories will necessarily be consistent with each other if they are proven true in themselves.

3.4 Natural law in the Oeconomica

3.4.1 A contractual reading of family life

Natural law, in Wolff's terms, functions less as a jurisprudential concept than a moral primer and a yardstick for more ephemeral customs and traditions. As a synthesis of elements from practical philosophy and traditional jurisprudence, Wolff fuses philosophical terms with concepts from the natural law tradition into one construct. This is already apparent where three key concepts of his natural law – natural (*status naturalis* or *originarius*), social (*status adventitius*) and political (*status civilis*) status – are directly associated with the Aristotelian categories of moral philosophy: ethics, *Oeconomica* and politics.[412] The blending of the two traditions is also palpable in terms of content. Most significantly, the three *societates* of the household, known

to Roscher's chagrin, Wolff even demonstrates that adultery is harmful for conjugal love. See Wolff, *Oeconomica* § 140, pp. 220–222; Roscher, *Geschichte der National-Oekonomik in Deutschland*, p. 349.

410 Wolff, *Oeconomica*, §. 114, p. 164: 'Maritus uxorem amore conjugali prosequi debet, etiamsi uxor eum non amet, & idem quoque valet de uxore, si maritus eum non amet.'

411 See ibid., § 114 *nota*, pp. 165–166.

412 The association between *status originarius* and *status civilis* with the *Ethica* and the *Politica* features in the 'Discursus praeliminaris'. See Wolff, *Philosophia rationalis sive logica*, §§ 63–65, p. 31; this is also anticipated in Thümmig's *Institutiones* whereby natural law is divided up into *jus naturae ethicum* and *jus naturae politicum*. See Thümmig, *Institutiones*, p. 48.

from the philosophical tradition, are reinterpreted as natural contracts stipulated by the universal order of the world; the rights and obligations for the household members do not arise from their communal living but from the theoretical concepts underpinning the *status adventitius*: property and power.[413]

This formal integration of natural law with moral philosophy has some visible consequences. For one, Wolff blends the concerns and language of two different literary traditions. In that grain, the *Oeconomica* reinvents its traditional content in a jurisprudential guise and social bonds within the household are reborn as natural pacts, *pacta naturalia*. By defining each relationship in this way Wolff creates the theoretical basis to deduce the rights and obligations of its members from the purpose of these putatively natural, tacitly formal relationships. The content of these rights and obligations do not tend to stray far from the traditional path; but the source of legitimacy is now shifted from experience, authority or religion to natural law as the science of good and bad with an inherent logic. In contrast, traditional examples of *Hausväterliteratur* establish a direct relationship between God's authority and the domestic sphere. In a household abiding by Christ, so Florinus, every task and be it as mundane as sweeping the floors, is understood to be a service to God.[414] Under the guidance of piety, the *paterfamilias* can rest assured that his prosperity and welfare is indeed a blessing by God, and legitimate.[415] Wolff dislocates not God but Scripture as the source of legitimacy and consequence and replaces it with natural law. This should be understood as a rationalisation more than secularisation of existing norms; after all, God is the explicit author and Christ the main interpreter of natural law.[416] Analogue to Christian counterparts, mundane dealings are imbued with a new cosmological relevance by reinterpreting them through natural law. A mother breastfeeding her child, for example, fulfils the bidding of natural law; and owing to the natural pact between parents and children, the baby has a formal right to her breastmilk.[417] This formalisation also defines a role, *persona*, for each person in a household, apart from his or her personality. This role is imposed directly by God, in Wolff's reading. Fulfilling the duties of a spouse therefore equates obedience to a divine bid-

413 Wolff, Christian, *Jus naturae methodo scientifica pertractata. Pars prima*, sig. b2: 'In statu originario naturali tantummodo obtinent obligationes seu officia & jura connata; in adventitio autem superaccedunt acquisita, quae ab introductione dominiorum & imperiorum privatorum in societatibus simplicibus, quae vocantur, pendent.'

414 Florinus, *Oeconomus prudens*, Ch. 1, § 11, p. 4: 'Denn erstlich wird solcher Gestalt eine jede Arbeit, so gering und verächtlich dieselbe an ihr selbst auch seyn mag, zu einem Gottesdienst geheiligt.'

415 Florinus, *Oeconomus prudens*, Ch. 1, § 11, p. 5: 'So ist auch zuletzt in einer solchen Haushaltung, wie hie beschrieben ist, dieses ein vortreflicher Vortheil und Vorzug, dass der Haus-Vatter 5. die Versicherung hat, dass der Gewinn, den er erlangt, ein Seegen Gottes, und eine Erfüllung seiner Verheissung ist.'

416 Wolff, *Oeconomica*, § 61 *nota*, p. 95: 'Quamobrem cum autor Juris naturae Deus sit (§. 275. part. 1. Phil. pract. univ.), & nos ad legem naturae servandam obliget (§. 276. part. 1. Phil. pract. univ), Christus vero legis naturae interpres adversus corruptelas Pharisaeorum...'.

417 Ibid., § 218, p. 363: 'Lactare infantem est debitum matris, ad quod jus competit infanti.'

ding.[418] The moral concept of the *societas* and the legal bind of *pactum* are fused into one construct to express human obligation on a universal scale.

In the *Oeconomica* this systematic assessment of norms stretches across custom, positive law and conventions alike. Wolff uses the immutable, ultimately rational order of natural law as a yardstick for man-made, ephemeral norms. Ideally, custom and legislation should always be consistent with natural law; but natural law itself obliges man to follow the rules and norms of his own body politic even where they are more restrictive than natural law would be.[419] The task of moral philosophy is therefore to distinguish natural law from positive legislation and custom to determine what is universally right and moral and what is merely man-made, relative and temporary. Natural law thereby provides a guideline for individual conscience and aids the observance of positive law.[420] It puts law and custom into perspective and gives Wolff a means to judge them by, and ostensibly so in the *Oeconomica.*

Applied to the household, natural law is sometimes less, often more permissive than positive law or custom. Wolff negates, for example, that infertile people have the right to marry, from a natural law perspective; however, he considers a union between blood relatives as merely subject to positive legislation, not universally illicit, arguing that no such restrictions are customary in China.[421] Wolff here departs from Pufendorf, who declares the marriage between blood relatives impure and naturally depraved.[422] Florinus, too, issues a warning against marrying too close a relative.[423] The Catholic side, however, seems to be less stringent, for once: the Council of Trent reserved the right for the Church to make dispensations in this matter.[424] Seemingly there was no united Christian front in this regard– and Wolff declares the issue culturally relative from the perspective of natural law.

Conversely, Wolff uses universal morality to reassess accepted legal concepts, for example the Roman legacy of *patria potestas*, a father's wide-reaching dominion over the life and death of his children. Grotius still considers it within the natural scope of

---

418 See, for instance, the role (*persona*) of the spouse, in Wolff, *Oeconomica*, § 83, p. 126: 'Persona conjugis a Deo matrimonium contrahentibus imponitur.' Ibid., § 84, p. 128: 'Obedientia erga Deum singulari quadam ratione influit in officia conjugum, quae ad personam conjugis recte gerendam requiruntur.'

419 See for example the case of legal restriction imposed on marriages beyond what natural law allows, Wolff, *Oeconomica*, § 45 *nota*, pp. 64–65.

420 Ibid., § 62 *nota*, p. 97: 'Et quamvis legibus positivis sit obediendum (§. 95. part 8. Jur. nat.), Jus tamen naturae manet regula pro conscientia & in observantia Juris civilis usum suum habet.'

421 Ibid., § 44 *nota*, p. 63.

422 Pufendorf, *De iure naturae et gentium*, Vol. 2, Bk VI, Ch. I, § XXVIII, p. 52.

423 Florinus, *Oeconomus prudens*, Pt. 1, Bk I, Ch IV, § 13, p. 15.

424 Calleja, Angel, ed., *Canones, et decreta sacrosancti oecumenici, et generalis Concilii Tridentini* (Alcalá de Henares: Andreas de Angulo, 1564), p. CLXXII: 'Si quis dixerit, eos tantum consanguinitatis, & affinitatis gradus, qui Leuitico exprimuntur, posse impedire matrimonium contrahendum, & dirimere contractum; nec posse Ecclesiam in nonnullis illorum dispensare, aut constituere, ut plures impediant & dirimant; anathema sit.'

a father's God-given power to pawn or sell his children where he cannot feed them.[425] Wolff vociferously argues against what he considers a parental overreach: the goal of the parental bond and by extension the *patria potestas* is the education of children; selling them into slavery, exposing or killing them, as the Romans and other ancients considered appropriate, would logically not contribute to this goal, that is, would not comply with natural law.[426]

Elsewhere, natural law helps to fortify the moral position vis-à-vis permissive legislation. Divorce, for example, is officially anathema to Protestant theology at Wolff's time; but owing to reality, there are a number of circumstances under which a divorce or separation is legally admissible, even if theologically unacceptable.[427] Within Wolff's natural law it is understood and never questioned that a marriage is a bond before God and indissoluble. Although he admits that irreconcilable differences can be cited as a reason for lawful divorce, it should not serve as a pretext to end an indeliberate marriage gone awry.[428] A person seeking divorce can thus act within the boundaries of positive law and break natural law, still. Where in the examples above, positive legislation is more restrictive than natural law, here natural law restricts the freedom permitted by positive legislation, in the name of morality. Wolff, in fact, extends the argument to a culture critique – the Jewish custom to break off a marriage on the grounds of mere antipathy is not in accordance with natural law and at least in this respect agrees with Florinus.[429]

Natural law as a universal yardstick thus is not only applied to the household but also to existing regulatory frameworks. Remarkable on this count is that the family is tied into a network of obligations towards the different members of the household but that the purpose of these obligations originates beyond, in the sphere of the state. Differently said: by getting married, the two spouses are obliged towards each other to fulfil the purpose of marriage as the ultimately felicitous one; yet the way Wolff positions these obligations makes it clear that the ultimate authority for safeguarding this pact is not some regulatory framework, but God – and the beneficiary of their morality is not just the family but, yet again, the state.

---

425 Grotius, *De iure belli ac pacis libri tres*, Bk. II, Ch. V, § V, p. 177.

426 Wolff, *Oeconomica*, § 203 *nota*, pp. 339–340.

427 Amongst those reasons are adultery, impotence or cruelty; the legal intricacy of the matter is described in Florinus, *Oeconomus prudens*, Pt. I, Bk. I., Ch. IV 'Rechtsanmerkungen' § 10, pp. 19–21.

428 Wolff, *Oeconomica*, § 7, p. 10.

429 Ibid., § 65, p. 100: 'Ast mos Judaeorum legi naturae minime consentaneus fuit, reprobatus ideo a Christo Matth. XIX. 7 & seqq.' See also the legal annotations in Florinus, *Oeconomus prudens*, Vol I, Bk. I., Ch. IV, § 10, p. 20.

3.4.2 Reconciling reason and religion

Wolff's lifetime endeavour was to prove that reason and religion necessarily were in accord with each other. In his opinion, reason as the one element common to all of mankind would provide the best basis for a shared, natural religion above the trappings of ritual and cult. The intention was not to invalidate Christianity by replacing it with a natural religion – rather the opposite, Wolff means to validate its tenets by means of his method as the universal, truly reason-based religion.[430] This intention permeates the *Oeconomica* likewise.[431] In the course of his mediation attempts, Wolff is never trying to reconcile natural law and the Gospel, directly. In fact, he openly disapproves of the idea.[432] Rather, the task of the philosopher and of the theologian is clearly divided in Wolff's universe: the philosopher contemplates the world as is by virtue of reason, the theologian explains revelation.[433] Where previously the Bible would have lent the only source for the interpretation of God's will, natural law as the correct analysis and interpretation of the world order, according to Wolff, yields an understanding of God's creation and his purpose behind each element: natural law *is* divine order. On the basis of this understanding, Wolff rationalizes existing norms and tries to solve confessional dissonance with the help of natural law.[434]

One example is Wolff's compromise between the Catholic and the Protestant position on whether marriage is obligatory. The medieval – Catholic – side of the story lends a voice to arguments against the idea of marriage as the barrier to a contemplative life. A number of works, such as *Utrum sapienti competat uxorem ducendam* by Engelbert of Admont (c.1250–1331), not only explore the question whether a scholar should marry but whether any man should marry at all. These works come as letters, dialogues, scholastic *quaestiones* or even poems which predominantly – and frequently in satirical tone – argue *against* marriage.[435] Erasmus' *Encomium matrimonii*, a letter to a friend written from the perspective of an unmarried scholar, picks up on this theme and converts it into what seems like a genuine argument for marriage – as a rhetorical challenge.[436] The Protestant side is virulently wedded to the opposite opinion: marriage – and now of the clerics, too – is a duty towards God. A celibate life

---

430 Schaper, Ein langer Abschied vom Christentum, p. 60.

431 In the *Oeconomica*, Wolff specifically cites this intention to achieve a 'consensus rationis ac fidei' in favour of his argument. See Wolff, *Oeconomica*, § 61, p. 96.

432 Wolff explicitly rejects selfsame attempt by another author to demarcate the difference to his own brand of natural law. See Wolff, *Oeconomica*, § 218, p. 364: 'Absit autem ut existimes, non sine absurditate officia hominis ex principiis Juris demonstrari, quasi hoc idem sit ac cum Autore Postillae Juridicae, cujus nomen non amplius succurrit, Evangelia ex corpore Juris civilis explicare velle.'

433 Ibid., § 225, p. 378.

434 Schaper, Ein langer Abschied vom Christentum, p. 62.

435 Blažek, Die mittelalterliche Rezeption der aristotelischen Philosophie der Ehe, p. 178.

436 See Erasmus, *Encomium Matrimonii* (Basel: J. Froben, 1518).

is practically a sin and a cause for adultery, as expressed in stark terms in Menius' *Oeconomia*.[437] Florinus proves more conciliatory, saying that no man should be forced to marry; the legal commentary on this section, however, highlights the traditionally difficult position of bachelors within societies ancient and contemporary.[438]

Wolff shares Menius' prejudice against a celibate life as a cause for fleshly desires.[439] But regarding the choice between a bachelor life and marriage, Wolff seeks a practical consensus in the middle: all fertile men should marry in order to produce progeny, except when the impediments of marriage would not allow them to pursue their intellectual occupations and they cannot find a wife to take on their share of the burden.[440] Ignoring the original, ideological debate, the matter is solved from a purely practical point of view, and quite successfully, it would seem.

The same pragmatic attitude governs Wolff's attempt at solving the separate confessional incarnations of ecclesiastic law. The ultimate difference between Protestant and Catholic marriage law sprang from the former's renunciation of the sacrament of marriage: although matrimony was still considered a divine institution – perhaps even more so than before – the justification thereof was drawn from a different interpretation than the Catholic notion likening the bond between husband and wife to that between church and man.[441] Seemingly a clerical distinction, it meant that the two confessions resorted to a different canon when it came to deciding private disputes: the Catholics drew the main body of regulations from the statements made at the Council of Trent, alongside Roman Law, Canon Law and the Bible. The Protestants resorted to a modified version of Canon Law and the Bible, including the symbolic books of the Church.[442] The resulting situation turned out to be quite unclear from a legal point of view. Particularly divorce and the dissolution of engagements caused a rift where Protestants and Catholics maintained a different set of rules. The Catholics considered an engagement confirmed by the consensus between man and woman, without the need for an official celebration. Two different kinds of agreements could be met, *sponsalia de praesenti* and *sponsalia de futuro*. The former essentially constituted a matrimony without celebration; the latter could be considered an engagement

---

437 Gause and Scholz, Ehe und Familie im Geist des Luthertums, p. 60.

438 Florinus, *Oeconomus prudens et legalis*, Ch. 4, § 2, p. 12: 'Es ist aber unsere Meinung hiebey gar nicht, daß wir dem Haus-Vatter wider seinen Willen das eheliche Leben aufdringen wollen. Denn obwohl die Ehe ein von GOtt verordneter Stand und Beruf ist, so ist sie doch nicht allen Menschen ohne Unterscheid befohlen.' Legal commentary to this paragraph follows on ibid., p. 18.

439 Wolff, Oeconomica, § 145, p. 231: 'Ad adulterium proni sunt, qui in coelibatu veneri vacarunt.'

440 Ibid., § 197, p. 326–327. Wolff here faces the conundrum to reconcile the celibate life of obvious role models like Leibniz and Descartes with the mandate of natural law to serve the propagation of the human race.

441 von Glück, Christian Friedrich, *Darstellung des Kirchenrechtes der Katholiken und Protestanten* (Augsburg: Jenisch und Stage, 1839), p. 221.

442 von Glück, Darstellung des Kirchenrechtes, pp. 222–223.

in modern terms, confirming a promise to marry in the future, with or without a conditionality clause. Mutual agreement to dissolve an engagement would have been considered a *justa causa* in the Catholic conception.[443] For the Protestants, true to their interpretation of Canon Law and the Bible, an engagement represented an absolute, binding contract and a divinely sanctioned bond resulting in an irrevocable obligation to marry.[444] Wolff, whose exposition on engagement and marriage rites strongly resembles the scholastic discourse on the topic, rejects the Protestant interpretation and argues his case from the point of view of natural law. In his reading, an engagement, *sponsalia*, is not naturally ordained – marriage only requires the consensus between the two parties involved but not a previous agreement. Seeing that it is not an obligatory part of the process, an engagement does not confer the same binding rights and obligations as a wedding would but only bears meaning as a pact in general.[445] The indissolubility of marriage, in contrast, derives from the duties and obligations of the marriage partners towards each other and their children. Transferring the idea of indissolubility of marriage to the naturally non-committal engagement pact is therefore a Protestant misconception, in Wolff's eyes – and impracticable and at odds with rationality insofar as it can force people into marriage who are likely to be unhappy and fulfil their role incorrectly.[446]

Wolff's reasoning strongly echoes the scholastic opinion represented by Francisco de Vitoria and Thomas Aquinas who argue from the same position: that an unhappy marriage is an ineffective one and that it would be preferable to allow the termination of an engagement to avoid such a scenario.[447] Vitoria further specifies that the Church has no real authority on the matter: an engagement, unlike marriage, does not require sanction from the Church and can only be tied or broken by the people in question; in fact, there is no historical precedent to suggest otherwise.[448] Wolff agrees with these arguments; his recommendation is for an engaged couple to be cooperative and dissolve an engagement where doubts arise, even if only one party would like to break it off. Yet differently from Vitoria, who makes a distinction between man-made bonds and Church-sanctioned bonds, Wolff judges the validity of all pacts – matrimony and engagement alike – on the basis of natural law which stipulates that *pacta sunt servanda*.[449] In that sense, Wolff transfers the power of the human pact of an engagement to the sphere of divine ordinance by pronouncing it a matter of natu-

443 Ibid., pp. 226, 229.
444 Ibid., p. 231; Wolff, *Oeconomica*, § 61, p. 94.
445 Wolff, *Oeconomica*, § 61, pp. 94–5.
446 Ibid., § 61, pp. 94, 96.
447 See Vitoria, *Relectiones*, p. 441 and Thomas Aquinas, *Commentary on the Sentences*, IV, d. 27 q. 2 a. 1 ad 2.
448 Vitoria, *Relectiones*, pp. 441, 443.
449 Wolff, *Oeconomica*, § 61, p. 95.

ral law, pact that it is; but since all pacts are therefore backed by God, it is not clear why an engagement should be dissoluble where a marriage is not.

The indissolubility of marriage, on the other hand, was not a feature exclusive but intrinsic to the Christian interpretation of matrimony, and Wolff's insistence on it betrays his fealty to Christian norms in the face of a culturally and legally varied landscape. The same bias rules his assessment of wedding rites and customs – at Wolff's time, subject to a potpourri of Saxon rites, local conventions and legislation. Wolff's analysis differentiates between rites and ceremonies within natural law, abstracted from any real custom. Only ceremonies are representative of the bond or contract in question and necessary for its validation; a rite does not have any representative power and as such is not essential to the procedure.[450] Ceremonies are mandated by natural law and morally immutable even where local custom or legislation might demand different forms of celebration.[451] Traditional Germanic wedding rites would foresee a host of ritualised gift exchanges as pledges to back up the marriage promise – a contract struck not between husband and wife, but groom and father of the bride.[452] Remnants of this tradition were still customary at Wolff's time, such as *arrha*, morning gift or dowry. The *Oeconomica* describes these rites but only writes those practices into natural law that spring from the understanding of marriage as a bond between the betrothed, not a contract between families. The wedding contract in principle only depends on the consensus of the two people involved.[453] The family background, Wolff clarifies elsewhere, does not contribute anything directly to marriage.[454] In this version of marriage, the traditional transactional elements, such as dowry, payments or pledges by the groom such as the so-called *arrha* and other ritualised exchanges between the two families, lose their validating function.[455] These swaps of gifts and material wealth were not legally required but merely based on convention, however, they communicated status alongside commitment and fulfilled a function within the broader social context.[456] The exchange and display of presents and the wedding banquet served not only as a form of ostentation and status display,

---

450 Ibid., § 67, p. 103.

451 Ibid., § 67, p. 103.

452 Schmidt-Wiegand, Ruth, 'Hochzeit, Vertragsehe und Ehevertrag in Mitteleuropa', in *Die Braut. Geliebt, verkauft, getauscht, geraubt. Zur Rolle der Frau im Kulturvergleich, Bd. 1*, ed. by Gisela Völger and Karin von Welck (Cologne: Rautenstrauch-Joest-Museum für Völkerkunde, 1985), pp. 264–73, pp. 266–7.

453 Wolff, Oeconomica, § 55, p. 82: 'Ad sponsalia celebranda sufficit mutua consensus personarum desponsandarum declaratio.'

454 Ibid., § 37, p. 52: 'Ad matrimonium nihil per se confert familia, ex qua nata est persona, quae in matrimonium accipitur.'

455 On blending of these originally Germanic elements with Christian traditions, see Schmidt-Wiegand, 'Hochzeit, Vertragsehe und Ehevertrag in Mitteleuropa', pp. 264–73, *passim*.

456 Sarti, Raffaella, *Europe at Home. Family and Material Culture 1500–1800*, trans. by Allan Cameron (London and New Haven: Yale University Press, 2002), p. 63.

but was in effect a 'circulation and exchange of goods that also had a symbolic function.'[457] Since Wolff's definition of marriage removes the family from the equation, these elements count as mere rituals in his analysis and not essential to the process.[458] As a consequence, Wolff can push for frugality – since size of gifts, *arrha* or dowry merely count as ritual offerings and bear no more than symbolic value, it would be 'absurd' to incur great expenses or take on debts in order to serve this custom.[459] The same goes for the wedding feast, which should only be as sumptuous as the hosts can afford.[460] The previously obligatory exchanges demanded by a Germanic understanding of marriage as the union between families and ritualised gift exchanges as a confirmation of bond and status between the families are formally downgraded by Wolff vis-à-vis the vision of marriage as the Christian, consensus-based union between the betrothed as individuals – and a nuclear household as part of a community.

The temporality of tradition is highlighted further with Wolff's definition of what actually defines a valid marriage. Historically, the validity of a marriage had not always been subject to an official ceremony. The Council of Trent sought to clarify legal uncertainties by codifying validation procedures: at least for Catholics, the presence of two witnesses was now required, additionally to the local priest, to confirm that bride and groom were, in fact, free to marry. The Lutherans also formalised procedures but conferred the mandate to a state official as representative of the ruler as the head of church.[461] This regulation naturally meant that a wedding was not a private affair anymore between couple, family and witnesses, but required the presence of an official or, in fact, a celebration outside the home. Furthermore, this legislative change brought some clarity into the considerations of what actually constituted a valid marriage: the officially witnessed consensus between just bride and groom before all else.[462] Wolff writes this procedure into his natural law, more specifically, the Protestant ruling that required a state official, not a priest, to represent the divine sanction of the marriage bond. This does not mean that Wolff considered marriage a secular affair. In fact, he expresses the hope that weddings would continue to be celebrated in full recognition of their divine meaning, and not be downgraded to a mere convention, excising God as the stakeholder in the union of husband of wife.[463] Yet while Wolff fearfully anticipates the demotion of what he considers a vital tradition,

---

457 Ibid., p. 68.

458 Wolff, *Oeconomica*, § 58, p. 87.

459 Ibid., § 59, p. 88–89; § 57, p. 86; § 59, p. 88.

460 Ibid., § 68., p. 105.

461 Eisenbach, Franziskus, 'Zeichen der Liebe und Treue Gottes. Die christliche Ehe aus katholischer Sicht', in *Die Braut*, pp. 144–149 (144).

462 Kubach-Ritter, Ursula, 'Rituale zur Offenkundigung der Ehe', in *Die Braut*, pp. 294–98 (295).

463 Wolff, *Oeconomica*, § 67 *nota*, pp. 104–105: 'Optandum omnino foret, ut haec solennitas non in nudam consuetudinem abiret, sed ut eadem uterentur omnes ad dignitatem matrimonii agnoscendam.'

the *Oeconomica* itself pays witness to the demotion of customary elements from necessary ritual to mere convention.[464] The topic of wedding formalities has Wolff preserving a snapshot of traditions in transformation – albeit with the intention to record the universal, not fossilise the ephemeral.

3.4.3 Natural law beyond the home turf

Wolff is not the only philosopher beholden to his environment – natural law in its historical evolution has a proven track record of cultural incarceration. To some degree this is the direct consequence of the task it had set in early days already: the Spanish Scholastics, for example, did not mean to set out a new order of things – they sought to explain and rationalise their present-day custom through the lens of natural law, and in particular, 'to demonstrate the rational principles underlying the Christian message'.[465] In this respect, too, Wolff is no different – except he is not calling it the 'Christian message' but the 'rational world order'.

Still, there are some instances where Wolff challenges the mainstream worldview at his time with the help of natural law, getting close to upending the world order he set out to confirm.

One area where Wolff proves surprisingly emancipated is that of gender equality. In small but unmistakeable ways, Wolff's *Oeconomica* takes a step away from the conventional norms presented in typical *Hausväterliteratur*. The work as a whole is addressed not to the male breadwinner but to all members of the household, women included; in fact, the term *paterfamilias* is entirely absent and the majority of the section about spousal duties, *De officiis conjugum*, is phrased in a gender-neutral way: addressing not husband and wife but the spouses as *conjuges*, in general. The terminological break leads the *Oeconomica* astray from traditional *Hausväterliteratur* in topical respects, too. Florinus, Coler and Menius all separate out the wife's obligations from those of the husband, in both practical and emotional terms. Granted, Wolff divides up labour in general into different categories ascribed to husband and wife, but he describes them in abstract, deontological terms; no concrete tasks are ever specified and assigned.[466] When it comes to moral conduct, moreover, he argues that both spouses should pay the same regard towards each other – at least for the first part of the section, *De officiis conjugum*. The egalitarian wording changes as of

464 Ibid., § 54 *nota*, pp. 81–82.

465 Pagden, 'The Preservation of Order', p. 156.

466 The husband can earn money through his labour or from his capital; the wife can contribute to the household through handiwork (*operae artificiales*) or administrative support (*operae ministeriales)*, so to speak, whilst being responsible to preserve frugality. As such, the husband is the main breadwinner and the wife is obliged to contribute to his work and life with her labour where she can. See Wolff, *Oeconomica*, § 131, p. 202.

§ 116, where Wolff starts using the words *maritus* and *uxor*. So far, husband and wife, as per natural law, had been granted the same rights and powers within wedlock: the *imperium conjugale*. § 120 brings theory into step again with Wolff's patriarchal reality, with the introduction of the *imperium maritale*: the dominion of husband over wife. The confirmation of female subordination puts the *Oeconomica* back in line with the conventions pushed by his predecessors. This recalibration, however, starts with a big if. *If* a husband, tacitly or by convention, possesses the *imperium maritale* over his wife, she is obliged to be obedient and subordinate to him.[467] The subordination of a wife to her husband is thus not a natural fact, but depends on the cultural circumstances, in Wolff's opinion. Yet even though conditional, the introduction of the *imperium maritale* allows Wolff to cover the traditional cant about spouses, almost identical with the norms endorsed by Florinus, Menius and Coler. Still, questioning the fact that rather than how women were subordinate to their husbands is a clear departure from the literary tradition.[468]

Previous examples of household literature underwrite the subordination of the wife under the husband with biological or religious arguments. For example, the physical and intellectual weakness and wickedness of women is cited as a justification for male leadership within the household in Alberti, Florinus and Coler.[469] The Protestant perspective in Menius derives the subordination of women from the Bible, as a consequence of Eve's role in the fall from grace.[470] To Wolff, natural law discounts the physical inferiority as an argument *for* authority; and a lengthy historical account of Maria Cunitia (1610–1660) and her conversion of Kepler's Rudolphine tables serves as evidence why women can have the same intellectual capacity as men (if educated accordingly).[471] Given the logical rejection of the physical and the historical refutation of intellectual weakness, therefore, Wolff concludes that in theory men and women are naturally equal. Accordingly, natural law attributes the *imperium conjugale* in matrimony to both spouses alike, even though in reality there is no culture known to Wolff where such an equality is actually put into practice.[472] He explains this discrepancy between reason and reality as a cultural trope rather than universal norm. In the case of Christianity, he argues, original sin provides the explanation for why the wife has lost her right to the *imperium conjugale*; the tale of Eve's vindictive behaviour is

467 Ibid., § 120, p. 177; § 123, p. 185.

468 Erasmus, who acknowledged the intellectual capacities of learned women he met, is an exception to the rule. See Rummel, Erika, 'Desiderius Erasmus', *The Stanford Encyclopedia of Philosophy*, ed. by Edward N. Zalta <https://plato.stanford.edu/archives/win2017/entries/erasmus/> [accessed 28 July 2019]

469 Alberti, *Über das Hauswesen*, p. 133.

470 Gause and Scholz, Ehe und Familie im Geist des Luthertums, p. 85.

471 Wolff, *Oeconomica*, § 120, pp. 179–182.

472 Ibid., § *nota*, p. 182: 'Quamvis vero nulla ratio naturalis detur, cur uxor marito subjecta esse debeat, mores tamen omnium, quantum constat, gentium uxorem potestati mariti subjiciunt...'.

used to justify the traditional inequality in marriage.[473] By implication, Wolff declares that an argument from the Gospel underwrites a cultural, man-made trope that departs from the logic of natural law. As said before, he does not invalidate the Bible overall; in fact, in some instances he uses it as an authoritative source. Moreover, his natural law does not prohibit the submission of a wife to her husband even if it does not logically support it. But by interpreting marriage as a naturally equal partnership which custom has rendered unequal and explaining this development with the Christian religion he only skirts challenging the ecclesiastic authority by not touching upon this issue any further.

Leaving aside the inconsistencies, Wolff brings in a surprisingly modern perspective by doing away with the myth of the inferior gender. Still, the discussion of gender equality never upends the existing cultural practices and that is telling of the general thrust of Wolff's discourse: the mere existence of traditional conventions serves as a self-stabilizer because they present the reality he seeks to rationalize. Still, Wolff robs these traditional norms of their logical foundation whilst struggling to supply another. He can neither give a rational explanation for why men should rule over women nor can he offer an alternative vision for an egalitarian marriage, even though he discredits the assumption of *praestantia sexus*, the superiority of the male sex.

Elsewhere, as a way out of the culture trap, Wolff uses cross-cultural comparisons. Some examples in the *Oeconomica* go beyond his own socio-political environment to corroborate principles of natural law – typically with references to China. This provides an interesting contrast to traditional tendencies in natural law: on occasion, natural law scholars had used different cultures to demarcate natural from unnatural, typically declaring their own society as the 'naturally correct' one.[474] Wolff attempts the same affirmation of his own discourse – yet not by demarcation but by association: he employs examples of Chinese culture to prove what is right and good in the European context. Just like he uses natural philosophy to scientifically inform the idea of a rational world order, China's laws and practices, in Wolff's eyes perfectly representative of an order in tune with natural law, are used to support his arguments – sometimes constructively, sometimes less so.[475] The two main works of reference on China in the *Oeconomica* are Noël's translation of Confucius of 1687 and the *Legatio Batavica* by Johan Nieuhof (1618–1672), published in Dutch in 1665 and translated to Latin in 1668. Confucius lends himself more easily as a source to Wolff's arguments, perhaps for the fact that the translation by Jesuits as were Noël and Couplet was already adjusted to the normative expectations of a Western, Christian reader.[476] In con-

473 Ibid., § 120, p. 179.

474 Pagden, 'The Preservation of Order', p. 163.

475 See also Michael Albrecht's introduction to the *Oratio*, p. LXXXVIII; Albrecht, however, does not discuss the curious disparity between Confucianism and China's social reality and the resulting split between the Jesuit's and the Dutch traders' accounts.

476 Kanamori, 'Christian Wolff's Speech on Confucianism', p. 301.

trast, the *Legatio Batavica*, a travel report by Nieuhof, describes the geography, history and customs of China from the point of view of an outsider. Whilst the sententious works of Confucius lend themselves well to Wolff's moral viewpoint, the travel reports are written with a view to the difference rather than similarity to European culture and do not readily provide fodder for a natural law discourse. This seems to have passed unnoticed by Wolff. Yet it becomes glaringly obvious where he argues for the irrelevance of beauty, riches and nobility in the choice of a potential marriage-partner, vis-à-vis the relevance of fertility, virtue and legal eligibility.[477] In that context, Wolff employs Chinese culture as an affirmative example on two occasions. Firstly, when trying to argue against the importance of status, he cites the Chinese emperor's habit of choosing the most beautiful rather than noblest girl in the country, and be her father of humble origin.[478] The Chinese custom is used to question the universal validity of custom or legislation barring intermarriage between different social strata. This anecdote supports Wolff's idea of the irrelevance of family background. But a choice made purely on account of beauty hardly implies a selection process based on moral virtue and economic acumen. Whilst serving as an argument *against* status, the argument corrodes Wolff's bid to choose virtue before beauty. Elsewhere, Wolff cites the fact that the size of a dowry is not an eligibility factor in China as the groom, quite literally, purchases the bride from the parents and can sell her off at will.[479] This excerpt might help to dismiss wealth as a relevant factor for the choice of a wife but stands in jarring contrast to Wolff's Christian ideal of marriage, and the reach of *patria potestas* besides. His concession here that the power of a husband over his wife can be more drastic in foreign lands, again, does not fit with his later comment echoing Aristotle who pronounced the undue subordination of women to the point of slavery the sign of a barbaric country.[480] The sale and resale of women would objectively qualify for that judgment; and Wolff's Chinese evidence against a wealthy match thus dissolves into a non-sequitur.

The *Legatio Batavica* contains more hints that the Chinese fashion on the ground might not necessarily be a model proponent of Wolff's natural law. The practice amongst poorer parts of the population to breed children for sale, for example, if anything, is at odds with Wolff's rejection of the Roman law allowing parents to sell their children into servitude.[481] Successful or not, Wolff is not using these examples to steer natural law *away* from what is conventional in his own society – rather, he is using these examples to affirm norms accepted but ignored. In a way, therefore, Wolff's cultural relativism joins hands with a reactionary stance. This impression is confirmed

477 Wolff, *Oeconomica*, § 9, p. 11, and § 44, p. 63.
478 Ibid., § 44, p. 64.
479 Ibid., § 46, p. 68.
480 Ibid., § 46, p. 68; § 120, p. 182.
481 Ibid., § 204, pp. 341–342 and the respective passage in Johannes Nieuhof, *Legatio Batavica ad Magnum Tartariae Chamum Sungteium* (Amsterdam: Jacob Meursius, 1668), p. 44.

by Wolff's treatment of a culture alien to him but in full view in Prussia: the Jewish. Samples of Jewish customs are not used for the sake of cross-cultural comparisons in the *Oeconomica* but as negative examples demonstrating the breach of natural law. One such case is the supposed Jewish fashion to divorce a wife solely for her looks or her cooking.[482] Judging from the *Legatio Batavica*, Chinese wives would not fare much better; yet far as Wolff's reason-based culture critique is concerned, some cultures are more equal than others in the eye of his natural law.

Rather than invalidating Wolff's work as a whole, such inconsistencies help to illustrate the fundamental problem of constructing an objective, universally valid moral yardstick decoupled from canonical moral literature or tacit assumptions. One would be hard-pressed to blame Wolff for a bias one way or another and a modern critique of his hard-coded prejudices is just as likely to arise from cultural predispositions. Such an analysis does show, however, that his scientific method is not a warrant for universality, partly for its incapacity to probe a critical comparison and partly also for its permissive epistemology: Wolff's natural law follows a rationalist format; however, it subsumes content not exclusively rational in origin but also accepted wisdoms and intuitions, combining judgment and prejudice alike. The ideological thrust of his natural law largely confirms existing norms but is made up of composite matter: Christian trappings, sometimes of distinctly Protestant fashion, sometimes siding with Catholic sources; a *carte blanche* to Chinese and a red card to Jewish culture and every once in a while an actual break with the mould of his own time and day.

3.5 Summary

Christian Wolff's methodological overhaul of the *Oeconomica* shows the transposition of many a familiar trope from wisdom literature into the rarefied sphere of reason. In a sense, Wolff's household morality is not a radical departure from common opinions of his own time. Yet his way of rephrasing known arguments into formal syllogisms newly affirm accepted wisdoms through seemingly fool-proof logic. The weight of legitimacy is shifted from authority and experience to the self-evidence of scientific discourse. This is not only a methodological departure from the lay wisdom literature but also the scholarly trend of *Oeconomica*. Rather than providing a scholarly treatment of canonical sources – like Keckermann, Avenarius and the Herborn encyclopedists did – Wolff incorporates arguments from a range of authors and disciplines into one demonstrative discourse: debates and topics from Aquinas to Florinus, from biology to theology, all stripped of reference and put on a logical footing. The *Oeconomica* as formerly purely practice- and experience-based discipline now presents a purely generalised science, abstracted from cultural or practical context.

482 Wolff, *Oeconomica*, § 65 *nota*, p. 100.

The majority of the arguments is not advising the reader on how to do something, as an advice book typically would – it affirms a roster of duties, i.e. that something is to be done. Indeed, the *Oeconomica* and its frequent lamentations about *nostro saeculo*, the vapid ways of the crowd and the thankless task of the philosopher to drive education still mark the work out as a corrective enterprise. Topically, Wolff reworks mostly accepted wisdoms; methodologically, he is breaking new ground.

The inherent idea of an *Oeconomica* in scientific format is to lift household morality from the earthbound realm of the *mundus sensibilis*, from a mode of argument based on experience and authority, into the self-supporting realm of the *mundus rationalis*. Wolff tries to support a brand of morality in the abstract, through logic and format, that has otherwise been pushed by traditional discourse supported by religious overtones. But where the source of his arguments still is the world around him, logical abstraction stumbles over the inevitable limitation Wolff suffers through his own cultural trappings. In that sense, he proves a revolutionary in method only – in terms of content, he remains a reactionary. In fact, the universalist mandate of his system faces an interesting challenge when sizing up custom and culture. Man-made norms, Wolff argues, are subject to flux; they should conform to the immutable natural order but they cannot change it.[483] Yet in the end Wolff's attempt to codify his cultural commonplaces into natural law exactly illustrates how the immutable order of Wolff's *mundus rationalis* is shaped by the flux of his own socio-political reality where trying to rationally affirm the status quo.

As particularly the comparison to Florinus' work shows, Wolff's *Oeconomica* rebuilds arguments previously abutted by the Christian tradition on the basis of natural law. As that, the actual precepts hardly differ – but the source of legitimacy does. Although applied to the context of the domestic morality, these different modes of legitimacy correspond well with Max Weber's typology of political authority. Weber differentiated authority based on traditional grounds, 'resting on an established belief in the sanctity of immemorial traditions' from that based on rational grounds, 'resting on a belief in the legality of enacted rules', and charismatic grounds, 'resting on devotion to the exceptional sanctity, heroism or exemplary character of an individual person'.[484] He does not describe the transition between these states. Yet these concepts are a helpful lens to understand the paradigm shift that Wolff achieves on a private level, shifting the legitimacy of a discourse from traditional to rational foundations without changing the substance of the instruction – for in fact, the majority of the rules expounded indeed perfectly agree with traditional wisdoms and traditional Christian notions. On occasion, Wolff makes a foray beyond, such as in the case

---

483 Ibid., § 17 *nota*, p. 25: 'Leges positivae et consuetudo hominum res immutare nequeunt, quae formam a lege naturae recipiunt.'

484 Weber, Max, *Economy and Society*, Vol 1, ed. by Guenther Roth and Claus Wittich (Totowa, N.J.: Bedminster Press, 1968), p. 215.

of his proto-feminist leanings. Elsewhere, he uses his discourse to clarify legally or morally confusing situations, such as courting rituals, mourning and wedding rites. All in all, however, he does not push over an existing order with a new rational paradigm – he is re-digging trenches that have fallen into disrepair. One might ask why Wolff feels the need to rewrite traditional rules in a different format if the basic content has not changed. The clue may be in the sentiment throughout – the *Oeconomica* is glistening with moral disapproval, replete with laments about his depraved times, *nostro saeculo*, where morality has slackened beyond belief. The sentiment is familiar from post-Reformation political treatises that almost exclusively ascribe the dilapidation of society to the moral decay of its members.[485] In that sense, Wolff continues the same trudge with new, rational weapons.

Lastly, whether the categorisation of the *Oeconomica* with *Hausväterliteratur* is a fruitful one from a perspective of genre is a question of some ambiguity. There is a considerable overlap in concern and even direct replication of traditional content. Some features unique to Florinus are recycled in Wolff: the idea of a well thought-through marriage, the concerns about matrimonial harmony and the measures prescribed to preserve it. But the content of Wolff's *Oeconomica* is equally beholden to the Scholastics, contemporary issues, customs and also his own, idiosyncratic inventions. One definitive break with the tradition of *Hausväterliteratur*, however, is the systematic integration. Florinus, Coler and Menius provided individual books responding to a sense of practical utility – Wolff's *Oeconomica* only exists as part of a system. Given its conspicuous absence from the early, German cycle and Thümmig's *Institutiones*, it was included as an afterthought but integrated with Wolff's systematic predicaments still. This suggests that the idea for this work did not arise from the household as literary material – it came as a systematic reflection. Wolff's understanding of utility is not concerned with realities on the ground but aims for a perfection of the soul in the name of the state. As such, his focus is far removed from the practical realities that provided the core content of *Hausväterliteratur*. Still, Wolff's integration of the *Oeconomica* into his system preserved an aspect of *Hausväterliteratur* that was on the wane on the academic scene at Wolff's time: the moral focus of wisdom literature as a genre. Wolff not only reinstates this focus – he transliterates it into a grander context that puts the mundane realities of the household into a direct relationship with the next level of organisation: the state. The immediate consequence of Wolff's overhaul is the rationalisation of accepted custom; below the surface, moreover, the *Oeconomica* now calls upon personal responsibility not only in the name of individual welfare and piety, but now also for the sake of the body politic.

485 Simon, Thomas, 'Der Erziehungsgedanke in den frühneuzeitlichen Polizeiordnungen', in *Das erziehende Gesetz*, ed. by Eva Schumann (Berlin; Boston: De Gruyter, 2013), pp. 59–74, p. 61.

4 *Oeconomica*, natural law and social welfare in the absolutist state

4.1 Introduction

This chapter discusses the interlocking morality of Wolff's *Oeconomica* and his social welfare model. The previous chapter already specified that the ontological aim of the family is reoriented towards the state, from a private focus to a public purpose. A joint reading with Wolff's public policy further illustrates that although common good and individual happiness are reciprocal principles, the latter starts with the first – and citizens' welfare is defined by its utility to the state.

Unlike modern welfare states, Wolff's social policies are not backed by a legal framework intent on shoring up basic citizen rights; they are presented as an appeal to the moral conscience of the ruler and defended by their utilitarian appeal to the state. This is apparent when putting his philosophy back into the context of eighteenth-century Kingdom of Prussia which saw a centralisation of existing public welfare institutions – such as poor relief and education – and the establishment of state-governed measures promoting public health. Social welfare became integral to the cameralist notion of good government and spelled not only public provision but also behavioural control. The *Oeconomica* and Wolff's political theory are two complementary forces in that regard: the former strives to educate, the latter aims to regulate.

Collectively organised welfare institutions have their origin long before industrialisation and its discontents. In the European context, poor relief, education and hospitals had been the domain of religious orders throughout the Middle Ages. For the Catholic Church as an organising fulcrum of charity, beneficence was an imperative purpose that allowed benefactors to serve Christian values, and the Church to perform its duty to the poor.[486] The Reformation, with Luther's efforts, wrested these institutions from the Catholic domain and placed them into secular, municipal hands, at least in Protestant lands. The town of Leisnig, for example, transformed its poor relief with the help of Luther's consultation; it became a model for other municipal governments attempting the same.[487] Alongside ideological motives, practical considerations came into play. Social welfare combined with municipal interest meant not merely provision for individuals in need but preserving the health and wealth of the

---

486 Friess, Peer, and Thomas Max Safley, 'Poor Relief and Health Care Provision in South-German Catholic Cities during the Sixteenth Century', in *The Reformation of Charity: The Secular and the Religious in Early Modern Poor Relief*, ed. by Thomas Max Safley (Boston: Brill, 2003), pp. 76–91 (76).
487 Torvend, Samuel, 'Charity and Social Ethics', *The Oxford Encyclopedia of Martin Luther*, ed. by Derek R. Nelson and Paul R. Hinlicky (Oxford: Oxford University Press, 2017), p. 246.

https://doi.org/10.1515/9783110714098-004

community overall – and voluntary poverty lost the sheen of spiritual enhancement where towns sought to combat wilful mendicants with anti-begging laws.[488]

The Prussian rulers of the seventeenth and eighteenth century, like other territorial princes, sought to concentrate welfare measures in state hands. The institutionalisation of public welfare had some obvious advantages for their efforts to build a strong state, army and economy to buttress either. Central here is the term of *Gute Polizey*, good governance, developed in the cameralistic literature. A 'police state' or state with 'good police' in the eighteenth century sense was not a term of indictment. Akin to 'policy' more than 'policing' it 'did not imply force employed by the state to impose law and order but a more general system tasked with regulating a range of aspects of social life for the sake of stability and prosperity': amongst them economic activity, public health, private vice and social welfare.[489]

In early modern times the three key issues of poverty, disease and lack of education remain focal points of social welfare; and to some degree, the institutional responses tend to be similar to the pre-existing models of charity. There are, however, discernible changes as to who is in charge – and why. In that sense, Wolff's own welfare model presents a specific slice in welfare state history, and specific to his Prussian locale, too. Like the rest of Wolff's philosophy, his social policies are moulded from reality and ideology alike. In this case specifically, Wolff takes the moral narrative of Christian absolutism, provides it with a rationalist foundation in natural law and a moral-utilitarian backing from political discourse. In analogy to *Oeconomica* and *Jus naturae VII*, we would have expected Wolff's *Politica* to provide a thorough exploration of deontological and utilitarian motives for these policies. In the absence of this work, traces of either are identifiable in his natural law.

The reform efforts of the Prussian kings Frederick and Frederick William I from the end of the seventeenth century to the middle of the eighteenth are well-documented in Reinhold Dorwart's study of the Prussian welfare state.[490] The similarity between the institutions documented there and postulated by Wolff suggests that the political reality around him provided a good foil for a statist welfare in theory. Halle in particular, pre- and post-exile Wolff's primary city of residence, witnessed pioneering developments in the area of social welfare programmes, driven, ironically enough, by Wolff's local adversaries: the Pietists.

Pietism, a Lutheran rebel offspring, sought to reform society through religious experience and community activism, and Halle was home to a particularly stark

488 Witte, John Jr., 'Martin Luther's Influence on Legal Reforms and Civil Law', *Oxford Research Encyclopedia of Religion*, 2017 <http://oxfordre.com/religion/view/10.1093/acrefore/9780199340378.001.0001/acrefore-9780199340378–e-503.> [accessed 6 April 2019]

489 Nokkala, Ere, From Natural Law to Political Economy: J.H.G. von Justi on State, Commerce and International Order (Münster: LIT Verlag, 2019), p. 85.

490 Dorwart, Reinhold August, *The Prussian Welfare State before 1740* (Cambridge, MA: Harvard University Press, 1971).

champion of this ideology, August Hermann Francke (1663–1727). 'For the reborn Christian, a healthy body, in conjunction with sound vocational training and adequate financial resources, permitted the person to be more useful to God and his or her neighbor', as the Pietist conception would have it.[491] Although embedded in a deeply spiritual dimension, their promotion of health, wealth and education amongst the lower classes provided a model that suited the purpose of Prussian state-building project well. The nascent bureaucracy not only replicated and built on Francke's institutional model but readily utilised the supporting ideology. Thus, Frederick William I, the Calvinist ruler of Prussia made good on the confessional gap to the chiefly Lutheran populace whilst instilling them with a rigorous work ethic and obedience through methods and creed of the Pietists.

After his exile, Wolff did not return to Halle in Frederick William's lifetime, ignoring the king's official pardon. Only King Frederick II's ascent to power saw Wolff resume his professorship in 1740 – and finish his Latin cycle.[492] By that time, the pillars of public welfare had been well entrenched in the Prussian state. The fact that Wolff promotes welfare institutions is less progressive than conservative, seeing that they already existed; yet his practical philosophy supplies these existing institutions with a new, theology-free justification – and complements the top-down state structure of his welfare state with a bottom-up primer to civic virtue in form of the *Oeconomica* in the place of religion to guide household morality. The following analysis is an attempt to put Wolff's welfare state back into this historical context so as to decode the ideology behind its institutional structure. The first part will examine legitimacy and justification for state-led social welfare within Wolff's natural law system. This will give an idea of Wolff's universalised account of reciprocal rights and responsibilities between household and state. The three following parts will consider the central elements of Wolff's welfare: education, Wolff's pedagogical approach and his vision for scientific societies; policies for prosperity, namely, the regulation of livelihood and poor relief; and public health, including the regulation of practitioners and institutional responses to collective health problems.

---

491 Gawthrop, Richard L., *Pietism and the Making of Eighteenth-Century Prussia* (Cambridge: Cambridge University Press, 1993), p. 170.

492 Gagliardo, John G., *Germany under the Old Regime, 1600–1790* (London and New York: Longman, 1991), p. 223.

4.2 The theoretical foundation of social welfare in Wolff's natural law

4.2.1 The contract as a legitimising fiction

Wolff's natural law maps out a direct relationship between government and governed through a contractual interpretation of social and political frameworks. The contract serves as a fiction to rationalise and legitimise a specific model of private and public relations, and to derive expected duties from the purpose of the political community: the *bonum commune*, the common good. As described in the previous chapter, the *Oeconomica* as the practical expression of his natural law does not really present a departure from customary ideas of morality but mostly re-casts traditional norms in systematic terms, informed by science and Wolff's own ideas. The same could be said for the state whereby Wolff chiefly re-formulates existing practices in a pseudo-legal format, occasionally enriched with new ideas.

The question naturally beckons why one would need a fictive pact to describe an existing and arguably unchallenged norm. The syllogistic argument Wolff provides in support is arguably weak: he claims that there is no sufficient reason forcing us *not* to define a community through a contract or quasi-contract.[493] Arguably, there is no sufficient reason why Wolff should do so, either. In fact, the *Deutsche Politik* delivers a very similar idea of the state without resorting to a contractual fiction. It features the same three household communities, the *societates simplices* familiar from the *Oeconomica*, but with a lot less formality and although preceded by a general account of 'societies in general', the description of the household is devoid of the legal sheen in the Latin cycle. Yet Wolff, cognizant of this open question, stresses the importance of this model because we officially bind ourselves to do as we naturally ought.[494] In practice, it provides a framework allowing him to specify duties as part of these contracts that he considers generally overlooked in reality: not merely regulations but a proactive show of virtue, and not just with the family but the body politic in mind. Revisiting the contractual interpretation of the household community in the Latin cycle with this predicament in mind helps to understand how the contractual model allows Wolff to reorient the family's purpose: with God and the state now as stakeholders in these *societates*, their purpose experiences a shift from an inward-facing perspective in Wolff's earlier works to a state-oriented motive in the Latin cycle. The purpose of marriage, for example, is and remains procreation; but where the *Deutsche Politik* simply quotes the joy that are children and continuity of the family as the end,

493 Wolff, *Jus naturae methodo scientifica pertractatum. Pars septima*, § 1 nota, pp. 1–2: '...nulla tamen ratio sufficiens est, quae societatem per pactum, vel quasi pactum non definire nos cogat.'

494 Ibid., § 634, p. 438: '...per pacta enim nos etiam obligare possumus ad ea, quae jam naturaliter debentur.'

the *Oeconomica* and *Jus naturae VII* explicitly interpret marriage and procreation as a duty towards God and the state.[495] The socio-political relationships in Wolff's discourse sometimes defy his conceptual repackaging, both on domestic and state level. This is clear from the disparity between the general concept of a *societas* and its invocation in social theory. A *societas*, in Wolff's definition, is a pact or quasi-pact between a number of parties with the intention to achieve some common end with combined powers.[496] The *socii*, or partners, are obliged to do what contributes to achieving the common goal.[497] Since the obligation arising from these pacts is perfect, the *socii* have the right to compel each other to fulfil their obligations.[498] These obligations, crucially, are determined by the goal of the *societas*. The rights, true to Wolffian definition, arise from the obligations: a *societas* exists through a moral bond that constitutes obligations for either party, alongside rights arising therefrom.[499] The three *societates simplices* in the *Oeconomica* are understood to be social contracts but they prove a challenge to a clean categorisation. The purposes of parental and spousal relationship, for example, overlap. The relationship between master and servant is not described by its purpose at all but by its origin in the concepts of property (*dominium*) and the power resulting from it (*imperium*).[500]

The most problematic part remains the assumption of mutual consent as the basis for these natural bonds. The marital and the professional relationship are arguably entered on the basis of an officially sanctioned consensus between the contracting partners. The *societas paterna*, however, is not a real but merely an implicit natural pact based on the presumed agreement of an infant, a human not yet capable of entering a contract; it is a quasi-pact, therefore.[501] It is evidently stipulated by its assumed universality and the sanction of God as the authority behind this universal order rather than the active consent of the contracting partners. Moreover, the right of the *socii* to compel each other to perform their duties is not always actionable in practice, again, particularly so when it comes to the *societas paterna*. Since in Wolff's understanding, duties are prior to rights, the children's right to care is not universal but contingent upon the parents' commitment to their duties. The *societas paterna*

495 Wolff, Vernünfftige Gedancken von dem gesellschaftlichen Leben der Menschen, §§ 16–17, pp. 10–11; id., Wolff, Oeconomica, § 74, p. 114; id., Jus naturae methodo scientifica pertractatum. Pars septima, § 270, p. 187.

496 Ibid., § 1. p. 1: 'Societas in genere est pactum, vel quasi pactum de fine quodam conjunctis viribus consequendo.'

497 Ibid., § 7, pp. 3–4.

498 Ibid., § 9, p. 6.

499 Ibid., § 10, p. 6.

500 Ibid., §§ 1086–7, pp. 789–791.

501 Ibid., § 634, p. 437: 'Quamobrem cum conventio ficta, in qua consensus alterius partis tantummodo praesumitur, sit quasi contractus, aut quasi pactum ...; Societas paterna, quae inter parentes & liberos inita intelligitur..., est quasi pactum.', poses an appeal to the moral rectitude of its contracting partners more than stipulating conditions that can be enforced. In that sense it is telling that the obligations inscribed within are mostly qualitative, not definitive: they stipulate mutual love, respect and happiness.[502] Clearly a moral, not a legal concept this marks a clear contrast to the *patria potestas*.

The contractual interpretation of an absolutist state is subject to similar struggles. The social contract of a *civitas*, a state, draws its legitimisation from a piece of imagined history. Wolff describes the origin of the state as a coming-together of families, as a sort of joint decision in form of a pact.[503] Just as with the paternal quasi-pact though, the contract is an abstract fiction and not an operational principle, albeit with political ramifications: it is used to justify obligations – and power imbalances – between ruler and ruled. This is most visible in Wolff's declaration that the renunciation of civil liberty is 'tacitly contained' in this imagined construct.[504] This translation of power presumably comes after the imagined contract between the citizens-to-be, meaning, said pact is not made between ruler and ruled. It only legitimizes whatever constitution is to come, that being an absolutist monarchy in Wolff's normal world. Perhaps this is the reason why Wolff does not cite the well-worn analogy between father-child and ruler-subjects in his Latin cycle anymore: strictly speaking, it does not translate into his societal contract.

With a view to the internal organisation of the republic, Wolff's natural law corpus serves, for most of it, as a meta-legal morality primer, not a legislative blueprint. Universal obligation and positive legislation only touch upon one another where the ruler makes it so, as demonstrated.[505] Rather than perfect laws, natural law à la Wolff presents the immaterial, idealised version of socio-political living, perhaps inspired by and complementary with legislative realities but not intent on supplying a model constitution. Moral more than constitutional, the institutions presented in Wolff's natural law are not supported by the rule of law but a moral mandate to whichever form of government will come to be. Officially, Wolff does not settle on monarchy as definitive constitution, nor absolutism as its necessary incarnation.[506] Yet his descrip-

502 See, for instance, Wolff, *Jus naturae methodo scientifica pertractatum. Pars septima*, § 711, p. 498; § 719, p. 497; § 739, p. 521; § 745, p. 525; 748, p. 528.

503 Wolff, Christian, *Jus naturae methodo scientifica pertractatum. Pars octava* (Frankfurt and Leipzig: Societas Veneta, 1766), § 4, p. 3: 'Societas inter plures domus contracta eo fine, ut conjunctim sibi parent ad vitae necessitatem, ..., civitas dicitur. Atque adeo patet, pacto hominum civitates fuisse constituendas.'

504 Ibid., § 148 *nota*, p. 48: 'Renunciatio libertatis civilis tacite inest ipsi translationi imperii pleni, absoluti atque summi in alium, vel alios, ut ideo expressa minime sit opus (§. 211. part. 7. Jur. nat.).'

505 Ibid., § 982, p. 344: 'Si superior determinat modum, quo obligationi naturali satisfieri potest, aut ab eo praecavetur, ne eidem adversa committantur; ex lege naturali, unde obligatio ista venit, civilem efficit.'

506 Wolff admits for scenarios where the power transfer from people to ruler is temporary or limited, and where 'fundamental laws', *leges fundamentales*, restrict the power of the ruler; yet this case is

tions of state functions regularly paint a picture of absolutist make: the authority in question is not an abstract state bound by a legal framework but the personage of the *rector civitatis* as the supreme locus of power and obligation.[507]

'The term 'absolutism', as Gagliardo puts it, 'derives ultimately from a principle of Roman law which asserted that the right and power to make and execute law rested solely and absolutely with the prince and that no individual, group or agency external or internal to his jurisdiction had a legal claim to interfere with or call him to account for this supreme legislative and executive entitlement.'[508] At first sight there seems to be an implicit contradiction between the sweeping rights of absolutism and the exogenous, universal authority of natural law. Yet just as Wolff recasts social relationships as pseudo-legal pacts preserving their original form, he uses the natural contract as a metaphor not to upend but to legitimise an absolutist relationship between ruler and people – and inscribe the mandate for the people's welfare within: not as a universal right of its citizens but a moral mandate to the ruler.

In this body politic, the base unit is not the individual but the family. The household provides an intermediate structure between individual and state but eclipses the political importance of socioeconomic fabrics otherwise ubiquitous: towns, villages and corporations of economic nature. Although the village is mentioned as a conglomerate of families, municipal levels of organisation are absent from Wolff's natural law. What seems like a formality in theory evidently bears witness to a drastic centralisation drive whereby princely ordinances started superseding the old laws issued by cities and rural places.[509] This development was manifest in almost all of Europe whereby the territorial monarchs sought to avail themselves of key monopolies of public administration, such as the power over taxation and defence.[510] In Prussia in particular, Frederick William I's reign saw a significant effort to weigh in on municipal matters and thereby change the relationship between citizens and state – an indirect consequence of war and tax collection efforts. A new canton system was formed to enable sweeping military recruitment whilst in 1722–23, the Finance Directory and War Commissariat were merged into one administrative body, the General Directory; the effect was a consolidation of power over the towns in the royal bureaucracy which not only ruled over the cities immediately subject to the king but also interfered more

---

presented with an 'if', not as the norm. See Wolff, *Jus naturae methodo scientifica pertractatum. Pars octava*, §§ 74–77, pp. 23–4.

507 The introduction commends the guidance of natural law to the 'good prince', see Wolff, *Just naturae methodo scientifica pertractatum. Pars octava*, p. iii. Throughout the book, Wolff charges the personage of the *rector civitatis* or the *superior* with all responsibilities. See, for instance, ibid., §§ 720–721, p. 250; §§ 715–718, pp. 248–249; §§ 726–728, p. 253.

508 Gagliardo, Germany under the Old Regime, p. 94.

509 Gawthrop, Pietism and the Making of Eighteenth-Century Prussia, p. 19–20.

510 Vesting, Thomas, 'Absolutismus und materiale Rationalisierung: Zur Entstehung des preußischen Patrimonialstaates', *Archiv des öffentlichen Rechts*, 119.3 (1994), 369–99 (369–70, 374).

and more with local politics previously considered the domain of the nobility.[511] This spelled a tighter state control of financial matters but also business and immigration, under the auspices of state-employed bureaucrats. As Karin Friedrich describes it, '[s]oon no new houses could be built, no new burghers admitted, no urban properties leased, no taxes passed or abolished, no legal procedures initiated, and no salaries increased without the consent of the royal tax collector (*Steuerrat*).'[512] Despite these efforts, corporate structures still played a significant role as administrative bodies on a regional or local level in Prussia and the efficiency of the state bureaucracy was not as immaculate as classically perceived. Thus, the suffusion of social structures with state regulation can have been nowhere complete or comprehensive.[513] Wolff's natural order building states straight from houses still mirrors this centralisation effort – and contrary to what Backhaus claims, designs a model state less intent on subsidiarity than its eclipse.

Wolff's political theory did not meet universal acclaim. Emer de Vattel, in his *animadversiones*, or objections, appended to the eighth tome of Wolff's natural law, critically evaluates his contractual theory of the state. He calls attention to the fact that Wolff's definition of a citizen is not coherent with this myth of a state as the consociation of houses or families. In reality, so Vattel, it would be individuals who band together to a state, for the sake of practical utility.[514] He further notes that in Wolff's law, the ruler possesses the *imperium plenum, absolutum, summum* either by right of possession or by inheritance.[515] Yet the goal of a body politic is not the renunciation of freedom but the achievement of a common goal, so Vattel, and to confirm this end, this composite will of many needs to be expressed by vote.[516] Wolff's natural law, however, assumes the voluntary translation of power without demanding any expression of the popular will. Similar to the problems with the contractual interpretation of the parental bond, where an unequal power relationship is entered by birth, the citizens do not actually have a means to weigh in on the pact. In that context, Vattel points out that citizens are bound by a certain obligation – reminiscent of the parental relationship – of citizens vis-à-vis the state to whom they owe their existence and education; they ought not to disturb the peace of the body politic but if they don't like the laws,

511 Friedrich, Karin, 'The Development of the Prussian Town, 1720–1815', in *The Rise of Prussia: 1700–1830*, ed. by Philip G. Dwyer (Harlow: Pearson Education, 2000), pp. 129–50, p. 136.

512 Ibid., pp. 136–7.

513 Hellmuth, Eckhart, 'Der Staat des 18 Jahrhunderts. England und Preußen im Vergleich', *Aufklärung*, 9.1 (1996), 5–24 (13–14).

514 See Vattel's commentary to § 4 of the eighth volume of Wolff's natural law, in: Wolff, *Jus naturae methodo scientifica pertractatum. Pars octava*, p. xiii.

515 Ibid., § 91, p. 29.

516 Ibid., p. xvi: 'Jam vero mens hominum, ita coalescentium, non fuit, ut libertati naturali cederent; sed cum utile viderent vires conjungere, voluntatem tanquam unam componere constituerunt, ac pacti sunt, voluntatem hanc communem plurium suffragiis significari.'

they should leave.[517] Within Wolff's natural law, however, a citizen would ideally not be permitted to leave the state on their own account, only by public consensus.[518] In the absence of suffrage and free movement, a citizen born into a state can vote with neither hands nor feet. This the understanding of the state as a relationship of power and obedience, not mutual governance, is fundamental to Wolff's constitutional set up. The contract serves as a legitimising fiction more than an actualised principle, and its fulfilment is dependent on the ruler's moral fibre.[519] Similarly to the *societas paterna*, the Wolffian welfare state has to be understood within this pseudo-contractual narrative: not as universal right of the citizens but a moral obligation of the ruler.

For Vattel, Wolff might have made a logical error; from a modern point of view, however, Wolff's idea of the social contract seems like a mere apology for absolutism, granting sweeping powers to the state over the private lives of citizens – rationalising the loss of individual freedom, as Emanuel Stipperger puts it.[520] This is indubitably true. Yet differently from a liberal democracy, the final purpose of the Wolffian state is not the protection of individual liberty but communal welfare, the *bonum commune*; in that sense he is not failing to protect citizens' rights but merely codifying the status quo under the heading of this goal. Furthermore, vis-à-vis an unrestrained exercise of absolute power, Wolff provided a rational modification of the ruler's leeway to only act where it serves the common purpose; freedom of individual and families are only to be curtailed in the name of the common good, not purely by volition of the ruler.[521] Based on the idea of common welfare as the purpose of a body politic and the natural pact to bind all parties to do as they naturally ought, Wolff confirms the traditional moral barrier for monarchs backed by divine right through logical argument – at least in principle.

4.2.2 Patrimonial welfare: moral duty with an ulterior motive

As explained above, for Wolff the obligation of the ruler to promote the people's welfare is backed by the natural contract. Seckendorf's Fürsten-Stat promotes a similar if

517 Ibid., p. xvi: 'Privari sane nequeunt libertate, quam omnes homines a natura sortiuntur; sed socieati obstringuntur, cui ortum & educationem debent, & erga ipsam justa officia tenentur implere; imo etsiam si nihil societati deberent, non tamen liceret ipsis ejus ordinem & tranquillitatem & quietem turbare; si leges ejus minus placent, exeant e societate.'

518 Similarly to the subordination of the wife to the husband, the topic of restrictive emigration policy is introduced with an 'if'. See ibid., § 415, p. 143: '*Si lege sancitum, ut ne quis civium discedat, vel etiam incola; nec civis, nec incola jus discendendi habet, nec discedere licet, nisi populi consensu.*'

519 As, yet again, admonished by De Vattel: ibid., p. xix: '...ipsa vero pacta jure jurando firmata obstringere tantum conscientiam Principis validius.'

520 Stipperger, Freiheit und Institution bei Christian Wolff (1679–1754), p. 84.

521 Wolff, Jus naturae methodo scientifica pertractatum. Pars octava, § 47, p. 14; § 48, p. 15.

not identical idea: the purpose of princely, that is, Christian government is the common welfare and prosperity, in material and spiritual respects.[522] Wolff effectively transfers this obligation from a spiritual to a rationalist setting without changing the content significantly. Analogue to Florinus's cameo appearances in the Oeconomica, therefore, Wolff shifts state ideology built on the Christian creed to a natural law basis.

Like Seckendorf, Wolff does not define 'welfare' as a purely material issue. The principle postulating social welfare in natural law is the obligation to perfect others for the sake of the common good, the political analogue to the individual's duty to perfect oneself for the sake of rational self-love.[523] The state as a collective entity therefore has to cater to the means to make perfection possible, both in moral and material terms.[524] This obligation arises from the shortfall between reality and ideal, better said, the necessary imperfection of society. If everybody were perfectly virtuous, people would not only not stray from the right path, fall into poverty, stupidity and disease but remain happy and self-sufficient; moreover, perfect virtue would mean each individual would support the community as is its due. Given that this is never the case, the mandate of perfection provides legitimacy for both disciplinary action – perfecting the citizen – and welfare – filling in where the collective virtue is too lacklustre to pick up the needy. Wolff thus creates the theoretical basis for the two twin concerns of *Gute Polizey* in the eighteenth century: discipline and welfare. The promotion of these is ensured through two measures: moral education of those who are reasonable; and disciplinary action against those who are not.[525]

As noted above, the disciplinary powers of the state are still under the heading of the public good but given the idea of perfection it becomes clear how broad this range is. The state has the mandate to perfect its citizens, meaning, it has to promote virtue and curtail vice – and vice not only where it actively impacts the rest of society but as a moral defect in itself.

Here the progressive intervention vis-à-vis the natural state becomes apparent: in the natural state, nobody has the right to punish another for a vice of no consequence as the responsibility for moral bearing is left to the individual's conscience

---

522 Seckendorf, Veit Ludwig von, *Teutscher Fürsten-Stat* (Frankfurt: Thomas Mattias Götz, 1655), pp. 24–5: 'Es bestehet aber wie gedacht die Lands-Fürstliche Regierung in Erhaltung und Behauptung gemeines Nutzes und Wohlstandes in Geist- und Weltlichen Sachen.'

523 de Levie, Dagobert, *Christian Wolff und der Begriff der Menschenliebe* (Krefeld: Scherpe, 1972), pp. 45–6.

524 Wolff, Jus naturae methodo scientifica pertractatum. Pars octava, § 397, p. 137.

525 Dioni, Gianluca, 'Die innere moralische Pflicht bei Christian Thomasius', in *Das Naturrecht der Geselligkeit: Anthropologie, Recht und Politik im 18. Jahrhundert*, ed. by Frank Grunert and Vanda Fiorillo (Berlin: Duncker & Humblot, 2009), pp. 69–87, p. 83: 'Christian Wolff unterscheidet die moralische Führung durch die Vernunft, die in der *Deutschen Ethik* ...behandelt wird, von der politische Führung durch Zwang, der für die "Unvernünfftigen" notwendig ist und von dem in der *Deutschen Politik* ...die Rede ist.'

only.[526] The body politic, however, effectively possesses the right to punish acts of vice, even if they do not have a direct effect on another individual. Wolff's justification for this is the image of the state as one aggregate moral personality the integrity of which is harmed by the action of the individual, even if the act in question is a crime of no consequence.[527]

What seems like a criminalisation of vice in principle only has to be seen against the backdrop of Wolff's time: the regulation of inconsequential vice is based on a community-based legacy; ensuring the aggregate morality in a body politic also meant avoiding the wrath of God against the community, as Thomas Simon points out.[528] Rather than calling upon a religious reason, Wolff gives the practice of legislating vice a rational footing: the state is a *persona moralis*, a moral personage made up of the conduct of its individuals. And given the idea that in Wolff's rational universe, bad actions necessarily have bad consequences, the locally inconsequential vice of one person and their eventual demise would inevitably have an impact on the community losing a productive member or even having to cater for their welfare. Yet Wolff's state should not only curtail vice but also promote virtue.[529] This is an idea that he admires in the Chinese model.[530] But judging from the sparseness of legislation on that count, this promotion of good behaviour seems a principle difficult in practice. In Wolff's system, however, the promotion of virtue occurs through the popularisation of practical philosophy, steering people in the right way through education. This is where the purpose of the *Oeconomica* interlocks with the regulative scope of the state: as a didactic means to act upon the legal grey zone, that is, promote proactive virtue in the household.

The matter of population management – *Peuplierung* – is such a topic where the private sphere and the public interest intersect most dramatically. A populous land was a desirable goal for a state, and hence the promotion of marriage and childbirth makes sense on a public level but will inevitably be subject to the vagaries of private lives. As Wolff hints at in the *Oeconomica*, the legality of marriages is a matter of politics; yet whether the state should force people to marry and have children is questionable. Moral education, however, and this transpires in Wolff's *Oeconomica*, can put in a bid to convince people of the moral rectitude and enlightened self-interest of decisions otherwise left to private discretion.

Revisiting the *Oeconomica* from this angle explains some topical shifts in comparison to other works of the genre, such as the highly untypical questions of fertility and anatomical guesswork about the womb. The cameralists were discussing how to

---

526 Wolff, Jus naturae methodo scientifica pertractatum. Pars septima, § 652, p. 221.
527 Wolff, Jus naturae methodo scientifica pertractatum. Pars octava, § 653, p. 221.
528 Simon, 'Der Erziehungsgedanke in den frühneuzeitlichen Polizeiordnungen', p. 63–64.
529 Wolff, Jus naturae methodo scientifica pertractatum. Pars octava, § 456, p. 157.
530 Wolff, Oratio de Sinarum philosophia practica, p. 29.

grow the population in terms of strength and numbers through legislation, by promoting marriage, childbirth and economic sustainability through public intervention as the token centre of their discourse. Wolff seeks to tackle these issues through moral education, advising the family in the name of the state.

In that sense, private and common good do not mete out conflicting but congruent spheres of interest, and the distinction between the two is that by numbers: public good is that which refers to the community, private to the individual. And since, logically speaking, the public good is common to all where the private good merely arises to each single member, the promotion of the common welfare before private interest is a logical consequence, as he explains.[531] From the point of happiness, his *Oeconomica* demonstrates why the promotion of public interest contributes to private happiness, which, conversely, justifies the regulation of private behaviour. And where, as will be seen in the following discussion, Wolff brings a utilitarian argument for a welfare measure, this must be understood less as *raison d'etat* than the promotion of the *bonum commune* – the common welfare private felicity is lodged in by definition.

4.3 State education in philosophy and reality

4.3.1 Non scholae sed vitae – pedagogy in education

Wolff's natural law postulates that the state should cater to the education of its citizens – through universal, mandatory schooling with a curriculum steering clear of the traditional faculties. Taken together with the *Oeconomica*, this education path starts with parental care, complemented by a state school system. The idea of complementary structures already features in Seckendorf's *Fürsten-Stat*, albeit, as part of a specifically Christian *Policey*.[532] As it turns out, Prussian state policy at Wolff's time; from an institutional perspective, Wolff is less innovator than chronicler of his sociopolitical environment. In one crucial aspect, however, he probes a radical departure: he strips the idea of education from all traditional forms of erudition, removes religious teachings as a core requirement and offers instead a pedagogy built on his theory of the soul.

The ideal of education as the means to render a child socially competent is conform with the humanist ideal; catering only to bodily needs of a child and leaving pedagogical matters aside is only half the parents' fare, so Erasmus.[533] In the same spirit, the *Oeconomica* poses education as a central duty of the parents, and as that,

531 Wolff, Jus naturae methodo scientifica pertractatum. Pars octava, §§ 23–25, p. 8.

532 Seckendorf, *Teutscher Fürsten-Stat*, pp. 140–1.

533 Rener, Monika, 'Unordnung und frühes Leid', in *Das Kind in der Renaissance*, ed. by Klaus Bergdolt, Berndt Hamm, and Andreas Tönnesmann (Wiesbaden: Harrassowitz Verlag, 2008), pp. 11–26, p. 18.

both a right arising to the children and an obligation towards God and the state.[534] The preparation of children and adolescents for a real, a human life, views education in terms of moral more than practical skills and this ties back directly into Wolff's idiosyncratic definition of utility: utility is not referring to hands-on practicalities but is directed at the inculcation of intellectual and moral virtues as the basis for any learning and happiness. The focus of his universalist education, therefore, is not building skills but bending minds.

In reality, moral pedagogy not only competed with lack of care but also economic pressures and social stratification. Coler's *Oeconomia* discourages labour below the age of seven, so as to not impede a child's growth, making it implicit that children were very much expected to contribute economically from a young age onwards.[535] Indeed, the path towards a vocation was paved early on in life, specialised, and to some degree socially stratified. Whether a man became a priest or a layman, for example, depended not only on his fortune and abilities, but also on specified schooling – bad writing and lack of Latin knowledge, for example, would disqualify a contender from a church career.[536] The educational reality of early modern days not only wedded certain expectations to specific age ranges; far from universal, educational paths prepared children for very different career and life trajectories, depending on social status.

The twin aspect of social stratification and vocational specialisation in education is entirely absent from Wolff's school system. Rather, he focuses on the universal faculties on the soul that should be developed by parents from an early age onwards, and that define the classification of the school system. Yet far from a private affair, the *Oeconomica* expands the humanist ideal of education to civic purpose – the children are not only to be shaped into humans, but, expressly, citizens.[537] With regard to the school system, Wolff's chosen model is not found at home but in China. His speech on Confucius favourably mentions the Chinese school system, as described in Noel's translation of Confucius' work, and finds it in accord with his own idea of education. Here, too, the vocational aspect is entirely absent in a bipartite education system: the school for the 'Little Ones', for children 8–15 years, is dedicated to forming the senses and virtues like obedience, respect, modesty, humbleness – targeting the lower faculties of the soul, in Wolffian terms. The 'School for Adults' teaches stu-

534 Wolff, *Oeconomica*, § 176, p. 291.

535 Coler, *Oeconomia ruralis*, p. 359.

536 Schlotheuber, Eva, 'Die Bewertung von Kindheit und die Rolle von Erziehung in den biographischen und autobiographischen Quellen des Spätmittelalters', in *Das Kind in der Renaissance*, ed. by Klaus Bergdolt, Berndt Hamm, and Andreas Tönnesmann (Wiesbaden: Harrassowitz Verlag, 2008), pp. 43–69, pp. 50–51.

537 Wolff, *Jus naturae methodo scientifica pertractatum. Pars octava*, § 429, *nota*, p.148: 'In civitate vero educanda proles est, ut ex civibus geniti vitam quoque cives vivere possint, sicque genus civium propagetur & civitas conservetur.'

dents to reason and to rule by training the upper faculties of the soul.[538] Concretely, whilst primary school teaches all children respect and obedience, i.e. the basics of model citizenship, only those going through upper school are furnished with leadership faculties.

Wolff's school system in his natural law is laid out accordingly, focusing on the different intellectual and psychological faculties of human beings and the stages at which they ought to be developed: primary school, *scholae inferiores*, are dedicated to practicing the memory as basic lower faculty of the soul; the *Scholae superiores* focus on the upper faculties, intellect and comprehension.[539] This bifurcated education programme mirrors in its structure the Chinese school system that Wolff so admires but adjusts the virtue-based curriculum to his own theory of the soul. The main emphasis seems to be building a basis for the intellectual virtues by exercising first memory, then comprehension, implies that the function of state education system – just as within the private household – is geared towards a moral education as an abstractly sound citizen more than a professional future.

What seems strikingly modern about Wolff's school system is not merely the universality but also the fact that it should be state-sponsored: *Jus naturae VIII* postulates that the state needs to take care that the children be educated in all things useful and necessary without education posing a financial burden to the parents; where the parents do not have the means necessary for an education, the state needs to deliver financial support.[540] This refers specifically to the children of poor people: it is the task of the head of state to make sure that they are educated.[541] Institutions are to be founded specifically for that purpose, the *Orphanotrophia* and the *Schola Pauperum*, where orphans and children of parents living in poverty are given the necessary education.[542] Yet there is no indication that the type of education differs by status or station: here, too, Wolff seems to understand education in a universal sense. In comparison to his own times this spells a significant democratisation of education that should, however, not be misunderstood as a deliberate promotion of social mobility. The justification for a public education system is not the benefit accruing to the individual – it is in the state interest that the children be educated so that they can contribute to the common good.[543] Seeing that the question of education is so keenly placed at the centre of public interest, Wolff adds that school is not simply an option – rather, it is compulsory and given the state's power to coerce any citizen to conform with the law of nature, it is equally entitled to coerce parents to commit their children to school education. This requirement does not remove the parental obligation to educate the

538 Wolff, Oratio de Sinarum philosophia practica, pp. 38–43.
539 Wolff, Jus naturae methodo scientifica pertractatum. Pars octava, § 434, p. 323.
540 Ibid., § 429, p. 319.
541 Ibid., § 741, p. 258.
542 Ibid., §§ 742–3, p. 258.
543 Ibid., § 429, *nota*, p.148.

children; in fact, education as a whole is to be seen as a joint effort combining the forces of both parents and state.[544] State education therefore does not just provide a means to plug the hole caused by a failing family unit; it is a complementary process that picks up the intellectual development from where the parents left it. The state not only provides education or supports it financially – it enforces it across the board.

The idea of education to inculcate civic virtue has literary precedents before Wolff. Melanchthon, dubbed the *praeceptor Germaniae* for a good reason, saw the power of the state as an analogue to paternal authority; and with this patrimonial interpretation of the state he charged it with the responsibility for the church as an institution within the state and the inculcation of the subjects with the fear of God – through education.[545] Closer to Wolff's time, there are a number of figures in Wolff's local and literary environment who sought to promote Melanchthon's idea by word and deed. Pre-eminent amongst these was Francke, the aforementioned Pietist activist based in Halle, who founded a slew of educational institutions at the end of the seventeenth century. His *Orphanotrophaeum*, founded in 1695, was the first seed of what was to become a whole institutional complex in Glaucha, a poor district outside the city walls of Halle. Initially Francke's projects targeted orphans and destitute children, later expanding the programme to include students from all strata of society. In his eyes schools were a vehicle to cure society's illnesses bottom up, through education and the inculcation of religious and morally sound attitudes.[546] At its peak, the educational arm of the *Franckesche Stiftungen*, Francke's charitable foundation, contained an elementary school for orphans and other local children, a Latin school for the offspring of middle-class citizens, a Lyceum for the sons of aristocrats and a school for girls. Customary divisions between genders and rank were preserved within this order and more differentiated than in Wolff's school system which lacks all vocational and social distinctions. Social stratification within Francke's school system, however, seems to have catered to social reality more than his own ideology; in theory he was intent on a universalised and democratised educational experience across the board.[547] It is important to recognise that Francke's motive for broadening access to education was not just to support disadvantaged individuals but to build up a Christian society in step with his own vision, locally and beyond. This endeavour also pervades his pedagogical practice: the inculcation of strict norms ruled over the encouragement of individual traits in each child.[548]

Wolff's *orphanotrophaeum* recalls the model in Halle insofar as it is not just an institution intent on feeding orphans but also on delivering education to children liv-

---

544 Ibid., § 430, pp. 321–322.

545 Dreitzel, Protestantischer Aristotelismus, p. 91.

546 Raabe, Paul, ed., Vier Thaler und sechzehn Groschen: August Hermann Francke, der Stifter und sein Werk (Halle/Saale: Franckesche Stift, 1998), p. 106.

547 Ibid., p. 110.

548 Ibid., pp. 109–10.

ing in poverty, very much in Francke's sense. The fact that his institutions define themselves by their primarily educative function, targeted at orphaned and impoverished children alike, coheres with what seems to have been a genuinely local fashion in Halle. Zedler's universal lexicon, in contrast, defines the *Orphanotrophia* (rather than *-trophaeum*) by their putative inmates, orphans of more or lesser means.[549] The stress here is on sustenance, not education.

The focus of Wolff's teaching programme, untraditionally intent on building the basic faculties for moral perfection, agrees with Francke's curriculum which stressed pedagogy over education, in the belief that moral betterment of children through the inculcation of a hard-working attitude was the primary cure to the evils in society. The idea of building up modes of cognition, stimulation of children's innate capacity and inspire joy of learning as a self-starter to further progress is common to both and other theorists like Christoph Semler, the founder of the first *Realschule*, a new form of secondary schooling, in Germany.[550] Yet unlike Wolff's rationalist morality, spiritual experience and religious education presented the core of Francke's curriculum. The Christian creed was *raison d'etre* and end alike in this educational model.

Francke enjoyed Seckendorf's patronage and earned the goodwill of the Prussian rulers, perhaps for the readily authoritarian bent of his pedagogy. After all, Francke's idea of moral education deliberately started with breaking the individual will in order to achieve subordination under the will of God – and, by proxy, the will of the educator.[551] In pedagogical practice, labour doubled up as a pedagogical tool to promote the prime virtues of industry and diligence; and although Francke recognised the need for relaxation, idle games, jokes and other nugatory business were dismissed as primeval habits, unworthy of true Christians.[552] His vision for universal education provided a ready model for Prussia's rulers. King Frederick William I had grown up Calvinist, not Lutheran or even Pietist, but, according to Gawthrop, 'invested new dynamism into the long-standing definition of a ruling prince as "administrator for God" (*Amtsmann Gottes*) by applying to his office a Promethean understanding of vocation similar to that of Francke.'[553] His drive to take on his subjects' welfare was not purely based on utilitarian stimulus but also a sense of responsibility towards God. Piety or not, the drunk antics of his social club, the *Tabakkollegium*, imply that the

549 *Grosses vollständiges Universal-Lexicon aller Wissenschafften und Künste* (Leipzig and Halle: Johann Heinrich Zedler, 1731), p. 870: 'Waysen-Haus, Lat. Orphanotrophium, ist ein Gebäude darinnen gemeiniglich nur arme, jedoch nach Gelegenheit auch wohl andere Vater- und Mutterlose, zugleich aber auch noch unmündige oder minderjährige Personen beyderley Geschlechtserzogen und versorget…'.

550 Raabe, Vier Thaler und sechzehn Groschen, p. 114.

551 Ibid., p. 107.

552 Ibid., p. 109.

553 Gawthrop, Pietism and the Making of Eighteenth-Century Prussia, p. 211.

king himself had not internalised the Pietist severity to the full.[554] But in his function as a ruler he readily co-opted said ideology when it came to building up strict discipline in the army and inculcating a hard-working attitude in his population. What the king wanted from his subjects was not mere obedience but dedication and commitment, the way Francke demanded it from his pupils.[555] To that end, he recruited university officials from Pietist ranks and channelled the graduates from Pietist institutions like Halle's theological faculty into the clergy, transforming the Lutheran church from within to promote obedience and hard work as Christian values among the common people. With the help of his new provost Lambert Gedicke (1683–1736), a former instructor at Francke's *Paedagogium*, the king recruited theology graduates from Halle as army chaplains, using their spiritual impact to impose discipline on his corps.[556] According to Benjamin Marschke, Gedicke 'made explicit the correlation between being a good Christian and being an obedient and submissive subject', the conception underwriting the Pietist pledge to 'impose genuine submission and instill authentic loyalty in Friedrich Wilhelm's soldiers and subjects' in the name of Christianity.[557] Given that the army was to a large degree composed of involuntary recruits – men quite literally kidnapped from families rich and poor – a strong sense of subordination was needed to keep order and the shockingly low desertion rates pay testament to the success of this strategy.[558]

Apart from clergy and military, the Prussian school system was reformed in the image of the *Franckesche Stiftungen*. Previously, school education in German lands had been the domain of the church, explicitly separate from state administration.[559] Public education had first taken shape after the reshuffle of clerical responsibility after the reformation. When Protestant princes assumed the additional function as head of church, the administration of the school system was also translocated to each state authority, albeit introducing no more than nominal changes to the actual school system. The curricula retained their clerical character and were authorised by the church; teachers were not financed by the state but paid through voluntary contributions by parents, later on church collects.[560] Brandenburg-Prussia under Frederick I.

554 Spamer, Franz Otto, Aus dem Tabakskollegium und der Zopfzeit; oder, Wie man vor hundertundfünzig Jahren lebte und es trieb. Historische Erzählung aus der Regierungszeit des Königs Friedrich Wilhelm I von Preussen (Leipzig: O. Spamer, 1972), pp. 79–85.

555 Gawthrop, Pietism and the Making of Eighteenth-Century Prussia, p. 212.

556 Ibid., pp. 219–222; p. 225.

557 Marschke, Benjamin, Absolutely Pietist. Patronage, Fictionalism, and State-Building in the Early Eighteenth-Century Prussian Army Chaplaincy (Tübingen: Max Niemeyer Verlag, 2005), pp. 83–4.

558 Gawthrop, Pietism and the Making of Eighteenth-Century Prussia, p. 228.

559 Bornhak, Conrad, 'Das preussische Unterrichtswesen als Staatsinstitut in rechtsgeschichtlicher Entwicklung', *Archiv des öffentlichen Rechts*, 4 (1889), 101–46 (101).

560 Bornhak, 'Das preussische Unterrichtswesen als Staatsinstitut in rechtsgeschichtlicher Entwicklung', pp. 103–105.

made some progress when it came to the establishment of public institutions such as universities, *Gymnasia* and city schools for the children of middle and lower class citizens, as also the *Fürstenschulen*, specifically targeted at princes' education. The content of the education differed by the students' social status and prepared them for a vocational path appropriate to their rank. Religious education, however, was a core element to any teaching effort, as can be seen from the Latin schools' curriculum: 'essentially religious-based on a classical foundation'.[561]

It was Francke's Pietist school project, however, which provided the conceptual impulse for a universal elementary education that Frederick's successor Frederick William I would spread throughout his territories.[562] The king adopted the Pietist model for his new schools under public administration, with a universal mandate retaining the religious-confessional character of the curriculum. An edict of October 1717 made regular school visits compulsory and created a basic, supra-confessional framework for elementary schools; school fees were now mandatory, parents in need were supported by the public chest.[563] According to James van Horn Melton this decree was 'little more than an exercise in wishful thinking' as it did not solve the financial issues the schools experienced with regards to staffing and the building of facilities.[564] Yet in 1736 the king backed up the struggling school system with another edict, the *Principia Regulativa*, which formalised the remuneration of schoolmasters, stipulated state subsidies for construction costs and teachers' salaries, established a royal endowment to support education in poorer parishes and levied additional taxes to fund new parish schools in East Prussia.[565]

The strikingly modern-looking elements of Wolff's education programme, the concept of a universal, mandatory school system with financial support from the state was therefore well-established practice by the time he wrote his natural law. In institutional terms, therefore, his school system is simply in tune with developments on the ground. Wolff does probe a break with this fashion where he replaces the Christian creed as a foundation with his scientific curriculum, his rationalist pedagogy based on his theory of cognition and morality. The clash between Wolff and the Pietists in Halle – and Francke's friends at the university in particular – was pre-programmed insofar as it dispensed with the centrality of Christian philosophy in the ordination of human lives.[566] Years before, Tschirnhaus, inspired by Francke, had

---

561 Dorwart, The Prussian Welfare State, pp. 146–150.

562 Ibid., p. 181.

563 Bornhak, 'Das preussische Unterrichtswesen als Staatsinstitut in rechtsgeschichtlicher Entwicklung', pp. 109–110.

564 Van Horn Melton, James, Absolutism and the Eighteenth-Century Origins of Compulsory Schooling in Prussia and Austria (Cambridge: Cambridge University Press, 1988), p. 46.

565 Ibid., pp. 47–8.

566 Rosemarie Ahrbeck, in fact, considers Francke the main agitator against Wolff, even if university theologians like Lange provided the public face of the campaign that led to his expulsion. See Ahr-

helped in the conception of an educational programme in Halle – but encountered bitter enmity when proposing to remove religion from its central place in the curriculum.[567] The centrality of the Pietist education model for Prussian state policy further illustrates how a clash of pedagogical ideals could culminate in a political fallout to the point of Wolff's exile. The success of Gedicke's army chaplains inculcating discipline in Frederick William's soldiers exemplifies the king's stake in collaborating with the Pietists and co-opting their teaching model. As Marschke puts it, 'Friedrich Wilhelm's understanding that being a "good Christian" was a precondition for being sincerely loyal is clear, and his notion that "proper Christians" would make excellent soldiers follows along the same lines'.[568] Yet the appeal of Pietist education extended beyond the army barracks – as James Van Horn Melton contends, by virtue of its universality and appeal to range of social strata, it 'offered the absolutist state a potential instrument of control appropriate for every social milieu', aiding the integration of 'recalcitrant or anomalous social groups into changing patterns of economic production', cultivating self-discipline through spiritual renewal whilst promoting submission.[569] Wolff's rationalist curriculum and the removal of the religious core from teaching practice naturally ran counter to the spirit of this project.

Clashes permitting Wolff has to be considered part of a thriving discourse on pedagogy in Halle even though his rationalist makeover was a badly timed suggestion. No matter the upheaval, in one aspect king, philosopher and Pietist are in perfect agreement: the importance of universal schooling to create a solid civil order. This explains how the institutional similarity between Pietist model and Wolffian ideal can be so striking even though the ideological core of their pedagogy differed to the point of altercation. Wolff offered conformity through rationalism – but the king demanded obedience on spiritual terms.

4.3.2 Universities: theory in practice

Wolff's school system seems dedicated to character building more than vocation save for one paragraph listing the basic skills like reading and writing that children have

beck, Rosemarie, 'Wolff und Francke – Kontrahenten oder Weggefährten?', in *Christian Wolff als Philosoph der Aufklärung in Deutschland*, ed. by Hans-Martin Gerlach, Günter Schenk, and Burchard Thaler (Halle: Martin-Luther-Universität, 1980), pp. 101–10, p. 101.

567 von Tschirnhaus, E.W., Gründliche Anleitung zu den nützlichen Wissenschaften, absonderlich zu der Mathesi und Physica, wie sie anitzo von den gelehrtesten abgehandelt werden (Stuttgart-Bad Cannstatt: Frommann-Holzboog, 1729), p. ix.

568 Marschke, *Absolutely Pietist*, p. 84.

569 Van Horn Melton, Absolutism and the Eighteenth-Century Origins of Compulsory Schooling in Prussia and Austria, pp. 57–8.

to learn.[570] Yet his abstract notion of education has to be understood within the context of his definition of science in order to understand how mere cognitive development could feed into the promotion of useful knowledge. Tschirnhaus had nursed similar literary ambitions about a pedagogy corresponding with an approach to scientific discovery. The inductive method Tschirnhaus advocated was – just like Wolff's scientific method – strongly inspired by mathematics, and he recommended the encounter with mathematical demonstrations as purposeful training to sharpen the mind against falsehoods.[571] Faith still plays a central role in his idea of cognition, in fact, is portrayed as an active medium of obtaining the truth where both the senses and the intellect meet their boundaries.[572] In comparison, Wolff might prefer the deductive over the inductive method and has a decisively rationalist attitude to epistemics. The pedagogical zeal, however, sparked from the belief in a universal heuristic method, is palpable in either author. The comparison between Wolff's and Tschirnhaus's pedagogy, moreover, elucidates in what way either conceived of their theoretical concepts of education as a path to practically applied sciences.

Tellingly enough, the title of Tschirnhaus's pedagogical work is *Anleitung zu den nützlichen Wissenschafften*, that is, an 'introduction to the useful sciences'; in that sense it might seem puzzling that it is chiefly concerned with a theory of cognition only. The title nevertheless makes sense in the context of Tschirnhaus's and Wolff's stress on heuristics in science. The theory of knowledge is a prerequisite to the production of knowledge in practice and theoretical though it is, Wolff's abstract preparation of the mind is his pathway to furnishing an individual with the capacity to create useful knowledge.

Utility, although perhaps not in the Wolffian sense, indeed ruled the day under the Prussian education reform, and a similar shift had been set into gear in the German university landscape. The establishment of a chair of *Oeconomie* in Halle pays homage to the gradual reform of university faculties and curricula in response to the demands of the real world if not the demands of Frederick William I.[573] Christian Thomasius, in that spirit, sought to push reform at the university level with a pedagogical zeal, a state education to create urbane, sophisticated, independent-minded

570 Wolff, Jus naturae methodo scientifica pertractatum. Pars octava, § 431, p. 149: '...id imprimis curae esse debet, ut liberi, dum educantur & publice instituuntur, legere, scribere ac computare discant, nec permittendum parentibus, ut in hisce addiscendis illos negligant.'

571 von Tschirnhaus, Gründliche Anleitung zu den nützlichen Wissenschaften, p. 22.

572 Ibid., p. 7.

573 According to Andre Wakefield, the establishment of the chair in Halle arose out of the king's explicit frustration with his ministers. See Wakefield, Andre, 'Cameralism. A German Alternative to Mercantilism', in *Mercantilism Reimagined. Political Economy in Early Modern Britain and Its Empire*, ed. by Carl Wennerlind and Philip J. Stern (Oxford: Oxford University Press, 214AD), pp. 134–50, p. 138: 'Frederick William wanted more obedience, less disputation, and more economy.'

and responsible citizens.[574] Thomasius's endeavours in Halle sought to shift the focus towards building capacities directly relevant to public life, away from 'empty scientism' and overly theoretical schooling and supporting individual virtue and personal development instead.[575] The establishment of new faculties – such as the chair for *Oeconomie* – also testifies to a new trend putting university learning to the service of the newly transforming Prussian state.[576] The utilitarian idea of knowledge subliminally leaks into Wolff's design of higher education. Where the *scholae inferiores*, the elementary schools, are to cater to the lower faculties of the soul, the *scholae superiores*, also known as academies or universities, focus on the intellect in preparation for obtaining knowledge of all things necessary and useful.[577] Any mention of traditional and common university faculties is left out whilst the discussion is entirely limited to the basic faculties that enable further learning. Wolff's incarnation of utility hence does not respond to Thomasius's call for reformed university faculties. But it does correspond with Tschirnhaus's ideal for whom the key to practical education consists of a cognitive preparation for universal heuristics.

Wolff's academic vision, furthermore, institutionally decouples teaching from research – in a development following a fashion of his own times. Whilst education happens in universities, the advancement of knowledge is mandated to the *societates scientiarum*, the scientific societies.[578] These societies stand independently within the stately realm and have their own rules and charters.[579] Independence is a given but their purpose is geared towards the common good as they actively devote their energies to public matters of social or economic dimensions: agriculture, horticulture and animal husbandry, arts and crafts and all that under the heading of universal learning.[580] The *societates scientiarum*, devoted to theoretical science, are complemented with the *societates artium* that dedicate themselves to furthering the practical arts, by training painters, architects and other craftsmen, explicitly in the interest of the state.[581] In that sense, vocational education is split up between the *scholae superiores*, building the foundation for heuristic skills, and the *societates artium*, where vocational crafts are instituted. The traditional university faculties, however, seem to have no purchase in Wolff's higher education. The *societates*, however, correspond with a

574 Menzel, Vernakuläre Wissenschaft, p. 78.

575 Wundt, Die deutsche Schulphilosophie im Zeitalter der Aufklärung, p. 27.

576 Frauendienst, Christian Wolff als Staatsdenker, p. 31.

577 Wolff, *Jus naturae methodo scientifica pertractatum. Pars octava*, § 434, p. 149: 'Scholae autem superiores sunt, in quibus juvenes docentur ea, quae vi intellectus comprehendenda, consequenter ad scientiam rerum scitu necessarium, vel utilium perducuntur. Vocantur hae apud nos *Academiae*, vel etiam *Universitates*.'

578 Ibid., §§ 439–451, pp. 151–156.

579 Ibid., 444, p. 153.

580 Ibid., 449, p. 155.

581 Ibid., 451, p. 156.

trend of his own time. The early eighteenth century saw a number of such institutions cropping up across Europe, inspired by the pioneers in the field, the Royal Society in England and the Royal Academy in Paris. These learned societies corralled their members to devote their time and efforts to research and exchange about the scientific questions ruling the day.[582] Leibniz, who harboured the ideal of a *Gelehrtenstaat*, a state of scholars made up of such frameworks, ever so enthusiastically promoted theoretical and practical skills in chemistry, mechanics and glassblowing, but also book printing, textiles and metalwork. In a treatise of 1671 he suggested academies for sciences and the arts that were to explore practical issues of state administration, such as food supply, prison systems, trade and education.[583] These *societates*, inspired by the much-envied Royal Society in Britain, were core to his state ideal and together with Tschirnhaus, Leibniz pushed for the establishment of such institutions in Germany.[584] In the end, consummation of this wish proceeded through state initiative: Elector Frederick III of Brandenburg established the first Society of Sciences, later *Akademie der Wissenschaften*, in 1700 in Berlin, modelled on the Royal Societies in France and England.[585] Numerous other German cities followed the example in the decades to come, to name only Göttingen, Mannheim, Munich and Erfurt.[586] Traditional universities persisted in their usual role but the scientific societies and academies provided a new drive for cutting edge research – albeit research only, not teaching.[587]

Wolff himself harboured an ambiguous stance towards this development. He was made an honorary member of the Royal Society in London in 1710, of Berlin's scientific society in 1711, the St Petersburg Academy of Sciences in 1725, appointed one of eight external members of the Paris Académie royale des sciences in 1733 and in 1752 of the Academy of sciences in Bologna.[588] Still, he resisted the call to Berlin to take up an administrative function at the scientific society there; vested in teaching and writing he remained wedded to university life and whilst he acknowledged the importance of scientific societies for a flourishing state, he came nowhere near Leibniz' enthusiasm for institutions of this kind.[589] In one aspect, however, Wolff's natural law

582 Burns, William E., 'Academies and Scientific Societies', *Science in the Enlightenment: An Encyclopedia* (Santa Barbara, CA: ABC-CLIO, 2003), pp. 1–3, p. 1.

583 Bredekamp, Horst, Die Fenster der Monade: Gottfried Wilhelm Leibniz' Theater der Natur und Kunst (Berlin: Akademie Verlag, 2004), p. 23.

584 Winter, Der Freund B. Spinozas E.W. v. Tschirnhaus, p. 8.

585 Dorwart, Reinhold August, 'Medical Education in Prussia under the Early Hohenzollern, 1685–1725', *Bulletin of the History of Medicine*, 32.4 (1958), 335–47 (336).

586 Burns, 'Academies and Scientific Societies', p. 2.

587 McClellan III, James, 'Scientific Institutions and the Organization of Science', in *The Cambridge History of Science: Volume 4, Eighteenth-Century Science*, ed. by Roy Porter and David C. Lindberg (Cambridge: Cambridge University Press, 2003), pp. 87–106, p. 88.

588 Biller, 'Biographie und Bibliographie', p. 12.

589 Wolff, Christian, *Eigene Lebensbeschreibung*, ed. by Heinrich Wuttke (Leipzig: Weidmann, 1841), p. 66.

takes a stand for scientific societies that is redolent of his own philosophical conviction: namely, that the intellectual freedom of the *societates* should expand beyond the immediate control of the state. Wolff declares that scientific societies are to come with their own charters and follow internal laws, in full enjoyment of intellectual freedom – *libertas philosophandi* – in order to follow their task effectively.[590] The term *libertas philosophandi* crops up regularly in Wolff, demanding the freedom for philosophers and scientists to pursue their work without censure or state intervention.[591] Yet unlike the idea of freethinking, which was frowned upon at the time, Wolff's defence of intellectual freedom does not pose a critical but a corroborative force for state and society. In the 'Discursus praeliminaris' the conditions of philosophical liberty are qualified to that end: if *libertas philosophandi* is granted to those using his scientific method, it poses no danger to religion, virtue or state, as those philosophising in this way will not contradict revealed truth, morality or state rationale – by definition.[592]

There is an interesting parallel with a pronouncement in Seckendorf's *Christen-Stat*. Seckendorf, in a wording similar to Wolff's, defends the Christian religion: it is not a force undermining the state's integrity, but a reinforcement to a state built on Christian values; it does not seek 'outward equality' but respects existing hierarchies.[593] Seckendorf maintains that a Christian subject will readily obey the state, precisely for his Christian faith which teaches the subject to bow to authority and the ruler to govern with justice. Frederick William's promotion of Pietism as a state ideology, in fact, proves this point with all due force. Wolff's defence of the *libertas philosophandi* invokes the same mechanism but in the name of rationality-based, non-confessional pursuit of knowledge: the tenets of reason promoted through schools and *societates* will not subvert but only fortify a state built on rational principles. The same idea of education as political stabilizer also feeds into Wolff's assessment of the different constitutional forms a state can and should adopt. The choice essentially depends on the capacities of the ruler: a monarchy requires a wise ruler with competent advisers; an aristocracy a capable ruling elite; a *Politie*, however, or democracy, would require a

---

590 Wolff, Jus naturae methodo scientifica pertractatum. Pars octava, § 447, p. 154.

591 The 'Discursus praeliminaris' dedicates a whole section to the topic, see Wolff, 'Discursus praeliminaris', *Philosophia rationalis*, §§ 151–171, pp. 79–104

592 Wolff, *Philosophia rationalis sive Logica*, § 167, pp. 64–65: '*Si libertas philosophandi integra conceditur iis, qui methodo philosophica philosophantur, nullum hinc metuendum est religioni, virtuti ac Reip. periculum*. Qui enim methodo philosophica philosophatur, non contradicit veritati revelatae (§. 163), nec virtuti, nec statui publico contraria docet (§. 164. 165).'

593 Seckendorf, *Christen-Stat*, II. VII, § 1, p. 268: 'Christliche Obrigkeit ist unter einem Haupt Christi mit den Unterthanen verbunden. Daraus folget aber keine eusserliche Gleichheit/wie die aufrührerischen Bauern haben wollen.' Ibid., II. VII. § 5: 'Der Unterthanen Gehorsam wird aus Betrachtung der Christlichen zusammen Vergliederung auch gestärcket und aus gutem Hertzen geleistet. Der Regent büsset also nichts daran ein/sondern ist als ein Christ/in seinem Amt desto glücklicher und getroster.'

virtuous and educated populace.[594] Wolff supports this paradigm through the institutionalisation of education. The prerequisite to a democracy is the virtue of the populace, and the comprehensive education of the populace's youth in state institutions therefore the necessary groundwork to political maturity. Education therefore has a political function that serves *raison d'etat* in the first instance, the individual in the second – not just in a democracy but most necessarily so there.

4.4 Preserving prosperity, providing for the poor

4.4.1 Economic sustainability in the household

A single household, in Wolff's philosophy, is by definition not capable of procuring all that life's necessity, convenience and pleasure – in short, happiness – demands.[595] In fact, the origin of the state, in Wolff's reading, goes back to the moment when families banded together to better cater to their needs.[596] The prospect of improved living conditions is therefore his explanation for the existence of political communities, rather than just a sociable instinct. Once part of a body politic, however, a family's economic sustainability presents a responsibility towards the household and the body politic alike. Good householding as a duty is enshrined in the *Oeconomica* and complemented with support and regulation from the state in Wolff's natural law. As the demonstration goes, economic sustenance is a family's natural mandate but now also a moral obligation to the ruler – with the ulterior motive that a financially prosperous population makes for a prosperous state.

Wolff's *Oeconomica* provides a deontological, not a practical account of good householding. Simply said, since the subsistence of life requires spending, it naturally warrants earning the necessary money.[597] The husband is chiefly responsible for procuring the funds through labour, the wife naturally disposed to assist with household tasks, adjusting spending to earning and taking care to avoid unnecessary or wilful expenses.[598] The impact private fortunes evidently had on the public good casts a new light on the economic prudence that pervades Wolff's *Oeconomica*: financial discipline here needs to be understood as a prerequisite to fulfilling the household's

594 Hofmann, 'Recht und Staat bei Christian Wolff', p. 638: 'Wolff erklärt, er sei vergnügt, diesen "Wink" gegeben zu haben (§ 252). "Polit", diese Ableitung aus dem Griechischen, entspricht dem lateinischstämmigen "zivilisiert", meint also so viel wie: bürgerlich gebildet. Und die notwendige Bemühung um Verstand und Tugend steht für Aufklärung und (notfalls drakonische) Erziehung.'
595 Wolff, Jus naturae methodo scientifica pertractatum. Pars octava, § 1, p. 1.
596 Ibid., § 4, p. 3.
597 Ibid., § 130, p. 200: 'Ad oeconomiam pertinet tam pecuniae acquisitio, quam erogatio, & boni oeconomi est parta tueri.'
598 Ibid., § 131, pp. 202–203.

function within the community. This responsibility starts with the choice of the partner: before getting married, either potential spouse needs to be sure that their combined force and capacities can take on the financial burden of a household in general, and the onus of raising children in particular.[599] Granted the central importance of frugality, there is one marked difference to other works of *Hausväterliteratur*: in contrast to classic guides of home economics, Wolff never offers any advice on how to actually save or earn money. Rather, the matter is abstracted and described in mere deontological terms: a household is universally obliged to keep the finances stable and limit expenditures to never exceed income, and most importantly: avoid debts by all means. The scope of the *Oeconomica* is thus limited to the moral inculcation of this goal, not its practical consummation. This refers to the general running of a household but also special occasions, such as weddings, and by implication to a household's social circle. Wolff demonstrates that the festivities and gifts between the spouses have to be well within their means.[600] Even the wedding presents given to the couple by friends and guests should be considered under the maxim of collective frugality: if the couple really needs material assistance with their new shared household, friends may contribute with gifts – if the couple has no need, they should not accept such gifts, even if offered.[601] Altogether, this signals a paradigm shift from economically self-interested *Hausväterliteratur* to collectively – or even politically – oriented financial prudence. Coler complains about greedy guests ruining the *Hausvater*.[602] Wolff evidently worries about the financial stability of guests and hosts as the members of the same social composite. The recurrent judgment stresses how 'absurd' it would be to take on debts to cover expenses that are not primarily necessary, be they for the sake of gifts or other.[603] To further safeguard financial stability, the state intercepts with legislative measures against personal ruin: luxury cannot to be tolerated and even though not illicit as such, the dilapidation of citizens' goods cannot be allowed.[604] Thus, a profligate man should be divested of his goods which are to be handed over to an administrator.[605] Given that squander should not be allowed, Wolff makes a case for prohibiting lotteries or other forms of gambling.[606]

599 Wolff, *Oeconomica*, §§ 27–28, pp. 37–39.
600 Ibid., § 68, p. 105: ...luxus in conviis (sic) nuptialibus vitandus & pro modo facultatum convivium nuptiale apparandum, immo pauperioribus ab eo prorsus abstinendum.' See also ibid., § 59, pp. 88–92.
601 Ibid., § 70, pp. 107–108.
602 Coler, *Oeconomia ruralis*, p. 99: 'Sonderlich soll er sich wol versehen/wann er im selbst/oder seinen Kindern Hochzeit machen will/daß er bald im anfang seiner Nahrung nit mer verpanckerire/denn er hernach in etliche Jahren nit widerumm erwerben kan/wie jetzt der verfluchte vermaledeyte brauch in der Welt is/daß man Hochzeiten macht/die 1.2.3.4.5.6.7.8. oder mehr als 100.thaler kosten.'
603 Wolff, *Oeconomica* §. 70, p. 108; Wolff, *Oeconomica*, § 59, p. 90.
604 Wolff, Jus naturae methodo scientifica pertractatum. Pars octava, § 733, p. 255; § 751, p. 261.
605 Ibid., § 752, p. 261:'...prodigalitas in Rep. non ferenda, consequenter prodigis administratio bonorum suorum adimenda & curator dandus, qui administret.'
606 Ibid., § 755, p. 262.

From a modern perspective, this level of control over a private individual's financial affairs seems excessive. Looking at the historical context it is neither novel nor surprising: regulating spending behaviour had been a common municipal practice since medieval times. Although matters concerning property, family law and inheritance were officially beyond the reach of council jurisdiction, cities tried to regulate economic behaviour on a basic level through by-laws. An individual's disproportionate or immoderate expenditures or mismanagement of assets were not merely a private matter but a harm to the community: a ruined human meant another pauper or a whole family to cater for and one person less to tax.[607] Costly entertainment indeed posed another point of public concern. Weddings, baptisms and other festivities took on increasingly ruinous dimensions by the end of the seventeenth century and genuinely caused destitution amongst some families. Alongside a number of taxes levied on luxuries, there was an increasing range of state regulations seeking to restrict the numbers of guests at family occasions and other ways to curb spending on private level. Initially issued as municipal by-laws protecting the economic robustness of a community, luxury legislation moved into the domain of territorial legislation during the fifteenth and sixteenth century before its wane in the second half of the eighteenth century.[608] To the state, taxing vice as a source of income and regulation to safeguard the prosperity of communities presented a good reason in its own right; yet the Christian backdrop as moral justification for these measures is unmistakable. Seckendorff's *Christen-Stat*, for example, defines the combat against prodigality as a moral obligation to the Christian ruler. Like Wolff, Seckendorf condemns excess and luxury as morally reprehensible, in particular when it comes to wedding festivities.[609]

Seckendorf's treatise not only highlights the necessity to prevent ruin but also to cater to the livelihood of the populace. The God-fearing prince, on account of his Christianity and Christian love, will cater to the needs of his subjects so that they may have food, work, income and other forms of support.[610] The ulterior – openly ulterior motif – brought to the table is that a well-looked after populace will also procreate accordingly and that the actual mass of well-nourished people makes for the greatest wealth of a country.[611] Seckendorf's argument illustrates the ideological paradigm

---

607 Isenmann, Eberhard, 'The Notion of the Common Good, the Concept of Politics, and Practical Policies in Late Medieval and Early Modern German Cities', in *De Bono Communi: The Discourse and Practice of the Common Good in the European City (13th-16th c.)* (Turnhout: Brepols, 2010), pp. 107–48, pp. 138–139.

608 For an in-depth description of the types of legislation and their background in German principalities in the seventeenth and eighteenth century, see Stolleis, Michael, *Pecunia nervus rerum: Zur Staatsfinanzierung in der frühen Neuzeit* (Frankfurt am Main: Klostermann, 1983), with p. 18 in particular reference to weddings.

609 Seckendorf, *Christen-Stat*, II.II. § 11–12, p. 212.

610 Ibid., II. XIII. § 1, p. 433.

611 Ibid., II.XIII. § 1, pp. 433–434: 'Aus dem Christenthum oder der Christlichen Liebe fliesset die Vorsorge bey Gottesfürchtigen Regenten/daß die Unterthanen bey ihrer Nahrung und Gewerbe das

shift that happens with the change of audience from private to municipal to state level: from a self-interested concern to a community issue to a utilitarian reading by and for the ruler. Wolff's discourse essentially provides the rationalist translation of this Christianity-based principle into natural law. Simultaneously, Wolff makes the economic sustenance of the populace a state objective: by keeping the living costs low through provision and price regulation of goods essential to daily livelihood.[612] Within that context, the ruler's mandate to provide wood for the population may seem like a strangely specific predicament.[613] At Wolff's time, however, vicissitudes in the wood market and the lure of profit vis-à-vis the absolute dependence of every person on wood as a fuel propelled this commodity to the forefront of the political discussion. For the princes, the financial gain of exploiting their forests competed with the patriarchal mandate to secure affordable wood for the population, even though often enough the latter served as a political excuse to secure a monopoly on wood trade for the government.[614] Although Wolff's philosophy seeks to abstract away from circumstantial information, the socioeconomic issues of the day securely fasten Wolff's discourse to its historical background.

Price fixing of life essentials is not Wolff's invention but had been practiced by German municipalities and city councils for a long time, in the name of social order and justice. These measures also imposed qualitative regulations on food producers like butchers, brewers and bakers, to avoid malpractice and profiteering. Sometimes grain from the communal storage was put on the market to reduce prices and keep bread production up.[615] The practice of market intervention hence is not new. But the fact that Wolff mandates it to the ruler of the *civitas* rather than city councils may speak to the centralisation of these measures in the Prussian reality of his own times. As of the late seventeenth century, the Hohenzollern rulers stepped up their efforts to introduce standard weights and measures, and further control mechanisms to support both trade and protect consumers. An edict by Frederick William I in 1722, for example, established a standard bushel across all Hohenzollern territories and sought to enforce the new standards through tax commissaries and town officials.[616] Where previously town councils sought to regulate prices for the benefit of the community, the administrative centralisation of the Prussian state was further incentivised by trade benefits. In fact, the importance of towns to the Prussian economy

---

Auskommen und alle mögliche Beförderung haben & und ihre Anzahl sich eher vermehre/als vermindere/weil auff der Menge wohlgenehrte Leute der grösseste Schatz des Landes besteht/und dazu zielet nicht allein der eusserliche Friede/und die Mässigkeit der Obrigkeitlichen Macht/in Einbringung der Gefälle/Steuren/Schatzungen/Contributionen und Anlagen.'

612 Wolff, Jus naturae methodo scientifica pertractatum. Pars octava, § 727, p. 253.

613 Ibid., §§ 729–730, p. 254.

614 Radkau, Joachim, *Holz. Wie ein Naturstoff Geschichte schreibt* (Munich: Oekom Verlag, 2018), p. 139–140.

615 Isenmann, 'The Notion of the Common Good', pp. 145–146.

616 Dorwart, The Prussian Welfare State, p. 56.

prompted Frederick William to increase the scrutiny of municipal governments through special commissions, successively replacing the formerly elective town councils with salaried state officials. By 1740 this administrative switch had been all but completed. As Gagliardo argues, these local commissioners 'became almost municipal viceroys in this arrangement, vested as they were with very extensive powers and responsibilities: they inspected weights and measures, fixed prices on necessities, looked after orphanages and hospitals and, in short, exercised or supervised all functions of local police (in the very broad contemporary meaning of the term).'[617] The link between social welfare and economic management is complete in the institutionalisation of *Gute Polizey* at the local level.

Ironically enough, Wolff defines excessive alms-giving as the third threat to prosperity besides prodigality and market vicissitudes.[618] This must be understood in the religious context of traditional Christian charity: in medieval times, giving to the poor was the foremost and most straightforward way of buying into salvation, either by giving to the church or tending straight to the needy.[619] Given the lofty promise it is not surprising that many people ruined themselves financially in the here-and-now. Luther sought to nip what he considered an ideological misgiving in the bud. In his reading, only God could bestow grace, uninflected by worldly deeds. Accordingly, charity should be dispensed towards fellow humans as a general expression of Christian feeling, without ulterior motives in mind.[620] The change in interpretation also freed up space for economic considerations, negotiating between personal needs and charitable impulses. This new reading transpires in the decisively Protestant *Hausväterliteratur*. Florinus and Menius both dedicate a space to the *Hausvater*'s responsibility towards the indigent and these charitable concerns are directly coupled with admonitions about prudent householding: as Menius explains, the 'righteous use of goods' includes sale and purchase of goods, prohibits wastefulness, and thus also alms within due measure – better said, within the means of the household.[621] Alms-giving is cast as a pious deed but righteous only where sustainable. The paradigm shift from the Catholic idea of self-sacrifice and the glorification of poverty to Protestant poor relief as a Christian duty of pragmatic dimensions is clear. In Wolff, notably, alms or *eleemosyne*, are brought back from the domestic to the individual's sphere of responsibility – in theory. The mandate to give but to give within one's

617 Gagliardo, Germany under the Old Regime, p. 305.

618 Wolff, *Jus naturae methodo scientifica pertractata. Pars septima*, p. 260, § 747: 'Quamobrem cum eleemosynae nimiae exhauriant opes subditorum, facile contingit, ut multi in paupertatem, vel egestatem incidant, aut tandem ipsi ad mendicitatem redigantur. Cavendum igitur est in Rep. ne subditi nimiis eleemoysnis onerentur.'

619 Lindberg, Carter, *Beyond Charity: Reformation Initiatives for the Poor* (Minneapolis: Fortress Press, 1993), p. 26–27.

620 Witte, 'Martin Luther's Influence on Legal Reforms and Civil Law', p. 12.

621 Menius, *Oeconomia christiana*, pp. 133–135.

means is clearly formulated in the fourth part of the *Ethica* although it does not feature in the context of householding and economic prudence in the *Oeconomica* nor in *Jus naturae VII*. Still, Wolff stresses alms as an obligation of the individual, not a member of a social composite like a village or community, and this marks a clear contrast to the decisively Christian works of *Hausväterliteratur*. Wolff's nuclear family as the unit of provision is herewith absolved from communal responsibilities towards unaffiliated people in need. With a view to the integration in the state sphere, however, the association of *eleemosyne* with the individual rather than the household has further implications: it facilitates the mandate for the state to control acts of charity, as is to be seen.

The argument for the state to care for the poor is based on a mixed logic: on one hand, the ruler has a natural obligation to provide for those in need, also because private individuals cannot be expected to cover for all shortcomings in spite of the natural obligation.[622] On the other, taking on charity means protecting overly charitable individuals from private ruin.[623] Wolff further argues that *eleemosyne* is by nature a composite contribution as one person cannot cover the full living expenses of another.[624] Just in terms of numbers, the body politic as a collective is hence more suited to providing for the needy than an individual. As a consequence, the prerogative to dispense alms falls to the ruler, better said: the responsibility to provide to the poor what they need if they are unable to work and earn their own upkeep.[625] Not just a moral mandate, a state-sequestered poor relief system was also in the financial interest of the government, as Wolff expresses in straightforward terms: the poor formed a powerful burden to the state and the prospect of private charity was wont to exacerbate the situation.[626] Moreover, since the power of the state was now understood to rely with the economic strength of its population, a fall to ruin meant, doubly, sapping finances from one part of the population whilst feeding another that was not economically active.

---

622 Wolff, Jus natura methodo scientifica petractata. Pars octava, § 739, p. 257.

623 Ibid., § 747, p. 260: 'Quamobrem cum eleemosynae nimiae exhauriant opes subditorum, facile contingit, ut multi in paupertatem, vel egestatem incidant, aut tandem ipsi ad mendicitatem redigantur. Cavendum igitur est in Rep. ne subditi nimiis eleemoysnis onerentur.'

624 Wolff, Christian, Philosophia moralis sive Ethica, methodo scientifica pertractata. Pars quinta (Halle: Renger, 1753), § 396, p. 538: 'Qui egenis & mendicis subvenire possunt, singuli pro modo facultatum suarum contribuere tenentur, ideoque eleemosyne munuscula sunt (§ 51. part. 4. Jur. nat.), quae a pluribus petenda.'

625 Wolff, *Jus natura methodo scientifica petractata. Pars octava*, § 937, p. 324: *'Superiori competit jus de eleemosynis disponendi.'*

626 Ibid., § 726, p. 253: *'Quamobrem cum non modo superiori curae esse debeat, ut hoc faciant subditi (§. 395.), verum etiam Reip. intersit, ne iidem sint pauperes, egeni atque mendici, ut oneribus Reip. ferendis sint pares; superiori maxime curae esse debet, ne subditi in paupertatem vel egestatem incidant, aut ad mendicitatem redigantur.'*

One ambiguity remains with regard to this newly divided domain: the responsibility for relatives. The *Oeconomica* itself does not expand on the obligations of the nuclear family towards their relatives, associates or friends in need, nor seem Florinus or Menius to mention this topic. Wolff's *Jus naturae VII*, however, identifies the familial bonds and relationships by analysing degrees of relation, *affinitas*, loosely hinting at a general obligation of the family towards the relations, also in terms of physical welfare.[627] These obligations are not further defined but implicitly mentioned in Wolff's section on poor relief: the state is obliged to care for subjects where – literally – friends or family cannot provide, which implies that there is a grey zone of competencies.[628] Peter Laslett observes a similar situation in his case study of family support systems in early modern Europe and a tension between social reality and legislation. He argues that the burden of poor relief was not only significant but also significantly sponsored by the community chest, more so than the beneficence of remoter relatives where existent. In his opinion it is exactly the legislative efforts made to compel families to provide for poor relatives that suggests how the sphere of care was not expected to extend beyond the nuclear family.[629] The ambiguity within Wolff's discourse implies that the situation was not entirely clear here either – and although some hints in the natural law suggest the obligations of the family go beyond the nuclear sphere, the *Oeconomica* does not confirm this claim, be that because it is unfinished or else. The lasting impression is the *de facto* translation of Christian duty of poor relief into a natural obligation to the ruler – additionally backed up with the utilitarian argument that preventing citizens from charity means pre-empting more paupers. The fact that Wolff still uses the term *eleemosyne* may have less to do with the Christian thrust behind his natural law than the Christian thrust behind the beliefs of the population – and habits of charity that defied legislation. Prussian measures to curb begging and wayfaring relied on a considerable support of the population which, largely faltering, jeopardised the harsh legislation in practice. As Dorwart explains, '[t]o a certain extent the royal efforts were rendered nugatory by a popular opposition to the coercive measures of a bureaucratic government.'[630] Poor relief at Wolff's time hence has a problem to grapple with that does not seem to burden the modern state just as much: civil disobedience for the sake of thy neighbour.

---

627 See chapter III of *Jus naturae pars septima*, entitled 'De Cognationibus & affinitatibus', §§ 556–632, pp. 378–435.

628 See, for instance, those that qualify for a *ptochotrophium*, in Wolff, *Jus natura methodo scientifica petractata. Pars octava*, § 738, p. 257: '*Ptochotrophium* dicitur locus, in quo aluntur egeni, qui labore suo ea, quibus ad vitae necessitatem indigent, acquirere nequeunt, ac destituuntur cognatis, vel amicis, qui indigentiae ipsorum prospiciunt.'

629 Laslett, Peter, 'Family, Kinship and Collectivity as Systems of Support in Pre-Industrial Europe: A Consideration of the "nuclear-Hardship" Hypothesis', *Continuity and Change. A Journal of Social Structure, Law and Demography in Past Societies*, 3 (1988), 153–75 (164–166).

630 Dorwart, The Prussian Welfare State, p. 111.

4.4.2 The case for state-managed poor relief

The relocation of charity from the private to the public realm is not only a matter of keeping households financially viable but also a question of expertise: in Wolff's natural law, the 'right to beg', jus mendicandi, is reserved to the genuinely needy only. He differentiates between those who are not able to work or provide for themselves and those who would be technically speaking capable of labour. Charity, as Wolff repeatedly stresses, should only be dispensed to those with said right to beg; the able-bodied should be given a job or compelled to work.[631] In the light of this requirement, Wolff argues that sufficient resources are only one reason that makes public poor relief preferable to individual charity. The state is also better-equipped to tell the un- from the deserving beggar, to compel a mendicant to work and to punish illicit begging.[632] The decisive elements of his poor relief that speak for his own time are hence not only the central organisation and financing through the state but also the discrimination between different types of begging and the separate treatment of each category.

Wolff's separation of those who beg by necessity from those who beg by volition hits at the heart of a debate continuing from early poor relief movements of the church to secularised approaches. For the early church it was not poverty that posed a theological problem – it was wealth.[633] Monastic or mendicant orders, intent on the abandonment of worldly riches to achieve a truly Christian life, considered poverty one way of ensuring salvation, even where orders like the Benedictines preached spiritual rather than material asceticism.[634] In the dispensation of alms, the identity of a beggar or pauper was not immediately instrumental to the essence of the effort; in principle, therefore, the Catholic Church made no distinction between different kinds of beggars. With the reformation, this development originating with practical concerns gained ideological currency: Luther questioned the truthfulness of the motive behind church-organised charity, not only ideologically but also from the point of economic viability of such practices. According to him, unconditional poor relief not only supported but also attracted and hence created beggars. Furthermore, he questioned the purity of charitable giving where such an action was believed to have an impact on the donor's salvation: was it meant for the primary benefit to the charitable giver as a contribution to his or her eternal destiny, or genuinely focused on the person in need? In Luther's view, a Christian backed by the confidence of God's grace could and should do good on earth without ulterior motives.

Luther not only criticised the rationale behind the existing order but actively pushed for change in the practice of charity – and effectively the dismantlement of a

631 Wolff, Jus natura methodo scientifica petractata. Pars octava, §§ 736–737, p. 256.

632 Ibid., § 735 p. 256; 735 *nota*, p. 257; § 736 *nota*, p. 256.

633 Lindberg, Carter, *Beyond Charity*, p. 22.

634 Ibid., p. 25.

'thousand-year network of social welfare administered by religious orders ... in one fell swoop.'[635] In its place he sought to establish decentralised welfare institutions on a municipal level. By means of the new *Kirchenordnung*, church order, the dispensation of charity was effectively mandated to the local level, that is, to city councils and church parishes. Luther was called upon to provide a poor relief plan for the municipality of Leisnig. His model recommended the establishment of orphanages and support schemes for the elderly, chronically sick or homeless, including funds allocated to unemployed people to sponsor retraining and to support their families until they had found a new footing. These measures were financed through a community chest, income from church masses, the sale of church property and tax. The project in Leisnig became a model of 'structured generosity' for other Reformed territories in Germany where similar schemes were implemented.[636] The idea of sequestering 'deserving' from 'undeserving' beggar arose where the municipal mandate, decoupled from salvation but burdened with a practical responsibility, met with too many mouths to feed. With the increase in wayfaring – and often also violent – population after the crusades and the struggles of the reformation, begging and vagabondage became a social problem the towns increasingly struggled to keep in check. Discretionary giving was a means to solve this issue in numbers at least. The *Liber Vagatorum*, a treatise classifying beggars – re-issued with a new preface by Luther in 1528 'marked the starting point of systematic legislative measures directed against vagrancy and vagabondage in Germany.' Luther maintained that 'every town and village should know their own paupers – and assist them. But as to outlandish and strange beggars they ought not be borne with.'[637] Targeted poor relief combined with the suppression of unwanted mendicancy thus necessitated the gathering and use of information about these beggars – a new bureaucracy of knowledge.

Luther was not the only one to concern himself with the reorganisation of poor relief nor was the idea of discretionary charity confined to the Lutheran camp. A good counterexample is the humanist Juan Luis Vives; inspired by a sojourn in England, he decided to dedicate a treatise to the topic of poor relief, *De subventione pauperum sive de humanis necessitatibus*. Vives suggested that the public purse should be called responsible in this regard rather than consider poor relief, 'as it had been previously, an ecclesiastically approved corporal work of mercy.'[638] Divided into two parts, the treatise makes a case for the provision of the poor in general, followed up by a detailed and concrete set of recommendations directed at the Elders of the City of Bruges.

---

635 Torvend, 'Charity and Social Ethics', pp. 244–245.

636 Ibid., p. 246.

637 Dorwart, The Prussian Welfare State, p. 96.

638 Travill, A. A., 'Juan Luis Vives: The De Subventione Pauperum', *Canadian Bulletin of Medical History*, 4.2 (1987), 165–81 (166).

Vives sees the ideological foundation for poor relief grounded in the universality of Christian charity but dispensed by individual and municipal government, not the church. He preserves the right for the Christian individual to commit charitable deeds but simultaneously charges the institutional level as a direct stakeholder in social problems – poverty and pauperism, so Vives, are social problems in their own right but also fuel diseases, affecting larger swathes of society.[639] The core of this strategy is based on a stratification of different types of poverty, each category calling for a different approach, under the headline of man's god-ordained purpose to work for a living. People with full capacity to work should not be allowed to beg. In order to curb the numbers of those illicitly begging, a committee would be tasked to examine the state of the individual in question.[640] In that way the different groups of the needy would be adequately supported, impostors expelled and vagrants in good health given money to be sent on their way home. Beyond that, Vives also offered ideas for gainfully employing the impaired, suggesting simple manual labour for the blind, for example, rather than idly feeding them.[641] The insane, even if perhaps not put to work, should be treated with compassion and examined for possible recovery. Discernible in Vives, again, is the twin force of ideological backdrop and utilitarian argumentation.

Vives' shift from mercy, *misericordia*, in its own right to targeted munificence was not always kindly received. The Catholic Church was naturally unwilling to relinquish the domain of poor relief to state care. In that vein, the scholastic theologian Domingo de Soto's work 'In causa pauperum deliberatio' does not share Vives' trust in communal welfare but stresses that almsgiving is a matter of theologically inspired mercy, fuelled by the compassion arising from direct contact with the poor. Charity, de Soto stresses, should be unconditional and not confounded with moralising attitudes.[642] Other voices from the Catholic camp, such as the Spanish theologian Juan de Medina, challenged de Soto on this count. Yet although in agreement with Vives separating the un- from the deserving beggar he remained adamantly opposed to the idea of secularising the care for the poor.[643] Within Protestant ranks, attitudes also differed; as Torvend summarizes, where the alms box was the symbol of charity for the Catholic church, the Lutherans countered with the common chest – and Calvinists with the workhouse.[644] The questions at large were not only the source of finance and ranking the poor but also differing degrees of punitive measures. Moreover, the concept of the 'deserving' and 'undeserving' beggar was not merely a question of ability

---

639 Vives, Juan Luis, *De subventione pauperum sive de humanis necessitatibus libri II*, ed. by C. Matheeussen and C. Fantazzi (Leiden; Boston: Brill, 2002), pp. 88–95.

640 Vives, De subventione pauperum, pp. 95–99.

641 Travill, 'Juan Luis Vives: The De Subventione Pauperum', pp. 173–175.

642 Fantazzi, C., 'Introduction', in *De subventione pauperum sive de humanis necessitatibus libri II*, by Juan Luis Vives, ed. by C. Matheeussen and C. Fantazzi (Leiden; Boston: Brill, 2002), pp. ix–xl, p. xxvi.

643 Fantazzi, 'Introduction', p. xxvii.

644 Torvend, 'Charity and Social Ethics', p. 247.

but also locality: both Vives and Luther stress the necessity to care for local paupers whilst moving roaming beggars along. From an administrative perspective, discretionary poor relief presented not merely the spectre of assessment and distribution but a territorial dimension and the removal of people.

The issue therefore fluctuates between moral mandate of absolute charity and financial viability. The Catholic church as a large, extra-governmental and well-funded body with poor relief as a statutory function had a different stake in the issue than town councils and local parishes facing resource constraints. The problem, and this issue rings familiar in modern times, politically exacerbates if support for the needy is financed through public money. There is an inherent conflict of obligations at play: the Christian duty to help without reservation and the collective responsibility for financial prudence. Wolff solves this issue in logically moral terms by giving state and individual a mandate – in theory. The individual has a mandate to almsgiving, *eleemosyne*, but only in reference to the genuinely destitute; in case of doubt, however, it is better to give to an undeserving man than miss out on a person who is truly in need.[645] He thus positions himself somewhere between the Catholic idea of unquestioning assistance and the Protestant demand for a differentiated approach. Yet this proviso only exists in the *status naturalis* – in the *status civilis* of Wolff's natural law, the ruler has the right to decide over the *eleemosyne* of his subjects, so in spite of the moral mandate in theory, the individual is absolved from the question whatsoever. On the state level, then, discrimination is made between the able-bodied poor and the genuinely destitute. His institutional set-up mirrors this twin mandate: the *ptochotrophium* is a place where the poor are maintained who cannot provide for themselves, and who do not have relatives, families and friends to pick up the slack.[646] The *ergastulum*, however, is a workhouse for the able-bodied poor where they are put to work and to good use, in these very words.[647] Particularly the latter comment implies that the workhouse did not merely have a corrective function but a utilitarian one, that is, mobilising extra work force for the state.

Secularised poor relief might have started at the municipal level but migrated into the sphere of responsibility in the absolutist state before Wolff. Seckendorf translates similar policies into the ruler's realm of responsibility – meaning, centralised and more sweeping competencies coupled with additional sources of financing. Poor relief should be financed through tax and other forms of government

645 Wolff, Christian, *Philosophia moralis. Pars quinta*, §§. 393–394, pp. 535–537.

646 Wolff, *Jus naturae methodo scientifica pertractatum. Pars octava*, p. 257, § 738: '*Ptochotrophium* dicitur locus, in quo aluntur egeni, qui labore suo ea, quibus ad vitae necessitatem indigent, acquirere nequeunt, ac destituuntur cognatis, vel amicis, qui indigentiae ipsorum prospiciunt.'

647 Ibid., p. 256, § 737: '*Ergastulum* appellare lubet locum, in quo opus facere coguntur, qui cum laborare possint, mendicare malunt...; *in Rep. instituenda sunt ergastula, & in iis ad laborem adigendi, qui, cum laborare possint, mendicare malunt.*'

income.[648] Here, too, deliberate idleness and begging, is to be forbidden. Far from a literary spectre, the legislative reality of the seventeenth and eighteenth century showed how the state had centralised and concentrated poor relief on the ground: both with regards to almsgiving as also punitive measures of wilful mendicants and eviction of begging strangers. In Prussia, legislation to reduce begging had been in place since the 16th century, but the attempt to organise the poor relief through the state rather than municipal government came at the end of the seventeenth century. Frederick William resumed his programme of penal legislation of wayfarers after the Thirty Years War, issuing edicts in 1670, 1672, 1682 and 1684, insisting on the outlawing and deportation of 'gypsies', as a term presumably inclusive of a whole range of 'thieving and robbing' people.[649] With the help of the rural police, these undesirable elements were to be taken to the state borders to quite literally evict them, a policy that proved no more than mildly successful. In addition, the 'manufacturing edict' of March 1687 established prisons, spinning houses and correction facilities for 'idle, loose or unmarried women as well as beggars capable of work', which may have been effective against the bout of poverty but presumably less so against criminal wayfarers.[650] The Pietist influence on state poor relief was manifest in the personalia chosen to run the 'Permanent Commission for Poor Relief', founded in April 1699, and converted into a 'Directory for the Poor' in 1703: it included the prominent Pietist Philip Jakob Spener, who was put in charge of the anti-poverty program.[651]

Frederick William I's efforts were increasingly directed towards establishing harsher and harsher measures against vagabonds, quacks, gipsies, and other roaming mendicants. The king was, in fact, known for an unrelenting, Calvinist attitude in the matter, as Gagliardo illustrates: '[t]he symbol of his reign was not the sceptre, but the heavy walking-stick he carried, with which on more than one occasion he pounded the unfortunate persons of able-bodied beggars, idlers or drunkards he turned up during frequent walking tours of his capital.'[652] The king's tough love for his subjects was supported by utilitarian arguments from learned circles as well. Justus Nipperdey quotes a passage from the pastor Johann Peter Süssmilch's demographic work that soberly demonstrates the political pragmatism behind poor relief. Süssmilch had been an active member of the Royal Directorate of the Poor with the

---

648 Seckendorf, *Christen-Stat*, II.XIII. § 1, pp. 433–434: 'Aus dem Christenthum oder der Christlichen Liebe fliesset die Vorsorge bey Gottesfürchtigen Regenten/daß die Unterthanen bey ihrer Nahrung und Gewerbe das Auskommen und alle mögliche Beförderung haben & und ihre Anzahl sich eher vermehre/als vermindere/weil auff der Menge wohlgenehrte Leute der grösseste Schatz des Landes besteht/und dazu zielet nicht allein der eusserliche Friede/und die Mässigkeit der Obrigkeitlichen Macht/in Einbringung der Gefälle/Steuren/Schatzungen/Contributionen und Anlagen.'

649 Dorwart, The Prussian Welfare State, pp. 98–99.

650 Ibid.

651 Ibid., 101.

652 Gagliardo, Germany under the Old Regime, p. 304.

responsibility to look after the sick and destitute of Berlin. His defence of poor relief and medical care shows not a gleam of Christian charity. As Nipperdey quotes: '[i]f "we" – meaning the propertied classes as well as the state as a whole – want to enjoy the benefits of the existence of the poor, that is, the product of their labouring hands, "we" have to look after them. Without the workers the manufactories would stand still. Therefore, "we" must not let them become too poor, because they will be weak and die even in salubrious times.'[653]

This attitude to poor relief – as a prevention of economic loss to the state – clearly suited the king's purpose and is reflected in Wolff's description of workhouses, *ergastula*, specifically for his locale, *apud nos*: as a place where able-bodied mendicants are put to work and where 'people of no use are being corralled and forced to work so that they may become more useful.'[654] The state effort to put all idle labour to action also informs Wolff's policy to *supply* work to the able-bodied unemployed.[655] The objective is the mobilisation of additional work force rather than an altruistic motive. Wolff, in that context, may be strongly coloured by his socio-political – starkly Protestant – environment and not provide the supra-confessional account he is vowing to give. Even so, simply the personalia involved in Prussia's state-organised poor relief imply – Calvinist rulers and Lutheran administrators – that the ideological basis may have been fluid; the utilitarian grounds, however, shared.[656] The pre-Enlightenment rationalisation of social welfare might have been driven by financial scarcity, but the nascent realisation of the economic benefit for Prussia's increasingly centralised economy provided its own stimulus for poor relief programmes in the eighteenth century. Where social welfare had been a concern of the Catholic church for its own, and for salvation's, sake, people like Luther and Vives identified its central importance for the health of the municipal community. On a state level, finally, the utility of labour, and especially cheap labour, gives new purchase to the organisation of poor relief and Wolff's natural law evidently pays witness to that paradigm shift. A glimpse of the Christian legacy is still visible in the thematisation of *eleemosyne*. Yet the concept of genuine charity is swiftly removed from the individual sphere and mandated to the better-equipped and -informed state: a 'natural obligation' to the ruler, with the ulterior motive of economic benefit.

---

653 Nipperdey, Justus, 'Johann Peter Süssmilch: From Divine Law to Human Intervention', *Population*, 66.2 (2011), 611–36 (625).

654 Wolff, *Jus natura methodo scientifica petractata. Pars octava*, § 737 *nota*, p. 257: 'Ceterum usus ergastulorum apud nos etiam hic est, ut homines nullius frugis in ea detrudantur, & ibidem opus perficere cogantur, donec ad meliorem frugem redierint.'

655 Wolff, Jus naturae methodo scientifica pertractatum. Pars octava, §§ 736–7, p. 256.

656 Sigrun Kahl, for example, interprets the differences in modern welfare regimes as specific confessional legacies. Her analysis treats Calvinist and Lutheran approaches as separate, which would not have been the case in Prussia, as shown. See Kahl, Sigrun, 'The Religious Roots of Modern Poverty Policy: Catholic, Lutheran, and Reformed Protestant Traditions Compared', *European Journal of Sociology*, 46.1 (2005), 91–126 (112).

4.5 Public Health

4.5.1 Keeping the healthy healthy

Wolff's public health programme, similar to his poor relief, has a twofold purpose: providing the basic necessities for citizens in good health; and a set of institutions catering to the seriously ill. The main thrust of the programme spells preventative measures in form of a regulatory regime for medical practitioners. Conversely, two factors central to a modern view of healthcare are touched upon surprisingly lightly: medical research and hospitals.

As becomes clear at closer observation, one central problem of health care in the eighteenth century was that the medical profession itself suffered from a lack of public trust. In the absence of scientific certitude in the field of medicine, the available means boil down to market regulation and social control. The European Enlightenment had a divided view on how medical research should progress, empirically or theoretically – and Wolff's reticence in his natural law on matters of obvious importance seems symptomatic of his own position in the debate.

Wolff's *Oeconomica*, compared to his predecessors, keeps information on practical medicine very sparse. The works of Coler and Florinus contain a wealth of information on household remedies, physical as much as financial necessity, so as to keep expensive doctors away. They cover symptoms and remedies for specific illnesses affecting adults and children, discuss interference of supernatural creatures and specific provisions for pregnant women. For these authors care and cure is evidently a private concern – and there is no indication that the state or body politic carries an obligation towards the individual's state of health. Wolff's *Oeconomica*, in comparison, excels with an almost absolute lack of information on curing or healing. This does not mean that corporeal matters were not important; in fact, the natural obligation of the individual to look after his or her health is explicitly demonstrated.[657] But rather than making a practical appearance in the *Oeconomica*, the preservation of health is translocated from the family realm to the state sphere as a mandate to the *rector civitatis*. The image that presents itself is of an increasing professionalisation of the field of medicine as a sphere of care and regulation.

Coler's *Oeconomia* communicates something poignant about the state of medicine that, in its practical guise had not changed much to the days of Wolff. Whilst practical solutions at a household level fed from a mixture of experience, practice and superstition, medicine at an academic, professional level still followed two trends: the Galenic or the Theophrastian school.[658] Moreover, in the eighteenth century an

---

657 Wolff, Jus naturae methodo scientifica pertractata. Pars prima, § 393, p. 258.

658 Coler, *Oeconomia ruralis*, p. 3: 'Weil aber zweyerley Ertzte heute zu Tage seyn/als Galenisten und Theophrastiner/so solte man auch hier anzeigen/wie man etliche Arzneyen auff Galenische/etliche

education in medicine was still largely based on canonical literature, not empirical knowledge; in fact, medical training as a largely textbook-based exercise had not changed much since the middle ages. Central to the discipline were the 'institutes of medicine', composed of five subject areas: physiology, pathology, semiotics, therapeutics, and dietetics', later also botany and chemistry.[659] In the absence of practical training, 'the definition of the physician turned on his erudition as much (and perhaps more) as it did on his performance at the bedside', so Mary Lindemann – although the growing emphasis on 'medicine at the bedside' would transform medical education throughout the eighteenth century.[660] Around 1750 still, however, doctors were considered part of the learned class, alongside the clergy and jurists; they carried a social distinction less derived from their practical function as healers than their 'shared experience of a humanist education' stressing 'broad familiarity with ancient culture, an immersion in Latin and cultivation of the dignified bearing and eloquence of an educated man.'[661] In the *Oeconomica*, Wolff betrays his knowledge and interest in practitioners and empirical studies beyond this classical curriculum, citing contemporary scientists like William Harvey and Daniel Sennertus. Their works are not explored from a practical perspective though; they are used to corroborate Wolff's views on anatomy that in turn support moral arguments. Wolff's musings about the womb, concocted from Malebranchian philosophy, Harveyan anatomy and Chinese custom, betray that at his time medicine was anything other than a discrete discipline with methodological boundaries. What is more so, as Wolff laments, the field was still subject to woeful obfuscation, as even famous doctors would admit. Some have tried to lead it to 'mathematical certainty' but given how Wolff communicates the putatively unsuccessful status of this endeavour, it is clear that he himself has not found a way either – which would disqualify the discipline from his system *per se*.[662] It thus seems a logical consequence that Wolff does not elaborate much on practical medicine in the *Oeconomica*. In the abstract, however, private and public health remain an ethical concern enshrined in Wolff's philosophy. Self-preservation is a duty towards God.[663] Conversely, the ruler of a state has the mandate to 'conserve and restore' the health of his subjects.[664] Yet this duty is not of purely moral make but builds

aber auf Theophrastische weise zurichten solte/so darff ich mich doch nit zu weit ins Feld begeben/weil ich kein Medicus bin/und nit mehr von der Medicina schreiben und sagen kan/dann was ich fast wie ein ander Empiricus nur gesehen und erfahren habe/...'.

659 Lindemann, Mary, *Medicine and Society in Early Modern Europe* (Cambridge: Cambridge University Press, 1999), pp. 96–97.

660 Ibid., p. 97.

661 Bromann, Thomas, 'Rethinking Professionalization: Theory, Practice, and Professional Ideology in Eighteenth-Century German Medicine', *The Journal of Modern History*, 67.4 (1995), 835–72 (841).

662 Wolff, Jus natura methodo scientifica petractata. Pars octava, § 717 nota, p. 249.

663 Wolff, Philosophia moralis. Pars quarta, § 187, p. 241.

664 Wolff, Jus natura methodo scientifica petractata. Pars octava, § 715, p. 248.

on the proviso that sick people are not very productive; preserving subjects' health hence automatically suggests safeguarding the state's prosperity.[665] Private health a duty to individual, public health a mandate to the state, the argument differs significantly from the pledge of modern welfare states proclaiming health a universal right to each citizen the cost of which should be borne by society.[666]

The policies Wolff suggests in support of this mandate rely on a mixture of market regulation and economic intervention. Starting with food and drink, the ruler should prohibit the sale of insalubrious foodstuffs and the regulation of beer-brewing and winemaking but also curb indirect threats to health such as inordinate working hours.[667] Intervention extends to medical practice as a professional field as well. To ensure that citizens have all the means to stay healthy, the prices for medications are to be kept in check and affordable; moreover, the state needs to cater to an abundance of personnel – medics and surgeons, essentially – in the country. Although the role of professional doctors is essential to this plan, Wolff maintains an ambiguous relationship to the medical profession. He quotes Friedrich Hoffmann (1660–1742), professor of medicine in Halle, on the occasion: if you want to stay healthy, stay away from the doctors.[668] Although often the case, Wolff admits, this is not altogether true – and the key to the problem is to sift out those medics that are inexperienced and harmful. Only doctors with proper training should be allowed to practice their profession, following the proviso that a bad doctor does more harm than good.[669] The illegalisation of quackery pays implicit discredit to the propagation of home remedies as untested, unlicensed forms of healing, in tune with a paradigm shift of the period.[670] Public concern more than private affair, the Wolffian scenario casts medicine as a professionalised field, and the government's task in the provision and regulation of

665 Ibid., § 715 *nota*, p. 248.

666 De Renzi, Silvia, 'Policies of Health. Diseases, Poverty and Hospitals', in *The Healing Arts. Health, Disease and Society in Europe, 1500–1800*, ed. by Peter Elmer (Manchester: Manchester University Press, 2004), pp. 136–65, p. 136: 'Health is now recognised, at least in most European countries, as a universal right and many agree that its costs should be met by society as a whole and not just by those who are sick.'

667 Wolff, Jus natura methodo scientifica petractata. Pars octava, § 716, p. 248; § 720, p. 250.

668 Ibid., § 717 *nota*, p. 249: '...ita ut etiam Hoffmannus noster, qui praeclarum inter sui ordinis viros nomen adeptus, pro conservanda sanitate dudum hanc regulam praescripserit: Fuge medicum & medicinam, si vis esse sanus.'

669 Ibid., § 717 *nota*, p. 249.

670 Risse, Guenter B., 'Medicine in the Age of Enlightenment', in *Medicine in Society: Historical Essays*, ed. by Andrew Wear (Cambridge: Cambridge University Press, 1992), pp. 149–96, p. 154: 'Previous self-sufficiency in treatment based on superstition or lack of knowledge was to be transformed into dependence on qualified physicians and surgeons. From a superior knowledge about bodily processes in health and sickness to familiarity with measures for the prevention of epidemics, from expertise in individual wellness programmes to responsibility for care in hospitals and dispensaries, a new medical elite took charge and increasingly played a more prominent role in European society.'

the people involved in that field, not teaching subjects to care for themselves. And since the health of a body politic could not rely on self-medication anymore, professional education was to play a crucial role. A licensing regime should disqualify untrained persons from practicing as doctors; teaching institutions should only be staffed with professors with actual experience in their subject – albeit what kind of experience is not clear.[671]

The regulation of practical medicine was indeed a hot topic at Wolff's time. A number of dissertations submitted at German universities up to the middle of the eighteenth century highlight the regulation of food hygiene, alcohol abuse, contagious diseases, hospital conditions and inexperienced medical personnel as focal points for princely intervention, such as e.g. Conrad Berthold Behrens' *Medicus legalis oder Gesetzmässige Bestell- und Ausübung der Artzney-Kunst*, for example, who shares Wolff's concerns.[672] Given that universities clearly concerned themselves with the question of public health, the regulations found in Wolff must be understood as commonplace discussion points of the academic debate. Wolff, in fact, inspired parts of this discourse. He is mentioned by J.W. Baumer (1719–1788) on the matter of public health, legal medicine and animal medicine and by Wolfgang Rau's treatise who picks up Wolff's twin mandate to not only care for the sick but also the healthy, lamenting that 'the misuse of medicine by untrained persons is as harmful as the discovery of gunpowder'.[673] The idea that healthcare warranted the protection of the population from inexperienced or bad medics was clearly not an isolated opinion. On the political level this posed the problem that while the state relied on doctors to cater to the health of private citizens, the profession was not considered *a priori* trustworthy.

The practice of licensing presented a compromise for this situation, not just in the German territories, but also in France. Jean-Baptiste Colbert (1619–1683) had already established licensing regimes for practitioners, control of medicinal supplies and their prices, considered public sanitation concerns in urban planning and the promotion of education and research with regards to medical knowledge.[674] Yet there was an important difference between the German states and France, regarding the bureaucracy of staffing: in France, medical officers were attached to guilds and colleges; in Germany, the government provided salaried doctors in town and country, *Stadt- und Landarzt*, whose practice included both private patients and public service. These kinds of medical officers had existed before, albeit by municipal appointment. In the course of the eighteenth century, the shift from municipal to state level admin-

671 Wolff, *Jus natura methodo scientifica petractata. Pars octava*, § 717 *nota*, p. 249: 'Huc etiam pertinet, ne Professores Medicinae instituantur, qui nec ipsi satis intelligunt ea, quae alios docere debent, nec artem salutarem exercuerunt, destituti ea experientia, quae in Professore medicinae utique requiritur.'

672 Rosen, 'Cameralism and the Concept of Medical Police', pp. 37–38.

673 Ibid., p. 39, 41.

674 Dorwart, The Prussian Welfare State, p. 239.

istration was completed, and the local doctors were now appointed by and serving the state.[675]

The expertise for this level of medical policing was provided by centralised institutions, particularly so in Prussia. A first decisive step was Elector Frederick William's *Collegium medicum*, established in 1685. The board was the outcome of a development starting with a petition by a number of court physicians in Berlin in 1661 – first with the intention to protect the corporate interests, before an edict of 1685 expressly enlisted it in an effort to put public health under state control.[676] The medical board sought to establish firmer control over medical practitioners in the country, through licensing regimes, managing caps on fees and prices, issuing codes on professional conduct and supervision of pharmacies.[677] With the intention of establishing some order and control over the field of applied medicine, it actually ended up entrenching the hierarchical status of university-trained doctors even more, vis-à-vis personnel trained through practice. True to its origin as a lobbying effort, the board and its eventual offspring usually consisted of physicians, with midwives, surgeons or apothecaries in advisory positions at best. As a hierarchy keen to preserve itself, these institutions further perpetuated the bookish approach to medical training.[678] Conversely, the roster of duties of the state-employed town and country doctors, *Stadt- und Landärzte*, expanded significantly beyond the initial range of tasks of caring for the poor, testifying in court cases, monitoring public hygiene and advisory roles in epidemics. The expansion of duties now included substantial information gathering, such as the collection of information about diseases, demographic information like birth and death rates and, as mentioned, all-encompassing supervision of healing practices.[679] More recent opinions testify to the efforts of the state but note that the implementation of this regulatory regime was often hampered by socio-economic realities *in situ*. As Silvia de Renzi notes, 'the role of the *physicus* was in fact constrained by a complex web of competing authorities and vested interests – local communities, notables, physicians, other practitioners and representatives of the state. It was in this intricate and multi-layered social and political system, rather than in an ideal 'enlightened' political arena, that health politics were formulated and implemented.'[680] As Thomas Bromann further explains, the supervisory *physici*, embedded in local communities, depended to some degree on the collaboration with the practitioners they were sup-

675 Brockliss, Laurence William, 'Organization, Training and the Medical Marketplace in the Eighteenth Century', in *The Healing Arts. Health, Disease and Society in Europe, 1500–1800*, ed. by Peter Elmer (Manchester: Manchester University Press, 2004), pp. 344–81, p. 350; see also De Renzi, Silvia, 'Policies of Health', p. 161.
676 Dorwart, The Prussian Welfare State, p. 240.
677 Ibid., p. 243.
678 Bromann, 'Rethinking Professionalization', p. 860.
679 De Renzi, Silvia, 'Policies of Health', p. 161.
680 Ibid., p. 161.

posed to regulate; the expanded mandate in the eighteenth century was rarely matched by a pay rise to render them financially independent of bedside practice, which 'put them in the awkward situation of being neither fully bureaucratic agents nor fully local healers.'[681]

Public health measures at Wolff's time still attested to a considerable interest gap between medicine applied and theoretical, simply in terms of hierarchy. In that sense, Wolff's vision of a central regulation of medical practice may reflect princely preferences more than the reality on the ground. His blueprint could be classified amongst the string of publications that saw the solution to public health issues in centralised governance but were presumably waging a war on paper against complexities persisting on the ground. Whilst the legitimacy of self-medication wanes in the face of professionalisation of medicine, one element in the new mandate to the local *physicus* still testifies to the overlap between public health and private care: pregnancy and the care for infants. It is telling that, in spite of the studied lack of medicinal information in the *Oeconomica*, a number of precepts regarding sexuality and the health of children survive: cues to judging fertility, the mandate for a mother to breastfeed, to avoid unhealthy food during pregnancy, and the warning not to expose children to overly strong influences, such as strong light or loud sounds.[682] Advice on pregnancy, fertility, and childcare might be found in traditional *Hausväterliteratur* but not forays into sex education or scientific accounts for an embryo's deformation. Those particular topics, however, are perfectly acceptable within a different discourse and its central concern: cameralist literature and its zeal for promoting population growth. Literature about the causes for deformations in newborn children can be found in the cameralist bibliography of Georg Heinrich Zincke (1692–1769) – a seemingly unexpected choice amongst a list of demographic treatises.[683] More egregiously, the Frankfurt-based writer Johann Michael von Loën (1694–1776) sees the ultimate key to growing the population in increasing the number of marriages with one *caveat* in mind: 'the prevention of biologically detrimental marriages'.[684] In cameralist discourse, therefore, neither the birth of disabled or deformed children nor marriage were considered a private matter but political issues they sought to address through legislation, and legislation of particularly pervasive kind, such as Loën's suggestion of a mandatory medical check prior to marriage. This is not dissimilar to Wolff's insistence on fertility as a necessary prerequisite for marriage and some simple guidelines to check it. Interventionist possibilities of the state were clearly limited on this particular point. Wolff seeks to solve these problems from a different direction: moral education through the *Oeconomica*.

681 Bromann, 'Rethinking Professionalization', pp. 852–853.

682 See e.g. Wolff, *Oeconomica*, § 218, p. 363; §. 222, p. 373; §. 234, p. 390.

683 Nipperdey, 'Johann Peter Süssmilch', p. 619.

684 Ibid., p. 622.

4.5.2 A priori medicine contra institutional innovation

Wolff's ideal of medicine as a science and his view on public health institutions are predictably interrelated. This is evident when comparing Wolff's suggestions to new developments in the eighteenth century in the field of collective medicine, specifically in the field of hospitals and responses to epidemics. Wolff's own view is wedded to a systematic, universalist idea of medicine. Vested in an academic tradition he steers clear from practice-informed approaches that started setting the scene in Prussia.

At Wolff's time hospitals would not have been considered a classic calling point for a 'normal' individual. Instead, true to their medieval beginnings, hospitals in Europe were charitable institutions caring for more than curing specifically the destitute: lepers, cripples, paupers, vagrants and other individuals living at the fringe of society.[685] More recent studies have tried to revise the notion that these institutions did not perform therapeutic functions; either way, the impression remains that hospitals were not intended for the population at large but only the destitute. As that, they performed a function of social control by containing people with contagious diseases and separating the mentally unwell out from the rest of society to care for them in both physical and spiritual respects.[686] Wolff's brief treatment of hospitals in his natural law has to be understood in that sense: he only mentions *nosocomia*, institutions intended for specifically poor people with health issues, and also infirmaries for veterans. These institutions count as a mandate to the state even though Wolff acknowledges the involvement of the Church in that matter. The overall impression is descriptive of reality more than prescriptive of an ideal; as it is, however, the very brief treatment of hospitals may also be due to the fact that Wolff explicitly reserves the topic for the *Politica*, not natural law – an endeavour cut short by his own gout.[687]

Amidst religiously motivated health care initiatives, secular efforts over public healthcare had had their precedents. Already in the late Middle Ages, with the growth and consolidation of cities, the sheer volume could not be met by the efforts of the church only. The citizenry stepped in to fill gaps, with joint charitable and practical perspectives. Having an uncontrolled agglomeration of poor people heightened the danger of diseases and epidemics, therefore posing a risk to the rest of the population. Moreover, public health institutions, such as the *nosocomia*, were de facto functioning as *ptochotrophiae*, as feeding institutions for the poor who, ill or not, could not provide for themselves. On one hand, therefore, the reduction and proper care for the poor would reduce the risk of widespread illness in the first place; in the second instance, separating the poor from the ill and creating appropriate institutions for either

---

685 Lindberg, *Beyond Charity*, pp. 150–151.

686 Ibid., pp. 59–60.

687 Wolff, *Jus natura methodo scientifica petractata. Pars octava*, § 740, p. 257. Judging from his publisher's epitaph, Wolff indeed died of gout. See Wolff, *Oeconomica*, p. 412.

would mean freeing up resources for the latter, as Vives suggested.[688] The distinction between these institutions is also defined in Wolff's natural law although he does not spend an egregious amount of time on either. He merely mentions the *nosocomium* as a place where specifically sick paupers receive medical care, the *ptochotrophium* as a facility to feed the poor.[689] Entirely absent from this brief treatment is their function as places for scientific research – and this, in fact, corresponds with the view of medicine that Wolff himself harboured: as a field explored through theoretical, universalist discourse fostered in universities more than empirical research. As it turns out, he was siding with the traditional academic position rather than emerging trends that were to determine the future of medicine.

At Halle university, prominent figures like aforementioned Friedrich Hoffmann, a professor of medicine in Halle, or his colleague Georg Stahl (1660–1734) presented systematic views of medicine that sought to derive therapies not from empirical research but universalist theories of the body.[690] Wolff's own approach was not purely mechanical, as was Hoffmann's, but his teleological idea of nature very much conforms to the trend of *a priori*, rationally deduced medicine. His German work on physiology clearly positions itself in the Galenic tradition by deriving any ideas about the structure of human organs from their function.[691] As his discussion of genitals in the *Oeconomica* betrays, his view on medicine considers the body part within the cosmos and each organ imbued with teleological meaning that informs the inquiry, rather than empirical study. Wolff does refer to scientists like Harvey who explored medicine by actually examining real bodies. Yet in the overall picture, a genuinely scientific rendering of medicine in Wolff's understanding would have relied on a systematic approach ultimately verified through *a priori* thinking, not mere pathology.[692] In that sense, he is wedded to the theoretical, system-based medicine of his time that seeks and fails to progress on certain issues for its endeavour to argue from one moving principle behind living organisms.[693] For all of Wolff's complaints of insufficient doctoral training, his own conception was stuck on the view that a breakthrough in medicine required a cerebral investment, not empirical research.

688 Vives, De subventione pauperum, pp. 100–5.

689 Wolff, Jus natura methodo scientifica petractata. Pars octava, § 738, p. 257

690 Risse, Guenter B., 'Medicine in the Age of Enlightenment', pp. 158–161.

691 Favaretti Camposampiero, Matteo, 'Bodies of Inference: Christian Wolff's Epistemology of the Life Sciences and Medicine', *Perspectives on Science*, 24.3 (2016), 361–79 (368).

692 Judging from the publisher's epitaph in the *Oeconomica*, Wolff indeed plan to write a systematic work on medicine after completing his system, the *Novum Systema Medicinae*. Wolff, Oeconomica, p. 412.

693 Wolff's systematic medicine was not an outlier but in tune with conceptions of dominant physicians in Halle at the time, such as aforementioned Friedrich Hoffmann or Georg Stahl (1660–1734); see Risse, 'Medicine in the Age of Enlightenment', pp. 158–9.

Ironically, it is yet again Halle where pioneering moves were made to bring more practice to the theory, an effort seemingly ignored by Wolff. In collaboration with Francke's *Stiftungen*, Johann Juncker established a *Collegium clinicum* with practical training which was to influence later developments in Berlin.[694] For Francke, the impulse to build an orphanage and later a medicinal facility came from the notion that unhygienic environments sprang from and contributed to social problems on a larger scale. In collaboration with professors and students from Halle university's medical faculty, Francke set up a small, makeshift hospital in a former cattle barn on the premises of the *Halle Anstalten*, offering consultation hours and dispensing free medicines to the poor. Out of this collaboration arose a practice of informal medical training that eventually was included in the regular curriculum of the medical faculty. With the growing popularity of the *Collegium* with both patients and students, Francke sought to capitalise on their presence on the premises to intervene on their spiritual behalf. This endeavour is reflected in the clinic's ample regulatory framework, inspired by Francke's school system using permanent monitoring and control.[695] The medical facilities of the *Anstalten* thus had a twin purpose apart from actual cure: training new doctors and moral betterment of the patients. Sadly, Halle's *Collegium medicum* was not to last long after its founder's death.[696]

Francke's efforts in Halle anticipated a development on the state level. The Prussian rulers indeed picked up and improved the infrastructure of hospitals, creating new specialised branches, training and research facilities. Originally the domain of the church, the oldest hospitals of Berlin dated back to the thirteenth century and were mostly serving the destitute, elderly and infirm.[697] The second half of the seventeenth century saw additional hospitals specifically for the Huguenot community, for lepers, and plague victims and even an institution, the Dorotheen-hospital, for impoverished foreigners, which was later converted into an insane asylum. One of the major hospitals in Berlin, the *Charité*, was originally set up as an isolation hospital in case the plague should strike – and since it did not, it was turned first into an infirmary for the military and a general hospital for Berlin's poor in 1726, renamed *Charité* in 1727. So far these developments would not differ greatly from the traditional conception of hospitals as harbours to the fringes. Yet in the end, the *Charité* also served as a centre for medical research and had a number of especially established wards to cater to venereal diseases, a maternal ward, and the infirm.[698]

These new developments are not reflected in Wolff's philosophy. Granted, his apparent disinterest in the mobilisation of hospitals for state-led research may simply

694 Lindemann, Medicine and Society in Early Modern Europe, p. 99.
695 Gawthrop, Pietism and the Making of Eighteenth-Century Prussia, pp. 171–2.
696 Bromann, 'Rethinking Professionalization', p. 846.
697 Dorwart, The Prussian Welfare State, p. 258.
698 Ibid., p. 259.

be due to a literary life cut short; as it is, it is not clear whether the *Politica* as he planned it would have gone into greater detail on the matter. The way how his traditionalist view on medicine impacts his view on collective health care, however, surfaces more clearly on another topic of great collective urgency: epidemics amongst men and animals. In the absence of medical know-how, social control was the only means to combat spread and devastation of the plague, one of the 'capital enemies of the state', as Wolff calls it.[699] It is the state's responsibility to avert them, where possible, and avoid further spread, both amongst men and animals – even though no medicinal cure was known.

Epidemics amongst humans and animals such as *Rinderpest*, cattle disease, were of devastating effect since they posed an existential threat to people's livelihood, as Wolff explains.[700] Keeping their spread to a minimum was not only a matter of health concern but fed into the debate of livelihood and hence population management. The spectre of *Rinderpest* haunted Prussia in the eighteenth century to a devastating effect, first in the 1720s to return in the 1740s and last for two decades.[701] The mortality rate of the cattle was over 90% and its extremely rapid spread spelled a devastating effect on the livelihood of the population. The causes of *Rinderpest* remained undiscovered until well into the 19th century, not for the want of trying. An investigation of Halle's *Collegium Sanitatis* had decided that 'as far as the origin of this epizootic goes, it is caused by nothing other than the poisonous hot and foul miasmas that coagulate in the nightly dew and spread on the grass and meadows where animals consume them.'[702] The general medical opinion on the real origins and research on vaccines only started around 1779, even though a breakthrough only happened in 1890. In the meantime, culling, i.e. killing livestock was the only means to prevent a spread; in fact, self-medication was outlawed by the Prussian government by 1803 who also sought to control the process of butchering and disposing of the carcasses.[703] Influx and spread of disease by import restriction, quarantine and towns affected were isolated by use of force, where necessary, in order to minimise any movement of people or animals.[704] These measures proved effective yet Wolff does not make mention of any of them – he merely decries scientific shortcomings in battling the disease.[705] In the absence of weapons to combat the disease, as he puts it, the state still has to try

699 *Wolff, Jus natura methodo scientifica petractata. Pars octava*, § 718, p. 249: 'Pestis inter hostes capitales dudum relata…'

700 Ibid., §§ 719 nota, p. 250.

701 Brantz, Dorothee, '"Risky Business": Disease, Disaster and the Unintended Consequences of Epizootics in Eighteenth- and Nineteenth-Century France and Germany', *Environment and History*, 17.1 (2011), 35–51 (37).

702 Ibid., p. 47.

703 Ibid., p. 48.

704 Dorwart, The Prussian Welfare State, p. 288–9.

705 Wolff, Jus natura methodo scientifica petractata. Pars octava, §§ 718–719, pp. 249–250.

all that is within his power to minimise the damage.[706] In this way, Wolff communicates that social control is merely a compromise, not a fully valid solution; the 'weapons' society would need are the scientific understanding of the disease and effective therapies. The case is somewhat similar with human epidemics, specifically, the plague. Wolff presents the problem in fairly dramatic terms: The plague is the republic's worst enemy; finding a cure is the eternal, impossible desideratum, the medicinal equivalent of squaring the circle, finding the length of the sea or building a perpetuum mobile.[707] Whilst casting the issue in fairly dramatic terms, customary – even effective – measures against the plague are never mentioned. It has to be remembered that epidemics not only depleted the population but also caused a psychological fallout in the population, down to a breakdown of social order – not without the help of common superstitions. As De Riva stresses, 'when confronted with the problem of how to make sense of the diseases of the past, including their prevention and cure, we still need to engage with the moral and religious codes of belief and practice that fundamentally shaped this earlier world.'[708] Coler's *Oeconomia* illustrates how rational approaches to the topic were easily intermingled with religious or even apocalyptic readings: the spread of epidemics, so Coler, is due to comets spreading poison when they expire.[709] An outbreak was a sign of Judgment Day approaching, hence pious people should not worry but pray and look forward to the day of salvation.[710] Alongside this apocalyptic reading, however, Coler identifies a number of very pragmatic predicaments for the authorities: to prevent the breakdown of social order, priests, medics and pharmacists are to stay put whilst the cities are put under quarantine whilst still provided with victuals and the pharmacies well-stocked to prevent not only disease but inflation.[711]

In North-Eastern Germany, the last major epidemic occurred 1709–1711, fuelled by the war between the Russians and the Swedish. The eventual disappearance of the plague from the region is a testament to Prussia's state policy which oversaw the introduction of a centralised policy to combat epidemics. The more immediate measures, implemented towards the end of the seventeenth century, largely consisted in the closing of borders and isolating local outbreaks. These measures saved Berlin and Brandenburg in the plague of 1709–11, complete with quarantines and

---

706 Ibid., 719 nota, p. 250: 'Quamdiu vero desunt arma, quibus Reip. insensus hostis prosterni & profligari potest; ea tentanda sunt, quae in potestate sunt, ne quid culpa nostra praetermittatur, quod ad minuendum nocumentum fieri poterat.'

707 Ibid., § 718, p. 250: 'Hactenus tamen problema hoc de peste e civitate proscribenda mansit insolutum, perinde ac problema de quadratura circuli, de lognitudine maris, de perpetuo mobili…, multumque vexavit & hodiernum vexat.'

708 De Renzi, Silvia, 'Policies of Health', p. 162.

709 Coler, *Oeconomia ruralis*, p. 282.

710 Ibid., p. 285.

711 Ibid., p. 286.

travel bans. The danger at the time though spurred Frederick I to issue an edict, titled 'A Regulation and a Medical Plan on What to Do in Connection with the Current Dangerous Occurrences of the Plague in Towns, Villages, and Hamlets', essentially a worst-case-scenario plan. In the case of an outbreak in the city, the public health directors there would be overseeing medical and auxiliary staff necessary to diagnose, treat and contain the disease. This 'plague personnel' would live in isolation from the rest of the population, spot outbreaks, treat infected people and bury the dead, disinfect dwellings, whilst imposing restrictions on public gatherings and other measures. The funds for their salaries as also food, shelter for dislocated people and provisions for the poor were to come out of the public pocket. The directive also sought to issue information to these emergency staff, educating them on how to recognise and treat the illness, by whatever medical standards ruled the day.[712] The dawning recognition was that the successful prevention of the disease depended on certain hygienic standards, as a list of ordinances issued by Friedrich Wilhelm II still maintains.[713] Yet at the time this recognition must have come without a scientific explanation to go with, let alone the methodological certainty Wolff was hoping for. Instead, his discussion of the matter closes with a slightly obscure affirmation: the reader should not assume, Wolff says, that he would suggest anything that would *not* be possible – in the absence of any suggestions.[714] Silence may not be a strong indicator for Wolff's position on the matter. Yet it is striking given the fact that the rise of empirical medicine noticeably started changing the hospital landscape and that social control had a proven track record in the battle against epidemics. If anything, Wolff's silence on the matter tacitly confirms that these developments have no real purchase in the view of a philosopher approaching medicine *a priori*. On another note, it shows that traditional schools still ruled the day.

4.6 Summary

'The welfare state is the institutional outcome of the assumption by a society of legal and therefore formal and explicit responsibility for the basic well-being of all its members', as per Harry Girvetz' definition.[715] From this definition already it is clear why Wolff's welfare state, grounded in moral, not legal obligation, maps existing tradi-

---

712 Dorwart, The Prussian Welfare State, p. 285–6.

713 Friedrich Wilhelm II, *Instruction für die Kreisdirectorien in den fränkischen* Fürstenthümern (Berlin: 1797), § 27: 'Die fürchterlichste epidemische Krankheit ist die Pest; sie ist die gefährlichste Quelle der Entvölkerung. In einem Lande, wo alle Reinlichkeitsanstalten vorgekehrt werden, ist sie nicht leicht möglich.'

714 Wolff, *Jus naturae methodo scientifica pertractatum. Pars octava*, § 718, p. 250: 'Absit itaque, ut tibi persuadeas in propositione praesenti praecipi talia, quae in potestate non sunt.'

715 Girvetz, 'Welfare State', p. 512.

tions more than marking the dawn of a new era. His natural law presents the consolidation of Christian ideas of governance with cameralist utilitarianism in a new rationalised framework. The old, religiously motivated duties of the ruler but are preserved but rationalised through natural law.

Looking at Wolff's welfare state as the end- rather than starting point of the evolution of welfare institutions helps to identify the elements specific to his own point in time and place. The centralisation of welfare functions, shifting their mandate from municipal shoulders to territorial government, was accompanied by a number of differences: different modes of financing, using taxes and the ruler's own possessions; different administrative bodies, i.e. government bureaucrats; and finally, a shift in ideology. This is particularly evident in the case of poor relief where the initial idea of 'charity', in fact, the Christian ideal of 'caritas', is point-blank replaced by Wolff with a state-financed mandate capping the direct relationship between normal, presumably Christian citizens and the needy. It is interesting in that regard that the relegation of charity is the response to another concern of medieval origin: the financial sustainability of a community's members. Within the context of the absolutist state, however, the stability and prosperity of the populace held the additional incentive – taxability. Specifically, Wolff's fledgling public health programme is wedded to the challenges of his own time, a period where the professionalisation and the promotion of scientific and empirically supported medicine was only just about dawning.

The matter of education is the one matter where Wolff egregiously diverges from the reality, which explains the chagrin of the Halle Pietists. The radical aspect of universalised education had been well-entrenched in Prussian state policy, but Wolff's replacement of the religious with a rationalist core genuinely spelled a departure from accepted notions. Yet again, this should be understood as the culmination of a rationalised form of Christian philosophy, not liberal ideology. Although education should be for everyone, the primary purpose is to mould good citizens, not good freethinkers.

All these aspects taken into account, Wolff's welfare programme is based on an ideology derived from the *bonum commune*, the common interest, rather than intrinsic rights of the individual. This means that the right to certain welfare provisions only arise from the obligations of the ruler, not the dignity of the individual. Secondly, this means that *jura connata*, preexisting and innate rights accruing to every human in the natural state are progressively curtailed in *status adventitius* and *status civilis* – or curtailed where it serves the common good. This should not be understood as a fresh invasion into the private sphere in the name of absolutism. Private morality was subjected to regulation in the name of the common good long before. In fact, in the face of the historical background, Wolff actually presents a modification of sweeping regulatory mandates. And although there is a reciprocity between private felicity and *bonum commune*, Wolff very overtly adjusts the intentionality of the household not to the reason of state but to the purpose of state: the common welfare.

5 Michael Hanov's completion of the Wolffian system

5.1 Introduction

This chapter uses a comparison between Wolff and Hanov to demonstrate that Wolff's methodological principles were not always clear to his contemporaries – even to those who studiously continued his work, like Hanov. The contrast between their contributions to one and the same philosophical system illustrates how their joint discourse about social and political frameworks is unwittingly coloured by each author's tacit sense of normality – and by vested stakes in their own living environment. This provides further evidence that Wolff's philosophy was informed by external but local impulses, in spite of its abstracted guise.

Christian Wolff had a number of known acolytes. Scholars like Johann Christian Gottsched (1700–1766) or Alexander Gottlieb Baumgarten (1714–1762) sought to explore scientifically unploughed fields such as poetry or concepts of beauty with the help of his method.

Curiously, Michael Hanov, who eventually completed the philosopher's unfinished system, was not a classic Wolffian himself, judging from his publication history. Still, when it comes to his work on that account, Hanov was generally assumed to be a 'strict follower of Wolff's, a scholar furnished with versatile knowledge, and promoter of this at that time wide-spread philosophy.'[716] A closer examination of his completion of Wolff's cycle provides a litmus test to this assumption – and further illustrates where each author's ideas about social and political life may be more closely wedded to reality and local discussion than to a theory shared between them.

In the preface to the second part of the *Oeconomica* Hanov states quite frankly that he had no specific relationship with the *beatus philosophus*. Neither related, acquainted nor fellow citizens, Hanov admits that he never encountered or corresponded with Wolff in person.[717] Judging from the preface, he was appointed upon

716 Prantl, 'Hanow, Michael Christoph', p. 525: 'Seine Hauptwerke aber bestehen in einer Fortführung und Ergänzung der Wolff'schen Philosophie, nämlich: "Oeconomia Wolffiana" (1755) und "Philosophia civilis sive Politica, tanquam continuatio systematis philosophi. Christiani Wolff" (4 Quartbände, 1756–59), seine "Philosophia naturalis sive Physica dogmatica tanquam contin. syst. philos. Chr. Wolff" (4 Quartbände, 1762–68), in welchen Schriften er sich als strenger Anhänger Wolff's und als ein mit vielseitiger Gelehrsamkeit ausgerüsteter Erklärer und Förderer dieser damals weit verbreiteten Philosophie zeigt.'

717 Hanov, *Oeconomica*, sig.)(3: 'Neque enim ulla mihi est peculiaris conjunctio cum *Beato Autore* systematis Philosophiae, de quo loquar: quippe quem nullo jure cognationis, affinitatis vel civitatis, ad me referre possum, quem numquam vidi nec audivi, cum quo nullu mihi intercessit literarum commercium.'

https://doi.org/10.1515/9783110714098-005

recommendation by friends, bringing his qualifications as a teacher and editor of many years to the table.[718] Predestined or not, Hanov ended up delivering the rest of the *Oeconomica*, the *Philosophia civilis* and the *Physica*, completing the system in tune with the programme laid out in the 'Discursus praeliminaris'. These works were published under Hanov's authorship but self-consciously present themselves as a continuation of Christian Wolff's system. It is clear from the title that Hanov meant to complete the project in a Wolffian spirit more than his own and that the work as a whole was to stand as one consistent intellectual effort. Hanov's preface illustrates the glory associated with writing a comprehensive, internally consistent philosophical system. In his view, it is not only unprecedented internationally – it also provides a stable footing of knowledge for generations to come.[719] Already the fact that Hanov picked up the task where Wolff left it highlights how vital the completion of the work was in its own right – in fact, the importance of the project and its completion exceeds the significance of authorship itself.[720] Indeed, the completion by Hanov seems to have been considered a valid fulfilment in the more immediate reception history.[721]

Hanov may not have met Wolff in person but showed demonstrable interest in his work for a number of reasons. On one hand, both authors have a considerable zeal for carrying knowledge into the world. What is more, both share the intention to use the German language for that purpose. In a work of 1734, the *Erläuterte Merkwürdigkeiten der Natur*, 'Natural phenomena explained', Hanov specifically references Wolff as one of the few scholars writing scientific works in the vernacular. Hanov here defends his own choice of language, against the fashion of German scholars writing in Latin to make their works as widely accessible as possible – citing the express wish of 'the famous Mr Wolff of Marburg...that more works of this kind would be written.'[722] Ironically, although Hanov wished to promote the German language on an academic level just as his predecessor did, it was Wolff's Latin cycle that he was to complete.

---

718 Ibid., sig.)(4.

719 Ibid., sig.)(2v.

720 The preface to the first volume of Hanov's *Politica* betrays that he bitterly regretted taking on what turned out a monumental task. See Hanov, Michael Christoph, *Philosophiae civilis sive politicae pars prima* (Halle: Renger, 1756), sig. b2.

721 Short appraisals of Hanov's *Oeconomica* can be found in literary journals of the time, see for instance von Windheim, Christian Ernst, *Philosophische Bibliothek, Vol 9* (Nuremberg: George Peter Monath, 1757), pp. 212–218; *Freymüthige Nachrichten Von Neuen Büchern, Und Andern Zur Gelehrtheit Gehörigen Sachen, Vol. 13* (Zurich: Heidegger & Co., 1756), p. 131. Roscher, about a century later, cites from Hanov's part as 'Oec. II', without mention of any author other than Wolff which implies that he considered the two parts equally valid. See Roscher, *Geschichte der National-Oekonomik in Deutschland*, p. 450.

722 Hanov, Michael Christoph, *Erläuterte Merkwürdigkeiten der Natur: nach denen Grund-Sätzen derer neuesten Physicorum* (Danzig: Knoch, 1737), sig. A5: 'Weßhalb der berühmte Herr Wolff in Marpurg in der Vorrede der jüngsten Thümmigischen Versuche wünschet, daß solcher Art Schrifften mehr möchten verfasset werden.'

In spite of these shared interests, the two authors' ideal of science and learning is fundamentally different. The same goes for their priorities in terms of content, as the two parts of the *Oeconomica* betray. Hanov's part picks up where Wolff had left it, midway through the section dedicated to the *societas paterna*. But where Wolff's *Oeconomica* largely amalgamates Florinus's and Seckendorf's concerns, Hanov's *Oeconomica continuata* is informed by a mix of the canonical literature on the subject and his own experiences. The text frequently refers back to classical works of *Oeconomica* literature, including Xenophon and the Pseudo-Aristotelian *Oeconomica*. Although Hanov is not intent on his own authorship, legitimacy is sought from the authority of previous authors, rather than probing an escape from tradition by means of method, as Wolff would have it. The topical split is not all that intentional; in fact, Hanov vows to 'conform my additions to the principles and the natural method of the author'. Yet, as he himself admits, he did not always 'satisfy his own expectations in fulfilling the order and deducing the precepts'.[723] At first sight, Hanov's completion seems to indeed conform to the previous author's ideas. But a closer inspection reveals that Hanov has different assumptions driving his style and method – and that the *Oeconomica* and the later *Politica* are informed by a different socio-political environment. Hanov's hometown Danzig identified as Prussian in ethnic terms but was officially part of the Polish-Lithuanian Commonwealth. This area of so-called 'Royal Prussia' that the city belonged to was part of the Polish constitutional monarchy and hinged on a very different political paradigm than Wolff's ducal Prussia. As Karin Friedrich describes it, 'Royal Prussia was a typical early modern nation of estates, orders and parliaments, deeply rooted in European constitutionalist traditions' – and in spirit not wedded to an absolutist ideology but 'clearly linked to the principle that a ruler must be bound to positive law.'[724] Unsurprisingly, Hanov's political theory betrays this different ideological stake, even if unwittingly. He begs to openly differ where he does; in reality, his discourse departs from Wolff's path much more frequently and, as it seems, unintentionally. The following offers a short survey of Hanov's own scholarly convictions to then compare *Oeconomica* and welfare solutions in his *Politica* to Wolff's own work in order to show up just where the two authors agree or diverge.

723 Hanov, *Oeconomica*, sig.)()(2: 'Caeterum conatus quidem sum, conformare mea additamenta autoris praeceptorum principiis & methodo naturali; quod vero illud, uti volui, assequutus sim; id qui negaverit, a me non dissidebit. Neque enim mihi semper satisfeci tum in ordine concinnando, tum in deducendis praeceptis.'

724 Friedrich, Karin, *The Other Prussia: Royal Prussia, Poland and Liberty, 1569–1772* (Cambridge: Cambridge University Press, 2000), p. 9.

5.2 Hanov: From independent scholar to wavering Wolffian

5.2.1 Hanov's intellectual background

Like Wolff, Hanov was a polymath whose multifarious interests wind their way through his career path. Born 1695 in Zamborst, he studied in Danzig and Leipzig, enrolling for theology before switching to law, apparently on account of his weak memory.[725] After graduating, Hanov worked as a house teacher in Dresden and then Danzig before being appointed as a professor of mathematics and philosophy at the gymnasium there. His literary activity within this time was not restricted to his official faculty: Hanov published books of philosophical, theological, agrarian, mathematical and jurisprudential content, writing for academic and also lay audiences. Amongst his books are scholarly works written in Latin and also a number of treatises and works written in German, such as the *Erläuterte Merkwürdigkeiten der Natur* in 1734, the *Entwurf der Erfindungskunst, als der Vernunftkunst erster Abschnitt* in 1738 with a sequel in 1739, or his history of the Culmian law, the *Jus Culmense* in 1745.[726] Hanov thus actively made good on the new enthusiasm for the vernacular as a means to spread knowledge to new audiences. Unlike Wolff, however, Hanov did not develop or employ a uniform method throughout his works nor did he aspire to. The *Erläuterte Merkwürdigkeiten*, for example, a treatise on natural and physiological phenomena, is written in a narrative style framing his explanations of natural phenomena. A little fiction of 'Mr Frosty' and 'Mr Bear-Up' is used to illustrate human bodies' responses to cold temperatures in different environments.[727] Where Wolffian pedagogy uses infallible logic inculcating the mind with truths, Hanov conveys knowledge by playfully capturing the reader's attention. Yet it is not just the didactic method but also the heuristic approach where the two authors overtly differ. Apart from an early experiment on planting wheat, Wolff sought out science in the abstract, separate from what he termed 'historical knowledge', that is, facts and deeds in the here and now. Hanov, in contrast, made a name for himself conducting numerous practical experiments, apart from enduring efforts to promote and explain the history of Prussia to a broader audience.[728]

Hanov's *Entwurf der Lehrkunst*, or 'sketch of pedagogy', the sequel to the *Vernunft-Kunst* as the theory of cognition, lays out his official approach to teaching. Here a parallel between the two authors' ideas becomes clear – at least in theory. Hanov directly references Wolff's *Logica* with the proposition that we seek out correct statements and explanations either for the sake of furthering our own knowledge or improving that of

725 'HANOV, MICHAEL CHRISTOPH', in: Meusel, Johann Georg, *Lexikon der vom Jahr 1750 bis 1800 verstorbenen teutschen Schriftsteller* (Leipzig: Fleischer, 1805), Vol 5, pp. 135–139 (135).

726 Ibid., pp. 135–139.

727 See Hanov, Erläuterte Merkwürdigkeiten der Natur, f. B.

728 Meusel, Lexikon der vom Jahr 1750 bis 1800 verstorbenen teutschen Schriftsteller, p.139.

others.[729] Finding and explicating truth is very much the same process, he says, and goes on to lay said process out in detail in the following paragraphs. The borrowings from Wolff are unmistakeable. The *criterium veritatis* and *falsitatis*, in Wolffian fashion, is the identification of non- or contradiction of a statement; falsities have to be weeded out or have to be examined more closely to see 'whether 1. the main subject is possible and 2. the relationship expressed with the predicate/side subject is clearly expressed in the main subject and unambiguously determined by it'.[730]

The adoption of Wolff's truth criterion did not translate into the same methodological unity; Hanov, it seems, acknowledged the poignancy of logic within the context of heuristics but not as a sole method of science or teaching across the board. In fact, Hanov's *Lehrkunst* differentiates between history and systematic philosophy as educational means. History cultivates the description of facts, deeds, that is particulars, whilst didactic books purport knowledge in general terms. The former, so Hanov, is easier to understand and a useful way of passing on knowledge, and even though content should be guided by logic and method, the writing of scientific textbooks is an entirely separate matter.[731] The two approaches need not be mutually exclusive; in fact, a print emblem in the last edition of Hanov's *Jus Culmense* places the books of both Pliny and Euclid at the base of Danzig's coat of arms, suggesting a fruitful coexistence of either branch of learning.[732] Yet even where his works are written in a more systematic style than the prose in *Erläuterte Merkwürdigkeiten*, and conform to a more conventional scholarly format structuring the content into paragraphs, Hanov steers clear of applying a geometric method, as was the vogue amongst seventeenth and eighteenth century philosophers like Wolff. Rather, to Hanov method is not universal but dependent on subject matter: a treatise on the impossibility of squaring the circle is self-consciously based on syllogistic *a priori* arguments, where other works of historical content or treatises on natural phenomena resort to descriptive prose.[733]

The two authors' approaches to knowledge have to be seen within their respective lifetime trajectories. Wolff's zeal for developing a scientific method was inspired by a political conundrum of his own time: the rift between Catholics and Protestants over

---

729 Hanov, Michael Christoph, *Entwurf der Lehr-Kunst, aus der Vernunft-Kunst, anderer Abschnitt* (Danzig: Schreiber, 1740), § 222, p. 193.

730 Hanov, *Entwurf der Lehr-Kunst*, § 224, p. 193; § 230, p. 198: 'Oder man muß sehen, ob 1. der Hauptbegriff möglich und 2. das ausgedruckte Verhältnis desselben zum Nebenbegrif aus dem Hauptbegrif klar erhelle und unwidersprechlich bestimmet werden könne, oder nicht. Läßt sich das Verhältnis durch den Hauptbegrif, wie er hier angegeben ist, unwidersprechlich bestimmen, ist der Satz wahr...'.

731 Ibid., § 93, p. 189.

732 Hanov, Michael Christoph, *Jus Culmense ex ultima revisione, oder Das vollständige Culmische Recht*, (Danzig: Johann Friedrich Bartels, 1767), p. vii.

733 See e.g. Hanov, Michael Christoph, *Impossibilitas quadraturae circuli a priori adserta* (Danzig: Schreiber, 1741); Hanov, Michael Christoph, Hanov, Michael Christoph, *Seltenheiten der Natur und Oekonomie*, ed. by Johann Daniel Tietz, 3 vols (Leipzig: Lankisch, 1753).

theological issues and its social and political ramifications. Hanov is at least as publicly minded, yet his surroundings spell a different political objective – and he responds with different intellectual approaches. Confessional differences do not seem to be the stimulus behind Hanov's intellectual activities; indeed, the Polish-Lithuanian Commonwealth Danzig might have been dominated by Catholics but under the guise of relative religious tolerance.[734] Rather, his publishing history implies a twin concern: securing and supporting Danzig's traditional privileges within the Commonwealth through historical studies; and contributing to the promotion and dissemination of practical knowledge. Hanov's stake in history corresponds with a long-standing tradition of his own intellectual breeding ground. The Gymnasium celebrated the study of past with a view to the present, highlighting in particular the origin of the economic and political standing of Danzig in comparison to other Polish cities. The seventeenth and eighteenth century in particular witnessed Danzig's scholars turning to the study of Polish history in an attempt to instrumentalise it for the vocational education of young people preparing for their roles as merchants, city administrators and advisors to the Polish king.[735] The city had a strong incentive to keep historical memory alive: the city's prosperity and political stability was the direct consequence of its trade prerogatives and municipal self-governance, exceptional in comparison to other cities in Poland. These privileges had been granted by Poland's rulers to a string of cities in the 13th century in an attempt to spur immigration of chiefly German-speaking colonists so as to reverse the devastating effect of the Mongol raids.[736]

The continued stress on historical legacy at Hanov's time would have arisen from the peculiar socioeconomic positioning of Danzig within the Polish-Lithuanian Commonwealth. The city, whose port was estimated to process over 90% of Poland's exports in the eighteenth century, was chiefly inhabited by a Protestant merchant class. The German traders had no part in the legislative process unlike the nobility, the *szlachta*, who was in turn barred from trading by threat of losing privileges. Vested in agricultural trade and wanting to keep prices of imported goods down, the *szlachta* used their power to the significant detriment of the merchant classes.[737] The German-populated cities had a significant stake in cultivating the study of history so as to be able to call upon their historically enshrined rights.

734 Stone, Daniel, *The Polish-Lithuanian State, 1386–1795* (Seattle: University of Washington Press, 2001), p. 214.

735 Mokrzecki, Lech, Studium z Dziejów Nauczania Historii: Rozwój Dydaktyki Przedmiotu w Gdańskim Gimnazjum Akademickim Do Schyłku XVII w. (Gdansk: Zakład Narodowy imienia Ossolińskich, 1973), p. 201.

736 Roczniak, Władysław, 'Clashing Functions/Clashing Elites Negotiating Hospital Functions in Pre-Modern Poland (13th-18th Centuries)', *The Polish Review*, 51.3/4 (2006), 283–305 (291).

737 Klimesz, Henryk, 'Poland's Trade through the Black Sea in the Eighteenth Century', *The Polish Review*, 15.2 (1970), 55–80 (55–59).

Hanov's own self-consciously methodical approach to history was not unprecedented in Danzig. It was, in fact, Keckermann who left a powerful legacy a century before, introducing systematic approaches to historiography. Keckermann believed the writing of history to be a matter of method more than oratory: just like logic was not wont to expand unnecessarily, exaggerate or make use of rhetorical artifice, a historian should not invent, embellish or expand on sources beyond an executive summary. By keeping to these precepts, a methodical, self-evidently true account of history would be possible.[738] In Keckermann's view, history really was a discipline in support of practical philosophy, specifically political prudence. Scholars closer to Hanov's time, prominently Gottfried Lengnich (1689–1774), shifted their focus from political events to the history of jurisprudence. Across the stretch of time from Keckermann to Lengnich, however, most of these efforts were aimed at creating a sense of civic responsibility and political belonging amongst the Danzig populace, fostering allegiance to the Polish king as guarantor of Danzig's privileges and trying to weigh in on legislation with their findings.[739]

Hanov's *Jus Culmense*, the history of the law of Culm, the codex used in Danzig and select other Prussian towns in Royal – but not ducal – Prussia at the time is a deliberate continuation of this tradition in the spirit of Lengnich.[740] The overt purpose was to create a study with the same level of certainty and order as his chosen role-model, in order to support maintenance and survival, where not the completion and restitution of the Culmian law code.[741] Like his predecessors, therefore, Hanov pursued the study of history with a very immediate purpose in mind: preserving the very law that codified the privilege granted to Danzig.[742] The *Jus Culmense* tries to organise the broad scope of the material with the help of a systematic, concise order. The content is structured into short paragraphs that lead the reader along a train of history free from anecdotes or illustrations, much in the sense of Keckermann's ideal of logical history. Footnotes support the arguments and explain the logic of the author's progressive argument. Hanov very much creates the impression that history can be brought to a degree of certainty, rigour permitting. Like Wolff, he harbours the belief

738 Menke-Glückert, Emil, Die Geschichtschreibung der Reformation und Gegenreformation: Bodin und die Begründung der Geschichtsmethodologie durch Bartholomäus Keckermann (Leipzig: J. C. Hinrich, 1912), p. 129.

739 Mokrzecki, Studium z Dziejów Nauczania Historii, p. 202.

740 Hanov's deference to Lengnich is expressed in a footnote to the second paragraph, see Hanov, *Jus Culmense*, §. 2, footnote b, p. 3; on the usage of Culmian law in Royal Prussia, see Johanek, Peter, 'Alter Kulm', *Die deutsche Literatur des Mittelalters. Verfasserlexikon* (Berlin; New York: Walter de Gruyter, 1985), 267–70 **(269).**

741 Hanov, *Jus Culmense ex ultima revisione*, p. XII: 'Dabey wünsche ich, daß die Aufrechterhaltung der Culmischen oder Preußischen Rechte bis auf die spätesten Nachkommen fortdaure, und von Gott gnädiglich alles verhütet werde, was dieselben ferner schmälern oder mindern könnte. Vielmehr wolle er das weislich fördern, was zu deren Ergänzung und Wiederherstellung dienlich sein wird.'

742 Friedrich, *The Other Prussia*, p. 51.

that the internal coherence of the material guarantees the clarity and integrity of the argument, by illustrating necessary connections between deeds and their consequences, in congruence with the order of the world at large.[743]

Conceptual vicinity permitting, Wolff would have considered the study of history exempt from scientific pursuit because it is concerned with actual events, not abstract truths. Empirical evidence might be accepted, and Wolff does build on historical precedents at times but his arguments, self-professedly, do not consider the particulars of this world but only universal principles. 'Historical' and 'philosophical' knowledge classified as different types of discourse whereby only the latter really promised a path to certainty and truth.[744]

Classical jurisprudence, too, is not a 'science' in Wolff's world but merely a descriptive record of ephemeral, man-made norms.[745] Regardless a shared belief in rigour, the two authors clearly have different assumptions about what qualifies as science.

The same goes for their respective quest for utility in knowledge. Hanov's other research interests included the faithful recording of empirical data of many kinds, for example meteorological reports.[746] Wolff, again, did not disavow empirical evidence but restricted this to 'indubitable experience' and reproducible experiments, emphatically not data collection. The difference between the two authors comes to the fore in a field that Hanov pursued and that Wolff explicitly denied the status of a science: demographics.

Hanov had created a register of births and deaths in the city of Danzig in the conviction that such data could be profitably used for political and historiographical purposes. The basic of his reasoning was the in- and decrease of livelihood and its impact on population – rather, inhabitants' – numbers. In 1753 he published a guide to using this sort of data for practical purposes: "[a] statesman will easily be able to find the

---

743 'Die glaubwürdigsten Nachrichten sind also erstlich daran zu erkennen, wenn sie innerlich auf einer solchen Verknüpfung der Dinge beruhen, die kein Wanken zu befürchten hat. Darzu gehöret nicht nur eine unläugbare Möglichkeit alles dessen, was darinnen enthalten ist; sondern auch eine solche Uebereinstimmung mit der Natur aller dabey vorkommenden Dinge, und mit den Umständen und Verhältnissen zu andern Dingen, dergleichen nur bey wahren Begebenheiten statt findet.', Hanov, Michael Christoph, *Preußische Lieferung alter und neuer Urkunden, Erörterungen und Abhandlungen zur Erläuterung der Preußischen Geschichte und Rechte* (Leipzig: Lankisch, 1755), pp. 4–5.

744 Corr, Charles A, 'Christian Wolff's Treatment of Scientific Discovery', *Journal of the History of Philosophy Journal of the History of Philosophy*, 10.3 (1972), 323–34, (324).

745 With his *Jus naturae* Wolff means to deliver a scientific basis for positive legislation, but not a study of law *per se*. See Hofmann, 'Recht und Staat bei Christian Wolff', p. 641.

746 Hanov, Michael Christoph, Der Danziger großen Mondjahre monathliches voriges und künftiges Wetter oder Anweisung wie die Wetterprognostica aus dem Mondzirkel abzunehmen mittelst der Observationen des Jahres 1767 (Danzig und Wittenberg: Dürr, 1768).

causes of a decline of inhabitants and will try to eliminate them as far as it is in the power of man."[747]

The curious opposition between Wolff and Hanov in this regard circuitously surfaces in the legacy of Hanov's register. The pastor Johann Peter Süssmilch went on to use Hanov's data in a second edition to his work on population growth, in 1761–62. Wolff had provided the foreword for an earlier edition of Süssmilch's treatise, published in 1756. Here Wolff makes it clear that he valued the work as such but did not consider the use of statistics and demographic data as an actual science.[748] Wolff's *Oeconomica* and natural law show a clear concern for population management, but they also signal a different approach to the issue: not by gathering intelligence through statistics but through moral education based on *a priori* demonstration.

It is clear that Wolff and Hanov subscribe to different scientific discourses and the epistemological gist of Hanov's publications does not change much after his Wolffian adventure. Both the meteorological treatise mentioned and the demographic study, for example, were published after Hanov completed the *Oeconomica*. This implies that Hanov escaped epistemological conversion and retained an idea of scholarship pristinely different in spite of the Wolffian interlude. This is also apparent with a view to the definitive aspect of Wolff's systematic work, the idea that all arguments and disciplines should be interlinked, *pulchro nexu*. Rather, some of Hanov's work bears Ramist traces, with a tendency to divide and subdivide categories into mutually exclusive categories. The treatise on meteorology, for example, opens with a categorisation of causes into 'remote' and 'closer', and 'inner' and 'outer'.[749] This mode of structuring content was clearly familiar to the author and the habit of doing so did not change with the completion of the Wolffian cycle. Wolff's system structures knowledge horizontally, concatenating rather than categorising. As shown below, Hanov's occasional lapse into vertical modes of categorisation in the *Oeconomica* betrays that he, too, did not consciously complete the shift from one systemic mode of thinking to another.

In the end, the authors not only differ in theory but also in practice. Hanov's engagement with the material world and his desire to explain its various phenomena through hands-on approaches results in a different mode of study. Wolff seeks utility in universality, in abstraction. Hanov has a hunger for haptics and optics alike, approaching politics through the study of history and law, and nature through observation and experiment. This tactic is evidently informed by his teaching practice, his intellectual breeding ground at the Gymnasium and his activity as a member of the

---

747 Hanov cited in Nipperdey, 'Johann Peter Süssmilch: From Divine Law to Human Intervention', p. 621.

748 Süssmilch, Die göttliche Ordnung in den Veränderungen des menschlichen Geschlechts, pp. 11f.

749 Hanov, *Der Danziger großen Mondjahre monathliches voriges und künftiges Wetter*, p.1, § 1: 'Das Wetter auf unserm Erdboden hat zweyerley Ursachen. Einige kann man die nahen und theils innerlichen, andere die äusserlichen und entferneten nennen...'

local scientific society. His engagement as a member of that institution exemplifies how the intellectual elite could make their knowledge useful and accessible to the rest of society. Hanov's practically oriented *Wochenschrift*, or 'weekly journal', addressed scientists, householders and doctors in equal measure, in the conviction of the 'natural law' obliging every person to share and promote knowledge of the world in the honour of God.[750] In the same grain, Danzig's scientific society saw its purpose in promoting the sciences for the sake of the common weal and welfare. To promote public knowledge, they organised experiments, privately and publicly, published a ream of pamphlets with specific use cases and even lobbied for the establishment of educative institutions, such as a training facility for midwives.[751]

Hanov's activities for Danzig's scientific society not only show the ideological overlap with Wolff but the difference in practice. The Danzig scholar actively engaged in empirical science (which Wolff did sometimes, not always) and was wedded to the idea of providing hands-on, practical solutions to problems in the here and now. Even though there are *prima facie* overlaps in academic zeal and public-mindedness, the two authors are clearly vested in different traditions and approaches when it comes to the promotion and promulgation of knowledge.

5.2.2 Congruences and dissonances between Hanov and Wolff

The immediate reception of Wolff and Hanov generally casts their joint work as consistent; it might be for the prima facie similarity of the two parts that the coherence between them was not really called into question. Recent scholarship, however, has probed a more incisive comparison between the two authors. Francis Cheneval's study of Wolff's and Hanov's understanding of the *civitas maxima*, for example, clearly identifies a conceptual gap between the two authors' understanding of the term. As with a regular state, Wolff seeks legitimacy for this cosmopolitan body politic in an assumed quasi-contract – Hanov finds it in the will of God.[752] Hanov's branding, however, makes it clear that he did not understand his contribution to the Wolffian cycle to contradict his predecessor. Rather, the impression emerges that he considered his *Oeconomica*, *Politica* and *Physica* truthful complements to Wolff's begin-

---

750 Górska, Liliana, 'Die Naturforschende Gesellschaft in Danzig und die gemeinnützige Aufklärung', in *Die Entdeckung von Volk, Erziehung und Ökonomie im europäischen Netzwerk der Aufklärung*, ed. by Hanno Schmitt, Holger Böning, and Werner Greiling (Bremen: Edition Lumiere, 2011), pp. 97–114, p. 99: 'Er beruft sich auf das "natürliche Recht". Dieses verbinde jeden Menschen "wie mit andern Gütern, also auch mit dem Erkänntnisse, so wir von Gott durch seine Wercke haben, so viel möglich zu seiner Ehre zu wuchern."'

751 Górska, 'Die Naturforschende Gesellschaft in Danzig und die gemeinnützige Aufklärung', *passim*.

752 Cheneval, Francis, 'Auseinandersetzungen um die Civitas Maxima in der Nachfolge Christian Wolffs', *Studia Leibnitiana*, 33 (2001), 125–44 (133–137).

nings – and that discrepancies between the authors present a silent clash of tacit assumptions more than an open conflict of opinions.

In the preface Hanov mentions his career as a school teacher and is quick to point out his intellectual independence in that context: he describes himself as 'following the authority of no other teacher'.[753] The insistence on his intellectual independence raises an interesting question when it comes to the planned continuation of another man's work in said man's spirit. Wolff clearly conceived of his methodology as a non-ideological, self-explanatory tool suitable for any discourse and any reasonable person. It is absolved from the idea of authorship and individual judgment but merely aims to codify objective truths into a successive chain of statements. Hanov, the preface betrays, had a less absolute idea of knowledge, or rather, believed in the validity of rivalling opinions. On one hand this is signalled by his pride in his intellectual independence. On the other he freely admits that two people of different make will necessarily have different thoughts.[754] From the outset, therefore, there are indicators of an unintentional divergence given the two authors' different assumptions about a possible uniformity of knowledge. Hanov, in fact, admits himself to some uncertainty as to whether, goodwill permitting, he has executed the method to the Wolffian dot. He is intent on his duty to imitate Wolff's style when completing his work.[755] Yet it seems that Hanov, quite innocently, does not share the same conviction that Wolff's – or anyone's – scientific method provides a singular path to truth. This becomes clear in his proleptic exculpation for possible disagreements. Where he agrees with Wolff, so Hanov, he will not explicitly say so. Yet where he begs to differ, he will.[756]

The actual programme of Hanov's *Oeconomica* is modelled on his understanding of Wolff's intention, and proposed in the schedule he submitted to the publishers. The *Oeconomica continuata* completes the section on the *societas paterna*, the *societas herilis* on masters and servants and adds a fourth part dedicated to the composition of the family as a whole and the formation of villages from households, an intent he reads into Wolff's introduction to the *Oeconomica*. Hanov's preface furthermore lists the sources he means to use: Wolff's *praecepta vernacula*, that is his German works; and the Latin cycle, complete with Wolff's annotations.[757] Granted the differences between Wolff's German and Latin cycle, Hanov's source work is not a warranty for consistency.

---

753 Hanov, *Oeconomica*, sig.)(4: '...nullius ne magistri quidem autoritatem sequens...'.

754 Ibid., sig.)()(2: 'Neque enim fieri potest, ut duo sint a se invicem diversi, & tamen nihil differant in suis cogitatis, suaque rerum prospicientia.'

755 Ibid., sig.)()(v: 'Priori atque ac posteriori responderem, imitandum mihi fuisse *Philosophum*, cujus praecepta trado.'

756 Ibid., sig.)()(2. For instance, Hanov explicitly rejects Malebranche's theory of the womb that Wolff supports.

757 Ibid., sig.)(4v.

What is more so, the distribution of content betrays something poignant about the promise of Wolff's method and its application in practice. If method is order, as Wolff says, and order prescribes content, Hanov would necessarily fulfil the programme faithfully if he but derived one proposition from the other. The traces of traditional structures or Florinus's *Oeconomus* in Wolff's *Oeconomica* suggest that his own work was conceivably moulded by external influences, not just method. Likewise, a look at Hanov's half of the *Oeconomica* suggests that his personal interests might have shifted the balance in content. Merely by numbers, the second part of *Oeconomica* shows a disproportional interest in teaching and pedagogy. This section vastly outweighs the other two chapters on servants and the structure of the whole household.[758] Even within the chapters devoted to the *societas paterna*, the chapter about education, *De educatione liberorum*, is a whole 126 paragraphs long and by far the longest in the whole section even though it merely serves to complete Wolff's unfinished beginnings. *De liberorum pietate erga parentes* contains 84 paragraphs, still more than the two remaining chapters, *De vicariis tutoribus & curatoribus* and *De bonis fortunae liberorum procurandis*. The bias of content is not surprising in the light of Hanov's professional background: he spent several years of his life as a tutor himself in Dresden and Leipzig before teaching at the gymnasium in Danzig. His practical expertise and personal opinion on the subject would have been invariably richer than on the other, more theoretical subjects and it is not surprising for this predicament to weigh in on content. The stress on expertise also transpires in Hanov's preface to the first tome of his *Politica*, where he laments the lack of a helper with the necessary political know-how.[759] This suggests that Hanov did not consider Wolff's method a heuristic tool that could replace human knowledge and experience.

The two authors also significantly differ in their writing style. Wolff's sentences are marked by formalistic zeal where Hanov has a certain flourish to his pen that earned him an honourable mention in at least one literary review.[760] Their stylistic variance is particularly palpable when it comes to packaging content. Hanov abandons Wolff's fashion of creating long sentence structures by concatenating proofs and propositions for a less formal, more legible format. Consequently, the paragraphs of the *Oeconomica continuata* are considerably shorter than Wolff's and lack the internal stringency. Notable, too, is the fact that Hanov by no means furnishes every single

758 The half-section on the *societas paterna* counts 330 paragraphs whilst the treatment of *societas herilis* and the *societas domestica* or *domus* count only 163 and 154 respectively.

759 Hanov, *Philosophiae civilis sive politicae pars prima*, sigs. b2–b2v: 'Frustra optassem adjutores, perfectos rerum civilium Magistros, ipsoque usu recentissimo arcanorum aulicorum publicorumque instructos.'

760 Königliche Gesellschaft der Wissenschaften, *Göttingische Anzeigen von Gelehrten Sachen, Vol. 2* (Göttingen: Johann Friederich Hager, 1755), p. 1338: 'Die lateinische Schreibart des Hrn. Hanovs, und die Erläuterungen aus andern Weltweisen, den Geschichten u.s.w. unterscheiden Hrn. Hanovs Arbeit von der Wolfischen auf eine Art die der ersten zum Vortheile gereichet.'

paragraph with a footnote, unlike his predecessor. In fact, where Wolff frequently uses the *notae* to make his broader opinions known, Hanov's authorial intent remains comparatively muffled in the footnotes. Instead, he uses this space in the traditional fashion, that is by referring to authoritative sources to back up his argument.

Given that each author's outlook was slightly different in practice and theory, and granted that each had a different writing practice and range of interests, it would not be to anyone's surprise were the two halves of the *Oeconomica* to differ significantly; in fact, it seems more surprising to assume that Hanov's completion of Wolff's work would pass as entirely consistent. Yet the crucial difference between them is not merely stylistic but conceptual, with regards to the main pillars of Wolff's philosophical cycle: method, system and natural law.

5.3 Hanov's Oeconomica – method, system, natural law

5.3.1 Method

The hallmark of Christian Wolff's method is the syllogistic bearing, formalised with the help of the Principle of Non-Contradiction and the Principle of Sufficient Reason. Each paragraph follows a strict pattern and consistently ends with the opening statement – very much like the *quod erat demonstrandum* of a mathematical proof. Start and end enclose the chain of arguments proving the non-contradiction of the statement. Hanov's continuation, at first sight, seems to follow his predecessor's pattern faithfully. Some paragraphs indeed open with the proposition in question, followed by a line of corroborating statements, and close with the original statement affirmed.[761] More often than not, however, Hanov follows the Wolffian model in appearance less than substance. Often, the bulk of a paragraph serves to qualify rather than corroborate the principal statements; in those cases, the content does nothing to support the opening statement, which also is not as religiously repeated at the end of each paragraph.[762] On occasion, Ramist tendencies come to the fore where Hanov structures an argument into dichotomies rather than sufficient reasons.[763] And unlike

761 Select paragraphs preserve the *quod erat demonstrandum* structure. See, for instance, Hanov, *Oeconomica*, § 371, pp. 153–154: '*Parentum est, liberos quoque, quantum licite fieri potest, reddere vere fortunatos*....Liquet igitur, obligari parentes, ut liberos suos, quantum moraliter fieri potest, reddant fortunatos.'

762 This can be easily seen comparing the first and the last sentence of the paragraph as already in the second paragraph, see Hanov, *Oeconomica* § 245, p. 4: '*Cavendum quoque a parentibus, ne alii animum infantis impleant ideis & notionibus erroniis superstitiosisve*...Quarum quo major est inter homines numerus, eo magis parentes providere debent, ne qua superstitiosa notio vacuum occupet liberorum animum, difficulter deinde extirpanda.'

763 Hanov, Oeconomica, § 248, p. 7: 'Praeparatio alia est remotior, alia proprior, item alia interna, alia externa.'

Wolff, Hanov is not strictly intent on the grammatical adjustment of the content to the truth criterion and does not seem to share the same zeal for absolute rigour. Tellingly, Hanov is not afraid to use the otherwise common but strictly un-Wolffian phrase *as per hypothesin*, which implies that he lacked his predecessor's categorical fear of speculation.[764]

More poignantly, Hanov frequently lapses into the traditional ways of advice literature – oftentimes he ends up explaining how something is done, rather than proving that, as Wolff does. The instruction of how blind and deaf children should be taught to communicate is such an example. In the process, Hanov goes into detail about how this problem is to be practically solved: just as children normally learn to pronounce by listening, those short of hearing can be taught by drawing their attention to the actual movement of the lips and the use of breath. By encouraging them to imitate the actual physical manifestations of a speech act, they can be taught a way of forming words without actually being able to hear them.[765] Hanov here explains here not that children have to be taught but how and thus casually reverts to a format much more familiar to household literature: dispensing actual advice rather than stipulating duties. And unlike Wolff, Hanov's solution is not derived from epistemological theories about the soul – it is genuinely practical.

The Principle of Sufficient Reason has a similarly different function in the second half of the *Oeconomica*. Wolff himself, as is clear from his casual usage of the term, had a variegated idea of its application within his moral philosophy. A *ratio sufficiens* could be posed by a duty attesting to an obligation; a motive qualifying an action as moral; or as an 'efficient cause', in some scenarios. In all these cases, however, the Principle of Sufficient Reason only describes what is logically possible and contingent, not a material consequence. This is evident in the way Wolff creates moral arguments from biological facts: by declaring not what bodies do but what they should do in the possibly most perfect world.[766] In Hanov's arguments the idea of a sufficient reason seems equally broad but still not congruent with Wolff's. Intermingled with propositions that build obligation upon obligation as Wolff would we find arguments that simply explain a phenomenon by cause and consequence. An example for this is the very opening paragraph of the book which continues the chapter on education commenced by Wolff. Hanov describes here how to prevent that false notions embed themselves in an infant's mind – albeit, not by advising on abstract duties but by explaining

764 Ibid., § 282, p. 50: 'Etenim per hypothesin hi non forent negligentes, nisi existimarent, se jam ea esse adeptos & meritos…'.

765 Ibid., § 254, p. 13.

766 This teleological interpretation of biology is apparent from Wolff's discussion of genitalia – he demonstrates not what they do but what they ought to do. See Wolff, *Oeconomica*, § 11, p. 16: '*…habilitas physica maris requirit, ut semen prolificum generetur & in coitu ejaculetur.*'

how this happens in the first place.[767] In that sense, the Principle of Sufficient Reason, if indeed it is such, is not dedicated to justify a moral duty or obligation in the abstract *mundus rationalis*. Rather, Hanov's reasoning seeks explain the consequences of real-world phenomena so as to inform the actions promoting or preventing them.

It is this detail that reveals the conceptual difference of their respective understanding of morality and the function of a moral primer. Wolff's heuristic didactics work directly along the lines of his theory of the soul: since the motive is the sufficient reason to a moral action and intellectually pliable, Wolff's discourse is intent on providing logically fool-proof motives for a one-stop shop inculcation of virtue. This is particularly visible in his usage of the word *remedium*: under this heading Wolff offers not practical solutions to a problem, but a logically sound motive for a morally good action. Hanov, in contrast, does not have the same focus on *motivum* nor is he putting Wolff's theory of morality into practice. A *remedium* is understood as genuinely practical advice more than an argument to effectuate cognitive adjustment. Thus, the *remedium* where children are negligent out of arrogance or pride is to remove the root cause for this behaviour: their overweening self-esteem.[768] Notably often, a *remedium* presents itself as Hanov's prime pedagogical method: teaching by example.[769]

Hanov and Wolff employ different modes of authority in their pedagogical thought and practice: the latter builds on his systematic concept of morality – the former draws from know-how, his own and others', as the frequent 'teste experientia' suggests. Authority and experience as traditional elements of education culture also pervade Hanov's annotations. In the introduction to the *Oeconomica*, Hanov pledges to follow the authority of ancient authors, as he believes concurs with Wolff's own wishes.[770] What Hanov seems to misunderstand is that this is not a call for the resurrection of truths of old. Rather, Wolff here claims that the study of ancient wisdoms would prove them conform with his own philosophy. Yet true to his promise as he reads it, Hanov widely cites the actual classics of *Oeconomica* scholarship: Aristotle's *Politics*, Xeno-

767 Hanov, Oeconomica, § 244, p. 1: 'Ne infans per se falsam nomini notionem jungere adsuescat, parentibus vel ipsis observandum expiscandumque est, quaenam qualitates peregrinae in sensus infantis prae caeteris incurrant, ut has si fieri possit removeant, saltem aliam ista qualitate destitutam eidem substituant, atque nihilominus eodem nomine rem subinde compellent; vel aliis quibus suas partes commisere, idem injungendum.'

768 Ibid., §§ 282–283, pp. 50–51.

769 Ibid., § 353, p. 135: 'Praebent ergo excellentium, virorum vitae & facta praeclara tum documenta & adjumenta, tum incertamena ardoris partier aut magis excellendi.' Ibid., § 283, p. 50: '*Si nimia deprehendatur aviditas discendi, is non solum exemplis aliorum, qui sic sanitati, vitae & studiorum scopo obfuere, ab intemperie ista avocari poterit, sed & affectibus, quibus ad illam urgetur, imperandum esse docendus est, ut omnibus officiis satisfieri possit.*'

770 Ibid., sig.)()(: 'Animadvertens in nota §. 207. *B. Philosophum* optasse, ut quisquam sententias veterum colligeret, notaque luce philosophica collustraret, hujusque systematis veritates simul iisdem confirmaret; occasione eorum, quae hic tradenda fuere, consului praestantiores oeconomicae autores antiquos, hisque praeceptis mutuam foenerari lucem studui confirmationemque.'

phon's *Oeconomicus* and the Pseudo-Aristotelian *Oeconomica*. Cicero, Varro, Tacitus, Seneca and Livy are cited repeatedly but also contemporary voices on the subjects of jurisprudence, history and household management. Overall, Hanov takes recourse to a comparatively conventional catalogue in comparison to Wolff who does not quote a single canonical source from the field of ancient economics. By doing just that, Hanov harks back to the more traditionally academic approach of collating and referencing authoritative sources, away from the Wolffian style that neutralizes the provenance of arguments. What is more so, Hanov tacitly flouts Wolff's attempt to reconstruct a morality free from theology – in fact, references to Scripture occur throughout Hanov's *Oeconomica*.[771] In all those examples, samples from the Bible are used to illustrate or corroborate the argument at hand. In contrast, Wolff sought to separate traditional theology – speak, biblical exegesis – from philosophy to free the latter to explore moral matters in an unimpeded scientific fashion. Hanov's footnotes imply that he is free from this predicament. In other words, the moral authority of theology remains pristine in his discourse where the whole point of Wolff's lifetime endeavour was to wrest it free thereof.

The different understanding of morality, pedagogy and the application of logic within shows that the authors tacitly diverge in their understanding of the task at hand. On a more general note, too, Hanov's fulfilment of the *Oeconomica* is not playing to Wolff's definition of philosophia as a *scientia possibilium*. In Wolff's view, it is the philosopher's task not to record facts but explain the universal framework they relate to. And although his method allows for empirical and rational input alike, the ultimate aim is to report general principles, abstracted away from circumstance but universally applicable.[772] This also means abstracting away from imperfection: the first part of the *Oeconomica* is less a primer to fix than to pre-empt a less-than-perfect state of affairs by bringing the interrelation between the world order, motive and action into view. Hanov, in contrast, is happily wedded to the real world. Not only does he not restrict the discussion to Wolffian syllogisms; he also broadens the scope to discuss less-than-ideal phenomena in the real world. An example is his definition of the seemingly simple term 'children': the paragraph mostly serves to introduce categories for different levels of legitimacy or relatedness, that is children born out of wedlock, step- or adopted children.[773] Wolff's *Oeconomica* considers only the perfect world, describing the scenario of children born and educated in a married household; the question of illegitimate offspring would not feature. Hanov, however, does not build on an idealised, abstract cosmos but here as elsewhere just categorizes the

771 See e.g. Hanov, *Oeconomica*, § 295 *nota*, p. 68; § 790 *nota*, p. 626; § 851 *nota*, p. 683.

772 Wolff, *Oeconomica*, § 3 *nota*, p. 4: 'Oeconomica tamen tradit Principia generalia, quæ ad casus emergentes pro datis circumstantiis facile applicantur.'

773 Hanov, *Oeconomica*, § 492, p. 301: 'Liberi proprie dicti sunt homines ab aliis per generationem descendentem, seu ab aliis geniti homines.'

world as is. This is also visible in the two authors' treatment of social hierarchies. Wolff's *Oeconomica* is largely agnostic to status differences, or at least disavows their importance if we consider his general disinterest in the civil aptitude for marriage, *habilitas civilis*. Hanov's discourse is sensitive to and protective of traditional hierarchies, for instance, where he discusses the different conditions of upbringing depending on the parents' wealth – and that people of upward social mobility should not be ashamed of their retrospectively humbler parents or lament the adverse conditions of their upbringing.[774] Moreover, Hanov has no intention to boil down the breadth of the household down to singular, universal concepts. Some passages dwell on exactly the diversity of the domestic economy in all detail, with special reference to a topic very familiar to the genre of *Oeconomica*: nature and its cultivation. Separating out the different forms of life into animal, plant and mineral kingdoms, Hanov sets out to categorise the management of each realm.[775] Animal husbandry distinguishes between domesticated and wild animals, herding the former and hunting the latter, complete with the range of more specific professions.[776] The same goes for the cultivation of plants, divided into agriculture, forestry, horticulture, pasture land and vineries, followed by a range of professions such as farmers, foresters, oil-makers and wine-growers.[777] The whole discourse on human professions ends with a short argument that the description of best practices for each would take up the work of many volumes, beyond the scope of the present one; instead, Hanov refers to other authors and the works of the scientific societies, in Germany, England, France and Sweden, a comment presumably inspired by his own involvement in Danzig's scientific society and its numerous publications.[778] Granted, in the *Oeconomica* Hanov cuts short the breadth of topics in comparison to the material traditionally considered – but he still falls short of Wolff's level of abstraction.[779]

5.3.2 System

In contrast to the methodological divergence, the systematic integration of Hanov's *Oeconomica* into the Wolffian oeuvre seems to be more consistent with his precursor's

774 Ibid., § 561, p. 385; Hanov, *Oeconomica*, § 562, p. 388.
775 Ibid., § 798, p. 632.
776 Ibid., § 799, p. 632.
777 Ibid., § 800, p. 633.
778 Ibid., § 804, p. 636: 'Quid in singulis viate generibus sit optimum factu, id si Oeconomicae esse inserendum, magnis multisque opus foret libris conscribendis. Qui tamen uti per se patet, pro dignitate rerum nec dum confici possent, licet integrae Bibliothecae ejusmodi librorum jam prostent, quos exhibet de Rohr in Bibliotheca Oeconomica...'.
779 In comparison, Wolff's deontological account of work is almost entirely devoid of references to any professions or activities. See, for instance, Wolff, *Oeconomica*, §§ 130–131, pp. 200–205.

work. Hanov inherits Wolff's tendency to derive the necessity of a book, an argument or a chapter through the preceding framework. Thus Wolff considers the *Oeconomica* in itself a systemic requirement. The parts within, even where exogenously inspired, are presented as necessary elements of a chain of reasons. This mode of argument also features in Hanov's continuation, for example at the opening of the second chapter of the third section, *De virtutibus personarum herilium*. As Hanov states here in perfectly Wolffian fashion, if all requirements of the previous discourse are to be fulfilled, the discussion of servants' virtues are a necessary consequence of Wolff's practical philosophy, his *Psychologia empirica* and *Ethica*.[780]

The content of Hanov's *Oeconomica* self-consciously builds on previous parts of the system as Wolff prescribes in his own preface: *Jus naturae*, *Philosophia practica*, *Ethica* and *Psychologia*, which in turn presuppose the *Ontologia*, *Theologia naturalis* and the *Cosmologia*.[781] And even though Hanov announces in the preface that he will use material beyond the Latin cycle, his source work within the *Oeconomica* stays true to the style of his predecessor: the main paragraphs exclusively reference previous paragraphs of the *Oeconomica* and Wolff's Latin works. As was to be expected – and is consistent with Wolff's *Oeconomica* – *Jus naturae VII* is by far the most-cited work, followed by *Jus naturae I*; *Philosophia practica* and *Ethica* are mentioned with a similar frequency, appearing in a little over 100 paragraphs; *Psychologia empirica* and *rationalis*, taken together, appear in ca. 60 paragraphs – consistently, if significantly less often.

Hanov also follows Wolff's model quite closely when it comes to rebuilding certain topics with the help of the system's other disciplines, particularly with a view to pedagogy. Wolff had derived his pedagogical approach from the theory of intellectual virtues demonstrated in the *Ethica*. As far as his practical approach is developed in his part of the *Oeconomica*, ideas about the early stages of an infant are derived from his theories of cognition developed in both *Ethics* and *Psychologia*. Hanov first follows this train of thought, maintaining a close referentiality to the *Psychologia empirica*, *rationalis* and the *Ethica*. He lists all the intellectual virtues the parents need to cater to in the education of their children, as defined in the Wolffian cycle: a sharp mind, profundity, a sound imagination, memory and ingenuity, intelligence and prudence – all drawn from various Latin works, specifically the *Ethica*, *Jus naturae*, *Psychologia empirica* and *Psychologia rationalis*.[782] Hanov might look beyond the *Psychologia empirica* and the *Ethica* that are the sole sources of Wolff's pedagogical thought; yet all these pedagogical concepts hark back to the previous parts of the system. This is particularly evident in Hanov's discussion of education ends and means. Explaining the cognitive abilities that a child needs to acquire, Hanov frequently uses Wolff's *Logica* as a theo-

780 Hanov, *Oeconomica*, § 642, p. 472.
781 Wolff, *Oeconomica*, § 4, pp. 4–5.
782 Hanov, *Oeconomica*, § 286, p. 55.

retical foundation to his practice of teaching and inculcating children with strategies of cognition: in the respective section, the *Logica* is referenced in almost every single paragraph.[783] Hanov uses it to define the types of judgments and associations that can be made on a purely theoretical basis and that the child or adolescent will have to be taught to emulate and execute in order to understand *rationes* and *nexus*, the reasons and the linkages between truths. The first type of judgment is that of affirmative nature, the second of negative nature;[784] and on the occasion of explaining the third mode of judgment, Hanov employs the actual application of the truth criterion – determining the essential relationship of a predicate with the subject – within this pedagogy, as a form of judgment the child should be taught.[785] Rather than presenting formal logic as a specialist skill, therefore, it is recast as a mode of cognition fundamental to every human being's education as the basis to rational thinking, as already foreshadowed in Hanov's educational treatise, *Entwurf der Lehr-Kunst*.

Whether Wolff would have continued his pedagogical discourse in exactly this way is impossible to say. It is clear either way that Hanov shows awareness of the possibilities of the system as a resource and foundation, to the point that he picks up on inconcinnities in Wolff's own execution. In the first book of the *Politica*, for example, Hanov tries to rationalise a conundrum tacitly appearing in Wolff's part of the *Oeconomica*: that, if the *Physica* had preceded the practical philosophy, it could have served as an official basis for the biological facts of life presented in the *Oeconomica*. Instead, Wolff left the *Physica* to the end, leaving his biological facts in the *Oeconomica* without a scientific foundation. In a similar vein, Hanov concedes that if everything in the *Politica* 'would have to be rigorously demonstrated', the *Physica* and the *Technologia* would have had to precede politics.[786] As it is, however, the system is as it stands and it is only left to Hanov to rationalize, why the present order of things is justified even if impractical.

In the end, Hanov differs most from Wolff when it comes to the idea of a system in the sense of *systema*, as a metaphysical assumption serving as operational principle. He clearly departs from the Wolffian quest of practical philosophy and its main point of action, the logical modification of the *motivum* as the sufficient reason to will and action. Wolff had cast virtue as a habit: the habit of living according to natural law. Yet as becomes clear in the *Oeconomica*, it is less habituation that inculcates virtue than the rational formation of the requisite motive. Even though the notion of practice is involved, Wolff's moral theory lodges the Good Life with a cognitive, epistemic process. Hanov's idea of pedagogy mixes rational processes with quite literal, exogenously imposed habituation. This is concretely drawn out in his two-part ac-

783 Ibid., §§ 249–286, pp. 8–55.
784 Ibid., §§ 267–268, pp. 34–35.
785 Ibid., § 269, p. 35.
786 Hanov, Philosophiae civilis sive politicae pars prima, § 6, p. 7.

count of education: in the first instance, teaching basic principles of logic helps to build up the cognitive abilities needed to grasp the order of the universe, at least implicitly. Yet since a child still has a malleable intellect, the authority of parents and teachers is instrumental in inculcating moral practice for the time being: a habituation process, in the end, but not based on rational understanding but parental guidance.[787] This does not mean that Hanov disavows the importance of rational virtue. In his opinion, children should be taught to seek for a clearer, independent understanding of norms they know, even if the path has to lead via a simplified version of reality.[788] Wolff suggests an incremental process of learning modelled on a child's development stages which in turn is modelled on his theoretical vision of the faculties of the soul. Hanov adjusts educational practice not to the presence but the evident lack of these faculties. By implication, a sense of good and bad is not formed once children have enough rational understanding but they are taught the norms through authority first and then prompted to understand them *ex post*.

These diverging ideas about morality and virtue surface on a metatextual level, too. Hanov's discourse frequently draws on the aid of authority, more than Wolff's brand of intellectually self-sufficient rationality. When it comes to the education of young people in particular, Hanov insists on traditional modes of pedagogy based on lessons drawn from history or contemporary examples. As his *Lehr-Kunst* argues, particular facts of history are easier to understand than universal concepts.[789] Particularly when teaching young boys, real examples of deeds good and bad in history, even fictional tales, help to support the lessons.[790] This is very different from Wolff's idea that the abstract and irrefutably logical will lead the mind in the right direction. As his *Oeconomica* demonstrates by example, Hanov's strategy is not exclusive to the education of young people – the examples of famous men continue to serve as inspiration and stimulus to grown and aging men to aim for virtue and excellence.[791] Wolff, in contrast, sees the fates and deeds of famous men as a source of analysis of where virtue and true happiness really come into play, not in the sense of role-models by default.[792]

787 Hanov, *Oeconomica*, § 272, pp. 38–39.

788 Ibid., § 273, pp. 39.

789 Hanov, *Entwurf der Lehr-Kunst, aus der Vernunft-Kunst*, § 93, p. 189: 'Wie aber das [sic] Erkänntniß einzelner Dinge leichter ist, als das [sic] Erkenntnis algemeiner Dinge... so ist es auch leichter Geschichte als Lehren zu schreiben.'

790 Hanov, *Oeconomica*, § 324, p. 202.

791 Ibid., § 354, p. 135: '*Haec generosa aemulatio optimorum in virile sequentique aetate in omni virtutum genere numquam seponendo:* quia licito gloriae stimulo animus ad official nobiliora excitatur, ad scopum melius persequendum exacuitur, & a defatigatione sub onere emergentium difficultatum immunis redditur, *teste experientiae*.'

792 Wolff, *Oeconomica* §178, nota, p. 297.

This being said, there seems to be a slightly different understanding between the two authors what the good life really entails, judging from their respective usage of the term *bona fortunae*, good fortune. Wolff notes that when parents should imbue their children with the right ideas about virtue, the parents should have the right idea about real happiness themselves. Many parents, he observes, are intent on worldly happiness, wishing their children to obtain honours, marry rich wives or obtain wealth through other means; all the while they do not ask whether their children possess the kind of virtue that lets them fulfil their office well and be useful to the state, whether they have chosen their wives wisely or whether their riches have been obtained in a righteous fashion – the real source of happiness.[793] Hanov has a more pragmatic view towards the *bona fortunae* in general and quite straightforwardly mandates parents to obtain wealth, honours and ideally a good match for their children. The preservation of material wealth across generations is not only a concern of parents and the genuine hereditary line, but also – in case of bereavement – of the tutors who will have to preserve wealth in the name of their *pupilli*, their wards.[794] Hanov's idea of a good life is clearly not adverse to the material values Wolff dismisses. The difference between their outlooks may be due to tacit assumptions born in their social environments. Municipal legislation in Danzig was protective of patrician prerogatives and visibly so: the city defined regulations for the number of staff a household could have, the size of festivities and the types of clothes and ornament, setting patricians and ordinary burghers apart.[795] Moreover, Hanov had had a career as a house teacher, classically a position in an aristocratic or at least a well-heeled household.[796] His respect or at least support for social hierarchies and the values associated with them might relate to a professional stake in that regard.

Context permitting, there are cases other than *bona fortunae* where Hanov understands shared terminology in a different way. One such example is the concept of *charitas*. In Wolff's philosophy, *charitas* is officially introduced into the scientific canon of virtues in the fifth part of the *Ethica* as love in conformity with natural law, the basis for all virtues with regard to our behaviour towards others.[797] In that sense, Wolff reclaims the Christian virtue for his extra-theological, scientific discourse. The term is used to make a case for self-love, *charitas sui*, as a virtuous, not a selfish, stimulus.[798] Curiously, although Wolff talks about love in the *Oeconomica* aplenty, *charitas* as a virtue is not actually ever mentioned. Here, love only features as different forms of *amor*: *amor rationalis*, that is rational love inspired by virtue; *amor naturalis*, or instinctive, impulsive and sometimes defective love; and *amor universalis*, univer-

793 Ibid., §178, nota, p. 297.
794 Hanov, *Oeconomica*, §§ 451–467, pp. 244–264.
795 Stone, The Polish-Lithuanian state, p. 197
796 Gagliardo, Germany under the Old Regime, p. 194.
797 Wolff, Philosophia moralis. Pars quinta, sig. *2v.
798 Wolff, Philosophia moralis sive Ethica, methodo scientifica pertractata. Pars quarta, § 52, p. 66.

sal love mandated by natural law.[799] Where *charitas* featured prominently in the *Ethica*, its absence in the *Oeconomica* leads to assume that Wolff considered each category of love context-specific: *charitas* to the natural state of the individual in the *Ethica*, *amor* as a result to interpersonal affairs in the *status adventitius* in the *Oeconomica*. Hanov reintroduces the concept of *charitas* in both *Oeconomica* and *Politica* as the basis to cultivate benevolence and solidarity amongst the citizens.[800] It features alongside *justitia* and *aequitas* as the highest public virtues, safeguarding the state against injustice.[801] Hanov's emphasis on *charitas* in all aspects of practical philosophy spells a revaluation of a Christian virtue within all aspects of moral life. He replaces the enlightened self-interest driving rational morality with the traditional social glue Wolff meant to supplant with the glow of reason. The conceptual inconsistency between the two authors with regard to these two examples is understandable, if not a necessary consequence: If Hanov wanted to have the exact, idiosyncratically Wolffian understanding of every single term, he would have had to read every single work of the cycle in detail. As is clear from his own introduction, this is not what he did. Rather, he resorted to select Latin and German works. In that sense, testing Hanov's *Oeconomica* on systemic consistency simply shows that the exact same vocabulary can support a very different argument when employed by a person with different assumptions, experiences and connotations.

Conceptual misgivings permitting, Hanov's work shows a considerable effort to reconstruct the content of *Oeconomica* and *Politica* from the material Wolff had delivered. In one aspect the systematic integration of Hanov's *Oeconomica* misses a significant novelty introduced by his predecessor: the link between the domestic and the political sphere. Unlike the first part of the *Oeconomica*, the second half has not a single proleptic reference to the *Politica* that would communicate what Wolff laboured to demonstrate: the political relevance of domestic living. Wolff integrates the household very consciously with the political sphere, pronouncing it a proactive unit within the state which is responsible for its continuity and well-being. Hanov lets houses band together to villages but misses out entirely the impact of private lives on the body politic.

799 Wolff, *Oeconomica*, § 96, p. 143: '*Amor rationalis, quo conjugem prosequimur, virtute ejus concitatur.*' Ibid., § 184 *nota*, p. 307: '...naturalis iste amor insitus sit tam maribus, quam foeminis...'. Ibid., § 231, p. 384: '...amor universalis lege naturae praeceptus...'.

800 Hanov, Michael Christoph, *Philosophiae civilis sive politicae pars tertia* (Halle: Renger, 1758), § 166, pp. 191–192.

801 Hanov, Michael Christoph, *Philosophiae civilis sive politicae pars quarta* (Halle: Renger, 1759), § 123, p. 103; § 99, p. 86.

5.3.3 Natural Law

Natural law provides the theoretical backbone for Wolff's moral philosophy. In practice this means the provision of an extensive, morally absolute framework of rules and obligations to inform good practice. Genuine felicity, in Wolff's philosophy, is wedded to a deontological interpretation of the human condition: duty is intrinsic to man and its fulfilment a necessary condition for his happiness. Natural law serves as an ethical, not a legal guideline, blending and combining subjects native to jurisprudence to topics classical to moral and advice literature.

Judging from citations, Hanov faithfully builds his practical theory on Wolff's natural law as prescribed: Wolff's seventh tome of natural law is by far the most-cited work, followed by *Jus naturae, pars prima*. A lot of definitions are genuinely drawn from the Wolffian corpus and the material self-consciously derived from this declared theoretical foundation. Often, in a way that his predecessor would approve of, general statements from natural law are used to justify, explain or qualify some very specific pronouncements in the *Oeconomica*, rationalising the intrinsically mundane through the highly abstract. On a less literal level, however, Hanov does not adopt Wolff's trend of rewriting social relationships in jurisprudential terminology. And unlike his predecessor, he does not seem to have a pronounced interest in assessing existing legislation through the lens of universal natural law. Instead, he considers the relationship between existing legal concepts and constructible moral discourse in reverse. The difference between Wolff and Hanov's interpretation of the relationship between positive and natural law shows up most clearly on the example of the *patria potestas*: Wolff uses moral concepts to limit the extent of power assigned by this legal concept – Hanov advises not how the *paterna potestas* should be limited by but only modes of its employment, specifically education and the shaping of the moral will.[802] Although this is not entirely unlike Wolff's intention, the point of departure is subtly different: the original positive concept is not fenced in but left pristine in its traditional guise.

In a more general sense, Wolff uses natural law not only as a yardstick to judge man-made laws, but also customs, cultures and habits. In his work, it can serve to clarify (confessional) controversies and yields a rationality-based update to existing norms. This function transcends less in the main paragraphs than Wolff's accompanying annotations. In contrast, Hanov's footnotes are entirely free from general pronouncements about natural law as a measure of morality. True, the references in the main paragraphs refer back to Wolff's *Jus naturae* with reassuring regularity, yet unlike in the first part of the *Oeconomica* the majority of the commentary supplied by Hanov throws in the weight of historical evidence, ethnographic anecdotes, biblical references or, quite frequently and, as mentioned, the authority of the Ancients. In

802 Hanov, *Oeconomica*, § 281, p. 48; § 344, pp. 126–7.

terms of format he follows the Wolffian rule; in terms of the tacit assumptions beneath and what legitimates scientific discourse, it seems that Hanov has not quite wrested himself free from traditional scholarship. Rather than using natural law as a rational, irrefutable, self-evident yardstick Hanov gives purchase to traditional authority, as also in his education practice. In § 805 of the *Oeconomica*, for example, Hanov defines the concept of *autoritas moralis* as the dignity of a person whose opinion carries so much weight that we consider it accepted per se.[803] This would imply that the judgment of better men can function as a fully functioning guidance rather than the attempt to acquire said judgment on one's own accord. This idea of moral authority, to Hanov, is used to increase the weight of arguments that for Wolff should be supported by the force of logic. By implication, the concept of *autoritas* also transcends through the manner in which Hanov himself supports his arguments: with examples from authoritative scholarship. The idea of natural law as an exogenous, universally valid yardstick to verify and rectify practices is practically absent, even if very present in the formalistic execution; instead the weight of authorities ancient or modern is used to fortify its message.

Granted their different conceptual understanding of natural law, the two authors' tacit assumptions and also prejudices come to the fore in what they consider a value-neutral discourse. This is visible in Wolff's pronounced preference of some cultures over others. There is a Christian bias to his whole system, a natural legacy from the traditions Wolff subsumes; but there are also other, more personal opinions embedded in his discourse – and it is the comparison to Hanov that throws these respective blind spots into relief. Two egregious examples are the respective attitudes towards Chinese culture and philosophy, Wolff's pet interest, and the matter of gender roles. Wolff, as has been explained above, saw his natural law broadly in congruence with Chinese philosophy. Based on a somewhat sweeping assumption, he uses Chinese philosophy and cultural practices as corroborative evidence to his own ideas about wooing, schooling and pregnancy. Natural law is assumed to be in *a priori* congruence with Chinese thought and culture, so conversely any Chinese practice is an expression thereof. In contrast, Wolff uses his ideas on natural law on several occasions to identify unlawful practices from other cultures, such as the Jewish divorce policy.[804] This could count as a singular incident if references elsewhere did not signal

803 Ibid., § 805, p. 637: '*Quid sit autoritas moralis? Autoritatem dicimus* dignitatem tantam personae, qua illius sententiam nobis amplectendam esse censemus, sive qua mereri creditur, ut illius placita sequamur (§. 316. *seq.*).' The *nota* further explains that it is the authority we infer a person's intellectual capacity, experience and integrity from – rather than deriving authority from intellect and experience.

804 Wolff, *Oeconomica*, § 65 *nota*, p. 100: 'Judaei uxores dimittere poterant quavis de causa ex proprio arbitrio...Quamobrem patet matrimonium apud Judaeos perinde ac Jure Romano solo dissensu mariti dissolvi potuisse, idque privata autoritate. Multo minus itaque dubitandum est, quin ob eas, quas rejicimus, rationes sponsalia dissolvi potuerint. Ast mos Judaeorum legi naturae minime

other classic Christian prejudices against the Jewish at large – now justified by natural law.[805] Thc overly, sometimes grotesquely positive view of the Chinese empire is matched with what could well be described as a scientifically packaged prejudice against the Jewish. This relationship is not as firmly fostered in Hanov's continuation. Wolff's enthusiasm for Confucian philosophy does not find reflection in Hanov's works, although he does also use Johannes Nieuhoff's work for ethnographic references, such as in his description of the Chinese constitution.[806] This description, however, is devoid of any association of Chinese philosophy and culture with the concept of natural law; rather, it is presented as just one amongst a number of examples of constitutions in different countries, such as Japan, England, Bohemia and others. Thus, the contrast to Wolff's attitude vis-à-vis the Chinese is marked by Hanov's indifference rather than rejection; where Wolff singles out this particular culture as conform with universalist principles, Hanov does not seem to pick favourites. Rather than issuing moral judgments, his discourse displays a degree of cultural relativism. This value-neutrality largely includes Jewish customs. Whilst Wolff rejects Jewish law *a priori*, Hanov mentions it in a fairly disinterested fashion when covering different types of holidays.[807] In fact, Jewish legislation finds a positive mention in the context of population management.[808] This does not make Hanov a defender or specifically a pro-semite, as it were – in his opinion, the Jewish, 'whose own dogmata, as every Christian knows, are false', are not subject to admiration or emulation but toleration in a state.[809] Yet Jewish custom is not assumed to be morally wrong by definition.

The distance between Wolff and Hanov's attitudes towards the Jewish may just be reflecting the different social realities they encountered in their respective political environment. Whilst the Prussian regime under Frederick William I and Frederick the Great proved particularly intolerant of the Jewish minority, the city of Danzig, where Hanov lived, had a much larger Jewish populace. The Polish-Lithuanian Commonwealth the city belonged was not a consistently Jewish-friendly environment. In the seventeenth and eighteenth century, the Jewish were granted some economic rights

---

consentaneus fuit, reprobatus ideo a Christo *Matth.* XIX.7 & *seqq.*'. It is noteworthy that both Roman law and Jewish custom are negative examples, but only the latter is explicitly declared to be in breach with natural law.

805 See for example Wolff, *Jus naturae methodo scientifica pertractata. Pars prima*, §. 1033 *nota*, p. 683, using Jesus' defence of himself against 'Jewish defamations' as an example for the right to defend one's reputation: 'Quamobrem patet ratio, cur ipse Christus, qui convicia conviciis non rependebat, seu maledicta maledictis 1. *Petr.* II. 23. adversus calumnias tamen Judaeorum, qui famam ipsius lacessebant.'

806 Hanov, Michael Christoph, *Philosophiae civilis sive politicae pars secunda* (Halle: Renger, 1757), § 134, p. 139.

807 Hanov, *Oeconomica*, § 584, p. 414).

808 Hanov, Philosophiae civilis sive politicae pars secunda, § 272 nota, p. 370.

809 Ibid., § 60 *nota*, p. 66: 'Ideo enim quoque Judaei tolerantur, quorum dogmata ipsis propria falsa esse, nemo Christianorum nescit.'

exceeding those in other countries but there were also measures to limit interchange between Christian and Jews, particularly on an elite level. As Jacob Goldberg describes it, 'the general picture of the contacts between the *szlachta* and Jews in the period under consideration is characterised by a certain dualism, derived from oppressive acts against the Jews on one side, and growing mutual contacts on another'.[810] Hanov's display of measured tolerance seems to correspond with this complicated state of affairs and the situation of Danzig, which profited from Jewish (and other) immigration after periods of depopulation.

The two authors also differ with respect to some aspects of their own, ostensibly shared culture. Their respective views on gender relations are a good example in that regard. Wolff, as discussed above, nursed a surprisingly progressive view on the matter. Although he supports traditional gender roles in the household, he does so on a conditional rather than universal basis: women are not naturally inferior to men and a wife is subordinate to a husband only if the *imperium maritale* is a given in the couple's cultural understanding of marriage. As mentioned, he refers to both spouses in a gender-neutral way throughout most of his book, using the term *conjuges* rather than singling out husband and wife in his discourse. Even where their roles are separate, he takes care to explain that the same rules apply for either. The *Jus naturae* translates and defines *pater* and *mater* as *Hausvater* and *Hausmutter*, their German domestic equivalents; but the traditional Latin appellation of *pater-* and *materfamilias* is abandoned in his part of the *Oeconomica*.

This unusually progressive trend is reversed within Hanov's continuation, who strictly sticks to *paterfamilias* and *materfamilias*, and who remains faithful to traditional gender roles throughout. Although Hanov at no point sets out to logically refute Wolff's dismemberment of the superiority of men, the *praestantia sexus*, the usage of the term in a number of different contexts implies that the concept is a given in his world. Female inferiority is taken for granted in the discussion about the sale of male or female slaves, for example, or the status of widows and orphans in villages. Hanov's stance towards women also subliminally transpires in the index to the *Oeconomica* entire: where Wolff's *nota* to § 120 uses the example of Maria Cunitia to prove the intellectual capacity of women as the central point to his argument, the index in Hanov's *Oeconomica* lists her name only in reference to her solidity and modesty against Kepler. In that sense, he does not register the passage for its emancipative thrust but as an example of more traditional female virtues.[811]

---

810 On the treatment of Jewish people in the Polish-Lithuanian Commonwealth, see Goldberg, Jacob, 'Poles and Jews in the seventeenth and eighteenth Centuries: Rejection or Acceptance', *Jahrbücher für die Geschichte Osteuropas*, 22 (1974), 248–282 (262).

811 Hanov, *Oeconomica*, sig. Zzzz 2: '*Cunitiae* (Mariae) soliditas & modestia erga Keplerum 120 *not.*'; ibid., sig. Bbbbb 2: '*Kepleri*...investigavit orbitas planetarum ellipticas ex observationibus *Braheis*, cui superstruxit *tabulas Rudolphinas* ope demonstrationum difficiliimarum, & in *Epitome Astronom. Co-*

Hanov is hardly a misogynist. In fact, he uses the presumed weakness of women in order to strengthen their position in times of duress: women should be lent support in litigations and other business negotiations, both during and after termination of their matrimonial status. Yet in his view, women are not only unexperienced but also weak, belonging to the 'lesser sex', *sexus sequior* and hence have the prerogative of special assistance, as the Romans had already devised in their law code.[812] Hanov's discussion of beauty also brings worn clichés to the fore, where the idea of cosmetics and decking out the body is considered the *mundus muliebris*, a 'feminine world'.[813] Traditional stereotypes of this kind also weave their way through his political theory; in the second tome of the *Politica*, for example, Hanov discusses – very briefly – the role of men and women in the state. Even though, he admits, there are men of effeminate bearing and women of virile virtues, the general infirmity of the *sexus sequior*, the weaker sex, warrants protection, as in cases of bereavement. But given historical accounts where women ruled countries or fought in battle, 'it would not be entirely absurd' for them to partake in battle where there is a shortage of men. And given the thought experiment of women in combat he admits that women mixing in intellectual skirmishes would not be far from impossible either. Hanov's unbelieving tone, however, marks this as a purely hypothetical case that is not supported by actual precedent, as the annotation makes clear. The point is resolved by changing subject and making a case for allowing soldiers to marry, letting their wives earn their sustenance working in the army.[814] This, incidentally, was less a topic of gender relations than an appeal of cameralist writers to the state who wanted to explore an untapped source of population growth by letting soldiers marry.[815] This displays an altogether different attitude to Wolff who did not object to the idea of female suffrage – in theory.[816]

It seems a paradox that Hanov can logically derive statements from Wolff's source material that turn out so different from his predecessor's. In fact, the extensive references back to the *Jus naturae* show that Hanov works in the best of intentions of consistency. Yet the impression emerges that Wolff's natural law, universal or not, is not the warrant for the uniform practical philosophy he imagined it to be. Rather, either author utilizes the same base material to corroborate their own homegrown

pernic. Cujus calculum faciliorem dedit *Cunitia* 120 *not.*'. It must be said, however, that Wolff really does spend the majority of this note on explaining Kepler's merits rather than Maria Cunitia's.

812 Hanov, Philosophiae civilis sive politicae pars tertia, §. 585, p. 540.

813 Ibid., 552, p. 520: '*Mundus vero muliebris*, munditiem, cultum ornatumque earum complectitur, si *Livio* credimus *Hist. L. XXXIV. c. 7.*'

814 Hanov, *Oeconomica*, § 282, pp. 379–80

815 Nipperdey, Justus, 'Bevölkerungstheorie und Idee der Armenfürsorge im 17. und 18. Jahrhundert: Gesellschaftsanalyse, soziale Steuerung und soziale Sicherung', in *Soziale Sicherungssysteme und demographische Wechsellagen. Historisch-vergleichende Perspektiven (1500–2000)*, ed. by Thomas Sokoll (Berlin: Lit Verlag, 2011), pp. 169–97 (175).

816 Wolff, Jus naturae methodo scientifica pertractatum. Pars octava, § 329, p. 111.

beliefs and, at times, prejudices. Their diverging views on women, the Chinese and the Jewish people, in that sense, are just extant examples for the latent discrepancies that suffuse the two halves of the Wolffio-Hanovian practical philosophy.

5.4 Hanov versus Wolff – political systems in comparison

5.4.1 Legitimacy, power and levels of administration

Wolff's inclusion of the *Oeconomica* in the canon of practical philosophy not only spells the integration of domestic topics with natural law and ethics – it also betrays his conviction that the matters of the household are interwoven with the interest of the state. Getting married, having children and educating them, from a moral point of view, cease to be matters of personal choice only. As aforementioned, where Wolff's *Deutsche Politik* cited self-interested motives for procreation, the *Oeconomica* presents the matter primarily as a duty to the state and to God alike. In comparison, Hanov's *Oeconomica* is almost entirely devoid of references to the larger implications of private morality and lacks the Wolffian tendency to foreshadow the topics ostensibly reserved for political theory. Wolff's *Jus naturae VIII*, the natural law basis for what was to be the *Politica*, is referenced four times in total throughout the *Oeconomica continuata* and for unrelated matters: in the context of corporeal punishment; remuneration of servants in accordance with the master's status, the consociation of families for the sake of catering to their livelihood; and judgment and justice in the context of the village.[817] In all these cases, Hanov retrieves a general concept from the eighth, political tome of Wolff's natural law to corroborate an argument on a lower plane rather than render a political meaning to the domestic context. It seems that in no instance the reason of state informs or qualifies aspects of private lives the way it does in Wolff. From a systemic point of view, therefore, Hanov displays a different conception of civic virtue, better said, the relationship between state and individual. This impression hardens when considering their ideas about state, family and welfare in detail.

For Wolff, natural law defines progressive levels of obligation integrated with one another: the natural state of the individual and the pre-political composite of the family build the basis for the body politic as culmination of socio-political living. In that sense, the public and the private sphere do not present two realms in opposition but are complementary to each other. Hanov's idea of law in public and private sphere preserves commonplaces counter to this conception. In the first book of the *Politica*, Hanov declares that 'where the public and private welfare cannot be had simultane-

817 Hanov, *Oeconomica*, § 597, p. 432; § 618, p. 451; § 861, p. 692; § 889, p. 717.

ously, the public welfare is to be preferred to the private one'.[818] Wolff's public and private spheres are seamlessly integrated in one morality construct, which postulates that performing public duties contributes to private happiness. For Hanov, private welfare is not naturally lodged in the common good; a conflict between private and public interest is conceivable.

Moreover, Hanov has a different idea from Wolff about what defines a pact in a political context – better said, what constitutes a pact in the first place. Wolff uses the fiction of a contract to describe existing social and political relationships, therefore using the contract not as an actualised principle but as a moral fortification of natural obligations. Hanov takes the idea of a contract much more literally and seriously: according to him, '[a] republic cannot be better composed than by agreement through a public pact', specifically said, an explicit agreement publicly expressed.[819] Incidentally, the integration of Royal Prussia into the Polish kingdom happened with just such a declaration, the Incorporation Act of 1454 where the 'Prussian prelates, knights, burghers, nobles and all inhabitants of the Prussian lands' committed themselves in writing to the rule of the Polish king, Casimir Jagiellon, "spontaneously and voluntarily".[820] The fates of Royal Prussia thus crucially hinged on explicit, written translocation of power and as a historian Hanov's idea of legitimacy was certainly informed by this event.

Yet Hanov also differentiates between a pact as the founding moment of a state, and a pact defining the governing principles of a republic – a constitution, in essence.[821] Although this latter pact can be tacit in format or even a 'quasi-pact', an explicit agreement is customary and preferable, whether put down in writing or announced publicly.[822] What is clear from the above is that Hanov understands a contract as a principle in practice, not a moral concept in abstraction; in this understanding, a pact presents a means to mete out concrete rules rather than provide a moral yardstick, differently to Wolff's understanding. This does not mean that morality and law live separate lives in Hanov's republic. In tune with the trend of his times, legislation is a tool to improve not just citizens' lives but also their behaviour. Responsibility for moral reform resides with the state and Hanov charges law and authority to control and perfect the behaviour of citizens – more than through rational dis-

---

818 Hanov, Philosophiae civilis sive politicae pars prima, § 552, p. 207: 'Vbi salus publica & privata simul haberi nequit, publica privatae est anteferenda. '

819 Ibid., 258, p. 213: 'Respublica melius constitui nequit quam pacto publico conveniente. '

820 Friedrich, *The Other Prussia*, pp. 22–23.

821 Hanov, Philosophiae civilis sive politicae pars prima, § 259, pp. 213–214: 'Pactum, quo respublica sancitur, diversum est a pacto ineundae civitatis. '

822 Ibid., § 261, p. 215: 'Quo duplici pactum autem vel est expressum, vel tacitum, vel quasi pactum (§. 217): respublica quoque constitui potest pacto vel expresso, vel tacito, vel quasi pacto. Clarissimus tamen usitatissimusque modus statuendi rem publicam habetur in pacto expresso (§. 218.), sive nuncupetur illud, sive scribatur quoque (§. 221. seqq.).'

course, as Wolff would have it. Consistent with his ideas about education, the third volume of Hanov's *Politica* suggests that the betterment of citizens is best achieved through the authoritative force of role models. Exemplary behaviour, ideally by persons of high status such as rulers, magistrates and professors, inspires imitation and is easier and quicker to comprehend than a multitude of rules and long demonstrations; the better and more extant these examples are, the stronger their didactic force; ideally, the conviction caused by good example would even blot out bad influence from the wicked.[823]

Autoritas as a concept is not only used as a matter of weighing in on habits and opinions by example – it also describes the capacity of the state or an official to weigh in on private affairs. Hanov calls upon the authorities to intervene where justice is not observed between parents and children or husband and wife.[824] The level of interventionist mandate is a sign of its own times, or, as Marc Raeff puts it, '[f]or the state to interject itself into the legal aspect of family...was natural in this period because of the traditional concept of political authority as the protector of social norms and law'.[825] And although Wolff also gives the state primacy over family affairs, his idea of the law has a different intent in practice, as an educative force. What Wolff tried to solve with his didactic philosophy was exactly the problem that people failed to follow moral authority; his solution essentially provides cogent and internally valid reasons for the same precepts yet shifting the burden from traditional to rational foundations. Hanov does not seem to rely on the binding force of reason in the same way in his adult didactics. Instead, he matches traditional precepts with a traditional, top-down way of enforcement: the individual citizen is not guided to moral action by rational understanding but best led there through authority and example of those in elevated positions.

In that vein, Hanov also adopts the customary metaphor of the paternal bond between ruler(s) and citizens. This provides the foundation for the *commune bonum*, complete with a Christian sheen: imitating God the best they can, governors should rule with the common good as purpose, feeling happiness about the citizens' happiness and distress at their distress.[826] Yet unlike cameralist classics like Seckendorf, Hanov is not using the father-children metaphor to stand in for a legitimising fiction of absolutism or so it seems from a subtle detail in his discourse: unlike Wolff, Hanov's *Politica* is not talking about the *rector civitatis* in the singular but the *rectores civitatis*, the rulers in the plural. This is a subtle hint that Hanov naturally assumes the state executive to consist of a group of people – as was, in fact, the case in the Polish-Lithuanian Commonwealth, ruled by a parliamentary monarchy. He also har-

823 Hanov, Philosophiae civilis sive politicae pars tertia, § 116, pp. 129–131.
824 Ibid., § 237, p. 278; § 239, p. 279.
825 Raeff, Marc, The Well-Ordered Police State. Social and Institutional Change through Law in the Germanies and Russia, 1600–1800 (New Haven and London: Yale University Press, 1983), p. 76.
826 Hanov, Philosophiae civilis sive politicae pars quarta, § 100, p. 87.

bours a different notion about the way political communities come about. The foundation moment of a state, in his opinion, is the consociation of villages – not families, like Wolff postulates.[827] Hanov is not alone in this assumption; the village as pre-political, natural conglomerate of houses is an Aristotelian idea that resurfaces in the academic debate of the seventeenth century, for example in Keckermann's *Systema*.[828] From a scholarly point of view, Hanov is consistent with his local tradition, assuming Keckermann's books were still in fashion in eighteenth century Danzig. Yet this assumption poses a significant difference to Wolff's repeated assertion that families or households would make up the base units for a body politic.[829] To be sure, Hanov's concept of the logical genesis of the state from villages is not entirely at odds with Wolff: in the preface of the *Oeconomica*, when discussing whether the field counts as part of politics or qualifies as a separate discipline, Wolff argues that 'states consist of houses and villages, and those consist of smaller societies', that is spouses, parents, children, workers and masters.[830] Yet the similarity is only superficial. For Wolff, the relationship between citizen and ruler is immediate in nature. For Hanov, the village has considerable prominence in both his *Oeconomica* and the *Politica*, and not just as a pre-political pact between families and a pre-stage of the state, but also a unit endowed with the rights to certain judicative capacities and welfare functions.[831] This circumstance not only speaks of the fact that Hanov takes a different political order for granted; it furthermore corroborates the suspicion that Wolff's highly centralised state pays homage to a political discourse and reality specific to his own environment. Given Danzig's special position within the Polish-Lithuanian government, Hanov was indeed invested in a political order preserving the independence of cities to manage their own affairs, rather than be subject to a centralised state. And although the city's inhabitants were German more than Polish, the idea of incorporation into a centralised Prussian state need not be an appealing one for the cultural affinity. The example of Königsberg in the seventeenth century, in fact, provides a case where this municipal liberty was gravely eroded as a consequence of Frederick William's takeover of the city in 1657; his immediate efforts to take over control over trade and taxation and handle sumptuary legislation by ducal decree, not municipal council, was met with much resistance.[832]

827 Hanov, *Philosophiae civilis sive politicae pars prima*, § 31, p. 34: '*Civitatem* dicimus societatem vicorum liberam.'

828 Keckermann, Systema disciplinae politicae, p. 7.

829 See Wolff, *Jus naturae methodo scientifica pertractatum. Pars octava*, §1–4, pp. 1–3, particularly § 4: 'Societas inter plures domus contracta eo fine, ut conjunctim sibi parent ad vitae necessitatem, commoditatem ac jucunditatem, immo felicitatem requisita...*Civitas* dicitur. Atque adeo patet, *pacta hominum civitates fuisse constituendas.*'

830 Wolff, *Oeconomica* § 1 *nota*, p. 2: 'Quamvis enim Civitas, quae obiectum Politicae est ex domibus & vicis componatur, hae vero societates ex simplicibus conjugali nimirum, paterna & herili coalescant...'.

831 Hanov, *Oeconomica*, §. 889, p. 717.

832 Friedrich, *The Other Prussia*, pp. 49–50.

The return of the village does not mean the eclipse of the household in Hanov's work, even though he seems less intent on interpreting private activity with a view to public relevance. Yet rather than upgrading private to public virtue, his *Politica* duly picks up on an issue where the interests of the two spheres intersect: marriage politics and its importance for population growth. Wolff's *Oeconomica* was specifically intent on tying the topic of marriage into the context of national welfare, as a warrant for continuity. The *Oeconomica* pushes procreation as a civic virtue, as a mandate owed to the state even if a private matter. On a political, regulative level, this is complemented by emigration control safeguarding the state's interest.[833] Hanov's second volume of the *Politica* devotes a whole chapter to the question of population size and its growth. Starting with different types of citizen progeny – foreigners or native population – he also lists groups without citizen rights, such as slaves, for example. Hanov arrives at the conclusion that there are two ways of growing a citizen body: either by attracting immigration or stimulating marriage, preferably the latter as the more natural mode of replenishing the ranks of citizens.[834] Unlike Wolff, however, he uses not restrictive but permissive legislation: not keeping foreigners from leaving but attracting them; and not morally defining the framework of a socially productive marriage but legally stimulating it. Thus, in order to attract immigration and hence new citizens, the right to citizenship should be expanded.[835] In order to promote legitimate procreation, viz. in wedlock, the regulative and financial burden of marriage is to be lightened.[836] Hanov cites Moses' laws in the Jewish *civitas* as a positive example whereby the relative lack of restrictions on intermarriage are so few that a 'stupendous population growth' is achieved.[837] The benefits of natural population growth considered, the sensitive issue remains that legislation against certain types of marriage is possible, but legislating mandatory marriage is clearly beyond the scope of what is naturally right. Wolff makes it clear that from a natural law point of view, marriage – if all prerequisites are met – is the official path to virtue and felicity. His natural law, however, does not outlaw monasterial or self-chosen celibacy nor condemn it as harshly as some other Protestant sources do. Taking Leibniz and Descartes as an example, Wolff acknowledges that where intellectual contributions or public service may prohibitively limit a person in terms of time and resources available to bringing up children, a celibate life might be defensible.[838] Hanov, on the other hand, believes it justified by the state's need to impel the population with both sticks and

833 Wolff, Jus naturae methodo scientifica pertractata. Pars octava, §§ 402–405, pp. 138–139.

834 Hanov, Philosophiae civilis sive politicae pars secunda, § 270, p. 367.

835 Ibid., § 254, p. 354.

836 Hanov, Philosophiae civilis sive politicae pars secunda, § 272, p. 369.

837 Ibid., § 272 *nota*, p. 370: 'Ita legibus Mosaicis in Judaeorum civitate perpauca tantum conjugia interdicuntur & mature ineuntur, quae propterea quoque in tam stupendum hominum numerum excrevit, in quantum vix alia ulla.'

838 Wolff, *Oeconomica*, § 196 *nota*, p. 326.

carrots to procreate, particularly for a state in need that cannot procure citizens in any other way. In support, he quotes old German legislation putting confirmed bachelors under pressure and presenting them with financial disincentives to remain unwed or Roman policies offering privileges to citizens bearing and educating at least three children.[839] Although Hanov does not overtly praise or judge these policies, they are used as corroborative statements or at least cases of inspirational legislation to effectuate population growth in a state by 'natural' means. This is not to say that he discards all social taboos about marriage for the sake of political expediency. The *Politica* mandates the state to legislate against any illicit forms of marriage – such as polygamy or temporary marriages – and dissuades from a match against family consent, this all to the benefit of 'rudioribus civibus', the less educated specimen amongst the citizen body who would not follow this advice on their own account.[840]

With regards to his own situation, it is to be noted that Hanov remained unmarried to the end of his days – perhaps a reason for the somewhat dispassionate discussion of marriage and the omission of child rearing as a civic duty, in contrast to Wolff's frequent repetition thereof.[841] Yet even though celibate, Hanov has a confessional stake in the matter, judging from his hostility to Catholic monasteries. In fact, if at all possible, legislation should upend 'lecherous monkhood' *v.c. matrimonii*, 'by force of marriage', and thus prevent it from having its ranks and coffers replenished at the expense of the state.[842] As it turns out, Poland's clergy was predominantly Catholic, as opposed to Protestant Prussia; and Wolff, generally more dispassionate about confessional differences, does not seem to share Hanov's hostility against celibacy in that way. What is remarkable here, however, is that Hanov advocates mandatory marriage as a means of upending monkhood, but not a way to spur population increase. In the end, each author displays a different stake in political discourse and the family within, informed by exactly the different realities they live in and cater to. It is not surprising that both Hanov and Wolff would seek a universalist baseline in what each would consider normal. Yet the result are two very different constitutional models intended, believed but failing to support one and the same viewpoint.

---

839 See Hanov, Philosophiae civilis sive politicae pars secunda, § 273 nota, p. 371.

840 Hanov, Philosophiae civilis sive politicae pars tertia, § 309, pp. 358–9.

841 On Hanov's lifetime status as a single person, cf. the speech on occasion of Hanov's funeral: Rector Et Professores Nobilissimis Ac Politissimis Athenaei Gedanensis Civibus S. D. Eosqve Ad Funus Michaelis Christophori Hanovii Philosophiae Professoris Et Bibliothecarii, Jam Beate Fato Functi Secum Pie Celebrandum Ad Diem XII. Octobris Huius Anni MDCCLXXIII Convocant Et Invitant (Danzig: Schreiber, 1773).

842 Hanov, Philosophiae civilis sive politicae pars tertia, § 309, p. 359: 'Si recte inhiberi potuit pruritus coenobia replendi, ineundi & in immensum cum detrimento civitatis locupletandi (§. 284. nota): nil obstat, quo minus & alius abusus v.c. matrimonii, in detrimentum reip. & familiarum vergens, pactis legibusque impediatur puniaturque, quantum sufficere possit, ad eum tollendum.'

5.4.2 Social welfare programmes in contrast

The three pillars of the Wolffian welfare state rest on a number of arguments that link the ideological with the expedient. Health, wealth and education of the population are considered natural mandates to the ruler, with a utilitarian tangent in tow: the purpose of building an economically prosperous and rationally conform state. As is clear from Hanov's marriage politics, the idea of population growth is at the forefront of his political thinking and this may not be a surprise given his geography: depopulation posed a serious problem in Poland in the beginning of the eighteenth century. Yet as a burgher in a free city within the Polish-Lithuanian Commonwealth, Hanov evidently had no stake in the idea of a centralised state with a welfare mandate – and consequently has no space for the moral mandate of a ruler to care for his citizens. His *Politica* takes up on Wolff's welfare mandate in a more abstract guise in terms of poor relief and health care, whilst staying true to traditional ideas of education. Whilst there seems to be nothing visionary about many aspects of Hanov's welfare policies, there is one element that both approximates him to Wolff and sets him apart still: the proactive, voluntary involvement of citizens in the betterment of society.

The institutionalisation of health care is a topic Wolff's natural law specifically assigns to the *prudentia civilis*. Yet although Hanov duly picks up this mandate, his public health programme in the *Politica* looks markedly different from the institutional responses described by his predecessor. The Wolffian natural law showed a particular focus on the regulation of practitioners, and the introduction of food safety measures whereby the sale of insalubrious foods should be legally prosecuted. Hanov sees the state's involvement only partially vested in such permanent institutional responses – and, in fact, he cuts out the middleman by directing his regulatory efforts straight at each citizen. In fact, for Hanov the responsibility of a body politic to look after the health of their own is vested in the idea that individual and community are obligated to one another, with regards to both physical and mental health.[843] Since the care for mentally challenged exceeds the capacity of private citizens, *gyrgathi*, or insane asylums, should be established with public funds.[844] The same argument counts for hospitals to cure or care the physically destitute, which can be combined with mental institutions where possible, to save on expenses.[845] Whilst Hanov duly picks up on the institutions Wolff's natural law had foreshadowed, the impression is that of a municipal organisation mindful of expenses, more than a state-organised venture financed by taxation.

843 Hanov, Philosophiae civilis sive politicae pars tertia, §§ 455–456, pp. 466–467.
844 Ibid., § 459, p. 468.
845 Ibid., §. 460, p. 469.

The discussion of illness is dominated by concepts of health and takes up one chapter in the third volume of Hanov's *Politica*.[846] Hanov's interpretation of public health care seems to map straightforwardly to his understanding of the human body. To a large part, the end of his measures are aimed at the preservation of the bodily functions he defines, such as digestion, excretion, motion and breathing.[847] This quite literal understanding of public health results in a two-pronged approach that promotes the provision of goods alongside the promotion of knowledge. Quite simply, the health of citizens is promoted through the provision of goods such as safe housing, sufficient clothing and nutrition, as also the prevention of dangerous influences such as bad, even sulphurous or pestilential, air.[848]

Moreover, a healthy citizen body needs medicines and good doctors, thus first and foremost pharmacies and academies providing training in chemistry, surgery and other requisite skill sets.[849] Similarly to Wolff's licensing regimes, these pharmacies need to obtain the privilege to trade, so as to safeguard the quality, and are subject to a price cap, too.[850] Like Wolff, Hanov is concerned about the quality of doctors but he unsuspectedly lauds practical experience at least as much as academic training. The public considers a doctoral title often as a sufficient seal of professional knowledge; in reality, so Hanov's opinion, cases occur where doctors practice successfully who have acquired all skill and knowledge through their own initiative.[851] Given the difficulty to judge the pedigree of doctors, those of proven competence should be paid a salary to make their profession viable.[852] At this point, Hanov's discourse is still similar Wolff's, even if tinged by his own perspective. There is, however, one aspect in his public health programme that seems to dominantly relay his own experience and background. Since the scientific exploration of illnesses and their causes is an imperative in the state, Hanov wants it to be pursued not just by doctors and academic faculties but by 'curious citizens'.[853] The point of this is not only to educate medical personnel available to the citizens and to improve practices but also to educate citizens and inform legislation, in a joint effort with magistrates and 'teachers of moral truths', *moralium veritatum doctoribus*.[854] Hanov sees the crux in public health in the improvement of research and education, exactly as he himself practiced as a member of the scientific society. Regulation, in fact, means control over the indi-

846 See the chapter entitled 'De sapienti cura sanitatis reliquorum corporis bonorum', in: Hanov, *Philosophiae civilis sive politicae pars tertia*, §§ 450–560, pp. 462–524.

847 Ibid., §§ 484–7, pp. 482–5.

848 Ibid., §. 461, p. p. 469; § 474, p. 477; § 485, p. 483.

849 Ibid., §. 463–5, pp. 470–1; §§ 469–70, pp. 473–4.

850 Ibid., §. 467, p. 471; § 468, p. 473.

851 Ibid., § 472 with *nota*, pp. 474–6.

852 Ibid., §. 473, p. 476.

853 Ibid., §§. 476–7, pp. 478–9.

854 Ibid., §§ 488–93, pp. 485–489.

vidual so as to prevent him or her from bodily harm, an unhealthy lifestyle or doing harm to the health of other people.[855] Hanov inserts a whole catalogue of bodily functions that should not be harmed, and a whole set of individual activities that should be punishable by law as they affect the individual's health. In contrast, Wolff and the Prussian kings focus on exerting control on the business side, by licensing doctors and medications. Although both emphasise the professionalisation of medicine and the increasing importance of empirical research within the field, the respective political consummation is altogether different.

Hanov's prosperity politics are somewhat similar to his approach to public health: it starts with identifying needs and then lists the goods to be procured. For Wolff, the idea of financial sustainability, across private and public realm, comes under a twin heading: the reining in of personally ruinous habits and the provision for the poor as a state obligation. To Hanov, the matter of subsistence is simply equivalent to the question of provision, discussing what to procure rather than how to redistribute goods. He furthermore misses out the utilitarian point of Wolff's welfare: the political boon that is an economically self-sufficient and productive population. Hanov starts with the types of goods that need to be provided in a state to keep the citizens fed and healthy. The rulers of a state are to take care that all citizens are provided with food, clothes and shelter. This means the state will have to take precaution that the food, clothes, habitations and even the air are clean and healthy.[856] As it turns out, Hanov harbours quite a different idea about what 'necessity, joy and comfort' entails, the triple good communal life ensures for its members. The matter takes up some 110 paragraphs in the third volume of the *Politica*, devoted chiefly to a whole span of arguably essential goods. In that area he shows an incomparably kindlier attitude towards worldly pleasures than Wolff: beauty is intrinsic to welfare, thus public and private splendour are both encouraged and should be promoted in buildings, clothes, jewellery, and Hanov is not afraid to go into minute detail.[857] The same expansive approach governs the section about nutrition where Hanov describes the different types of nourishment humans tend to consume: all types of meat, fruit and vegetables, and 'natural' and 'artificial' forms of drink – including coconut water and coffee.[858] Still, with this broad expanse of offerings, Hanov maintains that only 'true' and 'innocent' pleasures should be promoted by the community.[859] It is clear that Hanov's idea of what counts as basic commodity caters to a different normality than

855 Ibid., §§ 479–481, pp. 480–1; §§ 496–7, pp. 491–2; §§ 499–505, pp. 493–497.
856 Ibid., § 396, p. 432: 'Quia rectori civitatis curae esse debet, ne desit rerum ad victum, amictum & habitationem necessariarum copia sufficiens (§. 420. P. VIII. *Jur. nat.*): patet, propter necessitate prospiciendi vitae praesidiis (§. 394), *operam dandam esse, quantum fieri potest, ut civitati, omnibusque civibus quam optime prospiciatur de aere, victu, amictu & domiciliis salubribus...*'.
857 Ibid., §§ 551–559, pp. 519–524.
858 Ibid., §§ 408–9, pp. 438–40.
859 Ibid., §§ 541–2, pp. 514–5; 548, pp. 517–8.

for Wolff. In contrast, the essential goods Wolff is interested in – safe buildings, food and wood – are of more existential nature. Where Wolff seems to be more supportive of luxury legislation and generally disapproves of unnecessary expenditures, Hanov seeks to actively promote the pleasantries of life in the state, in quite straightforwardly material terms: fragrant herbs, soft wool, singing birds and tasty (but healthy) foods. This casual ode to joy is a song somewhat alien to the Wolffian discourse. What is more so, at no point does Hanov argue from the point of utility for the state. The entire section on the comfort, necessity and pleasantness that a political community should safeguard is written from the perspective of the citizen, not the ruler; and from the perspective of the citizen, the ruler should provide these – more or less – basic commodities where this exceeds the power of the private individual.[860]

Hanov also discusses the other side of the coin: necessity. The state needs to safeguard through law, penal sanctions and diligence that no citizen should die of hunger – and to make sure that his extends to the needy as well, generosity towards beggars and paupers should be obligatory.[861] Yet again, this marks out a considerable difference to Wolff, whose prime concern in poor relief is to prevent the rest of the population from ruining themselves through charity. *Eleemosyne*, private charity, is delegated to and controlled by the state to that end in Wolff's natural law. The term *eleemosyne* does not feature in Hanov's *Politica* nor is he intent on its management by the state; rather, he leaves the Christian virtue of *charitas* intact and elevates it to an essential virtue of state and household. *Charitas* classifies as quite simply an interpersonal feeling that should be fostered amongst citizens. Hanov officially pushes it to extend beyond the primacy of the nuclear family; this is implicit where he argues, for example, that parents have the right to donate a part of their children's inheritance to particularly needy or particularly deserving people.[862] On the public level, moreover, Hanov does not restrict but promote the idea of mutual charity and benevolence of citizens towards one another.[863] Unlike Wolff, he does not seem to be worried about the ruinous effects of Christian charity: the remedy to poverty is not replacing private with public charity but, in fact, to foster it.

From an institutional perspective, Hanov's idea of social welfare reflects municipal responses to poverty: not a centralised, state-led approach financed through taxes and state income but a local effort to corral and utilise private funds. In that sense, his descriptions mirror the Lutheran idea of the public chest and targeted initiatives. Hanov's suggestion is not simply to provide alms but to make borrowing easier for those in need, financed either by a religious fund, *aerarium pium*, or a specific lending facility, a *mons pietatis*, funded by private citizens with superfluous funds or public

860 Ibid., § 530, p. 508.
861 Ibid., § 417, p. 444.
862 Hanov, *Oeconomica*, § 412, p. 199.
863 Hanov, Philosophiae civilis sive politicae pars tertia, §§ 567–8, pp. 528–531.

money.[864] The justification here is that single citizens carry obligations towards the community that the state ought to channel and direct at favourable conditions for the sake of the less fortunate ones.[865]

Conversely, in Hanov's *Oeconomica* the provision of extended family members seems to follow a more traditional path relegating responsibilities to immediate social communities than is obvious in Wolff's theory. That parents are obliged to care for children in material and intellectual terms is a given for both. But at least Wolff's *Jus naturae* does not lay out in detail how the obligations are to be interpreted beyond the context of the nuclear family and there are only marginal references as to how these relationships may have ramifications in terms of provision. Hanov's *Oeconomica* is, *passim*, more specific on this topic, in fact, establishes a hierarchy of provision: if parents are too poor to cater to their own subsistence, the first port of call should be their own parents, before relying on the resources their children can contribute and tertiarily, the grandchildren.[866] This provision comes with a number of caveats: if the children's contribution to their parents' comfort is more onerous than it is useful to the parents, the latter should not accept it.[867] This proviso is reminiscent of Wolff's command that wedding couples should not accept gifts they do not need. In other words, in both cases not merely the welfare of the immediate people in need is at stake but also the economic stability of the community – and in that sense, both giver and recipient have to be taken into account. Yet in spite of Wolff's contractual formula that bind the partners to do as they ought, the prime virtue at play in Hanov's work is *charitas*. Pre-political social communities also play a role when it comes to the provision of relative strangers, which is where the village as an organising level between state and family comes in. In Hanov's political account, the village as an association of families is a miniature commonwealth that bears not only certain rights but also obligations towards its administration and conservation. These rights are not sweeping; the death penalty, for example, is explicitly beyond the reach of the village community.[868] But with a view to social welfare Hanov's village picks up some responsibilities that Wolff had relegated to the state level – and brings the topic back to the realm of the *Oeconomica*, where the village is discussed. Thus communal agreements on the village level regulate the 'personal' and 'material' help that the villagers should lend to each other.[869] Since this warrants a level of organisation there needs to be some form of local

864 Ibid., §§ 655–6, pp. 590–1.

865 Ibid., § 656, p. 591.

866 Hanov, *Oeconomica*, § 556, p. 379.

867 Ibid., § 560, p. 384: 'Si beneficium liberorum ipsis magis est onerosum, quam parentibus utile, hi vel non acceptare illud, vel largius remunerari debent.'

868 Hanov, Philosophiae civilis sive politicae pars prima, § 120, p. 95–6.

869 Hanov, *Oeconomica*, § 880, p. 708.

government.[870] In the end, therefore, social welfare is the stimulus to undo the centralisation effort that Wolff's natural law maps out, at least on paper.

The village is a direct and practical network of provision that is essentially based on a pact of mutual solidarity. This is in stark contrast to the Wolffian idea of mandating public welfare provisions to the state level, as a 'natural' obligation of the ruler towards his citizens, rather than a solidarity-based act from one villager to another. It does, however, resemble the models Luther and Vives promoted whereby villages and even cities sought to solve local, social problems through basic infrastructures of provision, financed by municipal funds, donations and funds collected by the church. Although Hanov does not mention the role of the church in terms of financial procurement, the virtue of charity is emphasised on all levels of organisation, in the absence of a utilitarian argument.

Finally, the *Politica*'s model of public education shows a similar divergence from Wolff's universalist state education model. With a curriculum built on moral pedagogy, not vocational perspectives or traditional faculties, state education in Wolffian terms presented itself as a mandatory, universal and state-supported necessity – which in the perfect world of natural law starts with parents' moral education of their children. Hanov writes for and about a more realistic, traditional view of the world: as he remarks in the second volume of the *Politica*, it is clear that parents *should* cater to their children's early moral and intellectual education – but fact has it that this does not always happen, either because the parents die prematurely or are not suited to the task for a variety of reasons. These shortcomings – rather than an ideal state of things – are whence the necessity arises for the state to provide as much succour as possible so as to bring up and educate proper citizens.[871] For Wolff, schooling is a universal mandate and not just where the parental unit is failing. And although Hanov does not overtly explain whether education is to be sponsored by state or family, the placement of this topic in the *Oeconomica* suggests he considers it a matter of private choice and initiative – not public responsibility and private obligation. With regard to the actual curriculum, Hanov's *Oeconomica* already foreshadows a certain faithfulness to traditional vocational structures and the description of school and academic education is no exception. In the chapter dedicated to the household as a whole, Hanov describes to what he generally terms the *culturae animi*, the cultivation of the mind and its implication on professional lives.[872] Separating men of learning into those of practical and those of theoretical knowledge he further describes the sphere of academia by its traditional categorisation into the four liberal arts: theology, law, medicine, philosophy, taught in churches, gymnasia, schools and privately.[873]

870 Hanov, *Oeconomica*, §§ 884–5, pp. 712–3.

871 Hanov, Philosophiae civilis sive politicae pars secunda p. 401f., § 303.

872 Hanov, *Oeconomica* §. 792, p. 628.

873 Ibid., 793–4, pp. 629–30.

The public schools in the *Politica*, however, seem to mirror Wolff's China-inspired system, the *scholae inferiores* and *superiores*. Granted, this categorisation may not have been new but has equivalents in Hanov's German terminology, the *niedrige* or *untere Schulen* and *Oberschulen*.[874] Still, he initially picks up Wolff's rationality-based curriculum which is oriented on the superior and inferior faculties of the soul.[875] Only later does Hanov return to more traditional curricula, whereby the *scholae inferiores* are dedicated to basic skills like reading, writing, maths and religion, and the upper schools to the three liberal arts (grammar, rhetoric and poetics), together with the study of history and theology.[876] In that sense, Hanov lapses back to tradition, away from Wolff's idea that schools dedicate themselves to inculcating faculties to rule and obey.

Still, since schools are in the state's interest, Hanov proposes some regulation to ensure access to education. As with his approach to public health and prosperity, schooling is a matter of procurement: the state does not finance education but should cater to the right quantity of schools, which is defined by the number of parents in an area. As the logic goes, it is not the number of children that demand a number of teachers, but the combined financial capacities of the parents that can cover a teacher's salary; differently said, 'superfluous' are those schools that pose too much of a financial burden to the collective.[877] Like poor relief, therefore, education as a social welfare concern, therefore, is a community-bound venture, not a state-organised one.

One aspect of the cultivation of knowledge that Wolff and Hanov clearly agree upon is the importance of the scientific societies and the promotion of knowledge for specifically the common weal. Yet although both root for the same institution, their respective understanding subtly differs. For Hanov the focus of research should be all and everything that bears some kind of utility for the political community.[878] This idea is indubitably in tune with Wolff's idea of scientific societies. Yet Hanov's idea of utility in knowledge is remarkably different from Wolff's: to Wolff, truth lives in the abstract and should be taught as such – Hanov prefers observation, data collection and experiment combined with scholarship of a more traditional make. Judging from the afterlife of the material he collected, his approach to science was more readily sub-

---

874 Hanov, *Philosophiae civilis sive politicae pars secunda*, § 321 *nota*, p. 424: 'Scholae autem superiores distinctam rerum & rationum, cur res ita sint, explicationem praestant, ideoque excolunt intellectum. Scholae inferiores nostratibus dicuntur *niedrige Schulen*, vel *untere Schulen* aut simpliciter *Schulen*; superiores autem *Oberschulen* vel *hohe Schulen*.', signalling that this is common, not novel usage of the terms.

875 Ibid., § 321, p. 423.

876 Ibid., § 322, p. 424.

877 Ibid., § 323–4, p. 425–6.

878 Ibid., § 304, p. 402: 'Explorandum est, quaenam generatim, & speciatim pro indole civitatis in e salutis publiace causa conjunctis viribus instituenda sint.'

sumed, compared to the short afterlife of Wolffian philosophy. Far more remarkable, however, is Hanov's insistence on the voluntary involvement of citizens, the fact that citizens should show initiative to improve the living conditions of their *civitas*. In comparison, the stimulus for Wolff's academies and *societates* emanates from the state. They are to be specifically privileged with the *libertas philosophandi*, in the understanding that they will pursue science of Wolff's rationalist brand. Hanov's bottom-up civic engagement is still a very different endeavour, clearly informed by his own ambitions and circumstances, than a purely state-directed push for progress.

Interesting in that regard is the curious incidence of Danzig's scientific society's refusal to cooperate with the government after ducal Prussia's takeover on a project that it had called into life itself: an educational institution for midwives.[879] Whether it was specifically hostility against this particular government or the preference of civic engagement over centralised welfare, this example implies that a state-led push to improve medical conditions need not necessarily be in the civic interest.

5.5 Summary

Hanov's completion of the Wolffian system bears significant differences to the original part in execution and content, in spite of his promise of faithful adherence. Wolff had translated traditional norms of his time and place into a rationalist discourse – Hanov puts this rationalist discourse back into a traditionalist setting, and that of his own locale. This is evident in their respective understanding of content, sources and even terminology relevant to their joint discourse. Hanov seems to not have been aware of the conceptual divergence, even where he sets out to construct a completely different political set up on the basis of Wolff's natural law. He presupposes a constitutional rather than absolutist monarchy and his institutions rely on municipal structures, as would have been the reality of his own hometown Danzig, and the political stake of the learned circles Hanov was vested in. What is more so, Hanov calls upon civic engagement to solve social problems where Wolff mandates the ruler exclusively with this task. This is clear from Hanov's vision for scientific societies' contributions to medical research and individual charity as a backbone to poor relief as opposed to Wolff's state-led approach.

The comparison between the two authors is less intent on their 'correct' or 'incorrect' execution of the system; in fact, it would be more reasonable to assume that the two would necessarily diverge. Yet it is exactly the divergence that highlights how each author writes from a different vantage point and is unwittingly captive to their own environment: Wolff writes as a political philosopher, Hanov as an activist citizen. In that sense, incongruences between Wolff's and Hanov's work do not invali-

879 Górska, 'Die Naturforschende Gesellschaft in Danzig und die gemeinnützige Aufklärung', p. 105.

date one or the other. If anything, they corroborate the suspicion that Wolff's arguments were not part of a dominant discourse in the republic of letters that Hanov would have been familiar with but that they fed from the experience of his immediate surroundings and were moulded by personal interests. In that sense, the comparison throws into relief that in spite of a uniform method and the best of all intentions, consistency is not a given and that individual preference and socio-political realities leak into the discourse. Wolff's concern to solve confessional rifts is entirely absent from Hanov's half; and Hanov's zeal for historiography and municipal rights is anathema to Wolff's theory. In the end, it may also be that the subject matter – domestic morality and politics – is particularly susceptible to strong opinions and nurtured assumptions about normality and universality. The topic may throw these different conceptions into particularly stark relief. Yet it may also be an indication of how tacit assumptions can bear on an abstract, highly theoretical discourse as well, even if that would be much less discernible.

6 Conclusion

The starting point for this case study of Wolff's *Oeconomica* was the claim by a group of scholars that Wolff had 'consciously founded' the modern welfare state. As this study has argued, this is an *ex post* assumption, reading an innovative intent into an intrinsically conservative discourse. The social welfare framework Wolff proposes presents his normality more than a novelty when considered in its historical context, granted some exceptions. This is less on account of lacking originality than the point and purpose of his intellectual venture. Wolff's philosophy, by its very nature, is eclectic in conduct and essence; it subsumes the past to rebuild the present, not to prepare the future.

Wolff's method portends to be heuristic. In reality, it rarely serves to seek new truths but to codify existing opinions, knowledge and experiences in a logical format. As is evident from the traces of Christian dogma in his philosophy, Wolff's propositions build up to foregone conclusions– it is only the supporting argument that is rationalised by means of method. In this way, the method allows Wolff to subsume more recent approaches and findings and utilise them in support of traditional views, as can be observed in the *Oeconomica*. The same practice lends Wolff's political theory a hand where method writes the institutional reality of eighteenth-century Prussia into universal, natural law – excising the overtly religious foundation. On occasion, Wolff pushes beyond traditional boundaries to develop ideas ahead of his own time, such as in the case of secular pedagogy or gender equality. But by and large, the method serves to fortify pre-existing practices, norms and institutions.

Wolff's system as a programmatic impulse behind his work is a framework intent on epistemological conciliation. The *systema*, the operational principle behind Wolff's philosophy, proclaims the integration and interlocking of all disciplines and propositions across traditional boundaries. The fundamental presumption is that all truly scientific tenets, regardless the provenance, are compatible with one another. Yet the practice shows that this can lead to inconsistencies where arguments borne from different traditions of thought and practice defy reconciliation, such as is the case of Wolff's theory about love. The systematic integration of the *Oeconomica* not only spells a fresh injection of sciences into the household – it anchors domestic morality within the political realm. Here the ramifications of Wolff's project become fully visible: Luther had revalued family life from a theological, Wolff from a political perspective. Both promote the same moral conduct, but with a view to different ends. A joint reading of natural law and the *Oeconomica* demonstrates how Wolff seeks to promote prosperity and stability of the state through the political reorientation of the household and a set of systematic welfare programmes. In this scenario, a citizen's true happiness relies with public welfare but also -mindedness.

The rewriting of the old rulebook on the basis of natural law rather than Christian values furthermore signals not secularisation but rationalisation of the existing

https://doi.org/10.1515/9783110714098-006

framework within the spirit of its own times. By corroborating accepted norms through demonstration Wolff tries to counter moral decay and social disorder. To that end he deliberately mobilizes a force to prompt both individual and state to action: self-interest and utility. By demonstrating how a particular course of action is in the interest of the individual or serves the state, Wolff yokes together two impulses traditionally found at odds: public and private interest. The two are intertwined in an understanding of happiness and virtue built on the notion of obligation, as defined by natural law. The idea of utilising self-interest in the name of morality is not necessarily a cheap trick. Augustin saw no contradiction between self-love and devotion, even identified the two with one another. The same idea translates into Wolff's brand of civic-mindedness: the right kind of self-love equates to piety, and – in worldly terms – is important for the overall stability of the state; yet self-love is also extended to include a broader, politically informed type of happiness we all ought to strive towards, for our own sake.

Wolff's philosophy is synthetic in nature and composition and the same goes for the *Oeconomica* and the welfare policies in his natural law. The *Oeconomica* relies heavily on received wisdoms, even though presented in a rationalised format for effect – and fortified with a set of reverse-engineered motives to strengthen moral resolve by. Wolff's welfare state chiefly documents policies and discourse well in vogue at his own time. Only his education theory is probing a departure from the prevalent state ideology, by excising the theological component within. The family is encased as the base component of society – firmly if not always consistently. Yet the household is not only a unit of provision and duty but of inherent inequality, vis-à-vis the natural state of man. This inequality is naturally deepened in the theoretical transition from pre- to political community, as private hierarchies are declared subordinate to the public interest. Wolff's fiction of a social contract is not an actualised principle but a legitimising fiction, and the welfare principles arising therefrom not the universal right of individual citizens but a moral mandate to the ruler. These twin aspects – inbuilt inequality and welfare as a moral duty, not a legal right – pose the clearest conceptual difference to a modern understanding of social welfare.

In Wolff's social theory, the family provides the middling stage between the two poles of natural freedom and civil surrender. The household as a base unit is to be fostered morally and materially, ostensibly for the purpose of private happiness but with the common good as a prior goal. This makes for the most dramatic break with the purpose of *Hausväterliteratur*, the genre the *Oeconomica* arguably belongs to – the fact that Wolff's book argues from the perspective of the state, not householder himself. In that sense, Wolff presents an old order where the same practices are demonstrated for an ideologically updated purpose.

The differences between Wolff's and Hanov's parts of the philosophical system suggest that the two did not work within the same theoretical discourse. There is a demonstrable distance between their tacit assumptions which implies that each catered to a reality specific to his own surroundings – and that Wolff's vantage point as a political philosopher differed vastly from Hanov's view as a politically engaged citizen. Wolff writes about and for the absolutist state and his social welfare does not argue with individual welfare but the state interest in mind. The political contribution of citizens consists in a morally meritorious lifestyle, intended to serve the state in the newly defined self-interest of the individual. Hanov is equally concerned about the common good but his constitutional mindset does not translate into social welfare provision of the same kind. Instead, he sees the proactive engagement of citizens as a fundamental aspect to the community's welfare. By implication, and also with a view to the prehistory of social welfare programmes prior to Wolff, the idea of a state welfare programme is a utilitarian consideration to the ruler – but not necessarily a desideratum in the eyes of the subject, although one would assume this to be in their natural interest. The modern, democratic welfare state, in contrast, *does* argue for social welfare for the promotion of individual happiness, which poses not an institutional but an ideological break with paternalist welfare. Where the institutions might resemble each other on the surface, the political rationalisation is altogether different. A democracy advertises the utility of social welfare from the perspective of the individual, not from interest of the state, as Wolff would have it. State education is seen as a catalyst to social mobility where Wolff proclaims it a warrant for conformity. Health care is presented as a basic right, not a matter of maintaining a populous and prosperous country, likewise poor relief and social regulation.

This differentiation is poignant with a view to the current debate of how valid the concept of 'Enlightened Absolutism' really is, a term coined by historians since the 1930s and tenacious in its legacy. As scholars like Johan van der Zande now argue, the seemingly progressive policies by rulers like Frederick II or Catherine the Great did not present a shift in values on the political level but merely the consolidation of traditional patterns.[880] This corresponds with Wolff's political theory that is ostensibly rebuilt on tradition: he does not critically examine the regimental traditions of his own times but provides them with scientific legitimacy. It is Kant who probes the break by declaring that all humans intrinsically pose ends in themselves, never means. Read against the backdrop of eighteenth-century population management discourse and traditionally practiced social regulation this poses a more momentous tectonic shift in political ideology than otherwise obvious.

Ideological continuity between Wolffian welfare theory and post-Kantian liberalism does exist, albeit in the negative. Liberal critiques of political systems often decry exactly what Wolff advertises: the utilisation of social structures and social welfare in the name of the state. Feminist theorist's Kate Millet's (1934–2017) *Sexual Politics*, for example, targets the nuclear family, the basic building block of Wolff's state, as a central tenet for the patriarchal structures she is wishing to demolish. The family is

880 van der Zande, Johan, 'Prussia and the Enlightenment', in *The Rise of Prussia: 1700–1830*, ed. by Philip G. Dwyer (Harlow: Pearson Education, 2000), pp. 89–107, p. 92.

'[p]atriarchy's chief institution. ... a mirror of and a connection with the larger society. Mediating between the individual and the social structure, the family effects control and conformity where political and other authorities are insufficient.', so Millet.[881] 'The chief contribution of the family in patriarchy is the socialization of the young... into patriarchal ideology's prescribed attitudes towards the categories of role temperament and status', she adds, to then conclude that '[a]s co-operation between the family and he larger society is essential ... the fate of the three patriarchal institutions, the family, society and the state are interrelated.'[882] The mechanism of ideological socialisation Millet decries is precisely what the *Oeconomica* seeks to fulfil. The purposeful centralisation of education is another potential target of suspicion. The philosopher and social anthropologist Ernest Gellner (1925–1995) discusses the matter in a book dedicated to a phenomenon of particular delicacy in a world post-World-War II: nation states and nationalism.[883] As a 'theory of political legitimacy' nationalism serves the 'organization of human groups into large, centrally educated, culturally homogenous units.'[884] In this scenario, state-led education systems do not act as a complementary but as an antagonistic force to the instruction received by family, tribe or other para-political social units. State education means socialising a human into the norms and working orders of the political community and, in this case, nationalist ideology, at the expense of the ideologically reproductive powers of more immediate social frameworks.[885] Where Wolff aligns the purpose of parenting to the public interest, Gellner sees a natural rift between house and state – and state education as a deliberate means to decide the battle for the latter.

The comparison between Wolff, Millet and Gellner is a perfectly anachronistic exercise. What is striking about it nevertheless is that the modern theorists view specific socio-political structures and institutions with the suspicion of an ulterior motive that Wolff postulates in broad daylight: the creation of conformity, homogeneity and social cohesion within a larger political structure. What needs to be distinguished in both cases is that it need not be the institution that is inherently suspicious – it is the combination with the ideology it serves. To Millet, the *patriarchal* society is shored up by the nuclear family; to Gellner, it is the spectre of *nationalism* that informs his view on state education. To both, however, the deliberate impact of a centrally organised, political structure on the living and thinking of its members poses grounds for suspicion – for Wolff and the absolutist mindset, it poses a fruitful, even benign spectre.

Whether family and state school really achieve what Wolff, Millet and Gellner postulate is a different question. The disparity in the ethical judgment of the same

881 Millet, Kate, *Sexual Politics* (London: Abacus, 1972), p. 33.
882 Ibid., p. 33; p. 35.
883 Gellner, Ernest, *Nations and Nationalism* (Oxford: Blackwell, 1983).
884 Ibid., p. 1, 35.
885 Ibid., pp. 29–38.

institutional mechanisms is remarkable either way. If anything, it signals a shift in what is considered legitimate within a socio-political order, and a shift in the locus of power. A liberal democracy seeks legitimacy in political participation and the safeguarding of individual rights and liberties; accordingly, a supporting ideology would have to appeal to the citizen, not the ruler, as the principal stakeholder and – in an ideal case scenario – participant driver of public policy. From this perspective, it is the ideological more than the institutional basis that divides the modern from the Wolffian welfare state. Ironically, the continuity between what is considered the foundation of Germany's welfare state through Bismarck shows just the opposite development: ideological continuity and institutional break. Bismarck was wedded to a conservative, patrimonial ideal of social welfare but designed a system based on social insurance, not direct provision. Institutional innovation aside, the ideological continuity is hardly the direct legacy of Wolff's work only. Rather, he can be considered a chronicler of values and ideologies that came to play a significant part in the discussion surrounding the birth of Germany's welfare state system in the 19th century. Wolff legitimated duty through natural order, including the government's obligation to social welfare. We find this link miraculously mirrored a hundred years later in a statement of the *Berliner Revue* made in an article titled 'Die Naturgeschichte der Arbeit', the natural history of labour, in 1855:

> Social policy recognizes God's order in the entirety of creation; not merely in the laws of nature but also in those laws on which the life and growth of society rests.[886]

Wolff's insistence on the family as base unit to the state equally lives on in the work of Adam Müller of about the same time who '...states clearly that every political philosophy has to begin with the theory of the family, and the family is actually the first social structure in which God's law became evident.'[887] Both quotes are part of Avraham Doron's study of the ideological, that is religious motivation behind conservative theories of public welfare in the nineteenth century, and their ultimate culmination in Bismarck's social policy reform. Doron's article features themes familiar from the Wolffian discourse and Prussian context, even if adapted to the particular situation of the nineteenth century – most notably the religious undertones with the deliberately supra-confessional bearing.[888] As a movement, the nineteenth-century idea of conservative social policy was a statist venture, by nature of the personages driving it but also the concepts it reinforced. The idea that privilege comes with responsibilities serves to legitimate the uneven distribution of riches as long as the better-endowed employ their resources – partly – to sustain the less fortunate. This idea is not

886 Quoted in translation in Avraham, Doron, 'The Religious and Moral Origins of German Conservative Social Policy', *Journal of Policy History*, 28, 133–61 (133).
887 Avraham, 'The Religious and Moral Origins of German Conservative Social Policy', p. 136.
888 Ibid., p. 143.

overtly represented in Wolff who does not see obligations necessarily arising from the difference in personal wealth, but from natural political hierarchies. Wolff converts the Christian tenet that the ruling power is legitimated through his patrimonial care into a natural law-based argument about the God-ordained order of society. A century later, the same nexus between privilege and responsibility served as a newly re-Christianised underpinning for social welfare policies designed to promote social order more than mobility.

The affinities of the passages above with Wolff's thought hardly arise because these authors drew on his philosophy. It is more likely that they fed from the same source. In fact, one reason why Wolff's philosophy seems prophetic and conservative at the same time might be that it subsumed such a multitude of ideas with an independent provenance and legacy outside his discourse. In a way, his entire work is simultaneously derivative and idiosyncratic, pre- and descriptive and the same can be said for his practical philosophy. Subsuming traditional views and contemporary concerns, Wolff hardly presents a change to traditional interpretations of the household or the state even. His merit, however, the novelty that comes with Wolff's practical philosophy is the systematic integration of the two realms previously treated separately: public and private. Hanna Arendt put the conflation of the two spheres down to a translation error in reception history. As Arendt puts it, 'The profound misunderstanding expressed in the Latin translation of "political" as "social" is perhaps nowhere clearer than in a discussion in which Thomas Aquinas compares the nature of household rule with political rule: the head of the household, he finds, has some similarity to the head of the kingdom, but he adds, his power is not so "perfect" as that of the king.'[889] In Arendt's view, the medieval interpretation of the relationship between body politic and household is also based on a misunderstanding: where 'the household covered the private, non-political sphere of material needs and necessity' in Greek philosophy, the public sphere stood for 'freedom, speech and persuasion.'[890] Arendt may be right and Aquinas' translation might not be mindful of original connotations. Yet translation errors such as that may also have arisen from a contextual shift of the terminology in question. Concepts like 'state' or 'household' are only stable on the surface. In reality, they are moving targets across time and space – and Aquinas's ideas about marriage or domestic morality may be as different from Aristotle's understanding as their respective view of politics.[891] The same issue would apply to Wolff's reception of ancient authors. His practical philosophy adopts Aristotelian commonplaces even though the ancient Greek scenario of a democratic *polis* and

889 Arendt, Hannah, *The Human Condition* (Chicago: University of Chicago Press, 1958), p. 23.
890 Haar, 'Tomás Sánchez and Late Scholastic Thought on Marriage and Political Virtue', p. 81.
891 Haar, in fact, suggests that with a particular view to the relationship between public and private realm, 'the Aristotelian source material remained unclear for subsequent interpreters, as illustrated in the thought of Aquinas.' See Haar, 'Tomás Sánchez and Late Scholastic Thought on Marriage and Political Virtue', p. 82.

Wolff's reality of an early modern monarchy are wildly different settings, in terms of size, legitimacy and political process. Likewise, it is probable that both authors harboured different assumptions about the inner workings of a household – in fact, this is implied in the usage of political metaphors within the domestic context: Aristotle compares the dominion of a husband over his wife to aristocratic rule, Wolff considers the *imperium maritale* akin to a monarchy.[892] Misgivings permitting, the peripatetic model building a body politic from families actually suits the absolutist purpose well, in theory and in practice. Wolff proclaims families the historical origin of the state, which casts the direct relationship between government and household the result of a natural process. In reality, the Prussian rulers did not build this bond from scratch but reconstructed it by centralising administrative powers, eclipsing intermediate levels of social, economic or political organisation. This is particularly manifest in the context of welfare. As the sociologist Ferdinand Tönnies claimed in 1914, patrimonial welfare, the care of the state for the happiness of its subjects complete with social control, shores up solidarity for the ruler whilst dissolving or displacing the authority of municipal government or para-political associations. In Tönnies' view, the similarity between a household and a kingdom is a curious incidence that only applies to smaller territories; the real purpose of the nascent welfare system is the formation of the great state, its citizens conform and homogenous.[893] Since the analogy between household and kingdom is a frequently recurring one it is indeed curious that Tönnies reserves it for smaller territories – and telling that Wolff avoids it for the contractual interpretation of his own, indubitably large and growing political domain. In fact, this may signal the wane of a political metaphor with the rationalisation of its Christian origins.

Shifting commonplaces may affect Wolff's reception of Aristotle, but also any modern interpretation of Wolff's philosophy. Overly negative and exceedingly positive assessments of his political thought seem to fall short of the same issue: they tend to analyse his philosophy from a modern vantage point, rather than filtering it through his own terminology and the problems that drove it at the time. Wolff is no traitor of civil liberties in a world where they had not legally existed in the first place. Even his reputation as an unoriginal truncator of Leibniz's thought seems exaggerated when considering the purpose of Wolff's work: by and large he aims to reconcile different schools of thought and to open up philosophy to broader audiences, not soar to new conceptual heights. In the same grain, following Backhaus and reading contemporary political concepts like subsidiarity into Wolff's philosophy means ignoring

892 Wolff, *Oeconomica*, § 122 *nota*, p. 184: 'Assimilatur status conjugalis, in quo omne imperium competit marito, uxori nonnisi obediendi gloria relicta, statui monarchico in Republica.' On Aristotle, see Haar, 'Tomás Sánchez and Late Scholastic Thought on Marriage and Political Virtue', pp. 84–5.

893 Tönnies, Ferdinand, 'Rechtsstaat und Wohlfahrtsstaat. Referat, erstattet auf dem III. Kongress der Internationalen Vereinigung für Rechts- und Wirtschaftsphilosophie', *Archiv für Rechts- und Wirtschaftsphilosophie*, 8.1 (1914), 65–70 (66).

purpose and legitimacy behind these institutions. In fact, a direct comparison even obscures – or at least does not highlight – the crucial difference between the two political systems. This is a precedented error, as Thomas Vesting notes. In his opinion, constitutional scholars and legal historians have regularly committed the same mistake by simply interpreting liberal democracies as the institutional outcome 'of a linear and continuous teleological development starting from absolute monarchy.' The consequence, so Vesting, is a 'twofold reduction': an all-too generous assessment of absolutism obfuscates its inherent limits and the impact of the hierarchies inscribed within; furthermore, it gives rise to a host of confusing notions and terminologies that inevitably miss the essence of what actually defines a liberal democracy – rather than some institutional semblance of one.[894]

To avoid a confusion of this sort, it may help to resort to a Wolffian paradigm, enlarged. It is not just the deed that counts as moral but the motive that drives it. On the political level, it is not the institution that qualifies an ideology, but the thought behind it.

894 Vesting, 'Absolutismus und materiale Rationalisierung', pp. 369–70: '...für viele Verfassungsrechtler und Rechtshistoriker ist der bürgerliche Nationalstaat häufig nichts anderes als das Produkt einer linearen und kontinuierlichen Höherentwicklung der absoluten Monarchie, die im 'Ursprung' und 'Geist' des Absolutismus bereits angelegt war.'

Bibliography

Primary sources

Alberti, Leon Battista, *Über das Hauswesen: Della Famiglia*, ed. by Fritz Schalk, trans. by Walther Kraus (Zürich: Artemis Verlag, 1962)

Alsted, Johann Heinrich, *Encyclopedia: Septem tomis distincta* (Herborn: Corvinus, 1630)

Avenarius, Johann, *Synopsis oeconomica* (Wittenberg: Selfisch, 1628)

Barbaro, Francesco, *Das Buch von der Ehe – De re uxoria*, trans. by Percy Gotheim (Berlin: Die Runde, 1933)

Budde, Johann Franz, *Bedencken über die Wolffianische Philosophie, nebst einer historischen Einleitung zur gegenwärtigen Controversie* (Freiburg: Schmaltz, 1724)

Calleja, Angel, ed., *Canones, et decreta sacrosancti oecumenici, et generalis Concilii Tridentini* (Alcalá de Henares: Andreas de Angulo, 1564)

Camerarius, Joachim, *Politicorum et Oeconomicorum Aristotelis Interpretationes et Explicationes accuratae : interpretationes et explicationes accuratae etc.* (Frankfurt: Andreas Wechel, 1581)

Casselmann, Philipp C., and Johann Hermann Fürstenau, *Desiderata oeconomica* (Rinteln: Enax, 1731)

Coler, Johannes, *Oeconomia ruralis et domestica* (Mainz: Nicolaus Heyl, 1665)

Cumberland, Richard, *De legibus naturae disquisitio philosophica* (Dublin: Jacob Carson, 1720)

Descartes, René, *Regulae ad directionem ingenii = Rules for the direction of the natural intelligence: a bilingual edition of the Cartesian treatise on method.*, ed. by George Heffernan (Amsterdam: Rodopi, 1998)

Döpler, Jacobus, *Theatri poenarum, suppliciorum et executionum criminalium oder Schau-Platz derer Leibes- und Lebens-Strafen Anderer Theil* (Leipzig: Heirs of Friedrich Lanckisch, 1697)

Erasmus, Desiderius, *De libero arbitrio diatribe, sive collatio* (Basel: Johann Froben, 1524)

Florinus, Franciscus Philippus, *Oeconomus prudens et legalis* (Nuremberg, Frankfurt, Leipzig: Christoph Riegel, 1750)

Freymüthige Nachrichten von neuen Büchern, und andern zur Gelehrtheit gehörigen Sachen, Vol. 13 (Zurich: Heidegger & Co., 1756)

Friedrich Wilhelm II, *Instruction für die Kreisdirectorien in den fränkischen Fürstenthümern* (Berlin: 1797)

Gasser, Simon Peter, *Einleitung zu den Oeconomischen Politischen und Cameral-Wissenschaften* (Halle: Verlag des Waisenhauses, 1729)

von Glück, Christian Friedrich, *Darstellung des Kirchenrechtes der Katholiken und Protestanten* (Augsburg: Jenisch und Stage, 1839)

Goclenius, Rudolph, *Lexicon philosophicum* (Frankfurt: Widow of Matthias Becker, 1613)

Grotius, Hugo, *De iure belli ac pacis libri tres: in quibus ius naturae et gentium, item iuris publici praecipue explicantur*, ed. by P.C. Molhuysen and Cornelis van Vollenhoven (Leiden: A. W. Sijthoff, 1919)

Hanov, Michael Christoph, *Oeconomica methodo scientifica pertractata. Pars reliqua* (Halle, Magdeburg: Renger, 1755)

Hanov, Michael Christoph, *Der Danziger großen Mondjahre monathliches voriges und künftiges Wetter oder Anweisung wie die Wetterprognostica aus dem Mondzirkel abzunehmen mittelst der Observationen des Jahres 1767* (Danzig and Wittenberg: Dürr, 1768)

Hanov, Michael Christoph, *Entwurf der Lehr-Kunst, aus der Vernunft-Kunst, anderer Abschnitt* (Danzig: Schreiber, 1740)

https://doi.org/10.1515/9783110553475-007

Hanov, Michael Christoph, *Erläuterte Merkwürdigkeiten der Natur: nach denen Grund-Sätzen derer neuesten Physicorum* (Danzig: Knoch, 1737)

Hanov, Michael Christoph, *Impossibilitas quadraturae circuli a priori adserta* (Danzig: Schreiber, 1741)

Hanov, Michael Christoph, Jus Culmense ex ultima revisione, oder Das vollständige Culmische Recht (Danzig: Johann Friedrich Bartels, 1767)

Hanov, Michael Christoph, *Philosophiae civilis sive politicae pars prima* (Halle: Renger, 1756)

Hanov, Michael Christoph, *Philosophiae civilis sive politicae pars tertia* (Halle: Renger, 1758)

Hanov, Michael Christoph, *Philosophiae civilis sive politicae pars quarta* (Halle: Renger, 1759)

Hanov, Michael Christoph, *Preußische Lieferung alter und neuer Urkunden, Erörterungen und Abhandlungen zur Erläuterung der Preußischen Geschichte und Rechte* (Leipzig: Lankisch, 1755)

Hanov, Michael Christoph, *Seltenheiten der Natur und Oekonomie*, ed. by Johann Daniel Tietz, 3 vols (Leipzig: Lankisch, 1753)

Harvey, William, *Exercitatio anatomica de motu cordis et sanguinis in animalibus* (Leiden: Johannes van Kerckhem, 1737)

Hemming, Nicolaus, *De lege naturae apodictica methodus* (Wittenberg: Crato, 1564)

Jablonski, Johann Theodor, *Allgemeines Lexicon der Künste und Wissenschaften* (Leipzig: Hartung, 1721)

Jensen, Mads L., *A Humanist in Reformation Politics: Philipp Melanchthon on Political Philosophy and Natural Law* (Leiden: Brill, 2019)

Justi, Johann Heinich Gottlob, *Staatswirthschaft oder Systematische Abhandlung aller Oekonomischen und Cameral-Wissenschaften, die zur Regierung eines Landes erfodert werden* (Leipzig: Breitkopf, 1758)

Keckermann, Bartholomäus, *Systema disciplinae politicae* (Frankfurt: Jacobi, 1625)

Königliche Gesellschaft der Wissenschaften, *Göttingische Anzeigen von Gelehrten Sachen, Vol. 2* (Göttingen: Johann Friederich Hager, 1755)

Leibniz, Gottfried Wilhelm, *Die Theodicee*, trans. by Robert Habs (Leipzig: Philipp Reclam jun., 1883)

Leibniz, Gottfried Wilhelm, *Kleinere philosophische Schriften*, ed. by Caspar Jacob Huth and Christian Wolff (Jena: Mayer, 1740)

Lemay, Helen Rodnite, *Women's Secrets. A Translation of Pseudo-Albertus Magnus's De Secretis Mulierum with Commentaries* (Albany, NY: State University of New York Press, 1992)

Ludovici, Carl Günther, 'Wolfische Philosophie', *Grosses vollständiges Universal-Lexicon aller Wissenschafften und Künste etc.* (Leipzig and Halle: Johann Heinrich Zedler, 1748), 883–1232

Menius, Justus, *Oeconomia christiana* (Nuremberg: vom Berg und Newber, 1556)

Meusel, Johann Georg, *Lexikon der vom Jahr 1750 bis 1800 verstorbenen teutschen Schriftsteller* (Leipzig: Fleischer, 1805), v

Nieuhoff, Johannes, *Legatio Batavica ad magnum Tartariae Chamum Sungteium* (Amsterdam: Jacob Meursius, 1668)

Pufendorf, Samuel Freiherr von, *De iure naturae et gentium, libri octo.* (Frankfurt and Leipzig: Knoch-Eslinger, 1759)

Pufendorf, Samuel, James Tully, and Michael Silverthorne, *On the Duty of Man and Citizen According to Natural Law* (Cambridge: Cambridge University Press, 1991)

Ramus, Petrus, and Walter J. Ong, *Scholae in liberales artes* (Hildesheim and New York: G. Olms, 1970)

Rector Et Professores Nobilissimis Ac Politissimis Athenaei Gedanensis Civibus S. D. Eosqve Ad Funus Michaelis Christophori Hanovii Philosophiae Professoris Et Bibliothecarii, Jam Beate Fato Functi Secum Pie Celebrandum Ad Diem XII. Octobris Huius Anni MDCCLXXIII Convocant Et Invitant (Danzig: Schreiber, 1773)

Seckendorf, Veit Ludwig von, *Christen-Stat in drey Bücher abgetheilet.* (Leipzig: J.F. Gleditsch, 1685)
Seckendorf, Veit Ludwig von, *Teutscher Fürsten-Stat* (Frankfurt: Thomas Mattias Götz, 1655)
Semler, Christoph, *Nützliche Vorschläge von Auffrichtung einer Mathematischen Handwercks-Schule bey der Stadt Halle* (Halle: Henckel, 1705)
Semler, Christoph, *Neueröffnete mathematische und mechanische Real-Schule* (Halle: Renger, 1709)
Semler, Christoph, *Die Stadt Jerusalem mit allen ihren Mauren, Thoren, Thürmen, Tempel, Pallästen, Schlössern, auch übrigen publiquen und privat-Gebäuden* (Halle: Verlag des Waisenhauses, 1718)
Spamer, Franz Otto, *Aus dem Tabakskollegium und der Zopfzeit; oder, Wie man vor hundertundfünzig Jahren lebte und es trieb. Historische Erzählung aus der Regierungszeit des Königs Friedrich Wilhelm I von Preussen* (Leipzig: O. Spamer, 1972)
Spinoza, Benedict de, *Die Ethik, nach geometrischer Methode dargestellt*, trans. by Otto Baensch (Hamburg: Felix Meiner, 1967)
Suárez, Francisco, *De pace, de bello: Über den Frieden, über den Krieg*, ed. by Markus Kremer and Josef de Vries (Stuttgart-Bad Cannstatt: Frommann-Holzboog, 2013), II
Süssmilch, Johann Peter, *Die göttliche Ordnung in den Veränderungen des menschlichen Geschlechts, aus der Geburt, dem Tode und der Fortpflanzung desselben*, ed. by Christian Jacob Baumann (Berlin: Verlag der Buchhandlung der Realschule, 1765)
Thomasius, Christian, *Historia juris naturalis* (Stuttgart, Bad Cannstatt: Frommann-Holzboog, 1972)
Thümmig, Ludwig Philipp, *Institutiones philosophiae Wolfianae, in usus academicos adornatae* (Frankfurt and Leipzig: Renger, 1760)
von Tschirnhaus, E.W., *Gründliche Anleitung zu den nützlichen Wissenschaften, absonderlich zu der Mathesi und Physica, wie sie anitzo von den gelehrtesten abgehandelt werden* (Stuttgart-Bad Cannstatt: Frommann-Holzboog, 1729)
Vitoria, Francisco de, *Relectiones theologicae* (Lyon: Jacob Boyer, 1557)
Vives, Juan Luis, *De subventione pauperum sive de humanis necessitatibus libri II*, ed. by C. Matheeussen and C. Fantazzi (Leiden and Boston: Brill, 2002)
'Waysen-Haus', *Grosses vollständiges Universal-Lexicon aller Wissenschafften und Künste* (Leipzig and Halle: Johann Heinrich Zedler, 1731), pp. 870–71
Weber, Max, *Economy and Society*, ed. by Guenther Roth and Claus Wittich, 2 vols (Totowa, N.J.: Bedminster Press, 1968), I
von Windheim, Christian Ernst, *Philosophische Bibliothek, Vol 9* (Nuremberg: George Peter Monath, 1757)
Wolff, Christian, *Ausführliche Nachricht von seinen eigenen Schrifften* (Frankfurt a.M.: Johann Benjamin Andreae and Paul Heinrich Hort, 1733)
Wolff, Christian, *Cosmologia generalis methodo scientifica pertractata* (Frankfurt and Leipzig: Renger, 1731)
Wolff, Christian, *De differentia nexus rerum sapientis et fatalis necessitatis, nec non systematis harmoniae praestabilitatae et hypothesium Spinosae luculenta commentatio* (Halle: Renger, 1737)
Wolff, Christian, 'Discursus praeliminaris', in *Philosophia rationalis sive Logica, methodo scientifica pertractata* (Halle: Renger, 1740)
Wolff, Christian, *Eigene Lebensbeschreibung*, ed. by Heinrich Wuttke (Leipzig: Weidmann, 1841)
Wolff, Christian, *Entdeckung der wahren Ursache von der wunderbahren Vermehrung des Getreydes, dadurch zugleich der Wachsthum der Baeume und Pflantzen überhaupt erläutert wird* (Halle: Renger, 1725)
Wolff, Christian, *Horae subsecivae Marburgenses anni MDCCXXIX, MDCCXXX et MDCCXXXI: quibus philosophia ad publicam privatamque utilitatem aptatur* (Frankfurt and Leipzig: Renger, 1735)
Wolff, Christian, *Horae subsecivae marburgenses quibus philosophia ad publicam privatamque utilitatem aptatur* (Verona: Marcus Moroni, 1770)

Wolff, Christian, *Jus naturae methodo scientifica pertractata. Pars prima* (Frankfurt and Leipzig: Renger, 1740)
Wolff, Christian, *Jus naturae methodo scientifica pertractatum. Pars septima.* (Halle: Renger, 1747)
Wolff, Christian, *Jus naturae methodo scientifica pertractatum. Pars octava* (Frankfurt and Leipzig: Societas Veneta, 1766)
Wolff, Christian, *Mathematisches Lexicon* (Leipzig: Son of Johann Friedrich Gleditsch, 1716)
Wolff, Christian, *Oeconomica methodo scientifica pertractata* (Halle: Renger, 1754)
Wolff, Christian, *Oratio de Sinarum philosophia practica. Lateinisch-deutsch*, ed. by Michael Albrecht (Hamburg: Felix Meiner, 1985)
Wolff, Christian, *Philosophia moralis sive Ethica, methodo scientifica pertractata. Pars prima.* (Halle: Renger, 1750)
Wolff, Christian, *Philosophia moralis sive Ethica, methodo scientifica pertractata. Pars secunda* (Halle: Renger, 1751)
Wolff, Christian, *Philosophia moralis sive Ethica methodo scientifica pertractata. Pars tertia* (Halle, Magdeburg: Renger, 1751)
Wolff, Christian, *Philosophia moralis sive Ethica, methodo scientifica pertractata. Pars quarta* (Halle: Renger, 1752)
Wolff, Christian, *Philosophia moralis sive Ethica, methodo scientifica pertractata. Pars quinta* (Halle: Renger, 1753)
Wolff, Christian, *Philosophia practica universalis, methodo scientifica pertractata. Pars prior* (Halle: Renger, 1744)
Wolff, Christian, *Philosophia practica universalis, methodo scientifica pertractata. Pars posterior.* (Verona: Dionigi Ramanzini, 1742)
Wolff, Christian, *Philosophia prima sive Ontologia, methodo scientifica pertractata* (Frankfurt and Leipzig: Renger, 1736)
Wolff, Christian, *Philosophia rationalis sive Logica, methodo scientifica pertractata* (Halle: Renger, 1740)
Wolff, Christian, *Psychologia empirica, methodo scientifica pertractata* (Frankfurt and Leipzig: Renger, 1732)
Wolff, Christian, *Ratio praelectionum Wolfianarum in mathesin et philosophiam universam* (Halle: Renger, 1718)
Wolff, Christian, *Theologia naturalis methodo scientifica pertractata, pars prior* (Verona: Dionigi Ramanzini, 1738)
Wolff, Christian, *Vernünfftige Gedancken von dem Gebrauche der Theile in Menschen, Thieren und Pflanzen* (Frankfurt and Leipzig: Renger, 1723)
Wolff, Christian ———, *Vernünfftige Gedancken von Gott, der Welt und der Seele des Menschen, auch allen Dingen überhaupt, den Liebhabern der Wahrheit mitgetheilet* (Halle: Renger, 1743)
Wolff, Christian, *Vernünfftige Gedancken von dem gesellschaftlichen Leben der Menschen und insonderheit dem gemeinen Wesen* (Frankfurt and Leipzig: Renger, 1747)
Wolff, Christian, 'De differentia intellectus systematici & non systematici: Über den Unterschied zwischen dem systematischen und dem nicht-systematischen Verstand', trans. and ed. by Michael Albrecht, *Aufklärung*, 23 (2011), 229–301
Wolff, Christian, and Laurent David Bollhagen, *Philosophia practica universalis, mathematica methodo conscripta* (Leipzig: C. Goez, 1703)
Wolff, Christian, *Psychologia Rationalis*, ed. by Jean Ecole (Hildesheim and New York: Olms, 1972),
Zabarella, Jacopo, *Opera Logica*, ed. by Wilhelm Risse (Hildesheim: Olms, 1966)
Zedler, Johann Heinrich, ed., *Grosses vollständiges Universal-Lexicon aller Wissenschafften und Künste* (Leipzig and Halle: Johann Heinrich Zedler, 1731–1754)

Secondary literature

Agamben, Giorgio, 'What Is an Apparatus?', in *What Is an Apparatus? And Other Essays*, trans. by David Kishik and Stefan Pedatella (Stanford, CA: Stanford University Press, 2009)

Ahnert, Thomas, 'Introduction', in *The Law of Nations Treated According to the Scientific Method*, by Christian Wolff, ed. by Thomas Ahnert, trans. by Joseph H. Drake (Indianapolis: Liberty Fund, 2017), pp. ix–xxiv

Ahnert, Thomas, *Religion and the Origins of the German Enlightenment: Faith and the Reform of Learning in the Thought of Christian Thomasius* (Rochester, NY: University of Rochester Press, 2006)

Ahnert, Thomas, 'Zum "Epikureismus" im Naturrecht der deutschen Frühaufklärung', in *Das Naturrecht der Geselligkeit: Anthropologie, Recht und Politik im 18. Jahrhundert*, ed. by Frank Grunert and Vanda Fiorillo (Berlin: Duncker & Humblot, 2009), pp. 39–54

Ahrbeck, Rosemarie, 'Wolff und Francke – Kontrahenten oder Weggefährten?', in *Christian Wolff als Philosoph der Aufklärung in Deutschland*, ed. by Hans-Martin Gerlach, Günter Schenk, and Burchard Thaler (Halle: Martin-Luther-Universität, 1980), pp. 101–110

Aichele, Alexander, 'Naturrecht', in *Handbuch Christian Wolff*, ed. by Robert Theis and Alexander Aichele (Wiesbaden: Springer, 2018), pp. 269–90

Albee, Ernest, 'The Ethical System of Richard Cumberland I.', *The Philosophical Review*, 4.3 (1895), 264–90

Albrecht, Michael, 'Die philosophischen Grundüberzeugungen des Wolffianismus', in *Christian Wolff und die europäische Aufklärung: Akten des I. Internationalen Christian-Wolff-Kongresses, Halle (Saale), 4.-8. April 2004. Teil 5*, ed. by Jürgen Stolzenberg and Oliver-Pierre Rudolph (Hildesheim, Zürich and New York: Georg Olms Verlag, 2010), pp. 13–30

Antognazza, Maria Rosa, *Leibniz: An Intellectual Biography* (Cambridge: Cambridge University Press, 2009)

Arendt, Hannah, *The Human Condition* (Chicago: University of Chicago Press, 1958)

Avraham, Doron, 'The Religious and Moral Origins of German Conservative Social Policy', *Journal of Policy History*, 28.1, 133–61

Backhaus, Jürgen G., 'Christian Wolff on Subsidiarity, the Division of Labor and Social Welfare', *European Journal of Law and Economics*, 4 (1997), 129–46

Backhaus, Jürgen G., *The Beginnings of Political Economy: Johann Heinrich Gottlob von Justi* (New York, NY: Springer, 2009)

von Bauer-Kayatz, Christa, *Einführung in Die Alttestamentliche Weisheit* (Neukirchen-Vluyn: Neukirchener Verlag des Erziehungsvereins, 1969)

Beck, Gunnar, *Fichte and Kant on Freedom, Rights and Law* (Lanham, MD: Lexington Books, 2008)

Bianco, Bruno, 'Freiheit gegen Fatalismus. Zu Joachim Langes Kritik an Wolff', in *Halle. Aufklärung und Pietismus*, ed. by Norbert Hinske (Heidelberg: Lambert Schneider, 1989), pp. 111–56

Biller, Gerhard, 'Biographie und Bibliographie', in *Handbuch Christian Wolff*, ed. by Alexander Aichele and Robert Theis (Wiesbaden: Springer, 2018), pp. 5–31

Biller, Gerhard, 'Die Wolff-Diskussion 1800–1982. Eine Bibliographie', in *Christian Wolff 1679–1754. Interpretationen zu seiner Philosophie und deren Wirkung, mit einer Bibliographie der Wolff-Literatur*, ed. by Werner Schneiders (Hamburg: Felix Meiner, 1986), pp. 321–45

Bissinger, Anton, *Die Struktur der Gotteserkenntnis: Studien zur Philosophie Christian Wolffs* (Bonn: H. Bouvier, 1970)

Blažek, Pavel, *Die mittelalterliche Rezeption der aristotelischen Philosophie der Ehe: Von Robert Grosseteste bis Bartholomäus von Brügge (1246/1247–1309)* (Leiden and Boston: Brill, 2007)

Bornhak, Conrad, 'Das preussische Unterrichtswesen als Staatsinstitut in rechtsgeschichtlicher Entwicklung', *Archiv des öffentlichen Rechts*, 4.1 (1889), 101–46

Brantz, Dorothee, '"Risky Business": Disease, Disaster and the Unintended Consequences of Epizootics in Eighteenth- and Nineteenth-Century France and Germany', *Environment and History*, 17.1 (2011), 35–51

Bredekamp, Horst, *Die Fenster der Monade: Gottfried Wilhelm Leibniz' Theater der Natur und Kunst* (Berlin: Akademie Verlag, 2004)

Brockliss, Laurence William, 'Organization, Training and the Medical Marketplace in the Eighteenth Century', in *The Healing Arts. Health, Disease and Society in Europe, 1500–1800*, ed. by Peter Elmer (Manchester: Manchester University Press, 2004), pp. 344–81

Bromann, Thomas, 'Rethinking Professionalization: Theory, Practice, and Professional Ideology in Eighteenth-Century German Medicine', *The Journal of Modern History*, 67.4 (1995), 835–72

Burns, William E., 'Academies and Scientific Societies', *Science in the Enlightenment: An Encyclopedia* (Santa Barbara, CA: ABC-CLIO, 2003), pp. 1–3

Casula, Mario, 'Die Beziehungen Wolff-Thomas-Carbo in der Metaphysica latina: Zur Quellengeschichte der Thomas-Rezeption bei Christian Wolff', *Studia Leibnitiana*, 11.1 (1979), 98–123

Catana, Leo, *The Historiographical Concept 'System of Philosophy': Its Origin, Nature, Influence, and Legitimacy* (Leiden: Brill, 2008)

Cerman, Ivo, 'Die Rolle der Akademie im naturrechtlichen Staatsrecht Christian Wolffs', in *Aufgeklärte Sozietäten, Literatur und Wissenschaft in Mitteleuropa* (Berlin; Boston: De Gruyter, 2019), pp. xxiv–xxx

Cheneval, Francis, 'Auseinandersetzungen um die Civitas Maxima in der Nachfolge Christian Wolffs', *Studia Leibnitiana*, 33 (2001), 125–44

Corr, Charles A., 'Christian Wolff and Leibniz', *Journal of the History of Ideas*, 36.2 (1975), 241–262

Corr, Charles A., 'Christian Wolff's Treatment of Scientific Discovery', *Journal of the History of Philosophy Journal of the History of Philosophy*, 10.3 (1972), 323–34

Cossar, C. D. M., ed., *The German Translations of the Pseudo-Bernhardine 'Epistola de Cura Rei Familiaris'* (Göppingen: A. Kümmerle, 1975)

Darge, Rolf, *Suárez' transzendentale Seinsauslegung und die Metaphysiktradition* (Leiden and Boston: Brill, 2004)

De Renzi, Silvia, 'Policies of Health. Diseases, Poverty and Hospitals', in *The Healing Arts. Health, Disease and Society in Europe, 1500–1800*, ed. by Peter Elmer (Manchester: Manchester University Press, 2004), pp. 136–65

Dioni, Gianluca, 'Die innere moralische Pflicht bei Christian Thomasius', in *Das Naturrecht der Geselligkeit: Anthropologie, Recht und Politik im 18. Jahrhundert*, ed. by Frank Grunert and Vanda Fiorillo (Berlin: Duncker & Humblot, 2009), pp. 69–87

Dorwart, Reinhold August, 'Medical Education in Prussia under the Early Hohenzollern, 1685–1725', *Bulletin of the History of Medicine*, 32.4 (1958), 335–47

Dorwart, Reinhold August, *The Prussian Welfare State before 1740* (Cambridge, MA: Harvard University Press, 1971)

Dreitzel, Horst, *Protestantischer Aristotelismus und Absoluter Staat: Die 'Politica' des Henning Arnisaeus (ca. 1575–1636)* (Wiesbaden: Steiner, 1970)

Duve, Thomas, 'Der blinde Fleck der "Oeconomia"? – Wirtschaft und Soziales in der frühen Neuzeit', in *Wirtschaft und Wirtschaftstheorie in Rechtsgeschichte und Philosophie*, ed. by Heinz Mohnhaupt and Jean-François Kervégan (Frankfurt am Main: Klostermann, 2004), pp. 29–61

Dyck, Corey, 'Power, Harmony, and Freedom: Debating Causation in 18th Century Germany', in *Oxford Handbook of Eighteenth Century German Philosophy*, by Frederick Beiser and Brandon Look, (forthcoming)

Eisenbach, Franziskus, 'Zeichen der Liebe und Treue Gottes. Die christliche Ehe aus katholischer Sicht', in *Die Braut: geliebt, verkauft, getauscht, geraubt: zur Rolle der Frau im Kulturvergleich*, ed. by Gisela Völger, Karin von Welck, and René König, 2 vols (Köln: Rautenstrauch-Joest-Museum für Völkerkunde, 1985), I, 144–49

Epstein, Julia, 'The Pregnant Imagination, Fetal Rights and Women's Bodies: A Historical Inquiry', *Yale Journal of Law & the Humanities*, 7 (1995), 139–62

Ewald, William, 'The Biological Naturalism of Richard Cumberland', *Jahrbuch für Recht und Ethik /Annual Review of Law and Ethics*, 8 (2000), 125–41

Fantazzi, C., 'Introduction', in *De subventione pauperum sive de humanis necessitatibus libri II*, by Juan Luis Vives, ed. by C. Matheeussen and C. Fantazzi (Leiden; Boston: Brill, 2002), pp. ix–xl

Favaretti Camposampiero, Matteo, 'Bodies of Inference: Christian Wolff's Epistemology of the Life Sciences and Medicine', *Perspectives on Science*, 24.3 (2016), 361–79

Frängsmyr, Tore, 'Christian Wolff's Mathematical Method and Its Impact on the Eighteenth Century', *Journal of the History of Ideas*, 36.4 (1975), 653–68

Frauendienst, Werner, *Christian Wolff als Staatsdenker* (Berlin: E. Ebering, 1927)

Friedrich, Karin, 'The Development of the Prussian Town, 1720–1815', in *The Rise of Prussia: 1700–1830*, ed. by Philip G. Dwyer (Harlow: Pearson Education, 2000), pp. 129–50

Friedrich, Karin, *The Other Prussia: Royal Prussia, Poland and Liberty, 1569–1772* (Cambridge: Cambridge University Press, 2000)

Friedrich, Markus, 'Das Verhältnis von Leib und Seele als theologisch-philosophisches Grenzproblem vor Descartes: lutherische Einwände gegen eine dualistische Anthropologie', in *Spätrenaissance-Philosophie in Deutschland 1570–1650: Entwürfe zwischen Humanismus und Konfessionalisierung, okkulten Traditionen und Schulmetaphysik* (Tübingen: Niemeyer, 2009), pp. 211–49

Friess, Peer, and Thomas Max Safley, 'Poor Relief and Health Care Provision in South-German Catholic Cities during the Sixteenth Century', in *The Reformation of Charity : The Secular and the Religious in Early Modern Poor Relief*, ed. by Thomas Max Safley (Boston: Brill, 2003), pp. 76–91

Gagliardo, John G., *Germany under the Old Regime, 1600–1790* (London and New York: Longman, 1991)

Gause, Ute and Stephanie Scholz (eds.), *Ehe und Familie im Geist des Luthertums: Die Oeconomia Christiana (1529) des Justus Menius* (Leipzig: Evangelische Verlagsanstalt, 2012)

Gawlick, Günter, *Wolff-Index: Stellenindex und Konkordanz zu Christian Wolffs 'Discursus praeliminaris de philosophia in genere'* (Stuttgart-Bad Cannstatt: Frommann-Holzboog, 1999)

Gawthrop, Richard L., *Pietism and the Making of Eighteenth-Century Prussia* (Cambridge: Cambridge University Press, 1993)

Gellner, Ernest, *Nations and Nationalism* (Oxford: Blackwell, 1983)

Gerlach, Hans-Martin, 'Christian Wolff – seine Schule und seine Gegner', *Aufklärung*, 12.2 (2001), 3–8

Girvetz, Harry, 'Welfare State', *International Encyclopedia of Social Sciences*, ed. by David L. Sills and Robert K. Merton (New York, NY: MacMillan, 1968)

Goldberg, Jacob, 'Poles and Jews in the 17th and 18th Centuries: Rejection or Acceptance', *Jahrbücher Für Die Geschichte Osteuropas*, 22.2 (1974), 248–82

Goldie, Mark, and Robert Wokler, eds., *The Cambridge History of Eighteenth-Century Political Thought, Vol 1* (Cambridge: Cambridge University Press, 2006)

Górska, Liliana, 'Die Naturforschende Gesellschaft in Danzig und die gemeinnützige Aufklärung', in *Die Entdeckung von Volk, Erziehung und Ökonomie im europäischen Netzwerk der Aufklärung*, ed. by Hanno Schmitt, Holger Böning, and Werner Greiling (Bremen: Edition Lumiere, 2011), pp. 97–114

Gray, Marion, *Productive Men, Reproductive Women: The Agrarian Household and the Emergence of Separate Spheres during the German Enlightenment* (New York, NY: Berghahn Books, 2000)

Haar, Christoph P., 'Tomás Sánchez and Late Scholastic Thought on Marriage and Political Virtue', in *The Concept of Law (Lex) in the Moral and Political Thought of the 'School of Salamanca'*, ed. by Kirsten Bunge, Marko J. Fuchs, Danaë Simmermacher, and Anselm Spindler (Leiden and Boston: Brill, 2016), pp. 81–105

Hahn, Philip, *Das Haus im Buch: Konzeption, Publikationsgeschichte und Leserschaft der 'Oeconomia' Johannes Colers* (Epfendorf/Neckar: Bibliotheca Academica Verlag, 2013)

Hairston, Julia L., 'The Economics of Milk and Blood in Alberti's Libri Della Famiglia: Maternal versus Wet-Nursing', in *Medieval and Renaissance Lactations: Images, Rhetorics, Practices*, ed. by Jutta Gisela Sperling (Farnham, Surrey: Ashgate, 2013), pp. 187–212

Hellmuth, Eckhart, 'Der Staat des 18 Jahrhunderts. England und Preußen im Vergleich', *Aufklärung*, 9.1 (1996), 5–24

Hinrichs, Carl, Preussentum und Pietismus. Der Pietismus in Brandenburg-Preußen als religiös-soziale Reformbewegung (Göttingen: Vandenhoeck & Ruprecht, 1971)

Hochstrasser, Tim J., *Natural Law Theories in the Early Enlightenment* (Cambridge: Cambridge University Press, 2000)

Hofmann, Hasso, 'Recht und Staat bei Christian Wolff', *JuristenZeitung*, 59.13 (2004), 637–43

Hotson, Howard, *Commonplace Learning: Ramism and Its German Ramifications, 1543–1630* (Oxford: Oxford University Press, 2007)

Hotson, Howard, 'The Ramist Roots of Comenian Pansophia', in *Ramus, Pedagogy and the Liberal Arts: Ramism in Britain and the Wider World*, ed. by Emma Annette Wilson and Steven J Reid (Farnham: Ashgate), pp. 227–52

Isenmann, Eberhard, 'The Notion of the Common Good, the Concept of Politics, and Practical Policies in Late Medieval and Early Modern German Cities', in *De Bono Communi: The Discourse and Practice of the Common Good in the European City (13th-16th c.)* (Turnhout: Brepols, 2010), pp. 107–48

Israel, Jonathan I., *Radical Enlightenment: Philosophy and the Making of Modernity, 1650–1750* (Oxford: Oxford University Press, 2001)

Johanek, Peter, 'Alter Kulm', *Die deutsche Literatur des Mittelalters. Verfasserlexikon* (Berlin; New York: Walter de Gruyter, 1985), 267–70

Kadelbach, Stefan, Thomas Kleinlein, and David Roth-Isigkeit, eds., *System, Order, and International Law: The Early History of International Legal Thought from Machiavelli to Hegel* (Oxford: Oxford University Press, 2017)

Kahl, Sigrun, 'The Religious Roots of Modern Poverty Policy: Catholic, Lutheran, and Reformed Protestant Traditions Compared', *European Journal of Sociology*, 46.1 (2005), 91–126

Kanamori, Shigenari, 'Christian Wolff's Speech on Confucianism: Confucius Compared with Wolff', *European Journal of Law and Economics*, 4 (1997), 299–304

Keller, Vera, *Knowledge and the Public Interest, 1575–1725* (New York, NY: Cambridge University Press, 2015)

Klimesz, Henryk, 'Poland's Trade through the Black Sea in the Eighteenth Century', *The Polish Review*, 15.2 (1970), 55–80

Kohlmeyer, Ernst, *Kosmos und Kosmonomie bei Christian Wolff: Ein Beitrag zur Geschichte der Philosophie und Theologie des Aufklärungszeitalters* (Göttingen: Vandenhoeck & Ruprecht, 1911)

Komm, Martina, 'Zu einigen Aspekten von Christian Wolffs Ökonomik', in *Christian Wolff als Philosoph der Aufklärung in Deutschland*, ed. by Hans-Martin Gerlach, Günter Schenk, and Burchard Thaler (Halle: Martin-Luther-Universität, 1980), pp. 83–89

Krause, Gunter, 'Christian Wolff and the Classics of "Scientific Socialism"', *European Journal of Law and Economics*, 4 (1997), 285–97

Kubach-Ritter, Ursula, 'Rituale zur Offenkundigung der Ehe', in *Die Braut: geliebt, verkauft, getauscht, geraubt: zur Rolle der Frau im Kulturvergleich*, ed. by Gisela Völger, Karin von Welck, René König, and Rautenstrauch-Joest-Museum für Völkerkunde, 2 vols (Köln: Rautenstrauch-Joest-Museum für Völkerkunde, 1985), I, 294–98

Kusukawa, Sachiko, 'Nature's Regularity in Some Protestant Natural Philosophy Textbooks, 1530–1630', in *Natural Law and Laws of Nature in Early Modern Europe*, ed. by Lorraine Daston and Michael Stolleis (Farnham: Ashgate, 2008), pp. 105–21

Laslett, Peter, 'Family, Kinship and Collectivity as Systems of Support in Pre-Industrial Europe: A Consideration of the "nuclear-Hardship" Hypothesis', *Continuity and Change. A Journal of Social Structure, Law and Demography in Past Societies*, 3.2 (1988), 153–75

de Levie, Dagobert, *Christian Wolff und der Begriff der Menschenliebe* (Krefeld: Scherpe, 1972)

Lichtblau, Klaus, Das Zeitalter der Entzweiung: Studien zur politischen Ideengeschichte des 19. und 20. Jahrhunderts (Berlin: Philo, 1999)

Lindberg, Carter, *Beyond Charity: Reformation Initiatives for the Poor* (Minneapolis: Fortress Press, 1993)

Lindemann, Mary, *Medicine and Society in Early Modern Europe* (Cambridge: Cambridge University Press, 1999)

Linke, Paul Ferdinand, *D. Humes Lehre vom Wissen: ein Beitrag zur Relationstheorie im Anschluss an Locke und Hume* (Leipzig: Wilhelm Engelmann, 1901)

Loemker, Leroy E., 'Leibniz and the Herborn Encyclopedists', *Journal of the History of Ideas*, 22.3 (1961), 323–38

Luig, Klaus, 'Leibniz's Concept of Jus Naturale and Lex Naturalis, Defined with Geometric Certainty', in *Natural Law and Laws of Nature in Early Modern Europe: Jurisprudence, Theology, Moral, and Natural Philosophy*, ed. by Lorraine Daston and Michael Stolleis (Farnham: Ashgate, 2008), pp. 183–98

Lüthje, Hans, 'Christian Wolffs Philosophiebegriff', *Kant-Studien*, 30 (1925), 39–66

Lutterbeck, Klaus-Gert, *Staat und Gesellschaft bei Christian Thomasius und Christian Wolff: Eine historische Untersuchung in systematischer Absicht* (Stuttgart: Frommann-Holzboog, 2002)

Maclean, Ian, *The Renaissance Notion of Woman: A Study in the Fortunes of Scholasticism and Medical Science in European Intellectual Life* (Cambridge; New York: Cambridge University Press, 1980)

Maier, Hans, Die ältere deutsche Staats- und Verwaltungslehre (Polizeiwissenschaft) (Neuwied am Rhein: Luchterhand, 1966)

Maifreda, Germano, *From Oikonomia to Political Economy: Constructing Economic Knowledge from the Renaissance to the Scientific Revolution* (Farnham, Surrey: Ashgate, 2012)

Marschke, Benjamin, *Absolutely Pietist. Patronage, Fictionalism, and State-Building in the Early Eighteenth-Century Prussian Army Chaplaincy* (Tübingen: Max Niemeyer Verlag, 2005)

McClellan III, James, 'Scientific Institutions and the Organization of Science', in *The Cambridge History of Science: Volume 4, Eighteenth-Century Science*, ed. by Roy Porter and David C. Lindberg (Cambridge: Cambridge University Press, 2003), pp. 87–106

Menke-Glückert, Emil, *Die Geschichtschreibung der Reformation und Gegenreformation: Bodin und die Begründung der Geschichtsmethodologie durch Bartholomäus Keckermann* (Leipzig: J. C. Hinrich, 1912)

Menut, Albert Douglas, 'Maistre Nicole Oresme: Le Livre de Yconomique d'Aristote', *Transactions of the American Philosophical Society*, 47 (1957), 783–853

Menzel, Wolfgang Walter, *Vernakuläre Wissenschaft: Christian Wolffs Bedeutung für die Herausbildung und Durchsetzung des Deutschen als Wissenschaftssprache* (Tübingen: Niemeyer, 1996)

Mercer, Christia, 'Leibniz, Aristotle and Ethical Knowledge', in *The Impact of Aristotelianism on Modern Philosophy*, ed. by Ricardo Pozzo (Washington, DC: Catholic University of America Press, 2004), pp. 113–47

Meynard, Thierry, *The Jesuit Reading of Confucius: The First Complete Translation of the Lunyu (1687) Published in the West* (Leiden and Boston: Brill, 2015)

Millet, Kate, *Sexual Politics* (London: Abacus, 1972)

Mohnhaupt, Heinz, '"Lex Certa" and "Ius Certum". The Search for Legal Certainty and Security', in *Natural Law and Laws of Nature in Early Modern Europe: Jurisprudence, Theology, Moral, and Natural Philosophy*, ed. by Lorraine Daston and Michael Stolleis (Aldershot: Ashgate, 2008)

Mokrzecki, Lech, *Studium z Dziejów Nauczania Historii : Rozwój Dydaktyki Przedmiotu w Gdańskim Gimnazjum Akademickim Do Schyłku XVII w.* (Gdańsk: Zakład Narodowy imienia Ossolińskich, 1973)

Moll, Konrad, 'Der Enzyklopädiegedanke bei Comenius und Alsted, seine Übernahme und Umgestaltung bei Leibniz – neue Perspektiven in der Leibnizforschung', *Studia Leibnitiana*, 34 (2002), 1–30

Müller, Rainer A., 'Die Oeconomia ist ein Monarchia. Der (deutsche) Fürstenhof der Frühmoderne als Objekt der Hausväter- und Regimentsliteratur', in *Hof und Theorie. Annährungen an ein historisches Phänomen*, ed. by Reinhardt Butz (Cologne: Böhlau, 2004), pp. 145–64

Neveu, Sébastien, 'Secondary Authors' Influence on the Formation of the Wolffian "System of Truths"', in *Handbuch Christian Wolff*, ed. by Robert Theis and Alexander Aichele (Wiesbaden: Springer, 2018), pp. 55–71

Nipperdey, Justus, 'Bevölkerungstheorie und Idee der Armenfürsorge im 17. und 18. Jahrhundert: Gesellschaftsanalyse, soziale Steuerung und soziale Sicherung', in *Soziale Sicherungssysteme und demographische Wechsellagen. Historisch-vergleichende Perspektiven (1500–2000)*, ed. by Thomas Sokoll (Berlin: Lit Verlag, 2011), pp. 169–97

Nipperdey, Justus, 'Johann Peter Süssmilch: From Divine Law to Human Intervention', *Population*, 66.2 (2011), 611–36

Nokkala, Ere, *From Natural Law to Political Economy: J.H.G. von Justi on State, Commerce and International Order* (Münster: LIT Verlag, 2019)

Obert, Marcus, *Die naturrechtliche 'politische Metaphysik' des Johann Heinrich Gottlieb von Justi (1717–1771)* (Frankfurt am Main: Peter Lang, 1992)

Pagden, Anthony, 'The Preservation of Order: The School of Salamanca and the "Ius Naturae"', in *Mediaeval and Renaissance Studies on Spain and Portugal in Honour of P.E. Russell*, ed. by F.W. Hodcroft, D.G. Pattison, R.D.F. Pring-Mill, and R.W. Truman (Oxford: The Society for the Study of Mediaeval Languages and Literature, 1981), pp. 155–66

van Peursen, C.A., 'Ars inveniendi im Rahmen der Metaphysik Christian Wolffs: Die Rolle der ars inveniendi', in *Christian Wolff 1679–1754. Interpretationen zu seiner Philosophie und deren Wirkung, mit einer Bibliographie der Wolff-Literatur*, ed. by Werner Schneiders (Hamburg: Felix Meiner, 1986), pp. 67–88

van Peursen, C.A., C. A., 'E.W. Von Tschirnhaus and the Ars Inveniendi', *Journal of the History of Ideas*, 54.3 (1993), 395–410

Poppi, Antonino, 'Zabarella, or Aristotelianism as a Rigorous Science', in *The Impact of Aristotelianism on Modern Philosophy*, ed. by Ricardo Pozzo (Washington, DC: Catholic University of America Press, 2003), pp. 35–63

Prantl, Carl von, 'Hanow, Michael Christoph', *Allgemeine Deutsche Biographie* (Leipzig: Duncker & Humblot, 1879), 524–25

Priddat, Birger P., and Christoph Meineke, 'Ökonomie', in *Handbuch Christian Wolff*, ed. by Robert Theis and Alexander Aichele (Wiesbaden: Springer, 2018), pp. 291–313

Raabe, Paul, ed., *Vier Thaler und sechzehn Groschen: August Hermann Francke, der Stifter und sein Werk* (Halle/Saale: Franckesche Stiftungen, 1998)

Radkau, Joachim, *Holz. Wie ein Naturstoff Geschichte schreibt* (Munich: Oekom Verlag, 2018)

Raeff, Marc, *The Well-Ordered Police State. Social and Institutional Change through Law in the Germanies and Russia, 1600–1800* (New Haven and London: Yale University Press, 1983)

Reinert, Erik, and Arno Mong Daastøl, 'Exploring the Genesis of Economic Innovations: The Religious Gestalt-Switch and the Duty to Invent as Preconditions for Economic Growth', *European Journal of Law and Economics*, 4 (1997), 233–83

Reinert, Erik S., 'Steeped in Two Mind-Sets: Schumpeter in the Context of the Two Canons of Economics', in *Joseph Alois Schumpeter: Entrepreneurship, Style and Vision*, ed. by Jürgen Backhaus (Boston: Kluwer, 2003), pp. 261–92

Reinert, Erik S., and K. S. Jomo, (eds), *Origins of Development Economics: How Schools of Economic Thought Addressed Development* (London and New York: Zed Books, 2005)

Reinert, Erik S., and Rainer Kattel, *The Visionary Realism of German Economics: From the Thirty Years' War to the Cold War* (London: Anthem Press, 2019)

Rener, Monika, 'Unordnung und frühes Leid', in *Das Kind in der Renaissance*, ed. by Klaus Bergdolt, Berndt Hamm, and Andreas Tönnesmann (Wiesbaden: Harrassowitz Verlag, 2008), pp. 11–26

Risse, Guenter B., 'Medicine in the Age of Enlightenment', in *Medicine in Society: Historical Essays*, ed. by Andrew Wear (Cambridge: Cambridge University Press, 1992), pp. 149–96

Roczniak, Władysław, 'Clashing Functions/Clashing Elites Negotiating Hospital Functions in Pre-Modern Poland (13th-18th Centuries)', *The Polish Review*, 51.3/4 (2006), 283–305

Rodriguez-Pereyra, Gonzalo 'The Principles of Contradiction, Sufficient Reason, and Identity of Indiscernibles', in *The Oxford Handbook of Leibniz*, ed. by Maria Rosa Antognazza (Oxford: Oxford University Press, 2018), pp. 204–215

Roscher, Wilhelm, *Geschichte der National-Oekonomik in Deutschland*, Bd. 14 (Munich: R. Oldenbourg, 1874)

Rosen, George, 'Cameralism and the Concept of Medical Police', *Bulletin of the History of Medicine*, 27.1 (1953), 21–42

Rummel, Erika, 'Desiderius Erasmus', *The Stanford Encyclopedia of Philosophy*, ed. by Edward N. Zalta, <https://plato.stanford.edu/archives/win2017/entries/erasmus/> [accessed 28 July 2019]

Sarti, Raffaella, *Europe at Home. Family and Material Culture 1500–1800*, trans. by Allan Cameron (London and New Haven: Yale University Press, 2002)

Schaper, Annegret, *Ein langer Abschied vom Christentum: Johann Christian Edelmann (1698–1767) und die deutsche Frühaufklärung* (Marburg: Tectum Verlag, 1996)

Schlotheuber, Eva, 'Die Bewertung von Kindheit und die Rolle von Erziehung in den biographischen und autobiographischen Quellen des Spätmittelalters', in *Das Kind in der Renaissance*, ed. by Klaus Bergdolt, Berndt Hamm, and Andreas Tönnesmann (Wiesbaden: Harrassowitz Verlag, 2008), pp. 43–69

Schmidt-Wiegand, Ruth, 'Hochzeit, Vertragsehe und Ehevertrag in Mitteleuropa', in *Die Braut. Geliebt, verkauft, getauscht, geraubt. Zur Rolle der Frau im Kulturvergleich*, ed. by Gisela Völger and Karin von Welck, 2 vols (Cologne: Rautenstrauch-Joest-Museum für Völkerkunde, 1985), I, 264–73

Schneider, Norbert, *Geschichte der Ästhetik von der Aufklärung bis zur Postmoderne: eine paradigmatische Einführung* (Stuttgart: Reclam, 1996)

Schneider, Ulrich Johannes, 'Leibniz und der Eklektizismus', in *Neuzeitliches Denken: Festschrift für Hans Poser zum 65. Geburtstag*, ed. by Günter Abel, Hans-Jürgen Engfer, and Christoph Hubig (Berlin: Walter de Gruyter, 2002), pp. 233–50

Schneiders, Werner, '"Deus est philosophus absolute summus." Über Christian Wolff's Philosophie und Philosophiebegriff', in *Christian Wolff: 1679–1754: Interpretationen zu seiner Philosophie und deren Wirkung*, ed. by Werner Schneiders (Hamburg: Felix Meiner Verlag, 1983), pp. 9–30

Schöffler, Herbert, *Deutsches Geistesleben zwischen Reformation und Aufklärung: von Martin Opitz zu Christian Wolff* (Frankfurt am Main: Vittorio Klostermann, 1974)

Schüling, Hermann, *Die Geschichte der axiomatischen Methode im 16. und beginnenden 17. Jahrhundert* (Hildesheim: Olms, 1969)

Schumpeter, Joseph A., *History of Economic Analysis: With a New Introduction*, ed. by Elizabeth Boody Schumpeter (New York: Oxford University Press, 1996)

Schwaiger, Clemens, 'Christian Wolff', *Bloomsbury Dictionary of Eighteenth-Century German Philosophers* (London: Bloomsbury Academic, 2016), pp. 862–67

Senn, Peter, 'What Is the Place of Christian Wolff in the History of the Social Sciences?', *European Journal of Law and Economics*, 4.2/3 (1997), 147–232

Simon, Thomas, 'Der Erziehungsgedanke in den frühneuzeitlichen Polizeiordnungen', in *Das erziehende Gesetz*, ed. by Eva Schumann (Berlin and Boston: De Gruyter, 2013), pp. 59–74

Stipperger, Emanuel, *Freiheit und Institution bei Christian Wolff, 1679–1754* (Frankfurt am Main: Lang, 1984)

Stolleis, Michael, *Pecunia nervus rerum: Zur Staatsfinanzierung in der frühen Neuzeit* (Frankfurt am Main: Klostermann, 1983)

Stone, Daniel, *The Polish-Lithuanian State, 1386–1795* (Seattle: University of Washington Press, 2001)

Szyrwińska, Anna, 'Die Pietisten', in *Handbuch Christian Wolff*, ed. by Robert Theis and Alexander Aichele (Wiesbaden: Springer, 2018), pp. 383–403

Thomann, Marcel, 'Christian Wolff', in *Staatsdenker in der frühen Neuzeit*, ed. by Michael Stolleis and Notker Hammerstein (Munich: Beck, 1995), pp. 257–83

Thomann, Marcel, 'Ideologische Aspekte der praktischen Philosophie Wolffs', in *Christian Wolff, 1679–1754: Interpretationen zu seiner Philosophie und deren Wirkung*, ed. by Werner Schneiders (Hamburg: Felix Meiner, 1983), pp. 193–202

Tönnies, Ferdinand, 'Rechtsstaat und Wohlfahrtsstaat. Referat, erstattet auf dem III. Kongress der Internationalen Vereinigung für Rechts- und Wirtschaftsphilosophie', *Archiv für Rechts- und Wirtschaftsphilosophie*, 8.1 (1914), 65–70

Torvend, Samuel, 'Charity and Social Ethics', *The Oxford Encyclopedia of Martin Luther* (Oxford: Oxford University Press, 2017) <https://www.oxfordreference.com/view/10.1093/acref/9780190461843.001.0001/acref-9780190461843-e-366> [accessed 25 September 2019]

Travill, A. A., 'Juan Luis Vives: The De Subventione Pauperum', *Canadian Bulletin of Medical History*, 4.2 (1987), 165–81

Tribe, Keith, *Governing Economy: The Reformation of German Economic Discourse, 1750–1840* (Cambridge; New York: Cambridge University Press, 1988)

Tribe, Keith, *Strategies of Economic Order* (Cambridge: Cambridge University Press, 1995)

Tully, James, 'Introduction', in Pufendorf, Samuel, *On the Duty of Man and Citizen according to Natural Law*, ed. by J. Tully, tr. by Michael Silverthorne (Cambridge: Cambridge University Press, 1991)

Van Horn Melton, James, *Absolutism and the Eighteenth-Century Origins of Compulsory Schooling in Prussia and Austria* (Cambridge: Cambridge University Press, 1988)

Vesting, Thomas, 'Absolutismus und materiale Rationalisierung: Zur Entstehung des preußischen Patrimonialstaates', *Archiv des öffentlichen Rechts*, 119.3 (1994), 369–399

Vidal, Fernando, *The Sciences of the Soul: The Early Modern Origins of Psychology*, trans. by Saskia Brown (Chicago and London: University of Chicago Press, 2011)

Waibel, Violetta L., 'Natur als "Aggregat" und "System". Kants implizite Auseinandersetzung mit Wolff und Lambert in der Ersten Einleitung in die "Kritik der Urteilskraft"', in *Kant und die Berliner Aufklärung: Akten des IX. internationalen Kant-Kongresses*, ed. by Ralph Schumacher, Rolf-Peter Horstmann, and Volker Gerhardt (Berlin: De Gruyter, 2001), pp. 667–675

Wakefield, Andre, 'Cameralism. A German Alternative to Mercantilism', in *Mercantilism Reimagined. Political Economy in Early Modern Britain and Its Empire*, ed. by Carl Wennerlind and Philip J. Stern (Oxford: Oxford University Press, 214AD), pp. 134–50

Wehler, Hans-Ulrich, *Deutsche Gesellschaftsgeschichte, erster Band: Vom Feudalismus des alten Reiches bis zur defensiven Modernisierung der Reformära 1700–1815* (Munich: Beck, 1989)

Winter, Eduard, *Der Freund B. Spinozas E.W. v. Tschirnhaus: die Einheit von Theorie und Praxis* (Berlin: Akademie Verlag, 1977)

Witte, John Jr., *Law and Protestantism: The Legal Teachings of the Lutheran Reformation* (Cambridge: Cambridge University Press, 2002)

Witte, John Jr., 'Martin Luther's Influence on Legal Reforms and Civil Law', *Oxford Research Encyclopedia of Religion*, 2017 <http://oxfordre.com/religion/view/10.1093/acrefore/9780199340378.001.0001/acrefore-9780199340378-e-503.> [accessed 6 April 2019]

Wundt, Max, *Die deutsche Schulphilosophie im Zeitalter der Aufklärung* (Hildesheim: Olms, 1964)

van der Zande, Johan, 'Prussia and the Enlightenment', in *The Rise of Prussia: 1700–1830*, ed. by Philip G. Dwyer (Harlow: Pearson Education, 2000), pp. 89–107

Maecenata Schriften

Previous publications:

Volume 18
Rupert Graf Strachwitz, Eckhard Priller, Benjamin Triebe (Ed.)
Handbuch Zivilgesellschaft, 2020
ISBN 978-3-11-055129-7, e-ISBN (PDF) 978-3-11-055347-5,
e-ISBN (EPUB) 978-3-11-055140-2

Volume 17
Siri Hummel
Anstifter zur Beteiligung? Die Förderung politischer Partizipation durch gemeinnützige Stiftungen, 2019
ISBN 978-3-11-065238-3, e-ISBN (PDF) 978-3-11-065650-3,
e-ISBN (EPUB) 978-3-11-065249-9

Volume 16
Rupert Graf Strachwitz (Ed.)
Religious Communities and Civil Society in Europe – Analyses and Perspectives on a Complex Interplay, Volume II, 2020
ISBN 978-3-11-067299-2, e-ISBN (PDF) 978-3-11-067308-1,
e-ISBN (EPUB) 978-3-11-067314-2

www.degruyter.com